seventh edition

STATE AND LOCAL POLITICS

Government By The People

James MacGregor Burns
Williams College

J. W. Peltason
University of California

Thomas E. Cronin
Colorado College

David B. Magleby
Brigham Young University

Prentice Hall, Englewood Cliffs, New Jersey 07632

Library of Congress Cataloging-in-Publication Data

State and local politics : government by the people / James MacGregor
  Burns . . . [et al.]. — 7th ed.
    p. cm.
  Rev. ed. of State and local politics / James MacGregor Burns. 6th
ed. 1990.
  Includes bibliographical references and index.
  ISBN 0-13-845694-1
  1. State governments—United States. 2. Local government—United
States. I. Burns, James MacGregor. II. Burns, James MacGregor.
State and local politics.
JK2408.S79 1993
320.973—dc20   92-36158
                                                                    CIP

Acquisitions editor: Julia G. Berrisford
Editorial/production supervision and interior design: Serena Hoffman
Prepress buyer: Kelly Behr
Manufacturing buyer: Mary Ann Gloriande
Cover designer: Karen Marsilio
Cover photos: (top) UPI/Bettmann; (middle) Courtesy Governor's Office;
        (bottom) AP/Wide World

© 1993, 1990, 1987, 1984, 1981, 1978, 1976 by Prentice-Hall, Inc.
A Simon & Schuster Company
Englewood Cliffs, New Jersey 07632
as chapters 3, 23, 24, 25, 26, 27, 28, 29, 30, and 31
of **Government By The People, Fifteenth Edition**

Printed in the United States of America
10 9 8 7 6 5 4 3 2 1

ISBN 0-13-845694-1

Prentice-Hall International (UK) Limited, *London*
Prentice-Hall of Australia Pty. Limited, *Sydney*
Prentice-Hall Canada Inc., *Toronto*
Prentice-Hall Hispanoamericana, S.A., *Mexico*
Prentice-Hall of India Private Limited, *New Delhi*
Prentice-Hall of Japan, Inc., *Tokyo*
Simon & Schuster Asia Pte. Ltd., *Singapore*
Editora Prentice-Hall do Brasil, Ltda., *Rio de Janeiro*

Contents

3 State Constitutions: Charters or Straitjackets?   58

4 Parties and Elections in the States 73

5 State Legislatures 99

6 State Governors   133

7 Judges and Justice in the States   158

8 Local Government and Metropolitics 187

9 Staffing and Financing State and Local Governments 234

10 State and Local Policy Making   261

Glossary of Key Terms   293

Index   300

Preface

This book is about the political forces that shape policy making and policy outcomes in state and local communities. To those of us who are students of American politics, states and their 87,000 subdivisions are fascinating political laboratories that allow comparisons among different political systems. State and community governments pose certain problems more sharply than others. The party system is much weaker in some regions of the country than in others. State legislatures in some of the smaller or rural states meet for just a few months a year, whereas in other states they meet all year. The importance of interest groups and the media varies from state to state and from city to city. Generalizations are sometimes difficult, yet we try in this book to summarize what political scientists know about state and local politics.

States and cities are struggling in the 1990s. Our governance arrangements are being tested as they have rarely been in the past. Those who want better government in their communities and states will not achieve it by sitting around and waiting for it. If government by the people, of the people, and for the people is to be more than just rhetoric, activists must understand state and local politics and must be willing to clarify the issues for debate, form political alliances, respect and protect the rights of those with whom they differ, and be willing to serve as citizen leaders, citizen politicians. We hope this book will motivate students to the view that every person *can* make a difference, and that all of us should work toward that end.

This book consists of the last nine chapters plus the chapter on federalism from the fifteenth edition of *Government By The People*, National, State and Local Version (1993). We have had the benefit of useful criticisms and suggestions from Professors Thad Beyle, University of North Carolina, and Roy E.

Thoman, West Texas State University. We also wish to express our sincere thanks to our production editor at Prentice Hall, Serena Hoffman.

We would be pleased to hear from our readers with any reactions or suggestions. Write to us at our college addresses or in care of the Political Science Editor, Prentice Hall, Englewood Cliffs, New Jersey. Thanks.

James MacGregor Burns
Williams College
Williamstown, MA 01267

Thomas E. Cronin
Colorado College
Colorado Springs, CO 80903

J. W. Peltason
University of California
Oakland, CA 94612

David B. Magleby
Brigham Young University
Provo, UT 84602

1

State and Local Politics: Who Governs?

tate and local governments flourished before the U.S. government was even dreamed about. Indeed, the framers of the U.S. Constitution shaped the national government largely according to their practical experience with state, village, or community governments. Today this is still true. What happens in the 87,000 state and local governments continues to influence the forms and policies of the national government. The reverse, of course, is also true: The national government and its policies have an important impact on local and state government.

The national government's activities—dramatic diplomatic maneuvers, key Supreme Court decisions, major congressional debates—receive most of the publicity, so we often overlook the countless ways governments closer to home affect our lives. The quality of the air we breathe, the purity of the water we drink, the character of our schools and universities, the effectiveness of law enforcement, and decisions about how we will pay for all these things—these are just a few examples of policies determined by state and community governments.

"Who really runs things around here?" "Who has the clout?" "Who counts?" "Who is left behind?" These are important questions, especially for a nation that is committed to the idea of a government by the people and for the people.

In 1924 two sociologists from Columbia University, Robert and Helen Lynd, studied a typical American city as though they were anthropologists investigating a tribe in Africa. For two years they lived in Muncie, Indiana—at the time a city of 38,000—asking questions and watching how people made their living, brought up their children, used their leisure time, and joined in civic and social associations. The Lynds reported that despite the appearance of democratic rule, a social and economic elite actually ran things.[1] Their work stimulated a series of studies by social scientists and journalists in all kinds of communities to find out how government works and whether power is concentrated in the hands of the few, dispersed among the many, or somewhere in between.

Studying American state and local governments to find out how they operate and who governs them in the 1990s presents major problems. It is one thing to study the national system, vast and complex as it is; it is something else to study 50 separate state governments, each with its own legislature, executive, and judiciary, each with its own intricate politics and political traditions. Moreover, the state and local governments are only part of a much larger picture. To discuss the government of Mississippi or of the city of Detroit without mentioning white-black relations, the government of New York City or of Los Angeles without noting the politics of ethnic groups, or the government of Texas without referring to cattle and oil would be to ignore the real dynamics of the political process. State and local governments, just like the national government, cannot be properly analyzed and assessed as organizational charts. They are systems of politics and people. And the great variations among the states and localities—in population, economic resources, environment—make comparisons and generalizations difficult.

Every government system is part of a larger social system. A government is a structure and a process that resolves, or at least manages, conflicts. Further, it regulates, distributes, and sometimes redistributes items like income and property. It is also a device to achieve certain goals and to perform services desired both by those who govern and by those who are governed. Many outside factors are often more important than the structure of the government system itself or even the nature of its political processes. The economic system, the class structure, and the style of life are sometimes more important in determining the policies adopted by a particular state or municipality than are the government structures it has adopted.[2] Obviously, the economic circumstances and objectives of a city influence what is discussed and often what is decided.[3] However, the interrelations among the economic, social, and political systems are so complex that it is often difficult to unscramble them and to decide which is cause and which is effect.

This already complex picture is complicated still further by the fact that more than 87,000 cities, counties, towns, villages, school districts, water-control districts, and other governmental units are piled one on top of another within the states. If all states or cities or towns were alike, the task might be manageable. But of course they are not. Each city, like each state, is unique. Our states, cities, and counties do not fit into simple categories; we must discover the patterns and search for the uniformities underlying all the variation before we can begin to understand how these governments operate, who most influences their operations and policies, who benefits, and who pays.

The Location of Power

How can we grasp the operations and problems of state and local government without becoming bogged down in endless detail? We can do so by calling attention to the core problems of democratic governance: citizen participation, liberty, constitutional checks and balances, representation, and responsible leadership. Further, we can emphasize a question that throws light on all these problems: *Who governs?* Does political power in the states and localities tend to gravitate toward a relatively small number of people? If so, who are these people? Do they work closely together, or do they divide among themselves? Do the same people or factions shape the agenda for public debate and dominate all decision making, or do some sets of leaders decide certain questions and leave other questions to other leaders or simply to chance?

ANALYZING PATTERNS OF POWER

Relying on a mix of research methods, social scientists have studied the patterns of power in communities and have come up with varied findings. Floyd Hunter, a sociologist who analyzed Atlanta in the 1950s, found a relatively small and stable group of top policy makers drawn largely from the business class. This elite operated through shifting groups of secondary leaders who sometimes modified policy, but the power of the elite was almost always important.[4] In contrast, Robert Dahl, a political scientist at Yale, studied New Haven at the same time and concluded that although some people had a great deal of influence and most others had little, there was no permanent hard-core elite. There were, instead, shifting coalitions of leaders who sometimes disagreed among themselves and who always had to keep in mind what the public would accept when making their decisions.[5]

Of the two cities, Atlanta and New Haven, which is more typical of the distribution of influence in American communities? Or could it be that the differences between Hunter's and Dahl's findings stem from the questions they asked? Clearly, the assumptions of investigators and the techniques they use produce some of the differences in what they find.[6]

RULE BY A FEW OR RULE BY THE MANY?

One group of investigators, chiefly sociologists such as Hunter, have been mainly concerned with **social stratification** in the political system; in other words, how politics is affected by the fact that in any community, people are divided among socioeconomic groups. Are the upper classes the ruling classes? These social scientists, assuming that political influence is a function of the socioeconomic structure of the community, try to find out who governs a particular community by asking a variety of citizens to identify the persons who are most influential in it. Then they study these influential people to determine their social characteristics, their roles in decision making, and the interrelations among themselves and between them and the rest of the citizens. Those who use this technique report that the upper socioeconomic groups make up the **power elite,** that elected political leaders are subordinate to this elite, and that the major conflicts within the community are between the upper and the lower socioeconomic classes.

Another group of investigators questioned these findings, raising objections to the research techniques used. The evidence, they contend (even that contained within the stratification studies themselves), does not support the conclusion that communities are run by a power elite. Rather, the notion of a power elite is merely a reflection of the techniques used and the assumptions made by the stratification theorists. Instead of studying the activities of those who are *thought* to have "clout," one should study public policy to find out how, in fact, decisions are made. Those who conduct community studies in this manner usually find a relatively open **pluralistic power structure.** Some people do have more influence than others, but influence is shared among a rather sizable number of people and tends to be limited to particular issues and areas. Those who have much to say about how the public schools are run may have little influence over economic policies. And in many communities and for many issues there is no identifiable group of influential people. Policy emerges not from the actions of a small group, but rather from the unplanned and unanticipated consequences of the behavior of a relatively large number of people, and especially from the countless contending groups that form and win access to those who make important decisions. According to these theorists, the social structure of the community is certainly one factor, but it is not the determining factor in how goods and services are distributed.

Here we have an example of how the questions we ask influence the answers we find. If we ask highly visible and actively involved citizens for their opinions of who is powerful, we will find they name a relatively small number of people as the "real" holders of power. But if we study dozens of local events and decisions, we frequently find that a variety of people are involved—different people in different policy areas. Still other students of local politics suggest that local values, traditions, and the structure of governmental organizations determine which issues get on the local agenda.[7] Thus tobacco, mining, or steel interests, they say, are so dominant in an area that tax, regulation, or job safety policies normal elsewhere will be kept off the local policy agenda for fear of offending the "powers that be." And those interests may indeed go to great lengths to prevent what they deem to be adverse policies. Such students of local politics urge us to weigh carefully the possibility that defenders of the status quo can mobilize power resources in such a way that "nondecisions" may be more important than actual decisions. In effect, they tell us to study who rules, but also study the procedures and rules of the game that operate to *prevent* issues from arising. Determine which groups or interests would gain and which would be handicapped by political decisions.[8] This is useful advice, although the task of studying nondecisions or nonevents is sometimes impossibly complex.[9]

Studies of communities and states have now produced enough findings that we can begin to see how formal government institutions, social structure, economic factors, and other variables interact to create a working political system.

The Stakes in the Political Struggle

Events have given the national government enormous influence over the destiny of the American people. By assuming the responsibility for protecting our civil rights, fighting inflation and unemployment, regulating great economic power groups such as airlines and drug companies, and subsidizing weaker sectors of the economy, not to mention war and peace matters, the national government has become the custodian of the nation's economic strength and security. Certainly, state and local governments cannot claim so central a role. Yet the role of the states and localities is increasingly large in domestic policy questions, not only in absolute terms, but even in relative terms compared with the national government. Since World War II state and local government activities have increased much faster than the nondefense activities of the federal government. Today two-thirds of the expenditures for domestic functions are made by the states and their subdivisions. And states have had to assume even greater responsibilities for raising taxes and setting economic and social priorities as a result of the significant cutbacks in federal funds to the states and cities in the Reagan and Bush years. For example, federal mandates force states to raise taxes to pay for programs like Medicaid. Moreover, while the national government retains overall regulatory and enforcement authority over environmental policy, the responsibility for implementation and for paying for a cleaner environment has increasingly fallen to states and localities.

Moreover, state and local governments have more intimate relations with the average person than the national government does, for neighborhood, school, and housing problems are closely regulated by state and local governments. The points at which we come into contact with government services and officials most often are in schools, on the highways, in playgrounds, at big fires, in hospitals, in courtrooms. (But even in many of these areas, the mix of national, state, and local programs and responsibilities is such that it is often hard to isolate which level of government does what to whom. Also, there are some national-to-individual relationships that bypass state and local governments altogether, such as the mail service and social security.)

Some areas of life might seem far removed from any government—for example, having a dog or a cat as a pet. But a dog needs a license and a collar, it must be confined, and it must be inoculated. And if anyone thinks that cats are beyond the reach of the law, one should remember Adlai E. Stevenson's famous veto of the "cat bill" when he was governor of Illinois. The bill would have imposed fines on cat owners who let their pets run off their premises, and it would have allowed cat haters to trap them. The governor said:

> I cannot agree that it should be declared public policy of Illinois that a cat visiting a neighbor's yard or crossing the highway is a public nuisance. It is in the nature of cats to do a certain amount of unescorted roaming. . . . I am afraid this bill could only create discord, recrimination, and enmity. . . . We are all interested in protecting certain varieties of birds. . . . The problem of the cat versus bird is as old as time. If we attempt to resolve it by legislation, who knows but what we may be called upon to take sides as well in the age-old problem of dog versus cat, bird versus bird, or even bird versus worm. . . .[10]

So the governor sided with cat supporters over bird lovers, while staying neutral between bird lovers and worm diggers. Such incidents illustrate how the complex workings of modern society can lead to government intervention in or overregulation of our lives.

THE MAZE OF INTERESTS

Special interest groups are found, in varying forms, in every state and locality. Even industrial Rhode Island has farm organizations, and rural Wyoming has trade unions. Influential economic pressure groups and political action committees (organized to raise and disperse campaign funds to candidates for public office) operate in the states much as they do nationally. They try to build up the membership of their organizations; they lobby at the state capitols and at city halls; they educate and organize the voters; and they support their political friends in office and oppose their enemies.They also face the internal problems all groups face: maintaining unity within the group, dealing with subgroups that break off in response to special needs, and maintaining both democracy and discipline.

One great difference, however, is that group interests can be concentrated in states and localities, whereas their strength tends to be diluted in the national government. Big business does not really run things in Washington, any more than Wall Street, the Catholic Church, or the American Legion do. But in some states and localities certain interests are clearly dominant because they represent the social and economic majorities of the area. Few politicians in Wisconsin will attack dairy farmers; candidates for office in Florida are unlikely to oppose benefits for senior citizens; and few African-American officeholders in Boston are likely to espouse strong Republican positions.

It is the range and variety of these local groupings that give American politics its special flavor and excitement. Such groups include auto unions and manufacturers in Michigan, corn and hog farmers in Iowa, French Americans in northern New England, gas and oil dealers in Texas, gun owners in New Hampshire and Idaho, tobacco farmers in North Carolina, poultry growers in Arkansas, aircraft employees in southern California, cotton growers in the

South, coal miners in West Virginia, and sheep ranchers in Wyoming. However, the power of these groups should not be exaggerated.

Different groups have different needs and aspirations, and we have to be cautious about lumping all labor unions, all businesses, all teachers, all Chicanos, and all blacks together. The union movement is sometimes sharply divided among the teamsters, building trades, machinists, auto workers, and so on; the business community is often divided between the big industrial, banking, and commercial firms on the one hand and small merchants on the other.

In New England Irish and Italian fraternal societies have long expressed the opinions of their respective groups on various public issues; other organizations claim to speak for people of French-Canadian or Polish descent. New England politicians have feared the power of such groups to influence elections, especially primaries. Yet there are examples of "Yankees" winning in heavily ethnic areas. Similarly, Asian-American, Latino, and African-American communities are playing an increasingly important role in California's elections. Compared to the other considerations affecting voters' choices, the ethnic factor may be small (although even if only a minute percentage of citizens vote according to their ethnic interests, that can, of course, be a decisive factor in an election). Much depends on the character of the candidates and their personal appeal.[11] Any group, no matter how strong, must cope with a variety of cross-pressures, including a general sense of the rules of the game, which suggest that the voter does not vote for "one of our own" merely on that ground alone.

Now, let us look further at interests that are more specialized and that have a closer relation to local government. Many businesspeople sell to the state or perform services for it—for example, milk dealers, printers, contractors, parking meter manufacturers, computer and communications technology firms, makers of playground equipment, and textbook publishers. Such people often formally or informally organize in order to improve and stabilize their relations with purchasing officials. At the local level, developers and home builders together with their lawyers press for zoning and planning commission action. Millions of dollars are often at stake, and the resulting action or inaction frequently shapes both the economic growth and the environmental quality of a community.

Business interests are inevitably involved in city and county politics and policy making. As one student of Atlanta found, the business elite has rarely been a passive or reluctant partner in setting local priorities. "Atlanta's postwar political experience is a story of active business-elite efforts to make the most of their economic and organizational resources in setting the terms on which civic cooperation occurs."[12] Downtown businesses everywhere are dependent on local governments for parking, good roads, safety, urban renovations, and much more. Business elites get involved in long-range planning efforts, are keenly interested in who gets elected, and are ever-watchful of any changes in the taxation structure.

Another type of group intimately concerned with public policy is the professional association. The states license barbers, beauticians, architects, lawyers, doctors, teachers, accountants, dentists, and many other groups. Associations representing such groups are concerned with the nature of the regulatory laws and with the makeup of the boards that do the regulating. They are especially concerned about the rules of admission to their profession or trade and about the way in which professional misconduct is defined. Stiffening licensing requirements for physicians will decrease the supply of new doctors, for example, and thereby raise the incomes of those in practice. Bar associations, for example, closely watch the appointment of judges and court officials.

Every state has its particular set of lobbyists, yet some of the more typical and important interests that are likely to be represented by their own associations at the state capitol are manufacturing businesses, banking and insurance industries, public school teachers, chemical companies, dairy farmers, cattle farmers, highway contractors, public employee associations, oil, gas, and mining producers, environmental and consumer interests, unions, and taxpayer groups. Today other groups of citizens are also likely to organize and send lobbyists to the state capital: those who are pro-life and those who are pro-choice; those who want stiffer sentences for drunken driving and for armed robbery. Even more specialized interests do not let what happens in a state capital go uninfluenced these days, so you are likely to find representatives from the Beauticians' Aid Association, the Funeral Directors' and Embalmers' Association, the Institute of Dry Cleaning, and the Association of Private Driver-Training Schools at the statehouse.

Many businesses, especially larger corporations, are likely to supplement their representation through a chamber of commerce or trade association with their own lobbyists—often called public relations or political consultants. Or they may hire a law firm to represent their business. One of the growth businesses in state politics is consulting, done usually by specialized lawyers or former state legislators. For a fee, political consultants help push desirable bills through the legislature or block unwanted ones.

Many law firms and an increasing number of political consultants offer a variety of services to those who are able and willing to pay the price. These services range from merely providing information about what is going on, to

"Where there's smoke, there's money."

Drawing by Joe Mirachi; © 1985 The New Yorker Magazine, Inc.

taking statewide polls on various issues, to overseeing concentrated lobbying efforts and campaigns to change elite and public opinion about a matter. This kind of activity again raises the question of who has clout or who governs. Clearly, those who can hire skilled lobbyists and other experts to shape the public agenda often wield more influence than citizens who rarely even follow state and regional governmental decision making.

LOBBYISTS AT THE STATEHOUSE

There is a widespread conviction that lobbyists have freer rein in state legislatures than they do in the United States Congress and, what is more, that bribery or informal "payoffs" by lobbyists is cruder, more basic, and more obvious in state legislatures. This may be because most states' lobbying restrictions are more relaxed than restrictions at the federal level, and also because there is less likelihood of media exposure at the state level—at least in many states. Still, kickbacks from highway contractors or from other firms doing business with the states reported in the media are often enough to give credence to these claims. Spiro Agnew was forced to resign from the U.S. vice-presidency back in 1974 because he took kickbacks while he was a county executive and later governor of Maryland. Florida, Illinois, Louisiana, New York, Oklahoma, Arizona, and South Carolina have all been plagued by indictments and convictions of public officials on grounds of corruption in the past generation.

Corruption of legislators and state officials is usually hard to prove. Insiders sometimes charge that legislators accept favors for votes. Exposure of scandals in several states, especially in the post-Watergate era, pushed many legislatures to curb election abuses and pass ethics codes with more stringent conflict-of-interest provisions. Several legislatures have enacted comprehensive financial disclosure laws, and today most state governments are more open, professional, and accountable than in the past.[13]

Washington lobbyists tend to spend more time with legislators who are sympathetic to their points of view, while lobbyists at the state level appear to be more prone to try to persuade the opposition or the undecided in the legislature to bolster supporters. Former President Jimmy Carter, who served for a few years in the Georgia state senate and then as governor, recalled that only a "tiny portion" of the 259 members of the Georgia legislature were not good or honest people. But Carter found that

> it is difficult for the common good to prevail against the intense concentration of those who have a special interest, especially if the decisions are made behind locked doors. . . . In the absence of clear and comprehensive issues, it is simply not possible to marshal the interest of the general public, and under such circumstances legislators often respond to the quiet and professional pressure of lobbyists.[14]

In a few states one corporation or organization has considerable influence; in others a "big three" or "big four" dominate politics. But in most states there is open competition among organizations, so that no single group or coalition of groups stands out. In no state does any one organization control legislative politics,[15] although the powerful Anaconda Company once came close in Montana. Lobbyists are present in every state capital, and they are there to guide through the legislature a small handful of bills their organization wants passed or to stop those their organization wants defeated. Legislators each year process hundreds or even thousands of bills, in addition to doing casework on behalf of constituents and worrying about party, district, and colleagues. The governor? "Governors come and governors go, but the lobbyists [or legislative representatives] stay on forever!"[16] Shrewd lobbyists usually get a chance—sometimes several chances—to influence the fate of their few bills.

In one recent year nearly 400 lobbyists were registered at the Arkansas state capitol. Of these, 125 represented utilities, and more than 200 lobbied on behalf of individual businesses, industry, or professions. Nine lobbyists represented labor interests, eight worked on behalf of senior citizens, and three lobbied for environmental interests. In the absence of strong parties in Arkansas, interest groups and their lobbyists are viewed as the most influential sources of information for state officials. Surveys in that state suggest that the Arkansas Power and Light Company, the railroads, the poultry and trucking industries, the teachers, and the state chamber of commerce are the most effective lobbyists. "It is still true that ordinarily those with greater economic resources, greater numbers, and higher status have far more impact than those who lack these attributes . . . ," writes political scientist Diane Blair. "Nevertheless, an increasingly complex economy has produced many more actors in the political system, and especially when there is division among the economic elite, some of the lesser voices can be heard."[17]

Some groups have a special role both because of their relations with government and because of the size and importance of the work they do. Consider public school teachers. They are both employees of the local government and an interest group exerting pressure on it. They must deal with many other organized groups in education—for example, parents in local and state PTAs; principals and superintendents, who often have their own associations; and parents of children attending private and parochial schools. Teachers across the nation are increasingly politically organized, and they now regularly interview and endorse candidates for public office at all levels of government. They are often a formidable political force in local campaigns. Sometimes, too, they use a strike or the threat of a walkout as a weapon to influence their wages and working conditions.

Participation Patterns in Small and Medium-Sized Cities

Citizens generally take less interest in, vote less in elections for, and are less informed about their local governments than they are about the national government. This might seem strange, for people are closer to city hall and to county

administration buildings than they are to remote government officials and bureaucracies in Washington. Nevertheless, there are some reasons for the lower
involvement in local government. Most of the time local governments are
preoccupied with relatively noncontroversial routines, such as keeping the
roads in shape, providing fire and police service, attracting businesses that can
create more jobs, or applying for state and federal financial assistance. Most
local communities want to keep their tax rates down and to promote their
cities as "nice places" in which to live, work, and raise a family.

Mayors and city officials generally try to avoid controversies and the kind
of favoritism that will divide the community. Although they do not always succeed, they go to considerable lengths to appear reasonable and work for the
good of the community. Few city authorities aggressively seek to alter the
status quo. Cities do not, as a rule, try to promote equality in the sense of taxing the well-to-do and redistributing various resources to needier citizens. City
officials tend to believe this is the job of the national or state authorities—that
is, if they think it should be done at all. Typically, they say their cities do not
have the funds for that type of program. They might add, "Go see the governor" or "Go talk to your member of Congress." In fact, this may be good advice, because various state and national programs (health care, educational
loans, unemployment compensation and disability assistance, and so on) were
explicitly designed to help the less fortunate. They may not do so, but frequently this was their original intent.

One result of the reality that local governments are less involved in **redis-
tributive policy** politics is that interest groups are less developed and lobbying
is more sporadic than at the state and national levels of government.[18] Local officials obviously have to be concerned about the political consequences of their
decisions, but they are often free to make decisions with less interference from
organized interest groups than are state and national officials. Indeed, many
mayors and county officials are able to make an impressive range of decisions
primarily on the basis of what they think is best for the community—guided
mainly by the professional and technical advice they get from city managers,
planners, and other community employees who help administer their cities.

Of course, there are exceptions to this generalization. Neighborhood
groups sometimes become very involved in protecting their areas and petition-
ing for improvements. But that kind of involvement often occurs only once or
twice every few years and affects only a minor portion of the city's budget. Or
a local school district may seek to close down a community elementary school
—almost always a controversial issue. Squeezed by declining enrollments and
shrinking funds, school board officials often become embroiled in heated community meetings. Still, attendance at local government meetings is usually low.

Those who have a major economic stake in a community actively participate in local campaigns and make it a point to stay in close touch with their
local officials. In most cities local developers and real estate groups customarily
want close ties with city officials because most zoning regulations are decided
at the local level. Likewise, the local chamber of commerce often has longstand-

ing ties to many members of city and and county government. Economic development, the property tax rate, the sales tax, and tourist promotion loom large as concerns for both local business leaders and local officials.

What about local newspapers? Most communities have only one newspaper, and in small communities it is often a weekly. Some newspapers, and some local radio and television stations, do a good job of covering city and county politics. But this is the exception rather than the rule. Most newspapers recognize that their readers are generally more interested in national news, and especially in sports, than in what is going on at municipal planning meetings or county commissioner sessions. Most of what takes place in local government is often dull. It may be important to some people, yet it strikes the average person as decidedly less interesting than what goes on at the White House, or whether Congress has really solved the health care problem, or whether the Chicago Bulls, the Miami Dolphins, or the Oakland A's won last night.

Further, in towns and medium-sized cities some local newspapers develop a rather cozy relationship with elected local officials. Sometimes the owners or editors are social friends or golfing buddies of local officials. Friendships and mutual interests develop, and close, scrutinizing coverage of what goes on in city hall takes a backseat to city boosterism. In effect, "newspapers boost their hometown, knowing that its prosperity and expansion aid their own. Harping on local faults, investigating dirty politics, revealing unsavory scandals, and stressing governmental inefficiencies only provide readily available documentary material to competing cities. . . ."[19]

It is expensive to cover community government properly. Most newspapers can afford to assign only a part-time reporter to city government, and often this person is relatively new to writing about government. In many instances reporters are intimidated by elected officials, who typically are successful business or professional leaders who are considerably older and more established in the community than are the reporters. Irreverent young reporters sometimes find themselves reassigned, perhaps because of the influence city officials have with the owners of the local paper. Also, we must remember that the lifeblood of many local newspapers is the ads they sell to local businesses. When these dry up, newspapers fold. Thus some rather basic economic realities partially account for how papers and stations cover, or fail to cover, local government.

Still, local officials are more dependent on the local press than are state and national officials, since all we know about what happens at meetings of our city council or what our mayor has done is what we read in the local newspaper. Although we have dozens of ways to find out about Congress and the goings-on at the White House, we usually have only one source to give us the story on the mayor or sheriff or school board. Of course we could attend the board meetings or even talk with our mayor, but this is not usually an option for most people.

Although a president can speak to us directly through television, we generally know about our local mayor or county commissioners only as their actions are filtered through the eyes and mind of a local, often inexperienced and sometimes critical, news or television journalist. Depending on how they cover or fail to cover city council or local police activities, a local radio or television station can play a major role in whether city and county officials get reelected or reappointed. Thus the relationship between local officials and the local media is often one in which the media are important players. Indeed, a critical local press is sometimes cited by local officials as one reason why the public is disillusioned with city and county politics.

APATHY IN GRASS-ROOTS AMERICA

Many important political and economic transactions in a community are ignored by both the press and the citizenry. Thus the influence of savings and loan associations on certain members of Congress and the lax state and national practices that led to the huge number of business and real estate bankruptcies in the 1980s were largely ignored or went unnoticed. Charter revision and annexation battles are similarly ignored by all but those directly affected by the new taxes or regulations. However, when a land-fill area or a prison construction project is announced, that often galvanizes the reaction that local officials call NIMBY, an acronym for "Not In My Back Yard!"

Even New England town meetings have difficulty getting people to participate—despite the fact that decisions made at these meetings have major consequences for the local tax rate and the quality of the schools, the police force, and the parks and recreational areas. Thomas Jefferson once proclaimed the town meeting to be the noblest, wisest instrument yet devised for the conduct of public affairs. Yet most towns find that only about 2 or 3 percent of the population care enough to come.

All these are contributing factors, yet the major reason for grass-roots apathy is that the average person is not interested in local politics. Most people are content to leave politics and political responsibilities to a relatively small number of activists while they pursue their private concerns—their crabgrass, their bowling leagues, their children's Little League or soccer games, their daughters' applications to college. Of course, it may be sensible for the many who are satisfied with their local governments' functioning to sit on the sidelines and leave civic responsibilities to those who are interested in and willing to deal with personnel boards and planning and zoning commissions.

Cynicism about the effectiveness and fairness of local political processes is sometimes reflected in the occasional use of the politics of protest—mass demonstrations, economic boycotts, even civil disorders—to make demands on government. When certain issues become intense, the population is often revitalized politically. African Americans, Hispanics, gays, and others in the inner city form political organizations to present their grievances and organize their votes more effectively. Neighborhood organizations form to work for better housing, enforcement of inspection ordinances, and anticrime and antidrug activity.

CIVIC INNOVATION IN STATE AND LOCAL GOVERNMENTS

Just as there will always be indifference toward politics and apathy about government, so also will there always be creative, entrepreneurial people who are willing to step forward and find new ways of solving problems. States such as Oregon and Minnesota seem to encourage a climate of innovation and civic enterprise, and a wider look at the United States finds buoyant, optimistic, creative problem-solvers in nearly every corner of the nation.

These "can-do" problem solvers have been described as flexible and willing to make mistakes, yet driven to improve their communities. They are especially good at collaborating with all kinds of people in government, in business, and in nonprofit organizations, across traditional professional and agency lines —always trying to find new ways to do things, and often devising new combinations of old ways. "They may have been motivated to innovate by a lack of money to fund even standard programs, but some money will be needed for innovation, and they likely will find ways to scrape it together from nonstandard sources."[20]

Urban League leader T. Willard Fair is a committed problem-solver for his Liberty City community in Miami. He is recognized as a one-man force trying to rid Liberty City of drug pushers. In the late 1980s Fair started a private/public collaboration to improve the quality of life in this inner-city community. Among many other results, his efforts led to 27 demolished crack houses, 3,500 arrests, many abandoned vehicles towed away, and trees trimmed to decrease the shade in areas where drug deals were made. But above all, Fair was able to get the neighbors in Liberty City to band together and have faith that their neighborhood could be rid of its pushers. "Fair started the program after reading about a young woman who had been shot. Residents were too fearful of drug dealers to cooperate with police." Fair became a catalyst for change, enlisting the help of government and school officials, police and fire officers, churches, residents, and local businesses. He also persuaded the national drug program to share some funds, and he raised other funds by whatever means he could. By 1992 he could declare, along with the Liberty City residents, that their 70-square-block, drug-free zone was "off limits" to what he calls "the drug boys."[21]

Other examples of local innovation include the remarkable community health clinics started by Parkland Memorial Hospital in Dallas. These clinics are pioneering outreach efforts in family and preventive care. And residents in the area of Seattle's Volunteer Park rallied to upgrade and beautify a park that had become a dumping ground for litter, used hypodermic needles, and condoms. "Volunteers raised nearly $100,000 for the task from door-to-door solicitations and donations from businesses and foundations."[22]

Not long ago school reformers and parents in Minnesota fought to introduce more competition and choice in the public school systems. They had to take on entrenched teacher organizations, but they eventually succeeded in allowing students and parents to decide which school they wanted to attend. Several other states and communities are following the lead of this Minnesota experience.[23]

Elsewhere, enterprising local activists have advocated and implemented cost-saving energy programs, environmental clean-up campaigns, recycling and solar energy initiatives, job training centers, AIDS prevention efforts, housing for the elderly, tutoring for the illiterate, and hundreds of other problem-solving and opportunity-enhancing community efforts.

In almost every case, one finds creative partnerships—partnerships among local community people with outsiders, sometimes with elected officials at city hall, sometimes with the Urban League or Chamber of Commerce, often with local foundations and business corporations. In Indianapolis, the Lilly Foundation has been a major supporter of efforts for urban change and renewal. In Colorado, the El Pomar Foundation and the Colorado Trust have been crucial. In Minnesota, the Twin-Cities Citizen League and the Minnesota Business Partnership have been central players. In New York City, the Fund for the City of New York has been a creative supporter for rehabilitating urban communities.

As a leading student of innovative activities in American cities writes:

> Often the community organization is sparked by an outsider—but the successful outsider hurries to make the effort the community's own. The vital element is community ownership. The jobs of reforming community and competence building seem best accomplished by neighborhood mediating institutions, churches, civic groups, community development corporations, and peer-to-peer counsel of disadvantaged people. Indeed, in a time of such vivid radical and ethnic separations in our ever-more-diverse society, peer assistance may be the indispensable ingredient if we hope communities can learn more self-sufficiency, and democratic governance, from the grassroots up.[24]

Minnesota has recently pioneered in devising health-care coverage for those excluded from existing health insurance options. Here a Republican governor teamed up with a Democratic-controlled legislature to tax health-care providers (hospitals and many physicians) to expand insurance coverage for those "too poor" to afford private insurance and "too rich" to qualify for state Medicaid.

Metropolitan areas are where most of the social and economic and racial problems are, and this is where most of our nation's problems have to be solved. Many students of leadership and problem solving are convinced that most problems are more likely to be solved at the community level than by legislators and policy makers in far away Washington. Neighborhood organization and a spirit of civic involvement are crucial to the vitality of our constitutional democracy. Thousands of neighborhoods have learned to help themselves.

So while elections, such as who is elected Chicago's mayor, are important, equally important are the stories of T. Willard Fair and Martin Luther King and the neighbors of Seattle's Volunteer Park, who regularly step forward to initiate community improvements.

Elections in Urban America

Perhaps the most distinctive features of American politics are the number and variety of our elections. Western Europeans, who are used to voting for one or two candidates at the national and local levels, and voting only once every two or three years, are flabbergasted on learning that Americans engage almost continuously in elections. Selection of town and local officials in the late winter may be followed by primaries to choose delegates to conventions, then primaries to choose party candidates, then general elections—all interspersed with special elections, special town or state referenda, and even, in some states, recall elections to throw an official out of office. Even more bewildering to Europeans is the number of offices voted on in a particular election, from president to probate judge, from senator to sheriff, from governor to member of the library board. This is the long ballot in operation. Europeans are more accustomed to electing a handful of key officials, who in turn appoint career officials.

Elections show some variability, yet experienced politicians would probably agree on the following rules of thumb:

1. By and large, the more local the election, the less the excitement and interest aroused among the electorate, and the lower the participation.

2. Except in the very few areas with strong party organizations, candidates usually run on their own—that is, through their personal organization rather than through the party organization. Partly because there are so many candidates running for so many offices, the party cannot give much help to any one of them.

3. Voter familiarity with names rather than issues is of relatively greater importance in local elections.

4. The candidates get most of their money from friends and interest groups, not from their parties.

5. Although there is no substitute for personal contact between the candidate and the voters, especially in local campaigns, more and more state and city elections are determined by the extent and quality of direct mail and radio and television ad campaigns. Hi-tech campaign strategies, once a major factor only in presidential and statewide elections in large, populous states, are now a factor everywhere except in *very* local races.

CAMPAIGNING FOR CITY HALL IN CHICAGO

For observers of roughhouse local politics, there is no place like Chicago. In recent years the city has had a black mayor, a woman mayor, machine politics, notable black-white divisions, and two famous mayors named Daley—Richard

J. Daley, the legendary mayor from 1955 until his death while still in office in 1976, and his firstborn son, Richard M. Daley, first elected to office in 1989 and reelected in 1991.[25]

Chicago politics has often defied the rules that govern local politics in the rest of America. In some ways, however, the city illustrates many of the patterns of party and organizational politics found elsewhere. In the past decade two candidates won city hall in upset victories. In 1979 Jane Byrne defeated the Chicago machine and its incumbent mayor, Michael Bilandic, who had succeeded Mayor Richard J. Daley when Daley died in office. Byrne's victory astonished people in Chicago, who had assumed that the famed Chicago Democratic political organization would continue in office as it had for nearly 50 years. But Jane Byrne beat the machine, and then she tried to put the pieces back together again. For the most part, she succeeded. Her four-year tenure was marked by controversy. Her critics said she was often too temperamental and that she frequently alienated the city's growing minority population. But she was also a tough and shrewd politician. After all, she knew the Chicago machine; she had worked within it for years, rising up through its ranks and holding high appointive office under Daley.

In late 1982, when Mayor Byrne prepared her reelection bid for city hall, most observers expected her to win easily. She had taken effective control of patronage, and in a city where at the time a few thousand jobs were still "controlled" by city hall, this was presumed to be a major advantage. She also proved to be an awesome fund-raiser, eventually raising $10 million for her bid to win a second term.

A major rival emerged when Richard M. Daley, state's attorney for Cook County (of which Chicago is the major city), announced his candidacy for the Democratic nomination in November 1982. As the son of a famous former mayor, and with considerable experience in state and local politics, young Daley was considered a serious candidate and challenger.

Soon a third candidate emerged in the primary—Congressman Harold Washington, a former state legislator who was then representing Chicago's First District in the United States House of Representatives. Washington, a Chicago-born attorney, was black. Some observers say he was a very reluctant candidate, and few thought he stood a chance against the Byrne machine. Some Daley campaign advisers believed Mayor Byrne actually encouraged Harold Washington's candidacy and even provided some of his early financial assistance because she thought a three-way race would ensure her victory. She reasoned, they charged, that in a two-way race young Daley would get most of the black and Hispanic vote, and that this would make him an extremely tough opponent. But with Washington in the race, Byrne's opposition would be divided and Washington would attract much of the city's growing black vote away from Daley.

All three candidates waged vigorous campaigns. The incumbent's record was scrutinized and attacked. The candidates engaged in four debates during the last stretch of the campaign—debates in which Harold Washington emerged as an impressive candidate. Expert observers said he "won" these debates. African Americans rallied to Washington in an unprecedented way. Some liberals swung in behind him as well. As the March 1983 primary election neared, experts were predicting a close race, but one in which Byrne was still the likely victor. Harold Washington, however, came from behind in the three-way race and emerged a clear winner.

Harold Washington had grown up in the black neighborhoods of Chicago. He had been a top student, worked hard, "paid his dues," and gradually worked his way up the social and political ladder. The son of a Democratic precinct captain, Washington himself had served in the lower ranks of the party and later had graduated from Northwestern Law School and practiced law. Then he worked in the Daley machine in a variety of capacities, and he—along with countless other black Chicagoans—had helped to deliver precincts and wards for the Democratic party for some 40 years or more. Now "it is our turn," said Washington, and he asked for the kind of support he and members of his race had given the white Democrats over the years.

Yet that white Democratic support was slow in coming. Old-line Democrats criticized Washington for tax evasion (of which he had been convicted in the past and for which he had even served a short jail sentence) and for running a campaign that mainly emphasized racial divisions. Whites in large numbers joined the campaign of Bernard Epton, the Republican nominee. Prior to the surprise outcome of the Democratic primary, he had virtually no name recognition and no chance to win. Epton's media advisers promoted his candidacy with the slogan: "Elect Epton—Before It's Too Late"—a blatantly racist slogan that angered African Americans and liberals alike because of its implication that the choice was between Epton and African-American control of city hall and Democratic party patronage.

The ensuing campaign was one of the most divisive the country had witnessed in at least a generation. Racism was rife and emotions ran high. National television and magazines featured the race prominently. Finally, in April 1983, in an election with high voter turnout, Harold Washington emerged the victor with about 51 percent of the vote. He won enormous backing from blacks and Hispanics as well as scattered white support, mainly from liberals and highly educated professionals. Epton got 82 percent of the white vote.

Chicago somehow endured, but the famed Democratic political machine was fractured. Mayor Washington tried in vain to revitalize the Democratic organization, but it would never be the same. A majority block of the 50-person city council opposed Washington on many issues and refused to act on the more than 50 nominations to boards and commissions he made during his first three years in office.[26]

Still, Harold Washington was easily reelected in 1987 and was credited with opening city government to many of Chicago's citizens who had long felt excluded and ignored. Although elected in a highly polarized contest that had deeply divided the city in 1983, Washington's subsequent performance had begun a healing process. When he died, shortly into his second term, City Councilman Eugene Sawyer, also a black, was chosen acting mayor by the white-dominated Board of Aldermen.

In February 1989 a new election took place to select a mayor to serve out the last two years of Harold Washington's four-year term. Cook County Prosecutor Richard M. Daley defeated Sawyer in a relatively low-key primary campaign in which both candidates repeatedly called for racial harmony. "But in this city, often regarded as the most residentially segregated in the country, racial tensions were never far below the surface, and charges of racism on both sides flared repeatedly in the final weeks of the campaign."[27] Daley won 91 percent of the white vote and only 5 percent of the black vote; Sawyer took 94 percent of the black and only 8 percent of the white vote.

Upon winning, Daley promised that he would have an open city hall and extend the hand of the city to all its citizens. He pledged, too, to improve Chicago's troubled school system, reduce crime, and work fairly with all segments of the city. Unlike his father, the new mayor controls only about a thousand of the more than 40,000 city jobs; the courts have outlawed most of the patronage that provided the muscle for his father's style of machine politics. Mayor Richard M. Daley has been less ruthless than his father in running city hall. He has appointed many more blacks, Hispanics, and women to key administrative positions than his father did. Daley easily won reelection in 1991. Another Daley era appears to be in the making.

These mayoralty campaigns suggest several patterns. The key to success in Chicago politics is still winning the Democratic primary. Money continues to be a crucial factor. A black candidate can win in a racially divided city only by putting together a coalition of committed African Americans and Hispanics along with at least some of the liberal white community. Chicago's election of a white mayor after a black had run city hall suggests that cities with large black populations will not necessarily win and retain a permanent hold on city hall. (This kind of changeover has also happened in Cleveland and Charlotte, North Carolina.) Although election campaigns in Chicago typify American party organizational politics in many ways, events in the city during the past decade illustrate how nothing can be taken for granted in politics—especially in Chicago.

The Challenges for State and Local Government

The 1990s have been a time of severe testing and strain in most states and communities. Budgets have been tight, taxes have been increased, and people have been dismayed by the lack of success in dealing with compelling urban and metropolitan area problems. What are the central issues in the states and local communities? Obviously, they vary depending on location, yet the following are the enduring challenges facing most cities and states:

1. *People want more services, but at the same time would like to see their taxes cut.* City and state officials are constantly trying to do more with less and introduce efficiencies into city and state operations. Voters in many communities have enacted tax cuts or spending limitations that constrain growth in public budgets.

2. *Racism still exists in many communities.* As our nation has become more diverse, most Americans have learned to mix, and share, and appreciate the strength that comes from multiple cultures and races. Yet the Ku Klux Klan and other racist groups still thrive in many areas, and bigotry and discrimination persist. Countless efforts have been made to improve social, civic, and economic opportunities for all Americans, but urban riots, such as the Los Angeles riots of 1992 after the Rodney King verdict, remind us of how much more needs to be done.

3. *Drugs, gangs, and drug-related crime in urban America pose tough policy challenges in the 1990s.* The costs of corrections and prisons have skyrocketed in recent years, and there are over a million people in U.S. jails and prisons on any given night, but gangs and drugs and crime are still increasing. Most state and local "wars on drugs" have failed, and the ravages and toll of drug abuse are enormously costly to the nation. Drug abusers fill our prisons; they lose their jobs; they make our streets and neighborhoods unsafe; they add to our welfare rolls; and in numerous ways they undermine the vitality of our cities and towns.

4. *Poverty in the inner cities is yet another persistent problem.* We have extremes of rich and poor within metropolitan regions, and often the wealthier suburbs turn their backs on the problems and poverty of the older cities. Indifference to these inequalities and lack of opportunities will come back to haunt the United States as this country attempts to compete with other world communities, such as Europe and the Pacific Rim nations, where concern for the advancement of the whole community is emphasized and where glaring inequalities are being diminished.

5. Another challenge is *the need to guarantee the best possible education for our young people.* As the American work force increasingly has to compete in a global economy, we are made aware of some of the deficiencies of our educational practices. Parents are demanding better quality education and more parental involvement. Schools for profit are being launched to compete with public schools. There is considerable talk about educational reform and choice and competition, but the salaries for public school teachers are often too low to attract and retain the best-qualified teachers. State and local governments have the responsibility to pay for public edu-

cation, not the national government, so educational reform and the search for excellent teachers and learning processes must remain a top state and local priority.

6. *Environmental regulation and recycling are also major challenges in grass- roots governments.* Every city and state wants economic growth and economic opportunities for its workers and businesses. But we have come to appreciate that many forms of economic development also have costs in terms of the quality of air, water, landscapes, and health. Every elected official and most appointed officials are faced with tough decisions about the need to balance economic and environmental concerns. Achieving a harmonious balance between the two is never easy.

There are many other critical challenges facing state and local governments. We have listed only the most urgent problems. They also illustrate the hard choices and political and budgetary realities that face elected officials and civic activists today. These are daunting problems and crises. They cry out for people to get involved in their solutions. In the chapters that follow, we will treat the political institutions, policy processes, and personnel and financial realities that shape how we govern ourselves in the states and localities.

Summary

1. American states and localities are characterized more by dispersion of political influence than by concentration. The diversity of elective offices gives influence to many different officials. In a positive vein, this gives people more openings in the system for access and innovation. In a negative vein, it makes it hard to bring about changes and to govern creatively.

2. Most states and localities today have reasonably porous systems that are a long way from rule by an establishment or by a boss. This does not mean every voter has roughly the same influence on political decisions. Power is often found in separate clusters of decision makers, and large numbers of people have little influence over these decision makers. Under the American system, ordinary people could have a more active role, but ignorance, lack of education, lack of time, and other factors keep many of them from wielding much influence.

3. Students should look at their own states and communities and ask hard questions. Who has influence and who does not? Who is excluded from the system? What are the rules of the game? Under what conditions is influence exercised? *How* is it exercised—through authority, friendship, propaganda, deals, manipulation, coercion? And in whose behalf is it exercised? What are the terms under which influence is pyramided and expended? What kind of influence do political leaders sacrifice in order to get the decisions they want? In short, if most of these political systems are marked by deals, bargains, and exchanges, then who gains and loses what? Does fragmented power prevent leaders from making joint efforts on behalf of the great mass of people? Finally, what are the available means of keeping public servants, elected and appointed, accountable and responsive between elections?

For Further Reading

DIANE D. BLAIR, *Arkansas Politics and Government* (University of Nebraska Press, 1988).

THOMAS E. CRONIN and ROBERT D. LOEVY, *Colorado Politics and Government: Governing the Centennial State* (University of Nebraska Press, 1993).

JOEL GARREAU, *Edge City: Life on the New Frontier* (Doubleday, 1991).

JOHN GAVENTA, *Power and Powerlessness: Quiescence and Rebellion in an Appalachian Valley* (University of Illinois Press, 1980).

VIRGINIA GRAY, HERBERT JACOBS, and KENNETH VINES, eds., *Politics in the American States*, 5th ed. (Scott, Foresman, 1990).

DAVID A. HAMBURG, *Today's Children: Creating a Future for a Generation in Crisis* (Times Books, 1992).

BRYAN D. JONES, *Governing Urban America* (Little, Brown, 1983).

DENNIS R. JUDD, *The Politics of American Cities: Private Power and Public Policy*, 3d ed. (Scott, Foresman, 1988).

DAVID OSBORNE and TED GAEBLER, *Reinventing Government: How the Entrepreneurial Spirit Is Transforming the Public Sector* (Addison-Wesley, 1992).

NEAL R. PEIRCE and JERRY HAGSTROM, *The Book of America: Inside Fifty States Today* (Norton, 1983).

GARY RIVLIN, *Fire on the Prairie: Chicago's Harold Washington and the Politics of Race* (Holt, 1992).

ALAN ROSENTHAL and MAUREEN MOAKLEY, eds., *The Political Life of the American States* (Praeger, 1984).

ROBERT A. SLAYTON, *Back of the Yards: The Making of Local Democracy* (University of Chicago Press, 1986).

CLARENCE STONE, *Regime Politics: Governing Atlanta* (University Press of Kansas, 1989).

JAMES D. THOMAS and WILLIAM H. STEWART, *Alabama Government and Politics* (University of Nebraska Press, 1988).

See also these useful journals: *Governing,* published monthly by Congressional Quarterly Press; *State Legislatures,* published 10 times a year by the National Conference of State Legislatures; and *Civic Action* and *The National Civic Review,* published by the National Civic League.

Notes

1. Robert S. Lynd and Helen M. Lynd, *Middletown* (Harcourt, 1929). See also their treatment of Muncie ten years later in *Middletown in Transition* (Harcourt, 1937).

2. Thomas R. Dye, *Politics in States and Communities,* 7th ed. (Prentice Hall, 1991); and Richard I. Hofferbert, *The Study of Public Policy* (Bobbs-Merrill, 1974).

3. See Paul E. Peterson, *City Limits* (University of Chicago Press, 1981).

4. Floyd Hunter, *Community Power Structure* (University of North Carolina Press, 1953). For a reassessment and rebuttal of Hunter's findings, see M. Kent Jennings, *Community Influentials: The Elites of Atlanta* (Free Press, 1964).

5. Robert A. Dahl, *Who Governs? Democracy and Power in an American City* (Yale University Press, 1961). For an example of the power elite or social stratification approach as applied to New Haven, see G. William Domhoff, *Who Really Rules? New Haven and Community Power Reexamined* (Goodyear, 1978).

6. See Nelson W. Polsby, *Community Power and Political Theory,* 2d ed. (Yale University Press, 1980), for the perspective of a critic of social stratification theorists. See Steven Lukes, *Power: A Radical View* (Macmillan, 1974), for a class conflict perspective, which differs sharply from the Polsby and Dahl analyses.

7. See the interesting study of San Jose, California, along these lines: Phillip J. Troustine and Terry Christensen, *Movers and Shakers: The Study of Community Power* (St. Martin's, 1982). See also Clarence N. Stone, *Regime Politics: Governing*

Atlanta 1946–1988 (University Press of Kansas, 1989).

8. See, for example Peter Bachrach and Morton S. Baratz, *Power and Poverty: Theory and Practice* (Oxford University Press, 1970); Matthew A. Crenson, *The Unpolitics of Air Pollution: A Study of Non-Decisionmaking in Two Cities* (Johns Hopkins University Press, 1971); and John Gaventa, *Power and Powerlessness: Quiescence and Rebellion in an Appalachian Valley* (University of Illinois Press, 1980).

9. Geoffrey Debnam, "Nondecisions and Power: The Two Faces of Bachrach and Baratz," *American Political Science Review*, September 1975, pp. 889–99.

10. Veto message, Governor Adlai Stevenson, to members of the Senate Assembly, Springfield, Illinois, 1949.

11. Michael R. Levy and Michael S. Kramer, *The Ethnic Factor: How American Minorities Decide Elections* (Touchstone, 1973).

12. Stone, *Regime Politics*, p. 232.

13. See, for example, Candace Romig, "Placing Limits on Political Action Committees," *State Legislatures*, January 1984, pp. 19–22; and "States Strengthen Campaign Finance Laws," *State Government News*, November 1984, pp. 7, 31.

14. Jimmy Carter, *Why Not the Best?* (Bantam Books, 1976), p. 101.

15. See L. Harmon Zeigler, "Interest Groups in the States," in *Politics in the American States: A Comparative Analysis*, eds. Virginia Gray, Herbert Jacob, and Kenneth Vines, 4th ed. (Little, Brown, 1983), pp. 97–131.

16. Jesse Unruh, "A Reformed Legislature," *Journal of Public Law* 16 (1967), p. 13. See also Kerry Drager, "The New Breed of Sacramento Lobbyists," *California Journal*, October 1980, pp. 393–97.

17. Diane D. Blair, *Arkansas Politics and Government* (University of Nebraska Press, 1988), p. 118.

18. Peterson, *City Limits*. The discussion in this section draws from insights developed in this book.

19. Ibid., p. 124.

20. Eileen Shanahan, "The Mysteries of Innovative Government," *Governing*, October 1991, p. 37.

21. Catherine Foster, "One Man Rallies a Neighborhood against Pushers," *Christian Science Monitor*, June 11, 1992, p. 7.

22. Shanahan, "The Mysteries of Innovative Government," p. 40.

23. David Osborne and Teb Gaebler, *Reinventing Government: How the Entrepreneurial Spirit Is Transforming the Public Sector* (Addison-Wesley, 1992), pp. 96–101.

24. Neal R. Peirce, "Affordable and Effective State and Local Government: Is It Possible: If So How?" An address at Princeton University, April 6, 1992, pp. 11–12.

25. For different insights into Mayor Richard J. Daley and his machine, see Mike Royko, *Boss: Richard J. Daley of Chicago* (Dutton, 1971); Milton L. Rakove, *Don't Make No Waves, Don't Back No Losers: An Insider's Analysis of the Daley Machine* (Indiana University Press, 1975); and Thomas M. Guterbock, *Machine Politics in Transition: Party and Community in Chicago* (University of Chicago Press, 1980).

26. For a detailed assessment of Mayor Washington, see Gary Rivlin, *Fire on the Prairie: Chicago's Harold Washington and the Politics of Race* (Holt, 1992).

27. Dirk Johnson, "Daley Wins Primary in Chicago," *The New York Times*, March 1, 1989.

2

American Federalism

A splendid way to guarantee a small attendance at a gathering, it is sometimes joked, is to hold a fund-raiser for a defeated candidate or schedule a meeting to discuss the merits of federalism.[1] Yet *federalism*—the constitutional division of powers between the national government and the states—is central to the workings of American government. And throughout much of the rest of the world, federalism issues are at the top of the political agenda. The very nature of Canada's federal system is at stake as the French-speaking province of Quebec demands special status and a considerable measure of autonomy.[2] The Soviet Union has changed from a highly centralized government that was federal only in form but not in fact to the Commonwealth of Independent States, a loose confederation of independent republics.

That ours is a federal system makes a lot of difference, even if we are not always aware that this is so. Almost every aspect of our lives is affected by several layers of government. Consider your college or university. About half the students are likely to be receiving some form of national or state financial assistance to help pay their tuition and fees. The institution itself is chartered by the state. Most of the funds that pay for the teachers, staff, and buildings at public institutions come from state appropriations, state bonds, private gifts encouraged by national tax laws, or a combination of national, state, and private sources. Faculty research, especially in the sciences, is likely to be supported by some combination of national, state, and private (yet tax-deductible) dollars. The conditions under which students are admitted, how their grades are posted and reported, and how faculty and staff are appointed and evaluated are subject to national and state regulations. The use of experimental animals is subject to governmental supervision, and national and state inspectors check to ensure that laboratories properly dispose of used chemicals.

Federalism was very much on the mind of Americans when our Constitution was being written. Most early Americans put at the top of their worry list a fear that governments might threaten their liberties. To them *federalism*, with its division of powers between national and state governments, promised to serve as a potent barrier against tyranny. If the newly formed national government threatened people's liberties, the states would protect them—and vice versa.

Federalism issues did not end with the founding period, though. In 1861, men and women fought and died for Virginia or Texas or for the Union (although it would be a mistake to think of the Civil War as merely a particularly heated debate over the principles of federalism). Federalism remains an important part of our political agenda, not merely in national elections but in Congress and before the courts of our land.

Today there are few doubts about the national government's constitutional authority to deal with issues affecting the nation, whether they concern civil rights, highway speed limits, or the sale of holiday lights. Nonetheless, we still argue about (1) whether Congress intended to regulate a subject completely or to leave some regulation to state discretion, and (2) whether, in the absence of congressional action, states may deal with subjects that affect commerce or people in other states.

Although couched in terms of federalism, such arguments reflect differences among various interests. The national and state governments are the arenas in which, and through which, clashes take place between consumers and producers, workers and employers, airlines and railroads, pro-choice and right-to-life advocates, progrowth and antigrowth forces, and all the other contending groups that make up our political system.

In this chapter we will begin by defining federalism and discussing its advantages and disadvantages, followed by a look at the constitutional basis of our federal system. Then we will see how the Supreme Court and political developments have shaped—and continue to shape—our modern system of federalism.

Defining Federalism

Scholars have argued and wars have been fought about what federalism really means. One scholar counted 267 definitions.[3] **Federalism,** as we define it, is a form of government in which a constitution distributes powers between a central government and subdivisional governments—usually called states or provinces or republics—giving to both the national government and the regional governments substantial responsibilities and powers, including the power to collect taxes and to pass and enforce laws regulating the conduct of individuals.

The mere existence of both national and state governments does not make

INTERPRETATIONS OF FEDERALISM

Federalism is a powerful but elusive concept, leading both scholars and politicians to add adjectives that reflect their ideas about the governmental relations within a federal system.

Dual Federalism interprets the Constitution as giving a limited list of powers—primarily foreign policy and national defense—to the national government, leaving most power to sovereign states. Each level of government is dominant within its own sphere. The Supreme Court serves as the umpire between the national government and the states in case of a dispute over which government is in charge of a particular activity. During our first hundred years, dual federalism was the favored interpretation most of the time by the Supreme Court, and it is echoed in the speeches of Presidents Reagan and Bush.

Cooperative Federalism stresses federalism as a system to deliver governmental goods and services to the people and calls for cooperation among various levels of governments in "getting the job done."

Marble Cake Federalism, coined by political scientist Morton Grodzins in 1966, conceives of federalism as a marble cake in which all levels of government are involved in a variety of issues and programs, rather than a layer cake with uniform divisions between layers or levels of government. As he wrote, "There is no neat horizontal stratification. Vertical and diagonal lines almost obliterate the horizontal ones, and in some places there are unexpected whirls and imperceptible merging of colors, so that it is difficult to tell where one ends and the other begins."[a]

The New Federalism, favored by President Richard Nixon and also used by Presidents Reagan and Bush, emphasizes their view that we should return fiscal resources and management responsibilities to the states in the form of large block grants and revenue sharing, and that we should more rationally sort out functions between national and state governments.

Competitive Federalism, a term created by Thomas R. Dye, brings to the fore the fact that federalism provides us with a national government, fifty states, and thousands of other units, each competing with one another in the way in which they put together packages of services and taxes and vying with each other for the support of citizens. Applying the analogy of the marketplace, Dye emphasizes that at the state and local levels we have some choice which state and city we want "to use," just as we have choices about which automobile we wish to drive.[b]

Permissive Federalism implies that although federalism provides "a sharing of power and authority between the national and state government, the states' share rests upon the permission and permissiveness of the national government."[c]

Intergovernmental relations is a term sometimes used as a synonym for federalism, sometimes in place of it. It came into vogue among political scientists in recent decades to emphasize that Americans have more than 87,000 different units of government and that governing our nation involves more than national and state officials. This view can be seen in the Advisory Commission on Intergovernmental Relations (ACIR), created by Congress to monitor the operations of the federal system and to make recommendations for its improvement. By undertaking studies, issuing publications, and drafting bills, ACIR has become a prominent part of the "intergovernmental landscape" and federalism's advocate. Its twenty-six members, who serve two-year terms each, represent Congress, the federal executive branch, state and local governments, and the public.

[a]Morton Grodzins, "The Federal System," in *Goals for Americans: The Report of the President's Commission on National Goals* (Columbia University Press, 1960), p. 265.

[b]Thomas R. Dye, *American Federalism: Competition among Governments* (Lexington Books, 1990), pp. 13–17.

[c]Michael D. Reagan and John G. Sanzone, *The New Federalism* (Oxford University Press, 1981), p. 175.

a system federal. What is important is that a *constitution divides governmental powers between the general, or national government and the constituent governments* (called *states* in the United States), giving substantial functions to each. Neither the central nor the constituent government receives its powers from the other; both derive them from a common source—a constitution. This constitutional distribution of powers cannot be changed by the ordinary processes of legislation—for example, by an act of either a national or state legislature. Both levels of government operate through their own agents and exercise power directly over individuals. Other countries that have federal systems include Canada, Switzerland, Mexico, and Australia. "Nearly 40 percent of the world's population now lives within polities that are formally federal; another third live in polities that apply federal arrangements in some way."[4]

Constitutionally, the federal system of the United States consists of only the national government and the fifty states. "Cities are not," the Supreme Court has reminded us, "sovereign entities." But in a practical sense, we are a nation of more than 87,000 governmental units—from the national government to the school board district (see Table 2-1). This does not make for a tidy, efficient, easy-to-understand system; yet, as we shall see, it does have its virtues.

ALTERNATIVES TO FEDERALISM

Among the alternatives to federalism are **unitary systems** of government in which a constitution vests all governmental power in the central government. The central government, if it so chooses, may delegate authority to constituent units, but what it delegates it may take away. Britain, France, Israel, and the Philippines have a unitary form of government. In the United States, state constitutions usually create this kind of relationship between the state and its local governments.

At the other extreme are **confederations** in which sovereign nations by a constitutional compact create a central government but carefully *limit* the power of the central government and do not give it the power to regulate the

TABLE 2-1
Number of Governments

States	50
Counties	3,043
Municipalities	19,296
Towns	16,666
School Districts	14,556
Special Districts	33,131
Total	86,743

Source: U.S. Department of Commerce, Bureau of the Census, *1992 Census of Governments.*

conduct of individuals directly. The central government makes regulations for the constituent governments, but it exists and operates only at their direction. The thirteen states under the Articles of Confederation operated in this manner, as did the southern Confederacy during the Civil War (see Figure 2-1).

To complicate this matter, the framers of our Constitution used the term "federal" to describe what we would now call a *confederate* form of government. Moreover, today the term "federal" is frequently used as a synonym for national; people often refer to the government in Washington as "the federal government." But it is the states and the national government *together* that make up our federal system.

WHY FEDERALISM?

In 1787, federalism was an obvious choice. Confederation had been tried and found wanting, but a unitary system was out of the question. Most of the people were too deeply attached to their state governments to permit them to be subordinated to central rule. Federalism was, and still is, thought to be ideally suited to the needs of a heterogeneous people spread over a large continent, suspicious of concentrated power, and desiring unity but not uniformity. Federalism offered, and still offers, many advantages for such a people.

Federalism Checks the Growth of Tyranny Although in the rest of the world federal forms have not been notably successful in preventing tyranny, and many unitary governments are democratic, Americans tend to associate freedom with federalism.[5] As James Madison pointed out in *The Federalist*, No. 10: If "factious leaders . . . kindle a flame within their particular states," national leaders can check the spread of the "conflagration through the other states." Moreover, when one political party loses control of the national government, it is still likely to hold office in a number of states. It can then regroup, develop new policies and new leaders, and continue to challenge the party in power at the national level.

Such diffusion of power creates its own problems. It makes it difficult for a national majority to carry out a program of action, and it permits those who control a state government to frustrate the consensus expressed through Congress and national agencies. To some of our Constitution's framers, this was an advantage. They were more fearful that a single-interest national majority might capture the national government and attempt to suppress the interests of others than they were that minority interests might frustrate the national will. Of course the size of the nation and the many interests within it are the greatest obstacles to the formation of a single-interest majority, a point often overlooked today (but emphasized by Madison in *The Federalist*, No. 10). If such a majority were to occur, having to work through a federal system would act to check its power.

Federalism Allows Unity without Uniformity National politicians and parties do not have to iron out every difference on every issue that divides us,

FIGURE 2-1   A Comparison of Confederation and Federalism

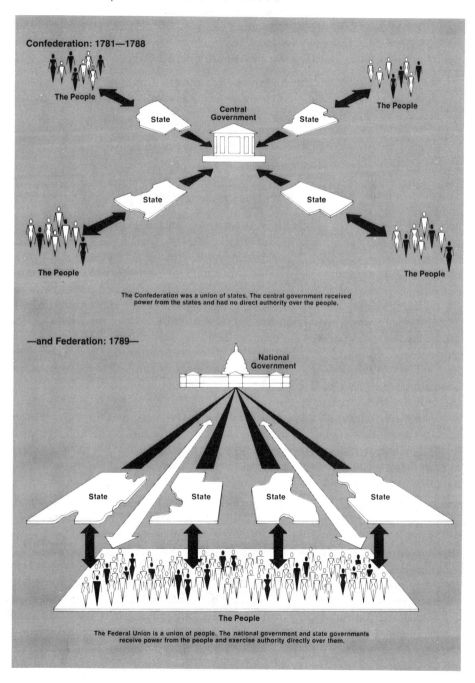

Confederation: 1781—1788

The People

State

Central
Government

State

The People

State

State

The People

The People

The Confederation was a union of states. The central government received
power from the states and had no direct authority over the people.

—and Federation: 1789—

National
Government

State

State

State

State

The People

The Federal Union is a union of people. The national government and state governments
receive power from the people and exercise authority directly over them.

whether it be divorce, gun control, capital punishment, education financing, or comparable worth. (**Comparable worth,** which mandates comparable pay for jobs requiring comparable skills, has been advanced as one way to correct pay inequities between higher-paying, male-dominated fields, such as plumbing, and lower-paying, female-dominated fields, such as teaching.) Instead, these issues are debated in state legislatures, county courthouses, and city halls.

Federalism Encourages Experimentation Supreme Court Justice Louis Brandeis pointed out that state governments provide great laboratories for public policy experimentation. States serve as proving grounds. If they adopt programs that fail, the negative effects are limited; if programs succeed, they can be adopted by other states and by the national government. Georgia, for example, was the first state to permit 18-year-olds to vote; New York has been vigorous in its assault on water pollution; California has pioneered air pollution control programs, especially automobile emission standards. After federal leadership on environmental matters waned in the 1970s, New Jersey assumed leadership in programs to handle toxic wastes; it initiated radon gas testing and was the first state to adopt a statewide mandatory recycling law. Many states legalized abortion under certain conditions before the Supreme Court acted. (Whether this is progress or regression depends, of course, on one's values, as do so many questions of politics.) "Sunset laws" (requiring periodic reauthorization for programs), equal housing, no-fault insurance, and "lemon laws" (providing consumer protection for faulty automobiles) are other examples of programs that originated in the states. Nevada is the only state, so far, to legalize statewide gambling, but legalized gambling is now found in parts of New Jersey, Iowa, Illinois, Wisconsin, North Dakota, and South Dakota. Not all innovations are widely adopted; Nebraska is the only state, for example, to use the unicameral legislature.

The states' role as laboratories of democracy has become even more important as the federal government in the 1990s faces "fiscal and political limits . . . and as the nation confronts such matters as . . . the revolution in family life, including, for example, surrogate motherhood, test-tube babies, adoption, and care of the elderly."[6]

Federalism Keeps Government Closer to the People By providing numerous arenas for decision making, federalism involves many people and helps keep government closer to the people. Every day thousands of Americans are at work running our governments by serving on city councils, school boards, neighborhood associations, and planning commissions. And since they are close to the issues and have firsthand knowledge of what needs to be done, they may be more responsive than the experts in Washington.

We should be cautious, however, about generalizing that state and local governments are necessarily "closer to the people" than the national government is. True, more people are involved in local and state politics than in national affairs, and in recent years confidence in the ability of state governments

From which level of government
do you feel you get the most for
your money — national, state, or local?

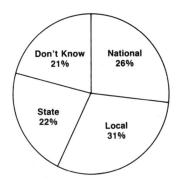

**Don't Know
21%**

**National
26%**

**State
22%**

**Local
31%**

FIGURE 2-2
The Most Popular Level of Government
Source: Advisory Commission on Intergovernmental
Relations, *Changing Public Attitudes on Governments
and Taxes, 1991* (Government Printing Office, 1992),
p. 7.

has gone up while respect for national agencies has diminished (see Figure 2-2.)
Yet national and international affairs are often more on the minds of most people than are state or even local politics. Fewer voters participate in state elections than in congressional and presidential elections. Still, states and their
local units remain an important part of the political life of those concerned
with public affairs.

The Constitutional Structure of American Federalism

Dividing powers and responsibilities between the national and state governments requires thousands of court decisions, hundreds of books, and endless
speeches to explain—and even then the division lacks precise definition. The
formal constitutional framework of our federal system, however, may be stated
relatively simply:

1. The national government has only those powers *delegated* to it by the Constitution (with one important exception of the inherent power over foreign
   affairs).

2. Within the scope of its operations, the national government is supreme.

3. The state governments have the powers not delegated to the central government, except those *denied* to them by the Constitution and their state
   constitutions.

4. Some powers are specifically denied to *both* the national and state governments; others are specifically denied *only* to the states; still others are denied *only* to the national government.

POWERS OF THE NATIONAL GOVERNMENT

The Constitution, chiefly in the first three articles, delegates legislative, executive, and judicial powers to the national government. In addition to these **express powers,** such as the power to appropriate funds, the Constitution delegates to Congress **implied powers,** such as the power to create banks, which may be inferred from express powers. (We will see an example when we discuss the famous case of *McCulloch v. Maryland.*) The constitutional basis for the implied powers of Congress is the **necessary and proper clause** (Article I, Section 8, Clause 18). This clause gives Congress the right "to make all Laws which shall be necessary and proper for carrying into Execution the foregoing Powers, and all other Powers vested . . . in the Government of the United States."

In the field of foreign affairs the Constitution gives the national government **inherent powers,** so that the national government has the same authority to deal with other nations as if it were the central government in a unitary system. These inherent powers do not depend on specific constitutional grants. For example, the government of the United States may acquire territory by discovery and occupation, though no specific clause in the Constitution allows such acquisition. Even if the Constitution were silent about foreign affairs, which it is not, the national government would have the right to declare war, make treaties, and appoint and receive ambassadors.

Together, these express, implied, and inherent powers create a flexible system that has allowed the Supreme Court, Congress, the president, and the people to expand the central government's powers to meet the needs of a modern industrial nation operating in a global economy. This expansion of central government functions has rested on four constitutional pillars.

National Supremacy Clause One of the most important pillars is found in Article VI of the Constitution: "This Constitution, and the Laws of the United States which shall be made in Pursuance thereof; and all Treaties made . . . under the Authority of the United States, shall be the supreme Law of the Land; and the Judges in every State shall be bound thereby; any Thing in the Constitution or Laws of any State to the Contrary notwithstanding." All officials, state as well as national, are bound by constitutional oath to support the Constitution of the United States. States may not use their reserved powers to override national policies. (This also applies to local units of government since they are agents of the states.) National laws and regulations of federal agencies *preempt* the field so that conflicting state and local rules and regulations are unenforceable.

The War Power The national government is responsible for protecting the nation from external aggression and, when necessary, for waging war. In today's world, military strength depends not only on troops in the field but also on the ability to mobilize the nation's industrial might and to apply scientific knowledge to the tasks of defense. The national government has the power to wage war and to do what is necessary and proper to do so successfully. This means the national government has the power to do almost anything not in direct conflict with constitutional guarantees.

The Power to Regulate Interstate and Foreign Commerce Congressional authority extends to all commerce that affects more than one state and to all those activities, wherever they exist or whatever their nature, whose control Congress decides is necessary and proper to regulate interstate and foreign commerce. *Commerce* includes the production, buying, selling, renting, and transporting of goods, services, and properties.[7] The **commerce clause**—Article 1, Section 8, Clause 3—packs a tremendous constitutional punch: it gives Congress the power "to regulate commerce with foreign Nations, and among the several States, and with the Indian Tribes." In these few words the national government has been able to find constitutional justification for regulating a wide range of human activity including agriculture, transportation, finance, product safety, labor relations, and the workplace. Few, if any, aspects of our economy today affect commerce in only one state and are thus outside the scope of the national government's constitutional authority.

The commerce clause can also be used to sustain legislation that goes beyond commercial matters. When the Supreme Court upheld the 1964 Civil Rights Act forbidding discrimination because of race, religion, or national origin in places of public accommodation, it said: "Congress's action in removing the disruptive effect which it found racial discrimination has on interstate travel is not invalidated because Congress was also legislating against what it considers to be moral wrongs." Discrimination restricts the flow of interstate commerce; interstate commerce was being used to support discrimination; therefore, Congress could legislate against the discrimination. Moreover, the law could be applied even to local places of public accommodation because local incidents of discrimination have a substantial and harmful impact on interstate commerce. "If it is interstate commerce that feels the pinch, it does not matter how local the operation that applies the squeeze."[8]

The Power to Tax and Spend Congress lacks constitutional authority to pass laws solely on the ground that they will promote the general welfare, but it may raise taxes and spend money for this purpose. This distinction between *legislating* and *appropriating* makes little difference most of the time. Congress, for example, lacks constitutional power to regulate education or agriculture directly, yet it does have the power to appropriate money to support education or to pay farmers subsidies. By attaching conditions to its grants of money, Congress may thus regulate what it cannot directly control by law.

When Congress puts up the money, it determines how the money will be spent. By withholding or threatening to withhold funds, the national government can influence—or control—state operations and regulate individual conduct. For example, Congress has stipulated that federal funds should be withdrawn from any program in which any person is denied benefits because of race, color, or national origin; subsequently the categories of sex and physical handicap were added. Congress has also used its power of the purse to force states to raise the drinking age to 21 by tying such a condition to federal dollars for highways.

Congress frequently requires states to do certain things—for example, provide services to indigent mothers, take action to clean up the air and water—or else Congress will take away federal funds or impose even more stringent federal regulations. These requirements are called **federal mandates.** Congress often does not supply the funds required to carry out these mandates.

These four constitutional pillars—the national supremacy clause, the war power, the power over interstate commerce, and, most especially, the power to tax and spend for the general welfare—have permitted a tremendous expansion of federal functions.

POWERS OF THE STATES

The Constitution reserves for the states all powers not granted to the national government, subject only to the limitations of the Constitution. Powers not given *exclusively* to the national government, by provision of the Constitution or by judicial interpretation, may be *concurrently* exercised by the states, as long as there is no conflict with national law. Each state has **concurrent powers** with the national government, such as the power to levy taxes and regulate commerce internal to each state (see Table 2-2).

Precisely how federalism limits the states' taxing powers is neither simple to explain nor simple to understand. In general, a state may levy a tax on the same item as the national government, but a state cannot, by a tax, "unduly burden" commerce among the states, or interfere with a function of the national government, or complicate the operation of a national law, or abridge the terms of a treaty of the United States. Who decides whether a state tax is an "undue burden" on a national function or commerce among the states? Ultimately, the Supreme Court decides.

Federalism issues are even more complicated when states act to protect the

TABLE 2-2   The Federal Division of Powers

Types of Powers Delegated to the National Government	Powers Reserved to the States	Some Concurrent Powers Shared by the National and State Governments
• Express powers stated in Constitution	• To create a republican form of government	• To tax citizens and businesses
• Implied powers that may be inferred from express powers	• To charter local governments	• To borrow and spend money
	• To conduct elections	• To establish courts
• Inherent powers that allow nation to present a united front to foreign powers	• To exercise all powers not delegated to the national government or denied to the states by the Constitution	• To pass and enforce laws
		• To protect civil rights

environment and the public health and well-being. When Congress has not preempted the field, states may even regulate interstate businesses, provided these regulations do not cover matters requiring uniform national treatment or unduly burdening interstate commerce. Who decides what matters require uniform national treatment or what actions might place an undue burden on interstate commerce? Congress does, subject to final review by the Supreme Court. When Congress is silent or does not clearly state its intentions, courts, ultimately the Supreme Court, decide if there is a conflict with the national Constitution or if there has been federal preemption by law or regulation.

CONSTITUTIONAL LIMITS AND OBLIGATIONS

To make federalism work, the Constitution imposes certain restraints on both the national and the state governments. States are prohibited from:

1. Making treaties with foreign governments
2. Authorizing private persons to prey on the shipping and commerce of other nations—what the Constitution refers to as granting letters of marque and reprisal, a practice common during times of war in the eighteenth century
3. Coining money, issuing bills of credit, or making anything but gold and silver coin a tender in payment of debts

Nor may states without the consent of Congress:

1. Tax imports or exports
2. Tax foreign ships
3. Keep troops or ships in time of peace (except the state militia, now called the National Guard)
4. Enter into compacts with other states or foreign nations that "tend to increase the political power in the States, which may encroach upon or interfere"[9] with the supremacy of the national government
5. Engage in war, unless invaded or in such imminent danger as will not admit of delay (Of course, an invasion of one state would be an invasion of the United States itself.)

The national government, in turn, is required by the Constitution to refrain from exercising its powers, especially its powers to tax and to regulate interstate commerce, in such a way as to interfere substantially with the states' ability to perform their responsibilities. Making this generalization about how the priciples of federalism limit national powers is easier than citing modern-day examples of the Supreme Court's striking down actions of the national government because they interfere with state sovereignty. Today, whatever

SECESSIONISM LIVES ON: A FIFTY-FIRST STATE?

Secession—an effort by a local region to break away from the parent state—recurs periodically in American and world history. England fought an unsuccessful war to prevent the 13 colonies from forming an independent nation. The United States waged the Civil War to prevent secession by the southern states. And the Soviet Union dissolved recently after failing to hold its member republics together.

In 1992 the citizens of southwestern Kansas authorized a constitutional convention to withdraw from Kansas and form the fifty-first state. In past years citizens of Alaska, Nantucket, Virginia, Nebraska, Colorado, and California have also made unsuccessful attempts to secede.

Source: Adapted from Kate Miniclier, "Irate Taxpayers Seek Secession from Kansas," *Denver Post,* April 19, 1992.

protection states have comes from the political process—in restraints that our system provides because individuals elected from the states participate in the decisions of Congress—rather than from judicially enforced limitations.[10]

The Constitution also requires the national government to guarantee to each state a *republican form of government.* The framers used this term to distinguish a republic from a monarchy, on the one side, and from a pure, direct democracy, on the other. Congress, not the courts, enforces this guarantee and determines what is or is not a republican form of government. By permitting the congressional delegation of a state to take its seat in Congress, Congress, in effect, acknowledges that the state has the republican form of government guaranteed by the Constitution.

In addition, the national government is obliged by the Constitution to protect states against *domestic insurrection.* Congress has delegated to the president the authority to dispatch troops to put down such insurrections when so requested by the proper state authorities. If there are contesting state authorities, the president decides which ones are the proper ones.[11] The president does not have to wait, however, for a request from state authorities to send federal troops into a state to enforce federal laws. Today it is hard to imagine a situation of domestic insurrection against a state that would not also involve federal laws.

HORIZONTAL FEDERALISM: INTERSTATE RELATIONS

Three clauses in the Constitution, taken from the Articles of Confederation, require states to give full faith and credit to one another's public acts, records, and judicial proceedings; to extend to one another's citizens the privileges and immunities of their own citizens; and to return persons who are fleeing from justice.

Full Faith and Credit The **full faith and credit clause** (Article IV, Section 1), one of the more technical provisions of the Constitution, requires that state courts enforce the civil judgments of the courts of other states and accept their public records and acts as valid. (It does not require states to enforce the criminal laws of other states; in most cases, for one state to enforce the criminal laws of another would be unconstitutional.) The clause applies especially to noncriminal judicial proceedings, such as enforcement of judicial settlements and court awards.

Interstate Privileges and Immunities Under Article IV, Section 2, states must extend to citizens of other states the privileges and immunities granted to their own citizens, including the protection of the laws, the right to engage in peaceful occupations, access to the courts, and freedom from discriminatory taxes. Further, because of this clause, states may not impose unreasonable *durational residency* requirements, that is, withhold rights to American citizens who have recently moved to the state and thereby have become citizens of that state. For example, a state may not set unreasonable time limits to withhold state-funded medical benefits from new citizens or to keep them from voting. How long a residency requirement may a state impose? A day seems about as long as the Court will tolerate to withhold welfare payments or medical care, fifty days or so for voting privileges, and one year for eligibility for in-state tuition for state-supported colleges and universities.

Extradition In Article IV, Section 2, the Constitution asserts that when criminals have fled from one state to another, the state to which they have fled is to deliver them to the proper officials upon the demand of the executive authority of the state from which they fled. This process is called **extradition.** "The obvious objective of the Extradition Clause," the courts have claimed, "is that no State should become a safe haven for the fugitives from a sister State's criminal justice system."[12] Congress has supplemented this constitutional provision by making the governor of the state to which fugitives have fled the agent responsible for returning them. Despite the use of the word "shall" in the Constitution, an 1861 Supreme Court decision, based on an antiquated view of federalism, controlled extradition until 1987, and federal courts would not order governors to surrender (extradite) persons wanted in other states. This is no longer so, since the 1861 decision has been reversed.[13] Usually federal courts do not become involved, and extradition is a routine matter. Recently, however, disputes over the custody of children that sometimes lead to criminal charges of parental kidnapping have complicated extradition procedures.

Despite their constitutional obligation, governors of asylum states on occasion have refused to honor a request for extradition. So far in modern times no federal judge has had to try to enforce an extradition request. When the governor of Indiana refused to extradite Bobby Knight, the celebrated Indiana University basketball coach who had been convicted in absentia by a Puerto Rican court of assaulting a police officer during the Pan-American Games in Puerto Rico, the governor of Puerto Rico decided not to force the matter.

Interstate Compacts　The Constitution also requires states to settle disputes with one another without the use of force. States may carry their legal disputes to the Supreme Court, or they may negotiate **interstate compacts.** More often, interstate compacts are used to establish interstate agencies to handle interstate problems. Before most interstate compacts become effective, congressional approval is required. After a compact has been signed and approved by Congress, it becomes binding on all signatory states, and its terms are enforceable by the Supreme Court. A typical state belongs to twenty compacts dealing with such subjects as environmental protection, crime control, water rights, and higher education exchanges.[14]

The Politics of Federalism

This outline of the constitutional structure of federalism is oversimplified and even misleading—especially in terms of the division of powers between the national government and the states. The formal structures of our federal system have not changed much since 1787, but the political realities, especially during the last half-century, have greatly altered how federalism works. To understand this, we need to look at some of the trends that spurred the growth of big government and continue to fuel the debate about the meaning of federalism.

THE GROWTH OF BIG GOVERNMENT

Over the past two hundred years there has been a drift of power from other institutions—families, churches and synagogues, the marketplace—to governments, and especially to the national government. "No one planned the growth," explains the Advisory Commission on Intergovernmental Relations, "but everyone played a part in it."[15] How did this come about? For a variety of reasons. One is that many of our problems became national in scope. Much that was local in 1789, in 1860, or in 1930 is now national—even global. State governments could supervise the relations between small merchants and their few employees, but only the national government can supervise relations between an international industry and its thousands of employees, all organized in national unions.

As industrialization proceeded, powerful interests made demands on the national government. Business groups called on the government for aid in the form of tariffs, a national banking system, and subsidies to railroads and the merchant marine. Farmers learned that the national government could give more aid than the states, and they, too, began to demand help. By the beginning of this century, urban groups in general, and organized labor in particular, pressed their claims. Big business, big agriculture, and big labor all add up to big government.

The growth of the national economy and the creation of a national transportation and communications network altered people's attitudes toward the national government. Before the Civil War, the national government was viewed as a distant, even foreign, government. Today, in part because of television, most people identify as closely with Washington as with their state capitals.

The Great Depression of the 1930s stimulated extensive national action on such issues as relief, unemployment, and agriculture surpluses. World War II brought federal regulation of wages, prices, and employment, as well as national efforts to allocate resources, train personnel, and support engineering and inventions. After the war the national government helped veterans and inaugurated a vast system of support for university research. Moreover, the United States became the most powerful member of the free world and maintains substantial military forces, even during times of peace.

The Great Society programs of the 1960s poured out grants-in-aid to states and localities. City dwellers, including African Americans who had migrated from the rural South to northern cities, began to seek federal funds for—at the very least—housing, education, and mass transportation.

Although economic and social conditions generated many pressures for expansion of the national government, so did political pressures. Members of Congress, presidents, federal judges, and federal administrators have actively promoted federal initiatives. And until the recent years of overwhelming budget deficits, Congress in particular encouraged this trend. True, when there is widespread conflict about what to do—how to reduce the federal deficit, adopt a national energy policy, reform social security, provide health care for the indigent—Congress waits for a national consensus and looks to presidents for leadership. But when an organized constituency wants something and there is no counterpressure, Congress "responds often to everyone, and with great vigor."[16] Once established, federal programs generate groups with vested interests in promoting, defending, and expanding them. Associations are formed; alliances are made. "In a word, the growth of government has created a constituency of, by, and for government."[17]

THE GREAT DEBATE—CENTRALISTS VERSUS DECENTRALISTS

The growth of big government was not without controversy. During the Great Depression of the 1930s, the nation debated whether Congress had the constitutional authority to enact legislation on agriculture, labor, education, housing, and welfare. Only 30 years ago some questioned the constitutional authority of Congress to legislate against racial discrimination. The debate continues between those who favor national action (**centralists**) and those who favor action at the state and local levels (**decentralists**), yet generally it does so outside the framework of constitutional principles. This victory for the nationalists is relatively recent and not likely to be the last word. Throughout our history and into the present, powerful groups have favored states' rights, and they still do today.

The constitutional arguments revolving around federalism grew out of specific political issues: Did the national government have the authority to outlaw slavery in the territories? Did states have the authority to operate racially segregated schools? Could Congress regulate labor relations? The debates were frequently phrased in constitutional language, with appeals to the great principles of federalism. But they were also arguments over who was to get what, where, and how, and who was to do what to whom.

Among those favoring the decentralist or states' rights interpretation, with varying emphasis, were Thomas Jefferson, John C. Calhoun, the Supreme Court from the 1920s to 1937, and more recently, Ronald Reagan, George Bush, Chief Justice William H. Rehnquist, and Justice Sandra Day O'Connor. Most decentralists contend the Constitution is a treaty among sovereign states that created the central government and gave it carefully limited authority. As a result, the national government is nothing more than an agent of the states, and every one of its powers should be narrowly defined. Any question about whether the states have given a particular function to the central government or have reserved it for themselves should be resolved in favor of the states.

Decentralists hold that the national government should not be permitted to exercise its delegated powers in a way that interferes with activities reserved for the states. The Tenth Amendment, they claim, makes this clear: "The powers not delegated to the United States by the Constitution, nor prohibited by it to the States, are reserved to the States respectively, or to the people." Decentralists insist state governments are closer to the people and reflect the people's wishes more accurately than does the national government. The national government, they add, is inherently heavy-handed and bureaucratic; to preserve our federal system and our liberties, central authority must be kept under control.

The centralist position has been supported by Chief Justice John Marshall, Abraham Lincoln, Theodore Roosevelt, Franklin Roosevelt, and throughout most of our history by the Supreme Court. (Chief Justice Rehnquist and Justice O'Connor, two of the strongest "defenders of states' sovereignty on the U.S. Supreme Court" of the last half century well may win enough converts from the Reagan and Bush appointees to veer the current Court back to a more decentralist position.)[18]

Centralists reject the whole idea of the Constitution as an interstate compact. Rather, they view the Constitution as a supreme law established by the people. The national government is an agent of the people, not of the states, because it was the people who drew up the Constitution and created the national government. The sovereign people gave the national government sufficient power to accomplish the great objectives listed in the Preamble to the Constitution. They intended that the central government's powers should be liberally defined, and that the central government should be denied authority only when the Constitution clearly prohibits it from acting.

Centralists argue the national government is a government of all the people and that each state speaks for only some of the people. Although the Tenth Amendment clearly reserves powers for the states, as Chief Justice Harlan

Stone said, "The Tenth Amendment states but a truism that all is retained which has not been surrendered."[19] The amendment does not deny the national government the right to exercise to the fullest extent all the powers given to it by the Constitution. On the other hand, the supremacy of the national government, it is argued, restricts the states, because governments representing part of the people cannot be allowed to interfere with a government representing all of them.

The Role of the Federal Courts

Congress and the political process ultimately decide how power will be divided between the national and the state governments. Still, the federal courts—and especially the Supreme Court—have often been called on to umpire the ongoing debate about which level of government should do what, for whom, and to whom.

MCCULLOCH VERSUS MARYLAND

In *McCulloch v. Maryland* (1819) the Supreme Court had the first of many chances to choose between a nationalist and a states' rights interpretation of our federal system.[20] Maryland had levied a tax against the Baltimore branch of the Bank of the United States, a semipublic agency established by Congress. James William McCulloch, the cashier of the bank, refused to pay on the grounds that a state could not tax an instrument of the national government. Maryland's attorneys responded that, in the first place, the national government did not have the power to incorporate a bank, but even if it did, the state had the power to tax it.

Maryland was represented before the Court by some of the country's most distinguished lawyers, including Luther Martin. A delegate to the Constitutional Convention, Martin left early when it became apparent that a strong national government was in the making. Basing his argument on the states' rights view of federalism, Martin said the power to incorporate a bank is not expressly delegated to the national government. He contended that the necessary and proper clause gives Congress only the power to choose those means and to pass those laws absolutely essential to the execution of its expressly granted powers. Because a bank is not absolutely necessary to the exercise of any of its delegated powers, Congress has no authority to establish it. As for Maryland's right to tax the bank, Martin's position was clear: The power to tax is one of the powers reserved to the states; they may use it as they see fit.

The national government was represented by equally distinguished counsel, chief among whom was Daniel Webster. Webster conceded the power to create a bank is not one of the express powers of the national government. However, the power to pass laws *necessary and proper* to carry out express powers is specifically delegated to Congress, and this should be interpreted to mean Congress has authority to enact any legislation convenient and useful in carrying out delegated national powers. Therefore, Congress may incorporate a bank as an appropriate, convenient, and useful means of exercising the granted powers of collecting taxes, borrowing money, and caring for the property of the United States.

Although the power to tax is reserved to the states, Webster contended that states cannot use their reserved powers to interfere with the operations of the national government. The Constitution leaves no room for doubt; in cases of conflict between the national and state governments, the national is supreme.

Speaking for a unanimous Court, Chief Justice John Marshall rejected every one of Maryland's contentions. He wrote:

> We must never forget that it is a constitution we are expounding . . . a constitution intended to endure for ages to come, and consequently, to be adapted to the various crises of human affairs. . . . The government of the Union, then, . . . is, emphatically, and truly, a government of the people. In form and substance it emanates from them. Its powers are granted by them, and are to be exercised directly on them, and for their benefit. . . . It can never be to their interest and cannot be presumed to have been their intention, to clog and embarrass its execution, by withholding the most appropriate means.

Marshall summarized his views on the powers of the national government in these now-famous words: "Let the end be legitimate, let it be within the scope of the Constitution, and all means which are appropriate, which are plainly adapted to that end, which are not prohibited, but consist with the letter and spirit of the constitution, are constitutional."

Having thus established the doctrine of implied national powers, Marshall set forth the doctrine of **national supremacy.** No state, he said, can use its reserved taxing powers to tax a national instrument. "The power to tax involves the power to destroy. . . . If the right of the states to tax the means employed by the general government be conceded, the declaration that the Constitution, and the laws made in pursuance thereof, shall be the supreme law of the land, is empty and unmeaning declamation."

The long-range significance of *McCulloch v. Maryland* in providing support for the developing forces of nationalism cannot be overstated. The arguments of the states' righters, if accepted, would have strapped the national government in a constitutional straitjacket and denied it powers needed to handle the problems of an expanding nation.

AN EXPANDING ROLE FOR THE FEDERAL COURTS

The authority of federal judges to review the activities of state and local governments has expanded dramatically in recent decades because of modern judicial interpretations of the Thirteenth, Fourteenth, and Fifteenth Amendments (especially the Fourteenth) and the congressional legislation enacted to implement these amendments. Today almost every action by state and local officials can be challenged before a federal judge as a violation of the Constitution or of federal law.

In carrying out their judgments, federal judges sometimes have, in effect, taken over the supervision of state prison systems, public hospitals, public schools, and other public facilities. The Supreme Court has gone so far as to sustain a federal judge's right to order a local school board to ignore a state's constitutional constraints and to raise taxes and sell bonds in order to fund the operation of a racially integrated magnet school. In his dissent, joined by Chief Justice Rehnquist and Justices Scalia and O'Connor, Justice Kennedy charged that the Court majority disregarded "fundamental precepts for the democratic control of public institutions," with its "casual embrace of taxation imposed by the unelected, life-tenured federal judiciary."[21]

One of the major instruments for opening these matters to federal court review is the Supreme Court's revitalization—some would say the rewriting— during recent decades of an 1871 civil rights act originally written to combat the Ku Klux Klan. This act, now called Section 1983 after its designation in Title 42 of the United States Code, permits individuals to go into federal court to sue cities and counties for damages or seek injunctions against any person acting under the color of law, that is in an official capacity, whom they believe has deprived them of any right secured by the Constitution or by any one of the several thousands of federal laws.[22] (Although federal judges can order states to stop acting in a manner that violates the federal Constitution or laws or treaties, the Eleventh Amendment constrains federal courts from hearing damage suits against the states—but not against local government officials.)

Federal judges spend a considerable portion of their time trying to decide which provisions of federal laws preempt state and local action. State and local laws are preempted not only when they conflict directly with federal laws and regulations, but also if they only touch a field in which the "federal interest is so dominated that the federal system will be assumed to preclude enforcement of state laws on the same subject."[23] **Preemption** occurs when a federal law or regulation takes over and precludes enforcement of a state or local law or regulation. Examples of federal preemption include the Coast Guard Authorization Act directing the secretary or transportation to develop standards for determining when people are considered intoxicated while operating a marine recreational vessel; dozens of laws regulating hazardous substances, water quality, and clean air standards; and many civil rights acts, most especially the Civil Rights Act of 1964 and the Voting Rights Act of 1965.

Over the years federal judges, under the leadership of the Supreme Court, have favored national powers (including their own). However, recently the Supreme Court has returned to the states several explosive political issues. Perhaps most notably, in 1989 the Court in *Webster v. Reproductive Health Services* gave states considerable latitude to regulate abortion, setting off intense clashes between pro-choice and right-to-life groups in the state legislatures.[24]

Despite the Supreme Court's bias in favor of national over state authority, few would deny the Supreme Court the power to review and set aside state actions. As Justice Oliver Wendell Holmes once remarked: "I do not think the United States would come to an end if we lost our power to declare an Act of Congress void. I do think the Union would be imperiled if we could not make that declaration as to the laws of the several States."[25]

A MESSAGE FROM GARCIA:
FEDERALISM AS A POLITICAL AND NOT A LEGAL CONSTRAINT

In 1985, by a 5–4 vote, in *Garcia v. San Antonio Metro* the Supreme Court said, in essence, that the federal courts should get out of the business of protecting the states from congressional interference. Congress, not the courts, said the court majority, decides which actions of the states should be regulated by the national government. The Court, in this case, upheld the application of the federal minimum wage and hours regulations to the employees of the San Antonio transit system.[26] Three years later, the Court, although noting that "some extraordinary defects in the national political process might render congressional regulation of state activities invalid," reaffirmed that nothing in the Constitution "authorizes courts to second-guess the substantive basis for congressional legislation 'affecting state action.' " "The States," said the Supreme Court, "must find their protection from congressional regulation through the national political process" rather than look to judges to shield them from it.[27]

Justice Sandra Day O'Connor, with the Chief Justice Rehnquist's concurrence, predicted "this Court will in time again assume its constitutional responsibility" of defining the scope of state autonomy protected by federalism.[28] She is probably right. Justices since nominated by Presidents Reagan and Bush—Scalia, Kennedy, Souter, and Thomas—are likely to be more sympathetic to her version of federalism than the majority in *Garcia*. The message from Garcia is not likely to be the final word on this matter. In fact, the Rehnquist Court has already started to modify the Garcia doctrine. It refused to apply the Age Discrimination in Employment Act of 1967 to set aside a provision of the Missouri Constitution mandating the retirement of judges at the age of seventy because Congress, although specifically making the law applicable to state employees, had not plainly stated it intended the law to apply to state judges.[29] Yet even the conservative justices acknowledged that if federal courts resume the task of protecting the states, the set of activities protected by state sovereignty from the reach of the national government "may well be negligible."[30]

Whether Congress can be counted on, as the Court argued in *Garcia*, to protect the states from being overwhelmed by the national government is not clear. State governments do not appear to have great influence in the halls of Congress. Members of Congress have their own constituents and are no longer dependent on state political parties for funds or electoral help. Congressional voting on federalism issues suggests moderate levels of support for the concept of federalism,[31] yet it does not appear to be an overwhelming concern for most members of Congress. And although a few senators have suggested a constitutional amendment to reverse *Garcia,* the movement to do so has not generated much support.

Federalism and the Use of Federal Grants

Congress always has the most to say about whether federal or state standards or some combination of them will prevail. Congress authorizes programs, establishes general rules for how the programs will operate, and decides whether and how much room should be left for state or local discretion. Most important, Congress appropriates the funds for these programs and—until recently—has had deeper pockets than even the richest states. One of Congress's most potent tools for influencing policy at the state and local levels has been the federal grant.

GOALS AND TYPES OF FEDERAL GRANTS

Federal grants serve four purposes, of which the most important is the fourth:

1. To supply state and local governments with revenue
2. To establish minimum national standards for such things as highways and clean air
3. To equalize resources among the states by taking, through federal taxes, money from people with high incomes and spending it, through grants, in states where the poor live
4. To attack national problems yet minimize the growth of federal agencies.

Even after the "Reagan revolution" resulted in the "devolution" of some functions back to the states, the national government continues to do much more than it did even two decades ago. Still, the number of federal employees is about the same today as it was then. Congress has chosen to use the states, the cities, the counties, the universities—and at times even private agencies—to administer programs, deliver services, and carry out federal mandates.

There are four types of federal grants: categorical-formula grants, project grants, block grants, and revenue sharing.

1. **Categorical-formula grants.** Congress appropriates funds for specific purposes—welfare, school lunches, the building of airports and highways. The funds are allocated by formula and are subject to detailed federal conditions, often on a matching basis; that is, the government receiving the federal funds must put up some of its own dollars. There are hundreds of grant programs, but two dozen, including Medicaid and Aid to Families with Dependent Children, account for almost 90 percent of total spending for categoricals.[32]

2. **Project grants.** Congress appropriates a certain sum, but the dollars are allocated to state and local units—sometimes to nongovernmental agencies —based on applications from those who wish to participate. Examples are grants by the National Science Foundation to universities and research institutes to support the work of scientists or grants open to states and localities to support training and employment programs.

3. **Block grants.** These grants, favored by recent Republican presidents and most governors, but opposed by most Democratic members of Congress and big city mayors, are broad grants to states for prescribed activities— elementary and secondary education, social services, preventive health, and health services—with only a few specific strings attached. During the first year of his presidency, Ronald Reagan was able to convince Congress to consolidate fifty-seven categorical grant programs, constituting 10 percent of federal aid to state and local governments, into nine block grants. But that was as far as Congress was willing to go.

   President Bush, outdoing Reagan and reviving New Federalism, selected from among the $140 billion in federal grants to the states a list of $22 billion dealing with education, human services, housing, law enforcement, and the environment, and urged Congress to put $15 billion into a single block grant program. Within these broad areas states would be free to decide how to spend the money. This would, argued the president, move "power and decision-making closer to the people."

   Big city mayors oppose proposals for block grants because such grants threaten to take both dollars and discretion from them. They also deprive members of Congress of the opportunity to announce and take credit for grants to their particular districts.[33] As a result, Congress paid little attention to the Bush proposals.

4. **Revenue sharing.** This program involves federal grants to state and local governments to be used at their discretion and subject only to very general conditions. From 1972 to 1987 substantial revenue sharing funds were given to state and local governments. When in the second Reagan administration federal budget deficits soared and "there was no revenue to share," revenue sharing was terminated—to the states in 1986 and to local governments in 1987.

THE POLITICS OF FEDERAL GRANTS

Arguments about the forms of federal aid involve more than questions of efficiency. They reflect differences about what constitutes desirable public policy, where power should be located, and who will gain or lose by the various types of grants. Republican presidents "have consistently favored fewer strings, less federal supervision, and the delegation of spending discretion to the state and local governments, whereas Democratic presidents have advocated the opposite. Congress has divided similarly, with Democrats generally voting for centralization, and Republicans for decentralization."[34]

Although chief executives—governors and presidents—generally tend to urge the consolidation of categorical-formula grants into larger blocks, legislators who prefer to decide where the funds are to go and groups who benefit from existing programs are likely to resist, most of the time successfully. Consider the battle over libraries. "[The] Administration proposed the consolidation of several narrow library grants. The Congress resisted, and the reason is simple. It can be expressed quantitatively: 99.99 percent of the public is not interested in library grant reform. Of the .01 percent who are interested, all are librarians and oppose it."[35]

The debate over the form of grants is not just a dispute over whether state and local governments can be trusted to spend federal dollars wisely. It is also a debate about which state and local officials should be given control over the spending. Specialists who work for state and local governments often have more in common with specialists working for the national government than they do with their own governors, mayors, or state legislators. These specialists (highway engineers, welfare administrators, educators) confer at meetings, read common journals, and jointly defend the independence of their programs from attempts by "politicians" (elected national or state officials) to regulate them.[36] When interest groups, congressional committee staffers, and federal bureaucrats (who in turn are connected to state and local bureaucrats) join forces, they create powerful "guilds."[37] The result is **iron triangles,** or as they are sometimes called, *issue networks,* that can be effective in protecting their programs.

The battle over "which piper calls the tune when one government raises the money and another spends it" tends to be cyclical. A scholar of federalism has explained, "Complaints about excessive federal control tend to be followed by proposals to shift more power to state and local governments. Then, when problems arise in state and local administration—and problems inevitably arise when any organization tries to administer anything—demands for closer federal supervision and tighter federal controls follow."[38]

At the moment the national government is having such budgetary problems that the trend is toward the elimination or reduction of federal grants and the return of functions to the states. But despite the decentralist rhetoric of the White House and many congressional leaders, Congress has found ways to continue to regulate the states and local governments.

Regulatory Federalism and Federal Mandates

Fewer federal dollars has not meant fewer federal controls. On the contrary, the federal government continues to impose mandates on states and local governments. State and local officials complain that these new federal regulatory devices are far more intrusive than the more obvious conditions a state or local government must meet to get a federal grant.[39]

NEW TECHNIQUES OF FEDERAL CONTROL

Here are five new techniques used to regulate state and local governments:

1. *Direct orders.* In a few instances, federal regulation takes the form of direct orders that must be complied with under threat of criminal or civil sanction. Examples are the Equal Opportunity Act of 1982, barring job discrimination by state and local governments because of race, color, religion, sex, and national origin, and the Marine Protection Amendments of 1977, prohibiting cities from dumping sewage into the ocean. Because such direct orders raise mild constitutional concerns and more serious political ones, Congress favors other techniques for imposing the federal will on the states.

2. *Cross-cutting requirements.* The first and most famous of these requirements (so-called because a condition on one federal grant is extended to all activities supported by federal funds regardless of their source) is Title VI of the 1964 Civil Rights Act, which holds that no person may be discriminated against in the use of federal funds because of race, color, national origin, sex, or handicapped status. More than sixty cross-cutting requirements concern the environment, historic preservation, contract wage rates, access to governmental information, the care of experimental animals, the treatment of human subjects in research projects, and so on.

3. *Cross-over sanctions.* These sanctions permit the "feds" to use federal dollars in one program to influence state and local policy in another. One example is the Emergency Highway Energy Conservation Act of 1974, which prohibits the secretary of transportation from approving federal funding for highway construction in states having a speed limit in excess of fifty-five miles per hour (since amended to allow the limit to be raised to sixty-five miles per hour in certain rural areas). Another example is a 1984 act that threatened to reduce federal highway aid by up to 15 percent for any state that failed to adopt a minimum drinking age of twenty-one by 1987.

4. *Total preemption.* This kind of control rests not on the national government's power to spend but on its powers under the supremacy and commerce clauses to preempt conflicting state and local activities. Building on this constitutional authority, federal law in certain areas just preempts states and local governments from the field.

5. *Partial preemption.* In these instances federal law establishes basic policies but requires states to administer them. Some programs give states an option to participate, but if a state chooses not to do so, the national govern-

ment then steps in and directly runs the programs. Even worse from the state's point of view is mandatory partial preemption, in which the national government requires the state to act on peril of losing other funds but provides no funds to support the state action. The Clean Air Act of 1990 is an example of mandatory partial preemption; the federal government sets national air quality standards and requires states to devise plans and pay for their implementation and enforcement.[40] If a state fails to adopt air pollution plans that are deemed to be adequate, there are what are called "hammer" provisions requiring federal implementation plans to be imposed on the state.[41] State violations of the clean air requirements can be "punished" by a variety of sanctions, including withholding of federal funds for a variety of purposes. Medicaid is another example of the national government providing some dollars but mandating states to provide kinds of services that cost more than the federal funds cover.

These new forms of federal regulation accelerated during the 1970s and abated only slightly during the 1980s. More than half the federal statutes preempting state and local authority have been enacted in the last two decades.[42] Despite the Reagan-Bush emphasis on retrenchment of federal regulations, the Reagan administration pressured for national controls to force states to adopt drunk-driving legislation, to cut off federal funds to cities enacting rent controls, and to force on states and localities certain busing, abortion, and school prayer policies. Ninety-one preemption statutes were enacted during the Reagan administration.[43] The Bush administration supported major expansions of federal preemption in the administration of the criminal laws. Apparently liberals and conservatives alike favor fewer federal controls over state and local officials in the abstract yet are willing to make exceptions in policy areas when they feel strongly something must be done to correct or prevent an injustice. Because there are plenty of injustices, federal regulation of state and local governments remains a continuing feature of our political system.

THE POLITICS OF FEDERAL MANDATES

Federal laws are usually fairly general. And since they are the product of political compromises, they often do not specify how they are to be implemented. As a result, the president and federal administrators have great latitude in their enforcement of federal mandates.

Yet it should not be thought that states and local officials are merely passive partners waiting to learn from federal authorities what to do and how to do it. It is one thing to get a law through Congress; it is another to impose national standards on state and local officials and the people they represent. If local and state political groups fail to persuade Congress to build safeguards into a law to protect their interests, they may still use the ambiguities of the law to do what they want done rather than what the federal agencies intend. In the implementation battles that routinely follow the enactment of legislation, the greater political power may be with state and local officials.[44]

Politics and Federalism: A Look to the Future

The ongoing debate about federalism can be understood on several levels. On one level, it is an argument about which government can most effectively deal with a particular problem—the national government or the states. On another level, it is an attempt by interest groups to find the forum—Washington or their state capitals—where they have the greatest chance of a sympathetic hearing. And, on yet another level, it is a debate about the best way to protect liberty and promote equality.[45]

Until the civil rights revolution of the 1960s, for example, segregationists feared that national officials—responding to different political majorities—would work for racial integration. Thus they praised local government, emphasized the dangers of overcentralization, and argued that the protection of civil rights was not a proper function of the national government. As one political scientist has observed, "Federalism has a dark history to overcome. For nearly two hundred years, states' rights have been asserted to protect slavery, segregation, and discrimination."[46]

Today the politics of federalism, even with respect to civil rights, is more complicated than in the past.[47] With changing political power distributions, the national government is not necessarily more favorable to the claims of minorities than most state or city governments. With the Supreme Court's abandonment of rigorous constitutional protection for women's right to abortions and its refusal to extend marital privacy rights to gays and lesbians, some state constitutions and state courts now provide more protection for these rights than does the U.S. Constitution. State and local governments also "have become the principal agents for advancing the cause of comparable worth. This role challenges the conventional wisdom that only centrist alternatives can advance equal opportunity and civil rights for all citizens."[48]

Further, as states more actively regulate the economy, some business interests have been running back to Washington, arguing that conflicting state regulations are unduly burdening interstate commerce and asking for preemptive federal regulation to save them not only from stringent state regulations but from having to adjust to fifty different state laws.[49] Yet, in general, political conservatives still favor state and local action, while liberals continue to favor national action. Conservative theorists still tend to champion local autonomy as the "means of protecting individual freedom." Local autonomy continues to be suspect by representatives of minorities, feminists, and the disadvantaged in general as "an exclusive haven for white privilege."[50] These "solid" positions about the appropriate functions of the national government versus state and local governments are more confused today.

THE RISE—AND FALL—OF "CRAZY QUILT" FEDERALISM

One source of confusion, termed "crazy quilt federalism,"[51] emerged during the 1960s urban crisis, when the national government started in earnest to provide large-scale, direct federal aid to cities, counties, school districts, flood-control districts, and other kinds of local units. In some ways Congress "became the city council of the nation" and the "president—acting very much like a Mayor"—tried to solve some tough local problems.[52] As a result, there was "virtually no function of local government from police to community arts promotion, for which there [wasn't] a counterpart federal aid program."[53] The combination of a strengthened national-city link and the corresponding state bypass resulted—at least in part—from the belief that Congress and federal authorities are more likely than state officials to ensure that the poor and the black, especially the latter, will get their fair share from tax dollars.

The high point of federal aid in terms of real dollars occurred in 1978. By the beginning of the 1980s, as national budget deficits mounted, liberals and conservatives, Republicans and Democrats, all agreed the expansion of the national government had gone too far. First the Carter administration curtailed some federal programs. Then the Reagan and Bush administrations made the reduction of the role of the national government one of their domestic priorities. They wanted cities to look to the states—not the national government—for help, and they wanted states to take over greater responsibilities for welfare, transportation, health, and education (see Figure 2-3). Many programs have been eliminated, and even more have been sharply reduced. General revenue sharing was eliminated. Between 1980 and 1990 categorical-formula grants for states and local governments were reduced by one-third. More than half the eighty federal regulations the National Governors' Association targeted as especially burdensome to the states have been eliminated.[54]

FIGURE 2-3 The Curtailment of Federal Aid

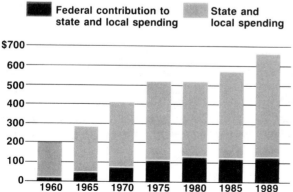

Source: Based on data from the Advisory Commission on Intergovernmental Relations, The New York Times, December 30, 1990, p.1. Copyright © 1990 by the New York Times Company. Reprinted by permission.

THE REEMERGENCE OF THE STATES

When the national government slowed the rate of growth of its domestic spending, the states took over some of its responsibilities.[55] "To a greater extent than almost anyone thought possible," Reagan "achieved his long-cherished goal of shifting the initiative and responsibility for domestic programs out of Washington and back to the states and cities."[56] "Instead of getting government off the backs of the American people," Reagan "presided over a huge growth of big government at the state level."[57] Not only were the programs shifted to the states, so were the costs of running them. For example, in 1970 Medicaid cost the states about 4 percent of their budgets; by 1995 it may reach 16 percent.[58]

Abandoned by the national government, cities and counties have also turned again to their own state capitals. The states have responded to this reduction in federal funding for urban governments with mixed results (see Table 2-3). Some states—Florida, Massachusetts, New Jersey, New York, and Oklahoma—tried with some success to replace the withdrawn federal funds for their cities and schools—until they, too, fell upon hard times in the early 1990s. Other states—California, for example—made little effort to replace the federal dollars or keep up the cut programs.[59] By the 1990s states were staggering under these additional burdens and being forced to raise taxes, lower the level of services,[60] or use mandates to make local governments provide additional services—without state aid.[61]

THE FUTURE OF FEDERALISM

In 1933, seeing state governments helpless during the Great Depression, one writer stated, "I do not predict that the states will go, but affirm that they have gone."[62] These prophets of doom were wrong. States are stronger than ever. Most have improved their governmental structures, taken on greater roles in funding education, launched programs to help distressed cities, and—despite

TABLE 2-3 Fiscal Capacity to Raise Revenue (from most able to least able)

U.S. average	100	Maryland	108	Maine	95	Indiana	87
Alaska	177	New York	107	Georgia	94	Wisconsin	86
Wyoming	151	Florida	105	North Dakota	94	Iowa	84
Nevada	147	Texas	104	Oregon	93	Tennessee	84
Connecticut	135	Minnesota	102	Missouri	93	Utah	80
Massachusetts	124	Virginia	101	Rhode Island	92	South Carolina	79
Washington, DC	122	Vermont	99	New Mexico	91	South Dakota	78
Delaware	121	Arizona	99	Nebraska	91	Idaho	77
New Jersey	121	Oklahoma	98	Ohio	91	West Virginia	76
New Hampshire	119	Washington	98	Louisiana	90	Kentucky	76
California	118	Michigan	96	Pennsylvania	90	Alabama	74
Colorado	117	Illinois	96	North Carolina	88	Arkansas	73
Hawaii	113	Kansas	96	Montana	88	Mississippi	65

Source: Advisory Commission on Intergovernmental Relations, *Intergovernmental Perspective,* 15 (Spring 1989), p. 17.

new constitutional limitations—expanded their taxing bases. Able men and women have been attracted to many governorships. "Today, states, in formal representational, policymaking, and implementation terms at least, are more representative, more responsive, more activist, and more professional in their operations than they ever have been. They face their expanded roles better equipped to assume and fulfill them."[63]

The national government, however, is not likely to retreat to a pre-1930 posture or even a pre-1960 one. The underlying economic and social conditions that generated the demand for federal action have not substantially altered. On the contrary, in addition to such traditional issues as helping people find jobs and preventing inflation and depressions that still require national action, countless new issues have been added to the national agenda by the growth of a global economy based on high technology, service, and information. Although it is worth remembering that in terms of gross national product, many American states are larger than many nations—California, for example, has an economy larger than that of Great Britain—most states still lack the jurisdiction by themselves to clean up the air, modernize the air traffic control system, regulate the economy, prevent pollution of our rivers, deal with drug abuse, or prevent the spread of AIDS and find its cure. And there are issues, such as the lack of decent housing for inner-city African Americans and Hispanics, that are beyond the capacity of the states to solve alone.

Most Americans have strong attachments to our federal system—in the abstract. They remain loyal to their states and show a healthy skepticism about the national government. Yet most of the time for most of the people, the concerns are about more immediate problems—clean air, safety in the streets, relations between men and women, jobs, the cost of medical care, heating fuel for their homes, and gasoline for their cars. They are not much concerned about the nature of federal grants or arguments about the virtues of national versus state action. They are willing to use whatever governmental agencies or combinations of agencies they feel can best serve their needs and represent their interests.

American federalism has modified and been modified by the political and social issues facing us during the last two hundred years. It will continue to shape our society. Our federal system remains firmly rooted in our political system as well as our constitutional democracy. We are not about to abolish it or modify it drastically. But just as the federalism of today is as different from that of 1787 as a jet airplane is from a stagecoach, so federalism will it continue to evolve as we move into the twenty-first century.

Summary

1. Our federal constitutional system has evolved into something only slightly different in form, yet significantly different in operation, from the 1789 version.

2. It is not possible to find neat and clear and noncontroversial divisions between the powers of the national and state governments.

3. Today the national government has the constitutional authority to do whatever Congress thinks is necessary and proper, and there are few if any judicially enforced limits to restrain Congress from interfering with the actions of the states.

4. The centralization of constitutional power at the national level does not mean that federalism is dead. Political power remains dispersed, and states remain active and significant political realities.

5. Ideological bias in favor of either national or state action is likely to reflect concrete political objectives. Conservative support for states' rights and the liberal preference for national action are no longer as predictable. Shifting political issues continue to lead to shifting allegiances among the various levels of government.

6. The drift toward increasing federal action has been fueled more by underlying economic and social changes than by concerns about federalism, but we detect a vigorous trend toward the view that federalism as a political principle is worthy of being preserved.

7. The major instrument of federal intervention has been various kinds of grants-in-aid, of which the most prominent are categorical-formula grants, project grants, block grants, and revenue sharing.

8. Additional forms of federal intervention to control the activities of state and local governments have become more important in recent decades. These include direct orders, cross-cutting requirements on federal funds, cross-over sanctions in the use of federal funds, total preemption, and partial preemption.

9. Beginning in the 1970s, accelerating in the 1980s, and continuing into the 1990s, there has been a substantial return of policy responsibilities to the states and a pause in the expanding role of the national government.

10. Today we no longer spend so much time debating the *law* of federalism; we have moved to the *politics* of federalism. As now interpreted, the Constitution gives us the option to decide through the political process what we want to do, who is going to pay, and how we are going to get it done.

For Further Reading

Advisory Commission on Intergovernmental Relations. *Intergovernmental Perspective.* (U.S. Government Printing Office, published four times a year).

THOMAS J. ANTON, *American Federalism and Public Policy* (Temple University Press, 1989).

RAOUL BERGER, *Federalism: The Founders' Design* (University of Oklahoma Press, 1987).

ANN O'M. BOWMAN and RICHARD C. KEARNEY, *The Resurgence of the States* (Prentice Hall, 1986).

Center for the Study of Federalism, *Publius: The Journal of Federalism.* (Temple University, published quarterly; one issue is an "Annual Review of the State of American Federalism.")

TIMOTHY J. CONLAN, *New Federalism: Intergovernmental Reform from Nixon to Reagan* (Brookings Institution, 1988).

THOMAS R. DYE, *American Federalism: Competition among Governments* (Lexington Books, 1990).

DANIEL J. ELAZAR, *American Federalism: A View from the States,* 3d ed. (Harper and Row, 1984).

————, *Exploring Federalism* (University of Alabama Press, 1987).

MICHAEL FIX and DAPHNE A. KENYON, eds., *Coping with Mandates* (Urban Institute Press, 1990).

PARRIS N. GLENDENING and MAVIS MANN REEVES, *Pragmatic Federalism: An Intergovernmental View of American Government,* 2d ed. (Palisades Publishers, 1984).

CHRISTOPHER HAMILTON and DONALD T. WELLS, *Federalism, Power and Political Economy* (Prentice Hall, 1990).

JEFFREY HENIG, *Public Policy and Federalism* (St. Martin's Press, 1985).

JOHN KINCAID, "American Federalism: The Third Century," *Annals of the American Academy of Political and Social Science* 509 (May 1990).

SCOTT M. MATHESON, with JAMES E. KEE, *Out of Balance* (Peregrine Smith Books, 1986).

SUE O'BRIEN and MARSHALL KAPLAN, *The Governors and the New Federalism* (Westview Press, 1991).

WILLIAM H. RIKER. *The Development of American Federalism* (Academic Publishers, 1987).

HARRY N. SCHEIBER, *Federalism: Studies in History, Law, and Policy* (Institute of Governmental Studies, University of California at Berkeley, 1985).

WILLIAM H. STEWART, *Concepts of Federalism* (Center for the Study of Federalism and University Press of America, 1984).

THOMAS R. SWARTZ and JOHN E. PECK, *The Changing Face of Fiscal Federalism* (M. E. Sharpe, 1990).

JOSEPH F. ZIMMERMAN. *Federal Preemption: The Silent Revolution* (Iowa State University Press, 1991).

Notes

1. See, for example, Charles Robb, quoted in *New York Times,* December 15, 1985, p. A80. See also Eugene W. Hickok, Jr., "Understanding Federalism, *Perspectives on Political Science* 19, No. 4 (Fall 1990), pp. 216–22.

2. Ronald L. Watts, "Canadian Federalism in the 1990's: Once More in Question," *Publius* 21 (Summer 1991), pp. 169–190; Robert C. Vipond, "The Canadian Constitutional Crisis: Who's Right on Rights?" *Intergovernmental Perspective* 17 (Fall 1991), pp. 49–52; Robert C. Vipond, *Liberty and Community: Canadian Federalism and the Failure of the Constitution* (State University of New York Press, 1991).

3. William H. Stewart, *Concepts of Federalism* (Center for the Study of Federalism and University Press of America, 1984).

4. Daniel J. Elazar, *Exploring Federalism* (University of Alabama Press, 1987), p. 6.

5. William H. Riker, *The Development of American Federalism* (Academic Publishers, 1987), pp. 14–15. Riker contends that not only does federalism not guarantee freedom but that the framers of our federal system, as well as those of other nations, were not animated by considerations of safeguarding freedom but by practical considerations of preserving unity.

6. John Kincaid, "State Constitutions in the Federal System," *Annals of the American Academy of Political and Social Sciences* 496 (March 1988), p. 17. See also David Osborne, *Laboratories of Democracy* (Harvard Business School Press, 1990) p. 1.

7. *Gibbons v. Ogden*, 9 Wheaton 1 (1824).

8. *Heart of Atlanta Motel v. United States*, 379 U.S. 241 (1964).

9. *U.S. Steel Corporation v. Multistate Tax Commission*, 434 U.S. 452 (1978).

10. *Garcia v. San Antonio Metro*, 469 U.S. 528 (1985); James R. Alexander, "State Sovereignty in the Federal System," *Publius* 16 (Spring 1986), pp. 1–15.

11. *Luther v. Borden*, 7 How. 1 (1849).

12. *California v. Superior Court of California*, 482 U.S. 400 (1987).

13. *Puerto Rico v. Brandstadt*, 483 U.S. 219 (1987). Kenyon Bunch and Richard J. Hardy, "Continuity or Change in Interstate Extradition? Assessing *Puerto Rico v. Branstad*," *Publius* (Winter 1991), pp. 51–67.

14. David C. Nice, "State Participation in Interstate Compacts," *Publius* 17 (Spring 1987), p. 70.

15. Advisory Commission on Intergovernmental Relations, *Restoring Confidence and Competence* (ACIR, 1981), p. 30.

16. Cynthia Cates Colella, "The Creation, Care and Feeding of the Leviathan: Who and What Makes Government Grow," *Intergovernmental Perspective* (Fall 1979), p. 9.

17. Aaron Wildavsky, "Bare Bones: Putting Flesh on the Skeleton of American Federalism," in Advisory Commission on Intergovernmental Relations, *The Future of Federalism in the 1980s* (ACIR, 1981), p. 79.

18. David O'Brien, "Federalism as a Metaphor in the Constitutional Politics of Public Administration," *Public Administration Review* 49 (September/October 1989), p. 411.

19. *United States v. Darby*, 312 U.S. 100 (1941).

20. 4 Wheaton 316 (1819).

21. *Missouri v. Jenkins*, 495 U.S. 33 (1990).

22. *Oklahoma City v. Tuttle*, 471 U.S. 808 (1985); *Mainer v. Thiboutot*, 488 U.S. 1 (1980); *Monell v. New York City Dept. of Social Welfare*, 436 U.S. 658 (1978). See Cynthia Cates Colella, "The United States Supreme Court and Intergovernmental Relations," in *American Intergovernmental Relations Today: Perspectives and Controversies*, ed. Robert J. Dilger (Prentice Hall, 1985), p. 66.

23. Joseph F. Zimmerman, "Federal Preemption under Reagan's New Federalism," *Publius* 21 (Winter 1991), pp. 7–28.

24. *Webster v. Reproductive Health Services*, 492 U.S. 490 (1989). See also Ann O'M. Bowman and Michael A. Pagano, "The State of American Federalism, 1989–1990," *Publius* 20 (Fall 1990), pp. 12–13.

25. Oliver Wendell Holmes, Jr., *Collected Legal Papers* (Harcourt, 1920), pp. 295–96.

26. *Garcia v. San Antonio Metro. Transit Authority*, 469 U.S. 528 (1985).

27. *South Carolina v. Baker*. 485 U.S. 505 (1988). Whether Congress is a reliable protector of federalism is a subject of research debate among political scientists. See also Rodney E. Hero, "The U.S. Congress and American Federalism: Are 'Subnational' Governments Protected?" *Western Political Quarterly*, 42 (March 1989), pp. 93–106.

28. Justice Sandra O'Connor, dissenting in *Garcia v. San Antonio Metro*. See also Paul J. Mishkin, "The Current Understanding of the Tenth Amendment," in *The Bill of Rights: Original Meaning and Current Understanding*, ed. Eugene W. Hickok, Jr. (University Press of Virginia, 1991), p. 473.

29. *Gregory v. Ashcroft*, 115 L Ed 2d 410 (1991).

30. Justice Sandra O'Connor, *Garcia v. San Antonio Metro*.

31. Rodney E. Hero, "The U.S. Congress and American Federalism: Are 'Subnational' Governments Protected?" *Western Political Quarterly* 42 (March 1989), p. 103. See, for greater skepticism, Martha Derthick, "Preserving Federalism: Congress, the States, and the Supreme Court," *Brookings Review* 4 (Winter/Spring 1986), pp. 32–37.

32. George J. Gordon, *Public Administration in America*, 3d ed. (St. Martin's Press, 1986), p. 149.

33. Kitty Dumas, "Governors, State Legislators Offer Block Grants," *Congressional Quarterly*, 49 (April 13, 1991), p. 923.

34. John E. Chubb, "The Political Economy of Federalism," *American Political Science Review* 79 (December 1985), p. 1005.

35. Richard P. Nathan, "Special Revenue Sharing: Simple, Neat, and Correct," unpublished paper.

36. Deil S. Wright, *Understanding Intergovernmental Relations*, 3d ed. (Brooks-Cole, 1982).

37. Harold Seidman and Robert Gilmour, *Politics,*

Position and Power, rev. ed. (Oxford University Press, 1985).

38. Donald F. Kettl, The Regulation of American Federalism (Johns Hopkins University Press, 1987), pp. 154–55.

39. Norman Beckman, "Developments in Federal-State Relations," The Book of the States: 1990–91 (Council of State Governments, 1990), p. 528.

40. Mel Dubnick and Alan Gitelson, "Nationalizing State Policies," in The Nationalization of State Government, ed. Jerome J. Hanus (D.C. Heath, 1981), pp. 56–57.

41. Timothy J. Conlan, "And the Beat Goes On: Intergovernmental Mandates and Preemption in an Era of Deregulation," Publius 21 (Summer 1991), p. 46.

42. John Kincaid, "American Federalism: The Third Century," Annals of the American Academy of Political and Social Sciences 509 (May 1990), p. 9. See also Zimmerman, "Federal Preemption under Reagan's New Federalism," pp. 7–28.

43. Michael A. Pagano, Ann O'M. Bowman, and John Kincaid, "The State of American Federalism, 1990–1991," Publius 21 (Summer 1991), p. 4.

44. Michael J. Rich, "Distributive Politics and the Allocation of Federal Grants," American Political Science Review 83 (March 1989), p. 209.

45. Thomas R. Dye, American Federalism: Competition Among Governments (Lexington Press, 1990), p. 199.

46. Ibid., p. 26.

47. Daniel J. Elazar, American Federalism: A View from the States, 3d ed. (Harper and Row, 1984), p. 241.

48. Debra A. Stewart, "State Initiatives in the Federal System: The Politics and Policy of Comparable Worth in 1984," Publius (Summer 1985), p. 83.

49. Martha M. Hamilton, "If You Want Something Done Right, Do It Yourself," Washington Post

National Weekly Edition, September 5–11, 1988, p. 31.

50. Gordon L. Clark, Judges and the Cities; Interpreting Local Autonomy (University of Chicago Press, 1985), p. 8.

51. W. John Moore, "Crazy-Quilt Federalism," National Journal, November 26, 1988, p. 3004.

52. H. F. Graff, "Presidents Are Now Mayors," New York Times, July 18, 1979, p. A23.

53. Neal R. Peirce, "The State of American Federalism," National Civic Review (January 1980), p. 32.

54. John Kincaid, "The State of American Federalism, 1987," Publius 18 (Summer 1988), p. 1.

55. John Herbers, "The New Federalism: Unplanned, Innovative, and Here to Stay," Governing 1 (October 1987).

56. David S. Broder, "What Reagan Did—and Didn't Do," Washington Post National Weekly Edition (January 23, 1989), p. 4.

57. Virginia I. Pastrel, "States' Rights, or Dereliction of Duty?" Washington Post National Weekly Edition July 22–28, 1991, p. 23.

58. Bowman and Pagano, "State of American Federalism, 1989–1990," p. 7. U.S. General Accounting Office, Federal-State-Local Relations: Trends of the Past Decade and Emerging Issues (GAO, March 1990).

59. Richard P. Nathan, "Federalism: The Great 'Composition," in The New American Political System, ed. Anthony King, 2d ed. (AEI Press, 1990), pp. 234–35.

60. Brad C. Johnson, "Washington Should Look at the Damage It's Doing," Washington Post National Weekly Edition, July 22–28, 1991, p. 24.

61. Susan A. MacManus, "Mad about Mandates: The Issue of Who Should Pay for What Resurfaces in the 1990s," Publius 21 (Summer 1991), pp. 59–75.

62. Luther Gulick, "Reorganization of the States," Civil Engineering (August 1933), pp. 420–21.

63. Osborne, Laboratories of Democracy, p. 363.

3

State Constitutions: Charters or Straitjackets?

T exas has a lengthy constitution. Adopted in 1876, it has been amended more than 330 times. The most recent effort to thoroughly revise it was in 1972, after political scandals brought in a new governor, Dolph Briscoe, and a reform-oriented state legislature. After pushing through a variety of reforms dealing with the ethics of officeholders, campaign practices, and registration of lobbyists, the legislature did an unconventional thing and called into being a constitutional convention consisting of members of the legislature rather than a specially elected body.

After working for seventeen months, the legislator-delegates came up with a much revised and shortened document intended to modernize many obsolete governmental practices. The convention deadlocked, however, over whether to give constitutional status to the state's right-to-work law, which prohibits labor contracts requiring union membership as a condition of employment, so this issue was referred to the voters. In the end, neither the AFL-CIO nor Governor Briscoe would support all of the convention's recommendations. The governor was especially opposed to the proposal for annual legislative sessions, which he argued would cause higher taxes. Advocates of the revised constitution tried to salvage their work by offering substantial parts of the new charter to the voters as amendments to the existing constitution. Conservatives praised the old constitution, claiming it had served Texas well for one hundred years. Progressives complained that the old constitution was elitist, permitted only the narrowest governmental objectives, and made real change nearly impossible. In November 1975, amid the charges and countercharges, Texas voters ultimately rejected the new amendments by a 2 to 1 vote.[1]

The experience of Texas illustrates just one reason some have charged that state constitutions seem less like charters empowering state governments and more like straightjackets that tie the hand of state officials with even the best of intentions. In this chapter we'll look at the roots of our state constitutions and some of the ways officials try to work around constitutional rigidity. Then we will look at the ways of amending state constitutions, ending with a few case studies of how some states have tried to revise their entire constitutions.

The Roots of State Constitutions

Now that our nation has finished celebrating the bicentennial of the ratification of the Bill of Rights of the U.S. Constitution, you might give some thought to your own state constitution. Although anniversaries of state constitutions are not usually observed with much fanfare, they deserve to be. State constitutions, like the federal one, are both *instruments of* and *limitations on* government. However, state constitutions, unlike the federal one, are not *symbols* of state unity. On a trip to your state capital you are unlikely to find the state constitution "displayed as is the federal Constitution, in a setting similar to a Shinto shrine."[2]

The first state constitutions were outgrowths of colonial charters. Virginia added its bill of rights to its constitution in 1776, thirteen years before the national one was proposed by Congress. Massachusetts and New Hampshire can boast of charters, still in effect, older than the federal document. In 1787 the framers of the federal Constitution drew heavily on their experience with these state charters and constitutions. "What is the Constitution of the United States but that of Massachusetts, New York, and Maryland!" remarked John Adams. "There is not a feature in it," he said, "which cannot be found in one or the other."[3]

Later state constitutions, in turn, benefited in large measure from their framers' experience with the federal Constitutions. As people moved westward and created new states, they copied the constitutions of the older states. The federal and the state constitutions were all adopted in conventions convened for that specific purpose. These conventions then submitted their new charters to the people for ratification.

Subject only to the broad limitations of the U.S. Constitution, the people of each state are free to create whatever kind of republican government they wish. Yet all state constitutions are similar in general outline (see Figure 3-1). No state has established a parliamentary system, and none has deprived its judges of the power of judicial review.

The usual state constitution consists of a preamble; a bill of rights; articles providing for separation of powers, a two-house legislature (except in Nebraska), an executive department (usually consisting of the governor and lieutenant governor and a half dozen or so more statewide elected officials) and an independent judiciary with the power of judicial review; a description of the form and powers of local units of government; an amendatory article; and mis-

FIGURE 3-1   Typical State Constitutions

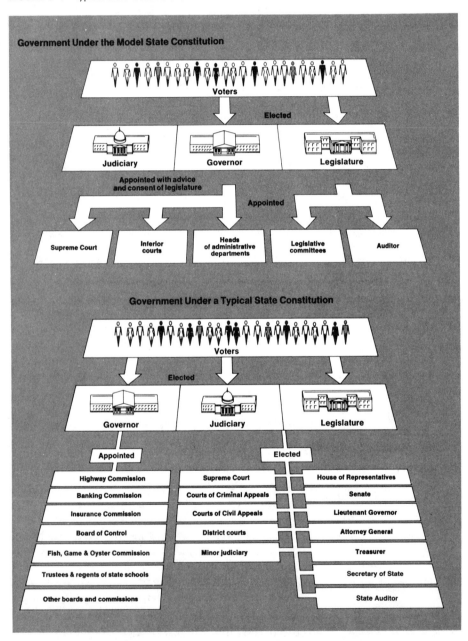

cellaneous provisions dealing with corporations, railroads, finances, and other specific topics.

Studying state constitutions obviously tells us much about how power is distributed within the states, and by studying them we learn of the essential similarity in the structure of state governments. Yet similarity of formal constitutions does not mean similarity in actual governmental processes. Much more has to be considered in determining who governs our states, as the preceding chapter suggests. The constitution is just a place to begin.

Constitutional Rigidity and Evasion

State constitutions contain more detail than does the national Constitution. They are longer and less flexible, and they require more frequent formal amendment. Further, states frequently change their constitutions. (Louisiana has had eleven constitutions; Georgia has had ten; South Carolina, seven; and Alabama, Florida, and Virginia, six.) State constitutions vary in length—from 6,600 words of Vermont's, the only state constitution shorter than the Constitution of the United States as amended, to the 174,000 of Alabama's.[4]

The U.S. Constitution grants powers in broad and sweeping terms, allowing each generation to write in the details and adapt the basic charter of government to new conditions. Most state constitutions, on the other hand, prescribe in detail what can be done and how it can be done. Compare, for example, the difference between how the federal and a typical state constitution spell out the way taxes can be levied and public moneys spent. The federal Constitution uses only one clause to authorize Congress to spend money, but state constitutions require dozens of pages to specify the purposes for which the money may be spent, how much may be spent, and in what manner. These details sometimes get in the way of action.

Although most state constitutional provisions deal with matters of significance, some deal with trivial subjects. California's much amended constitution (it has had more than 475 amendments since it was adopted in 1879), for example, goes into great detail about such matters as the taxation of fish and the internal organization of several major departments. The Oklahoma Constitution "embraces a vast amount of subject matter which in most of the older states, and the newest, is dealt with in their statutes."[5] It proclaims, for example, "Until changed by the Legislature, the flash test for all kerosene oil for illuminating purposes shall be 115 degrees Fahrenheit; and the specific gravity test for all such oil shall be 40 degrees." The South Dakota Constitution provides for authorizing a twine and cordage plant at the state penitentiary.

CONSTITUTIONS AS ROADBLOCKS

A written constitution sets forth, among other things, the terms upon which public officials are authorized to act on behalf of the people. The more detailed

87
TAXES. REDEVELOPMENT AGENCIES. LEGISLATIVE CONSTITUTIONAL AMENDMENT. Authorizes Legislature to prohibit property taxes for bonded indebtedness repayment from redevelopment agency use. Fiscal Impact: If implemented, property tax revenues received by redevelopment agencies would be reduced.

YES 163 ➡
NO 164 ➡

88
DEPOSIT OF PUBLIC MONEYS. LEGISLATIVE CONSTITUTIONAL AMENDMENT. Authorizes Legislature to deposit public moneys in any federally insured industrial loan company. Fiscal Impact: No direct fiscal effect. However, could result in greater interest-income by increasing competition for the deposit of public moneys.

YES 166 ➡
NO 167 ➡

89
GOVERNOR'S PAROLE REVIEW. LEGISLATIVE CONSTITUTIONAL AMENDMENT. Permits Governor to modify or reverse parole decisions involving murder convictions with indeterminate sentences. Fiscal Impact: Unknown state impact which depends on the actions of the Governor in granting or denying parole.

YES 169 ➡
NO 170 ➡

90
ASSESSED VALUATION. LEGISLATIVE CONSTITUTIONAL AMENDMENT. Authorizes homeowners over 55 certain transfer of assessed valuation to replacement dwellings in other counties. Fiscal Impact: The property tax revenue loss would not exceed $20 million in the first year if all counties participated and could be substantially less. Thereafter, the revenue loss would increase annually.

YES 172 ➡
NO 173 ➡

California voters are often presented with ballots that include constitutional amendments proposed by the legislature, initiatives, and bond issues. This ballot shows just a few of the legislative constitutional amendments on the ballot in the 1988 election.

the constitution, the less discretion public officials enjoy, and vice versa. The earliest state constitutions granted authority to the legislatures without much restriction on how their powers should be exercised. But after many legislatures gave special privileges to railroads, canal builders, and other interests, constitutional amendments were adopted to prevent such abuses. Reform groups, distrusting the legislatures, began to insist that their programs be incorporated into the constitution. In time, state constitutions became encrusted in layer after layer of procedural detail.

What does this mean for democratic government? Most simply, it means that state constitutions—intended as charters of self-government—are often like straitjackets imposed on the living present by the dead past. Listing powers in detail soon renders a constitution out of date. Some outdated provisions, of course, do no harm, but more often they are roadblocks to effective government. For example, fixed salaries do not reflect changing economic conditions, and a rigidly organized administrative structure is incapable of adjusting to new needs. Further, detailed and restrictive state constitutions enhance the position of those who wish to preserve the status quo.

Under these conditions the people's representatives—the legislature—cannot act on many problems; instead, voters are regularly asked to pass constitutional amendments on subjects about which they may know very little. Consider the overworked voters of Louisiana. Between 1921, when their next-to-the-most-recent constitution was adopted, and 1974, when their new one was adopted, they were presented with about 750 proposed amendments, two-thirds of which they approved. California voters are regularly given ballots that, in addition to a long list of candidates for national, state, and local offices, contain several legislature-proposed constitutional amendments, a dozen or so highly technical constitutional proposals submitted by the initiative process, as well as numerous bond issues. In the larger California cities it is not unusual for voters to be asked to consider 50 separate state, local, and special district ballot questions.

In recent decades many states have revised their older, more cumbersome constitutions and streamlined their operations (see Figure 3-2). Nonetheless, the very nature of a state government, where a state legislature has power to act unless the constitution takes it away, means that state constitutions are likely to be more detailed, more complex, and longer than the national Constitution.

GETTING AROUND THE CONSTITUTION

Does all this mean that state constitutions can forever prevent the wishes of the majority from being carried out? Not necessarily. The constitutional system of the states, like that of the national government, includes more than the formal written document. Unwritten rules, practices, political parties, and interest groups also shape events. When large groups of people want their officials to act, they usually find some way to overcome formal barriers.

One device for doing so is **judicial interpretation**, whereby judges can remove a constitutional provision's restrictive force by a narrow interpretation

FIGURE 3-2   Amendments to State Constitutions

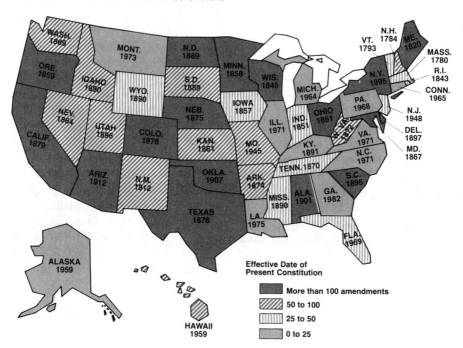

of its meaning. Also, the more complex the constitution, the easier it is for judges to veto legislation. Thus detailed state constitutions tend to increase the authority of judges. Actually, one reason for the growing length of some constitutions is that amendments are often required to reverse judicial interpretations. Furthermore, some sections of state constitutions have been invalidated by national action, especially in the area of civil rights and suffrage. Nevertheless, rigid state constitutions can inadvertantly create a "constitutional autocracy" by making it more difficult for new majorities to achieve their aims.

TAKING STATE CONSTITUTIONS SERIOUSLY [6]

In what is being called *New Judicial Federalism*, state constitutions have taken on a new importance. For decades, whenever both federal and state constitutional provisions were applicable, state judges tended to look only to the national Constitution and how it had been interpreted by the Supreme Court of the United States. But in recent decades, as the U.S. Supreme Court has become more conservative, some state supreme courts have started to use their own state constitutions—the entire constitution as well as its state bill of rights—to review the actions of state and local officials. This trend takes its inspiration, at least in part, from the U.S. Supreme Court, which has sent clear messages to state supreme court judges that they are free to interpret their own state constitution in order to impose greater restraints than does the U.S. Constitution. The U.S. Supreme Court and the U.S. Constitution set the floor, not the ceiling, for the protection of rights. [7]

State judges are now using state constitutions to require their state legislatures to provide better schools for children living in poor neighborhoods, force the building of more low-income housing, provide public financing for abortions of poor women, and regulate business enterprise in order to protect the environment. [8]

When state judges rely on their own state constitutions to protect rights beyond those required by the national Constitution, they do so at some political peril, since many are popularly elected. This peril has increased now that the Supreme Court requires state judges who wish to escape a review of their decisions by the Supreme Court to make it quite clear that they have decided a case on adequate and independent state constitutional grounds. [9] This seemingly innocent Supreme Court requirement means that when state judges apply a provision of their own state constitution, they must accept responsibility for their decision and cannot blame the U.S. Supreme Court if the state court's decision is unpopular. The Court's requirement was not, said Chief Justice William H. Rehnquist, an attempt to rein in state courts for going too far forward protecting the rights of criminal defendants but merely a recognition that if a state court wished to impose "a restraint on another branch of its state government . . . [it] should be willing to take the responsibility for doing so on its own authority and not because some justices in Washington require it." [10]

Amending State Constitutions

Constitutional amendments must first be *proposed* (initiated) and then *ratified.* There are three ways to propose amendments: by (1) legislative proposals, (2) initiative petitions, and (3) constitutional conventions. After an amendment has been proposed, it must be ratified. In all states except Delaware, where the legislature can ratify as well as propose amendments, ratification is by the voters. In most states, an amendment becomes part of the constitution when approved by a majority of those voting on the amendment. In a few states, however, approval by a majority of all those voting in the election is required. This makes ratification difficult, because some people who vote for candidates do not vote on amendments. Still, about 60 percent of all amendments submitted by legislatures to the voters are ratified.

LEGISLATIVE PROPOSALS

All states permit their legislatures to propose amendments; in fact, this is the most commonly used method. Although provisions vary, the general practice is to require the approval of two-thirds of the elected members in each chamber of the legislature. Some states, however, permit proposal of an amendment by a simple majority in two successive legislatures.

A legislature may appoint a **revision commission,** a commission to make recommendations for constitutional change that have no force until acted upon by the legislature. The legislature creates a commission of a relatively small number of people, some selected by the governor, some by the legislature, and charges it with presenting proposals for constitutional revision. If the legislature approves, it can then forward the recommendations for ratification by the voters.

A commission is less expensive than a full-blown constitutional convention (discussed below), does not require initial voter approval, and gives the legislature final control of what is presented to the electorate. Florida, Virginia, and Louisiana have used the commission procedure to bring about significant constitutional change. Mississippi has tried, so far unsuccessfully, to use commission device for changing its 1890 constitution, a constitution that had been designed to keep blacks out of the political process.[11] The California legislature is considering the possibility of calling a commission. Of special interest, the Utah Constitutional Revision Commission is a permanent body, required by law to submit recommendations for constitutional revision to the legislature sixty days before each regular session.[12]

In some states the revision commission has not worked well, perhaps because commissioners have not been responsive to political currents or representative of enough interests. Although a commission may provide a less partisan consideration of amendments and be less sensitive to the desires of single-interest groups than either the legislature or a convention, if it proposes changes that do not reflect political realities, these proposals will be rejected by the legislature or by the voters. Still, revision commissions are becoming more popular.

INITIATIVE PETITIONS

At the end of the nineteenth century, the prestige of state governments was at a new low. Out of this disillusionment came a variety of reforms. Among them was the constitutional **initiative petition,** a device that permits voters to force specific constitutional amendments onto the ballot. Seventeen states allow amendments to be proposed by initiative petitions, providing the petitions are signed by 4 to 16 percent of either the total electorate or the number of voters who voted in the last election. Once approved by the appropriate state official (attorney general or secretary of state), the amendment is placed directly on the ballot at the next election. In some states—California, for example—initiative proposals are limited to amending the state constitution, not to revising it, the distinction being that revision refers to "a substantial alteration of the entire constitution, rather than to a less extensive change in one or more of its provisions."[13] Revisions in California are limited to proposals by a constitutional convention or to proposals presented by the state legislature.

In recent years, voters have approved only about 30 percent of the amendments that originated as the result of citizen initiative procedures. This percentage compares with a slightly more than 60 percent approval rate for amendments proposed by state legislatures. Plainly, a variety of factors account for the low adoption rate of initiative measures. For example, initiatives tend to be used for controversial issues that have already been rejected by the legislature or that proponents believe do not have a chance of passing. Initiatives are also often proposed by a small number of interest groups or by reform-minded elites who lack broad support for their views. Sometimes measures are proposed more to launch educational campaigns than to win adoption.

Some critics charge that the initiative asks voters to make too many decisions for which they are not especially well prepared. Others argue that the use of the initiative petition can prevent elected representatives from exercising their proper authority. Still others hold that a constitution should be a blueprint that outlines not the rules for the moment but the overriding principles for an unknowable future. It should certainly not, they say, be too specific about how governments are to operate on a day-to-day basis. Critics also charge that the initiative process has recently become the tool of well-organized, single-interest groups that present voters with simplistic yes or no choices on complex taxation matters.

Defenders of the constitutional initiative petition contend that it is a valuable safety valve against unresponsive legislatures. When a legislature is tied so closely to special interests that it refuses even to acknowledge the real needs and demands of a majority of citizens, the initiative process can be used as a corrective. Defenders also contend that voters are much smarter than critics say and that they have, in fact, acted rather prudently when asked to decide most constitutional questions.[14]

CONSTITUTIONAL CONVENTIONS

Because amendments involve piecemeal change, people in many states advocate writing a new constitution rather than amending the current one. Americans love constitutional conventions; we have had more than 230 of them. One scholar has noted that calling conventions of the people is a uniquely American idea, emphasizing that even legislators cannot be trusted and that the supreme power belongs to the people.[15]

We have always insisted on written constitutions, viewing them as expressions of popular will and as fundamental law binding on all public officials. As such, they can be changed only by prescribed methods. Moreover, we have preferred to have our constitutions drawn up by some agency more in touch with the people's wishes than a legislature is. The constitutional convention has been by far the preferred method of writing new constitutions.

Forty-one state constitutions authorize their legislatures to submit the questions of calling a convention to the voters; in the other states the legislatures are assumed to have the power to do so. Fourteen state constitutions require the legislatures to submit this question to the voters at fixed intervals. If the voters approve, the next step is to elect delegates. Rhode Island, which in 1986 held the most recent state constitutional convention, is required to convene a convention every ten years.

Some state constitutions contain elaborate procedures governing the number of delegates, the method of election, and the time and place of the conventions. Others leave the details to the legislatures. The way convention delegates are selected seems to affect the kind of document the convention proposes. Nonpartisan, multimember district selection devices are more likely to result in a "reform" convention than those in which parties play a major role.[16]

After the delegates have been chosen for the specific job of drafting a new constitution, they usually assemble at the state capital. When the convention has prepared a draft of the new constitution, the document is submitted to the voters. But first the convention delegates have to make a difficult choice: Should the voters be asked to accept or reject the new constitution as a whole? Or should they be given a chance to vote on each section as though it were an amendment to the old constitution?

The advantage of the first method is that one provision of a constitution ties in with another and, in order to secure all the advantages of revision, the entire constitution should be adopted. The disadvantage is that those who oppose a particular provision may vote against the entire constitution in order to defeat the offending provision. When convention delegates know that a particular provision is controversial, they may decide to submit at least the most controversial provision separately. Whichever method they choose, the supporters of change must rally their forces to gain voter approval of their work.

The Politics of Constitutional Revision

Constitutions are not a neutral set of rules perched above the world of everyday politics; rather, they significantly affect who gets what from government. How a constitution is changed can help or hinder various groups; constitutional change is, therefore, a difficult process. "If the document is exceptionally innovative, those status quo supporting groups and interests who have lost in the selection and convention process will oppose and defeat the document. If the document is not innovative, those reform groups who initially lobbied for conventions will oppose and defeat the document."[17]

Many people simply do not care. It is difficult to work up much excitement in a campaign for revising a state constitution except among those with intense feelings, and they are more likely to oppose than to favor adoption. Those who like the status quo thus have a built-in advantage, which, combined with obstacles to the amending process in the constitution itself, helps explain the lack of action.

"Revision is time consuming, requiring sophisticated legal and drafting skills of the highest order, and involves negotiation and compromise. To be successful, revision requires gubernatorial as well as legislative leadership. . . . An effective political campaign is essential. . . . Success at the polls is not assured. Constitutional revision can be a high-risk endeavor and will continue to be."[18] Here are some brief case studies to illustrate the risky nature of constitutional revision, already demonstrated by the experience of Texas, as we saw at the beginning of this chapter.

RHODE ISLAND AMENDS ITS CONSTITUTION

Rhode Island's 1986 constitutional convention produced fourteen separate propositions for amending its 1843 constitution. On November 4, 1986, the voters approved eight of the fourteen provisions, rejecting attempts to increase compensation of state legislators, to provide for merit selection of judges, and to create a "paramount right to life without regard to age, health, function, or condition of dependency," which would have banned abortions or public funding of them. The voters approved provisions strengthening free speech, due process, and equal protection rights, and expanding fishing rights and access to the shore, as well as a statement that the rights protected by the Rhode Island Constitution "stand independent of the U.S. Constitution."

LOUISIANA REVISES ITS CONSTITUTION

The Louisiana constitutional revision commission set out during 1973 and 1974 to write a streamlined "people's constitution"—one the average person could understand.[19] The AFL-CIO, National Association for the Advancement of Colored People, League of Women Voters, Committee for a Better Louisiana, National Municipal League, and many other lobbying groups became involved in shaping the new constitution. It took well over a year to write, and it cost approximately $4 million. In the end, however, a readable 26,000-word document replaced the existing 265,000-word document that contained detailed legislative items and some 536 amendments. In April 1974, Louisiana voters approved the new charter by a large margin. The Louisiana Constitution could no longer be cited as the chief example of an unworkable state constitution.

CHANGING THE HAWAII CONSTITUTION (1978), AND LEAVING IT ALONE (1986)

Hawaiians take constitution making and constitution changing very seriously; Hawaii's constitution allows the voters to hold a constitutional convention every ten years. More than eight hundred proposals for constitutional changes were submitted to the Hawaii convention of 1978. The League of Women Voters and other groups conducted extensive information and discussion meetings, and the convention itself held many public hearings on key issues. The 102 delegates to the state constitutional convention met for nearly three months during the summer of 1978. After extensive debate, the convention narrowed the proposals down to 34 questions to be placed on the fall ballot. These questions reflected both traditional and new thinking in constitutional revision. Convention delegates rejected proposals for the initiative, referendum, and recall; for a unicameral legislature; and for an elected (instead of an appointed) attorney general.

The delegates were not opposed to all governmental "reforms," however, for they endorsed a two-term limit for governor and lieutenant governor, moved to make Hawaii party primaries more open by allowing voters to cast ballots without declaring party preference, and authorized the state legislature to provide partial public funding for election campaigns and to establish spending limits. The convention reflected current concern over government spending by setting tougher debt and spending limits for the state. It also strengthened environmental safeguards and gave further constitutional and financial protection to the special status of native Hawaiians.

When these and other recommendations were placed before the voters on November 7, 1978, in the form of proposed amendments to the Hawaii Constitution, all 34 were adopted. Seventy-four percent of the voters went to the polls; of those who voted, all but approximately 20 percent supported all the proposals as a package or individually by majority vote. The delegates had no sooner celebrated the favorable response to their work, however, than the election results were challenged in the courts. Opponents claimed, among other things, that the ballot contained an inherited bias toward a yes vote by making it harder to vote no than yes. The Hawaii Supreme Court rejected the challenge.

In November 1986, Hawaiians rejected the periodic question of whether to call a convention by a vote of 173,977–139,236. Hawaii's experiences with the revision process are reminders that constitution making is not just an experience in abstract argument or logical reasoning but flows directly from a state's political life.

ARKANSAS'S EIGHTH CONSTITUTIONAL CONVENTION

Arkansas's eighth constitutional convention was a protracted affair. The one hundred delegates who were elected in 1978 held their organizational session in the winter of that year but did not get down to work until the spring of 1979. Then, having reconvened in June 1980 to revise the final draft, they submitted the proposed constitution to the voters in November 1980.

Opposition later developed to a provision in the new constitution allowing the legislature, by a two-thirds vote, to set interest rates rather than limit them, as in the current constitution. Others opposed a new provision enlarging the taxing powers of the local governments. Even though the new constitution was endorsed by the governor, the Democratic party, and the Arkansas Bar Association, it was opposed by the AFL-CIO and the Arkansas Education Association. The voters rejected it by a 2 to 1 margin.

A CONSTITUTION FOR "NEW COLUMBIA"

Also of interest is the work of a constitutional convention of the District of Columbia. Forty-five delegates proposed a constitution that called for a unicameral legislature elected by a combination of single-member and at-large election districts, a relatively strong governor, a two-tier judicial branch with merit selection of judges for fifteen years, and a bill of rights similar to the U.S. Bill of Rights, except that an equality clause replaces the Tenth Amendment.

The proposed constitution was adopted by the voters of the District in November 1982 and subsequently submitted to Congress, along with a petition for the admission of the District as a new state, to be called New Columbia. After hearings and public discussion, the Council of the District of Columbia in 1987 approved a revised document for transmission to Congress, which continues to ignore these requests for statehood.

In a sense, then, constitutional conventions—and especially the constitutional initiative process—are yet other examples of the diffusion of power that characterizes our national and state political systems.

Summary

1. State constitutions attempt to spell out the fundamental laws of the states. Although they vary considerably in detail, each outlines the organizational framework of the state, vesting powers in the legislature and other departments. Each provides for a bill of rights, sets procedures for holding elections, provides for local governments, and contains a variety of provisions dealing with finances, education, and other state issues.

2. A constitution typically reveals little about the politics of a state. But to study the constitutional development of a state is to study its political heritage, the battles among interest groups, and the struggles to adapt to changing conditions.

3. Most state constitutions are cumbersome documents, containing more detail than the U.S. Constitution, and writing into "fundamental law" matters that most constitutional scholars believe should be left to statutory law. The distinction between fundamental and ordinary law is blurred. In many cases, the detail was introduced by reformers intent on preventing abuse.

4. There has been a flurry of renewed interest in state constitutions as they have been discovered to be additional instruments for protecting and expanding rights.

5. In what is known as the New Judicial Federalism, state judges are giving renewed attention to the provisions of their respective state constitutions.

6. State constitutions can be amended by ratification by the voters of proposals submitted to the voters by the legislature, by popular initiative petitions, or by constitutional conventions, which tend to revise the entire constitution rather than just amend portions of it.

7. Despite the considerable constitutional change brought about during the last half century through amendments, voters have often been resistant to sweeping constitutional revision.

8. In recent decades there has been an expanded use of the initiative process to bring about narrowly targeted constitutional change.

For Further Reading

Congressional Information Service, *State Constitutional Conventions, Commissions and Amendments 1979–1988: An Annotated Bibliography* (U.S. Congressional Information Service, 1989).

ELMER E. CORNWELL, JR., JAY S. GOODMAN and WAYNE R. SWANSON, *State Constitutional Conventions: The Politics of the Revision Process in Seven States* (Praeger, 1975).

PAUL FINKELMAN and STEPHEN E. GOTTLIEB, eds., *Toward a Usable Past: Liberty under State Constitutions* (University of Georgia Press, 1991).

JOHN KINCAID, "State Constitutions in the Federal System," *Annals of the American Academy of Political and Social Service* (March 1988).

JANICE C. MAY, "State Constitutions and Constitutional Revision: 1988–89 and the 1980s," *The Book of the States, 1990–91* (Council of State Governments, 1990), and equivalent articles in each edition of *The Book of the States.*

BERNARD D. REAMS, JR., and STUART D. YOAK, *The Constitutions of the States: A State by State Guide and Bibliography to Current Scholarly Research* (Oceana Publications, 1988).

ALAN G. TARR, *State Constitutions of the United States* (Greenwood Press). Fifty-two volumes are in publication, to be completed by 1995. Each will provide a comprehensive commentary on state constitutions.

ROBERT F. WILLIAMS, *State Constitutional Law: Cases and Materials* (Advisory Commission on Intergovernmental Relations, 1990, and annual supplements).

Because of this renewed interest in state constitutional law, the National Association of Attorneys General publishes a monthly bulletin on state constitutional law and sponsors an annual seminar, and the Advisory Commission on Intergovernmental Relations (ACIR) has published and keeps current the first modern casebook on state constitutional law.

Notes

1. Beryl E. Pettus and Randall W. Bland, *Texas Government Today* (Dorsey Press, 1979), pp. 34–36. See also Janice C. May, "Texas Constitutional Revision and Laments," *National Civic Review* (February 1977), pp. 64–69.

2. Gerald Benjamin, "The Functions of State Constitutions in a Federal System," paper presented to American Political Science Association Round Table, Washington, D.C., 1984.

3. John Adams, quoted in Judith S. Kaye, "Federalism's Other Tier," *Constitution* 3 (Winter 1991), p. 50.

4. Janice C. May, "State Constitutions and Constitutional Revision: 1988–89 and the 1980s," *The Book of the States: 1990–91* (Council of State Governments, 1990); John Kincaid, "State Constitutions in the Federal System," *Annals of the American Academy of Political and Social Science*, 496 (March 1988), p. 14.

5. Jack W. Strain, *An Outline of Oklahoma Government*, ed. Leroy Crozier and Carl F. Reherman (Edmond, Okla.: Bureau of Local Government Services, Department of Political Science, Central State University, 1984), p. 21.

6. This subhead is taken from an article of the same name by Robert Welsh and Ronald K. L. Collins, *Center Magazine*, September/October 1981, p. 6.

7. Kaye, "Federalism's Other Tier," p. 54. Judith Kaye is a judge of the Court of Appeals of the State of New York.

8. Miranda S. Spivack, "How States' Rights Can Rectify the Wrongs of the Supreme Court," *Los Angeles Times*, June 16, 1991, p. M2.

9. *Michigan v. Long*, 463 U.S. 1032 (1983). See also Justice Sandra Day O'Connor, opinion for the court, "Our Judicial Federalism," *Intergovernmental Perspective* 15 (Summer 1989), pp. 8–15. William M. Wiecek, "Some Protection of Personal Liberty: Remembering the Future," Kermit L. Hall, "Mostly Anchor and Little Sail: The Evolution of American State Constitutions," both in *Toward a Usable Past: Liberty under State Constitutions*, Paul Finkelman and Stephen E. Gottlieb, eds. (University of Georgia Press, 1991).

10. William H. Rehnquist, quoted in Randall T. Shepard, "State Constitutions: State Sovereignty," *Intergovernmental Perspective* 15 (Summer 1989), p. 20.

11. "Mississippi Begins Analyzing Its Racist Constitution of 1890," *New York Times*, December 12, 1985, p. B2. See also May, "State Constitutions and Constitutional Revision: 1988–89 and the 1980s," p. 23.

12. May, "State Constitutions and Constitutional Revision: 1988–89 and the 1980s," p. 24.

13. *Amador Valley Joint Union High School District v. State Board of Equalization*, 22 Cal. 3d 208, 1978 California Supreme Court, quoted in Eugene C. Lee, "The Revision of California's Constitution," *CPS Brief: A Publication of the California Policy Seminar* 3 (April 1991), p. 1.

14. See Thomas E. Cronin, *Direct Democracy: The Politics of Initiative, Referendum and Recall* (Harvard University Press, 1989), for a comprehensive discussion of these matters. See also David B. Magleby, "Taking the Initiative, Direct Legislation and Direct Democracy in the 1980s," *PS* (Summer 1988), pp. 600–11.

15. Caleb Nelson, "Majorities, Minorities, and the Meaning of Liberty: A Reevaluation of Scholarly Explanations for the Rise of the Elective Judiciary in Antebellum American," unpublished paper, Yale Law School, 1991, p. 51, elaborating the thesis of Gordon Wood, *The Creation of the American Republic, 1776–1787* (University of North Carolina Press, 1969), pp. 306–25.

16. Elder Witt, "State Supreme Courts: Tilting the Balance toward Change," *Governing* (August 1988), p. 33.

17. Elmer E. Cornwell, Jr., Jay S. Goodman, and Wayne R. Swanson, "State Constitutional Conventions: Delegates, Roll Calls, and Issues," *Midwest Journal of Political Science* (February 1970), pp. 105–30.

18. Lee, "Revision of California's Constitution."

19. Cecil Morgan, "A New Constitution for Louisiana," *National Civic Review* (July 1974), pp. 343–56.

4

Parties and Elections in the States

The African nation of Liberia has been heavily influenced by former slaves from the United States who settled there in the early nineteenth century. Most Liberians today are descendants of black Africans who came to the country in the 1400s; only about one in ten Liberians is a descendant of the freed slaves. Yet it was the descendants of those freed American slaves who governed Liberia until 1980, when a group of military officers identified with the original inhabitants killed the president and put one of their own, an army sergeant named Samuel K. Doe, in power.

Doe became head of state and chairman of the People's Redemption Council (PRC), which promised a return to civilian rule and a new constitution. In 1985, under pressure from the United States and other nations, Doe finally called a presidential election in which he was a candidate. Because Liberia did not have a democratic tradition, the first step in the transition to democracy was to agree on an election law—a set of rules by which the election would be run. This law was written by Cecilia Stewart, a Liberian lawyer; William Kimberling of the United States Federal Election Commission; and Sir John Boynton of Great Britain. The law permitted opposition parties, something that Doe had previously outlawed. The Lawyers Committee on Human Rights describes Doe's preelection opposition to democracy:

> First he banned the two most popular opposition parties. Then he issued Decree 88A, effectively outlawing criticism of his government. Then he shut down the *Daily Observer*, the most popular independent newspaper. Finally, he jailed some of

the most respected opposition leaders in the country, including Amos Sawyer and Ellen Johnson-Sirleaf.[1]

Liberians had no precedent for organizing an election. Political parties had not been legally recognized prior to the writing of the election law. And because there are no street names or numbers in Liberian cities and towns, it was difficult to construct a system of voter registration and designated voting places for geographic areas. Finally, because Liberia had no effective postal system, it was hard to communicate with voters and election officials about how this experiment in democracy would be conducted. Just as important, Liberians lacked experience in casting secret ballots at voting places staffed by officials trained in the democratic process.

Doe's behavior violated Liberia's new election law and the norms of fair elections everywhere. Violations included setting up unauthorized polling places in military barracks where soldiers friendly to Doe were permitted to "cast as many ballots as they wanted." At some rural voting places illiterate voters were denied the right to cast secret ballots and were intimidated by soldiers. Still, in the view of outside observers, "these instances appeared to be isolated."[2]

The real problem started when it became apparent which way the election was going. The new election law called for the ballots to be counted at the voting places and the results then reported to a central office. When Doe learned that he was trailing his opponent in some voting places, he ordered that all ballot boxes be brought immediately to his palace for counting by a central committee chosen by him. To no one's surprise, Doe won the election by the narrowest of margins.

His opponent and other Liberians offended by the way the election was won had no recourse to the courts, police, or an established government that valued democracy. In 1989 a rebellion of Doe's former colleagues led to his assassination, whereupon civil war broke out and engulfed the entire country by 1990. As many as 13,000 people have died and half of the nation's 2.5 million people have been displaced.[3]

Amos Sawyer, president of the interim government of Liberia, announced that Liberia would end the civil war through "free and fair elections under international supervision." In the spring of 1992, the competing factions in the civil war agreed to hold another election, one that hopefully would follow fair and free procedures.[4]

Liberia's election problems have something to teach us about our own democracy. Americans take free and fair elections for granted. It is unthinkable that the president would have ballots gathered and brought to the White House for counting. It is assumed that when election law violations occur, we have recourse to the courts and even the police to redress them. Americans take for granted the peaceful transfer of power from one politician and party to another. But U.S. citizens also know enough about events around the world to be certain that two of the most common alternatives to democracy are tyranny and anarchy. Unfortunately for Liberians, they have experienced both tyranny and anarchy in the period since the tainted election of 1985.

The Role of State Elections in American Democracy

The electoral process in the United States is decentralized in its rules and administration. All elections in the United States are administered by state and local governments, not by the federal government. The president and members of Congress are chosen in state elections conducted according to state rules. States differ, for instance, in the hours the polls are open, restrictions on campaigning near the voting place, and who may vote. With few exceptions, eligibility to vote is determined by state, not federal law.

There are heated debates over the wisdom of various democratic devices— the initiative, the referendum, teledemocracy—and these sorts of debates have been going since the inception of the American republic. The United States has already progressed further along the road to democracy than the founders intended. But how much further we go in the 1990s and the next century will depend on such things as who participates in the decision process, the quality of the deliberation, and the extent to which modern technology helps disseminate information and the recording of votes.

Political Parties in the States and Localities

Electoral politics focuses on the units of competition, and in our system these units are at the state and local levels. Because of the electoral college and the winner-takes-all rule, presidental candidates focus more on winning states than on winning individual votes. And, of course, state elections determine who will serve as U.S. senator, governor, and other statewide officials like attorney general, as well as the outcome of many ballot questions.

Our political federalism is noteworthy. State identities are important to both politicians and voters. Americans tend to think of themselves not only as citizens of the United States but also as citizens of a particular state. Each state has a distinctive political tradition and political culture.

It should not be surprising, then, that state parties are in many ways more important than the national parties. Indeed, the national parties, aside from their congressional campaign committees, are largely federations of state parties. And since our national parties have never been very strong, the activities they undertake often end up being done through the state parties. The independence of state parties also helps explain why, for instance, Democratic voters can be so different from one another, and why Republicans from different states can come down on different sides of some major issues.

ELECTION LAW AND PARTIES

Although political parties are not mentioned in the U.S. Constitution, they are vital not only to democracy but also to the functioning of the electoral system within the states. Parties organize the competition by recruiting and nominating candidates, function as the loyal opposition when out of power, unify and organize the electorate, and provide a link between the people and their government.

While political parties are extraconstitutional at the federal level, they are explicitly part of many state constitutions. Because it is the states that write the laws governing elections, they must deal with parties in those laws' provisions. One common legal provision regarding parties is ballot access. Before the turn of the century, parties printed their own ballots and voters brought these ballots with them to the voting place. The advent of the secret ballot forced the states to determine which parties or candidates would be included on the ballot.

Election rules are rarely neutral; almost always they favor some parties over others. In most states the two major parties have a "preferred position"— that is, their candidates can assume they will be placed on the ballot. But ballot access for minor-party and independent candidates is often a challenge. State law typically requires that in order to be on the ballot, minor parties must meet a minimal threshold of votes in the previous election or submit a prescribed number of signatures of supporters among registered voters. States vary in the difficulty of ballot access for minor parties, depending on three factors: the number of signatures required, the time allowed to collect them, and whether signatures must be distributed by county or area.

States choose one of two kinds of ballots. The **party column or Indiana ballot,** which encourages party-line voting, is organized by columns, with the party name and symbol at the top of a column that lists all the party's candidates running for offices in that election (see Figure 4-1). Typically there is a spot at the top of the column to make a single mark, and in so doing vote for all party candidates that appear under the mark. When voters make such a mark, or otherwise vote for only one party, they cast a **straight-party ticket.**

Partly to discourage straight-ticket voting, some states use the **office block or Massachusetts ballot,** which lists all the candidates running for an office together in one block, and then in another block all those running for another office, and so on (see Figure 4-2). If voters want to cast a straight-party ticket, they have to go through each office block hunting for the preferred party candidate. Office block ballots encourage **split-ticket voting,** or voting for candidates from more than one party.

At least 36 states prescribe the organization of the state parties, the means by which their officers are elected, and the nomination process for president and other offices.[5] In states that have some form of public financing of elections or parties, the state also regulates the distribution of public funds to the parties and the reporting of how those funds were spent.

FIGURE 4-1 A Sample Party Column Ballot.

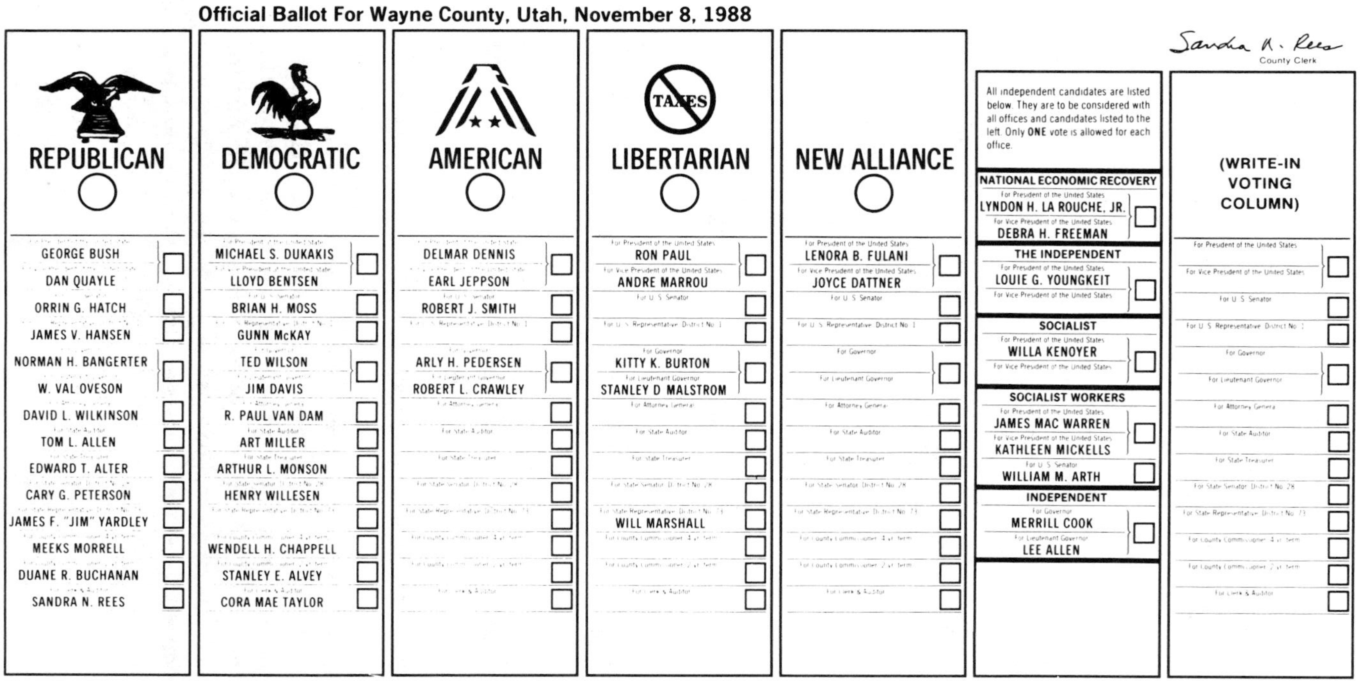

Official Ballot For Wayne County, Utah, November 8, 1988

REPUBLICAN

GEORGE BUSH
DAN QUAYLE
ORRIN G. HATCH
JAMES V. HANSEN
NORMAN H. BANGERTER
W. VAL OVESON
DAVID L. WILKINSON
TOM L. ALLEN
EDWARD T. ALTER
CARY G. PETERSON
JAMES F. "JIM" YARDLEY
MEEKS MORRELL
DUANE R. BUCHANAN
SANDRA N. REES

DEMOCRATIC

MICHAEL S. DUKAKIS
LLOYD BENTSEN
BRIAN H. MOSS
GUNN McKAY
TED WILSON
JIM DAVIS
R. PAUL VAN DAM
ART MILLER
ARTHUR L. MONSON
HENRY WILLESEN
WENDELL H. CHAPPELL
STANLEY E. ALVEY
CORA MAE TAYLOR

AMERICAN

DELMAR DENNIS
EARL JEPPSON
ROBERT J. SMITH
ARLY H. PEDERSEN
ROBERT L. CRAWLEY

LIBERTARIAN

RON PAUL
ANDRE MARROU
KITTY K. BURTON
STANLEY D MALSTROM
WILL MARSHALL

NEW ALLIANCE

For President of the United States.
LENORA B. FULANI
For Vice President of the United States.
JOYCE DATTNER
For U. S. Representative District No. 1

For Governor

For Lieutenant Governor

For Attorney General

For State Auditor

For State Treasurer

All independent candidates are listed below. They are to be considered with all offices and candidates listed to the left. Only **ONE** vote is allowed for each office.

NATIONAL ECONOMIC RECOVERY
For President of the United States.
LYNDON H. LA ROUCHE, JR.
For Vice President of the United States.
DEBRA H. FREEMAN

THE INDEPENDENT
For Vice President of the United States.
LOUIE G. YOUNGKEIT

SOCIALIST
For President of the United States.
WILLA KENOYER
For Vice President of the United States.

SOCIALIST WORKERS
For President of the United States.
JAMES MAC WARREN
For Vice President of the United States.
KATHLEEN MICKELLS

INDEPENDENT
WILLIAM M. ARTH

MERRILL COOK
For Lieutenant Governor
LEE ALLEN

(WRITE-IN VOTING COLUMN)

For President of the United States.

For Vice President of the United States.

For U. S. Senator

For U. S. Representative District No. 1

For Governor

For Lieutenant Governor

For Attorney General

For State Auditor

For State Treasurer

Sandra N. Rees
County Clerk

77

FIGURE 4-2 A Sample Office Block Ballot.

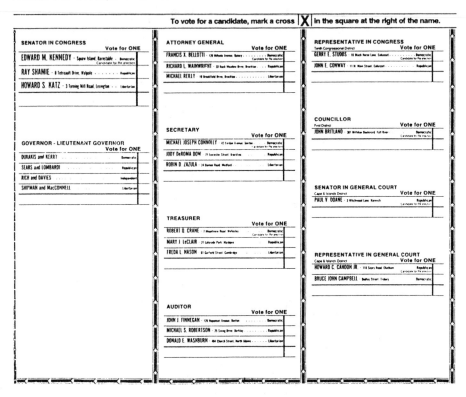

In sum, while the U.S. Constitution and federal laws have remarkably little to say about political parties, state constitutions and state laws do, and in some states the parties are regulated by law.

PARTY ORGANIZATION AT STATE AND LOCAL LEVELS

Although state party organizations are not all alike, in all states there is a party *chair*, who is elected by the party central committee or delegates to a party convention. Other statewide party officers include the *vice-chair*, who by state law or party bylaws generally must be of the opposite gender from the party chair, and officers like treasurer and party secretary. Party leaders generally answer to a *central committee*, which consists of a group of 20 or more persons who are elected or otherwise chosen for specified terms.

The party chair is the spokesperson for the party, who works at raising money for the party and its candidates and attempts to use the media to the party's advantage. The state party chair works closely with the governor when that party controls the governorship; indeed under these circumstances the chair is generally chosen by the governor. State party chairs often become leaders in setting party strategy. Because overt expressions of partisanship are thought to be unbecoming for a governor or a senator, it is often the party chair who defends the party and when necessary goes on the offensive against the opposition party.

The day-to-day operations of the party are usually carried out by the party's *executive director*, a full-time employee who oversees the staff, assists the chair, and coordinates the work of the central committee and other party officials. The executive director schedules functions and serves as a liaison to the national organizations.

At the local level, the political parties generally have county chairs and vice-chairs, a structure patterned after the state party organization. In some counties these organizations are fully staffed and functioning, but in most counties they are run by volunteers and are inactive until just before an election. Local parties provide opportunities for ordinary citizens to become involved in politics, which can eventually lead to running for office. One important characteristic of American parties at all levels is their permeability. They are extremely open to would-be candidates. Virtually anybody can run for any office anywhere in America. Some states, like Minnesota, have congressional district parties as well, further multiplying the number of party organizations.[6]

Although party bosses and strong local parties are virtually a thing of the past, in many of our largest cities local politics is still organized on a partisan basis. However, local politics is more often characterized by nonpartisanship. Two-thirds of cities with populations over 5,000 have nonpartisan elections.[7]

PARTY ACTIVITIES IN ELECTIONS

At all levels American politics is candidate-centered rather than party-centered like European and other democracies. Candidates create their own campaign organizations. Yet parties serve important secondary roles in elections. They provide the structure for elections; they are supposed to recruit candidates, help register voters, mobilize voters on election day, and provide some resources and campaign help to their candidates.

Structure for Elections Our election system would not function without parties to organize the competition. Parties narrow the field of candidate choices through a primary election or convention process, providing voters with candidate choices in the general election. These candidates, to one degree or another, have worked with party officials to secure their place on the ballot as the party's nominees for the offices they are seeking.

Candidate Recruitment Party officials are supposed to recruit candidates to run for office, help train them in how to run, and, to the extent they can, support them financially. In many states this is more fiction than fact. It may come as a surprise that many offices go uncontested in the United States. For instance, between 1984 and 1990 an average of 83 seats in the U.S. House of

Representatives had candidates who ran unopposed, evidence of a clear break-down in the parties' candidate recruitment role.[8] In most races for the House, candidates are *self-selected.* "As a result of these organizational weaknesses [in the parties] . . . the task of creating a successful campaign for a seat in the House of Representatives tends to fall to the would-be candidates," and usually only those with sufficient ambition start early enough and work hard enough to win.[9]

As one moves to state (except for the governorship) and local offices, the number of unopposed candidates increases the further down the ballot you go. To be sure, some of these incumbents have done such a good job that to oppose them would be an exercise in futility. Yet a lack of competition in elections violates American assumptions about democracy and is reminiscent of politics in the former communist states, where party officers ran unopposed. An important and often overlooked point, however, is that there could be far more unopposed candidates, especially at the local levels, were it not for the efforts of party leaders to recruit candidates.[10]

Voter Registration All states except North Dakota require that citizens register to vote before permitting them to vote. Some states, like Wisconsin, allow registration at the polls on election day. Twenty states not only record the voter's name, address, and other pertinent information, but also ask voters at the time of registration to register with a political party (in another nine states party registration is optional).[11] Voters, of course, have the option to decline to state their party at the time of registration, and a significant number of them do. In California in 1992 nearly 10 percent of the registered voters declined to state their party preference.

Political parties favor party registration for several reasons. First, it permits them to limit participation in their primaries to people registered in their party. Second, party registration creates voter registration lists, which parties find extremely useful for campaigning and fund raising. List vending—selling voter lists with addresses, phone numbers, and party preferences—is a multimillion-dollar industry. Third, voter registration helps the parties in the redistricting process because consultants, using party registration, voting, and other data, can project the impact of new legislative district boundaries.

Elections are decided by the people who vote, and to be able to vote, a person must be registered. Voter registration drives are sometimes run by civic-minded groups independent of a party or candidate; they urge citizens to vote without caring much for whom they vote. More often, however, *get-out-the-vote drives* are managed by people who target their efforts to registering and bringing out citizens they anticipate will vote for their party candidate. Both Democrats and Republicans do this. Voter registration drives targeted at blacks and Hispanics have been especially important to the Democratic party.[12] Such was the case in 1986 when Alan Cranston, then a senator from California, ran a drive financed largely by wealthy businessman-banker Charles Keating, which produced a lot of Democratic votes. Republicans have been just as aggressive in identifying and registering likely supporters. In 1988 the GOP hired college students to cruise beaches frequented by wealthy Californians, registering them to vote.

Voter Mobilization Registering citizens does no good if they do not turn out and vote. Only about 70 percent of eligible voters in this country are registered, and of that number only about 72 percent actually vote in presidential elections, meaning that only half of the voting-age population bothers to vote.[13] Get-out-the-vote drives are therefore a major activity of candidates and parties. Party workers, through telephone or door-to-door canvasses, identify registered voters who are likely to support their party and then contact these voters personally on election day, perhaps more than once, to encourage them to go to the polls. Where resources permit, the parties may even provide transportation to the polls or baby-sitting services.[14]

In states that permit registration by mail or by roving registrars, canvass and voter registration drives are often combined, so that volunteers register voters at the same time they learn these voters will support their party's candidates in the election. In states that permit absentee voting by mail, voter mobilization efforts can consist of helping voters fill out the form requesting an absentee ballot and then mailing the form for them. A few weeks later, the party volunteer will check to make sure the ballot has arrived and been filled out and returned. Because most voters prefer one party over another, it makes sense for candidates from the same party to consolidate their efforts. Sometimes, however, individual candidates conduct the canvas, registration, and mobilization activities.

Campaign Resources American political parties are organizationally weak. This is true of most state and local parties, with some notable exceptions; Colorado's Republican party, for instance, is "high tech" and well organized. Parties are often able to provide some campaign resources, and in better-organized states quite a bit of campaign help. They raise funds for their own organization and attempt to finance voter registration and mobilization efforts. A few parties raise enough money to help fund candidates for governor or other state offices. As at the national level, it helps with fund raising if the party controls the governorship because interest groups are much more likely to contribute to the governor's party.

Parties also help channel money from the national congressional campaign committees to local congressional candidates, especially incumbents. State parties have also been the beneficiaries of "soft money," which is money given to them, often in large amounts, that does not have to be disclosed under federal law but can be used for "party-building" purposes. In well-organized states, the parties train the candidates they have recruited. Wisconsin and New York have powerful state legislative campaign committees that distribute resources to candidates as the national party committee does to congressional candidates.[15]

Sometimes the state parties provide public opinion polling data to state and local candidates, help establish campaign themes, or prepare generic advertising that can be used in several state legislative districts. Despite their organizational weakness, parties are important to the outcome of state and local elections, and they play an important role in the day-to-day operation of state and local government.

PARTIES AND VOTING AT THE STATE AND LOCAL LEVELS

Voters base their choices on three factors: party identification, candidate appeal, and issues—listed in order of importance. But in many local elections party labels are absent from the ballot, and hence these elections have some peculiar dynamics.

Party Identification The single most important predictor of the vote is partisanship. In the election itself, parties provide a party label, which is a kind of endorsement that voters can use in making their decisions. Party is an especially important element in elections where most voters have little information, like contests for attorney general, state senator, state representative, or county commissioner. The simplifying device of party labels helps voters sort through the many candidate choices they encounter on election day.

People who identify themselves as Strong Democrats and Strong Republicans are remarkably loyal to their parties when voting for governor and other state and local offices. Independent leaners have clear partisan preferences in the direction of the party toward which they lean. Of the three types of partisans, weak partisans are the most likely to defect. Finally, the pure independents move most with changing circumstances, but there are few pure independents in the total electorate.[16]

Candidate Appeal Although partisanship is important, it is not decisive. Candidate appeal can be crucial. In the 1966 Maryland gubernatorial election, the Democrats ran a candidate who had made a racist appeal in the primary against the more moderate Republican Spiro Agnew. Maryland's black voters voted overwhelmingly for Agnew, although they had overwhelmingly given their votes to Democratic candidate Lyndon Johnson in the presidential election two years before. Thanks in part to the strong support of the black community, Agnew won.

In state and local elections name identification and the advantages of incumbency are also important. Candidates sometimes use creative means to generate positive name recognition. For example, Bob Graham, when he was governor of Florida, worked one day a week in different jobs around the state to demonstrate his desire to relate to his constituents. Candidates correctly assume that their success in state and local elections partly depends on voter recognition of who they are.

We The People

Who Are the People in Our Local Governments?

Elected Officials

Gender
Male	335,335
Female	83,739

Race
White	408,749
Black	8,267
Native American	1,710
Asian	348

Source: U.S. Dept. of Commerce, Bureau of the Census, *Census of Governments,* 1987, Vol. 1, No. 2 (Government Printing Office, 1988) pp. 1, 18.

Issue Voting Issues can also be very important to the outcome of elections at the state and local levels. Economic difficulties helped William Weld, a Republican, become governor in Massachusetts. State elections often focus on economic conditions as well as such issues as education, jobs, and the environment. New Jersey Governor Jim Florio and Virginia Governor Doug Wilder, both pro-choice on abortion, benefited from their opponents' "waffling" on that issue. While issues are important to state and local elections, however, it is fair to say that they are probably less important than at the national level.[17]

Nonpartisan Local Elections Progressive era reformers, angry at the corruption of city politics and party machines, sought to rid local government of political parties. They argued that city government was more administrative than political and that political parties were prone to graft in such matters as paving streets, picking up garbage, and providing police and fire protection.[18]

Some contend that the effect of nonpartisan local elections has been to make it more difficult for poor persons, minorities, and the less educated to participate effectively. For these people the party label serves as a way to identify politicians who share their values and perspectives on government. Better-educated, white, and better-off voters know more about who is running and what they stand for, even without party labels. For a time blacks seemed to be especially hurt by nonpartisan local elections in cities like Oakland, California, which for many years had a series of white mayors despite a black majority. More recently, blacks have been elected mayor of Oakland.

PARTIES IN STATE GOVERNMENT

With the exception of Nebraska, all state legislatures are organized along party lines (Nebraska's unicameral legislature is officially nonpartisan). All governors are elected as partisans, as are most statewide officials. This means that in state government, as in the national government, parties are one of the most important organizing devices. Patronage, while not as widespread as before civil service reforms, still allows governors and other elected officials to make a number of important appointments to reward fellow partisans with state government positions.

Parties in the Legislature Like the U.S. Congress, the state legislatures are organized largely along partisan lines. The *speaker of the house/assembly* and the *president of the senate* are generally elected by the majority party in each chamber. They preside over floor proceedings and make key assignments to standing committees, study committees, and other groups. In addition, most state legislatures have floor leaders, called *majority and minority leaders* and *majority and minority whips.* In most states the parties sit on different sides of the aisle in the chamber and are separated in committee meetings as well.

The *party caucus* is often important in state legislatures. This is where the party leaders and legislators in that house meet and discuss party policy. Because state legislatures typically meet for only a few months a year, it is often important to be able to hammer out agreements rapidly. Committee chairs in most state legislatures go to members from the majority party in that chamber, with the leaders of the majority party wielding great power in the final decision.

One area on which legislatures are predictably partisan is reapportionment and redistricting. Each decade, following the national census, state legislatures are constitutionally required to redistrict their congressional districts as well as both houses of their legislature. (We discuss this in greater detail in Chapter 5.) How the district lines are drawn can help or hurt a party for a decade or more. In states where one party controls both houses and the governorship, or where one party has a veto-proof majority in the legislature, the states can do pretty much whatever they want with district boundaries so long as they keep the districts equal in population and respect the rights of racial minorities. Where power is divided between the parties, the result is often a redistricting that protects the incumbents of both parties.

Parties in the Executive Branch Just as winning the presidency is the big prize at the national level, so is winning the governorship at the state level. When your party controls the state house, you can raise more money and build a stronger party than when you control only the legislature. Governors run as partisans and in many ways help to define the party for their state. It is not surprising, therefore, that governors are usually highly partisan. They customarily win office with the help of fellow partisans, and they know that from the day they take office, the other party is planning ways to defeat them in two or four years.

Governors are the leaders of the state party and often assist in recruiting candidates for the state legislature; they sometimes campaign on behalf of their party, even when they are not on the ballot. Presidential candidates court governors from their party for endorsements and support. Governors raise money for their next campaign, as well as for the state party. They generally have wide latitude in appointing boards, commissions, judges, and state administrators, and almost always take party affiliation and activity into account when making these appointments.

Parties in the Judiciary Despite the spread of merit selection, party affiliation remains a factor in the appointment and election of judges. In states where governors nominate judges, they pick people from their own party. In states where judges are elected on party ballots, partisanship is also important. Party matters less in nonpartisan ballots and judicial retention elections.

PARTIES AT THE LOCAL LEVEL

For many years the epitome of the political machine in America was Tammany Hall, the building where the Tammany Society (named after a Delaware Indian Chief) met and ran New York City politics. Tammany Hall was closely identified with the Democrats and was ruled by William Tweed, known as the boss of New York City politics.[19] A *boss* is a party leader who uses patronage, government contracts, and access to power to dictate policy. Some bosses, like Tweed, were never actually elected to office but were powers behind the scene who dictated their wishes to the mayor and other city officials. This system of party bosses was common in the period after the Civil War and well into this century. Other cities with prominent political machines were Chicago, Los Angeles, Boston, Pittsburgh, Cincinnati, Philadelphia, Indianapolis, San Francisco, and Baltimore.[20] A small elite ran the city of Atlanta at least until the late 1980s. While this elite was not always cohesive, it managed to dilute black opposition and maintain enough unity in the business community to get its way. The Atlanta "machine" worked with or without city hall, but usually with it.[21]

Overthrowing political machines was the principal objective of the urban reform movement active in the early twentieth century. Reformers advocated nonpartisan local elections, competitive bids for government projects, and civil service in place of patronage. They achieved their goals, although it is not clear whether these reforms ended the era of political machines or whether it was the rise of the New Deal, the "Americanization" of immigrants, or other social and economic forces that weakened the machines.

Political parties are still important in the politics of many cities, although they are in a much weaker position today. Mayors often lead city party organizations and play an important role in their state parties. They also often play a visible role in the election campaigns of presidents, senators, and, especially, governors. Moreover, the mayor's office is often a stepping-stone to other offices. California Governor Pete Wilson began his political career as mayor of San Diego, and U.S. Senator Richard Lugar was once mayor of Indianapolis.

PARTY BALANCE AND IMBALANCE

The major parties—the Democrats and the Republicans—dominate state and local politics just as they do national politics. The most important difference among state party systems is the extent of two-party competition (see Figure 4-3). State politics may be classified according to how the parties share public offices. In the *two-party* state the two parties share public offices rather evenly over the years; they alternate in winning majorities. In the *modified one-party* state one party wins all or almost all the offices over the years, but the other party usually receives a substantial percentage of the votes and sometimes surprises everybody—including itself—by winning. In the *one-party* state one party wins all or nearly all the offices, and the second party usually receives only a small proportion of the popular vote. Modified one-party Democratic states are mainly the border states plus a few other states such as Massachusetts, Florida, and Nevada. The one-party Democratic states are all in the South, except for Hawaii. There are no longer any one-party Republican states because such former stalwarts as Vermont and Kansas have chosen some Democrats for state office in recent elections.

Since the end of World War II there has been an accelerating trend toward two-party politics. In the South, Republicans have been making a contest of general elections. For a time the Republican resurgence in the South was mainly evident in presidential and congressional elections, but in recent years Republicans have been regularly elected to southern state legislatures. Arkansas, Tennessee, South and North Carolina, and Louisiana have elected Republican governors, although most of these states have reverted to the Democrats in the most recent elections. Republicans still have to make more significant gains in state and local elections before we can call most southern or border states two-party states. But the Solid South is no longer solid. Outside the South there has also been a gradual spread of two-partyism, with the rise of Democratic strength in the formerly solid Republican states of Iowa, Maine, and New Hampshire. The Democratic party has lost support in the South as more and more white southerners have moved into the Republican party. It has also lost strength in parts of the Rocky Mountain West. However, the party has been gaining loyalists in the midwest, northeast, and Pacific states.

What are the consequences of a fairly even party balance? When parties and their candidates compete on an even basis, they are more likely to be sensitive to slight changes in public opinion, for the loss of even a fraction of the voters can tip the scales to the other side in the next election. Party competition tends to push leaders within each party to work more closely together, at least as

FIGURE 4-3 Levels of Party Competition in the States (1960–1984)

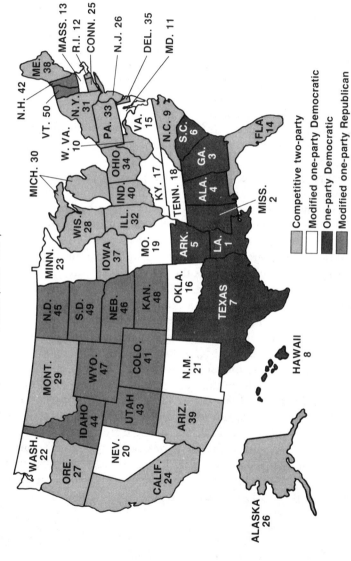

Competitive two-party

Modified one-party Democratic

One-party Democratic

Modified one-party Republican

Note: This index of two-party competition in the states helps one tell which states are most Democratic or Republican and which are about evenly divided. The index is based on the success rates the two parties achieved in state legislative, state-wide, and congressional and presidential elections (1960–1984). Numbers in the states tell exact rankings according to the most Democratic state (Louisiana #1) to the least Democratic state (Vermont #50).

Source: This index was prepared and shared with us by Robert D. Loevy of The Colorado College. See his, "The Two Party Index: Toward a Standard Statistic for Comparing United States Elections," *Social Science Journal* (April 1984). He has updated it through 1984 elections for this map.

elections draw near. Any defection may throw a race to the opponents, so competition generally produces more teamwork and efficiency in government. Doubtless it also generates more constituency work by legislators.

Party imbalance may have a serious effect on the dominant party in a one-party state. Because it is almost guaranteed a victory no matter how poor its record, the majority party may not keep itself in fighting trim. And the competition that otherwise would occur *between* the major parties often occurs *within* the majority party. Many contests in some southern states and in Massachusetts are not between Democrats and Republicans, but rather among Democrats—sometimes a handful of them—in the primary. In these intraparty fights issues may not be clearly drawn and personalities may dominate the campaign. Also, voters tend not to participate as much as they do in two-party contests. However, one has to be careful about drawing conclusions because lack of division on major issues within the community may in fact have caused the one-party situation.

If party imbalance disorganizes the dominant party, it pulverizes the minority party. Almost without hope of winning, minority leaders do not put up much of a fight. They find it difficult to raise money for campaigns or to persuade people to become candidates. They have no state or local patronage jobs to give out. Party workers and volunteers are slow to come forward. Young people wishing to succeed in politics tend to drift into the dominant party. And because the dominant party firmly controls the machinery of state and local affairs, the second party is likely to be concerned only with national politics and the patronage that could come its way if its candidate wins the White House.

We have been discussing *state* party imbalance, but imbalance can be found in even more extreme forms in cities and towns. Republicans hardly ever carry Chicago, Boston, Washington, Baltimore, Albany, Hartford, Pittsburgh, and many other cities throughout the industrial North. Democrats usually do not win in rural towns in the Rocky Mountain states. One result of this imbalance was the rapid growth, during the first half of this century, of nonpartisanship in local elections. Candidates were not able to run on major-party tickets, at least officially. The two parties were, in effect, blocked from exerting open influence on local politics. Adopted in the name of good government, nonpartisanship's effect on the major parties was probably to weaken them further as organizations. Nonpartisan elections sometimes help Republican candidates, especially in cities with populations of over 50,000.

Elections at the State and Local Level

In any year there are thousands of state and local primary and general elections in the United States—in some localities as many as five over a two-year period. They vary from statewide elections, to special elections for school boards, to recalls for mayors or school board members. Given this volume of election activity, it is fair to conclude that Americans like the idea of having elections, even though most of them choose not to vote in most of those elections.

ELECTION LAW AND THE ELECTORAL PROCESS

The U.S. Constitution provides only the most general guidelines to the states in the regulation of elections. Article I, Section 4, says, "The times, places and manner of holding elections for Senators and Representatives shall be prescribed in each State by the legislature thereof; but the Congress may at any time by law make or alter such regulations, except as to the places of choosing Senators." The constitutional language regarding presidential elections again defers to state law: "each State shall appoint, in such manner as the legislature thereof may direct, a number of electors."[22]

Amendments to the Constitution also recognize the central role of state law in this area by expressly forbidding the states to restrict the right to vote only to certain classes of people. States cannot deny the franchise on the basis of "race, color, or previous condition of servitude" (Amendment 15), gender (Amendment 19), failure to pay a poll tax (Amendment 24), or age for persons over age 18 (Amendment 26).

Modern technology makes it possible to vote by other means than in person at a voting place open on one day for a limited number of hours. Cities like San Diego and Berkeley, California, and Vancouver, Washington, have experimented with holding elections by mail. Voters are mailed a voter pamphlet that describes the question to be decided in the election and instructions on how to complete the ballot and return it by mail. Voters sign the return envelope, and their signature is compared against their signature on the voter registration form. There have been no major problems in administering these local mail-ballot elections, and the response rate (turnout) has been considerably higher than the norm for in-person special elections.[23]

A less dramatic reform of our election laws is permitting people to request absentee ballots through the mail and return them by mail. California and other states have already implemented this reform. In most of the country, in order to request an absentee ballot, a voter has to go to the county registrar and fill out a form, stating a valid reason for being unable to vote in the regular voting place on election day. Few citizens bother to request an absentee ballot under these conditions. But where the requirements for an absentee ballot have been liberalized, the voter no longer has to give a reason for requesting the absentee ballot, and can even do so by mail. The ballot is mailed to the voter and then returned by mail.

This change has significantly expanded the rate of absentee voting in California. It has been used especially by Republicans to activate retired and other voters who find it difficult to get from their homes to the polling places. Absentee ballots make up as much as 40 percent of all ballots cast in some California county elections today. Other states have also liberalized their absentee voting provisions. Oklahoma and Texas, for instance, have "early voting" whereby voters may vote for several days before an election at several locations in each county.

DIFFERENCES IN STATE ELECTION SYSTEMS

There are still some differences in state election laws, but these differences are not as great today as they were even 30 years ago. State law remains important in determining who may vote, in prescribing the means by which parties nominate their candidates, and in setting the timing and frequency of elections.

Who May Vote   States can limit suffrage. For instance, most states do not permit incarcerated felons to vote. Until the mid-1960s several states effectively limited the right to vote to white persons—often middle-class whites—despite the explicit constitutional guarantee that blacks and former slaves could not be denied the franchise (Fifteenth Amendment).

Before the Twenty-sixth Amendment was ratified, 4 states permitted 18- to 20-year-olds to vote, while the other 46 states set the voting age at 21.[24] Today, if a state wanted to permit 16-year-olds to vote, it could do so. The U.S. Constitution simply says that the right to vote cannot be denied to citizens over the age of 18; it does not preclude states from permitting younger persons to vote.

Voter registration rules can discourage people from participating in elections. States differ in the length of their residency requirement and office hours for registration, as well as in whether they permit roving registrars, postcard registration, or election-day registration. Most states require a periodic purge of the voter registration list to remove people who have moved or died. If registered voters have not voted in two or three general elections, their names are likely to be stricken from the registered voter list and they will have to register again in order to vote.

A much more common reason why people do not register is that they have moved and have not gotten around to registering at their new address. About one-third of Americans change their residence within a two-year period.[25] After moving, they may not realize that they need to register at their new address until only a few days before the election, and then it is too late. This is a commonplace occurrence among college students. Maryland, North Carolina, and the District of Columbia allow those who have moved within a city or county to vote without registering if they notify election officials of their move. All told, a state's registration rules can lower turnout by as much as 9 percent.[26]

Nomination Processes   State law establishes the process by which party nominees are selected. Most states use a primary election process, but some permit the parties to nominate their candidates through a caucus/convention system. In the caucus/convention system party delegates are elected in local voting district caucuses, which then meet and decide upon the party nominee. In some states the convention narrows the field to two candidates if no candidate can get a set percentage of the delegates.

The more widespread practice is for states to use primary elections to determine party nominees. States have two different approaches to primaries. One is the **closed primary,** in which only those voters registered in a party may vote in that party's primary. Such a system discourages **crossover voting**— voters from outside the party helping to determine the party's nominee— which is why partisans prefer closed primaries. In the **open primary** any voter can participate in any party's primary on primary election day. Wisconsin has long had open primaries. Some states, like Washington, even permit voters to vote for more than one party in the same primary election. Thus a voter can vote Democratic for governor and Republican for U.S. senator.

Primaries generally draw fewer voters than general elections, and in some cases the turnout is quite low. This raises concerns about the representativeness of voters in primary elections. Primary voters are generally better educated, earn more money, and are more likely to be white than the rest of the population.[27] Primary election turnout is also related to strength of partisan identification, the ease of voter registration, and the nature of the campaign.

In a primary election, where all the candidates are from the same party, voters make their choices based on candidate appeal and issues.[28] They may also vote for a candidate they perceive will win the nomination[29] or who has the best chance of winning the general election.

The dynamics of winning a nomination in a state with a caucus system are different from those in states with a primary. In a caucus system, having a grass-roots organization that can mobilize voters to attend a neighborhood meeting or local caucus is essential for candidates. Perhaps the state best known for this system is Iowa, whose party caucuses are the first decision in our quadrennial presidential election system. Some form of the caucus/convention system is used in eight states.

Louisiana has a unique system. All candidates, regardless of party, run in a single election. If no candidate gets a majority of the votes, there is a runoff election to determine the winner. It is not uncommon for both candidates in a runoff to be from the same party.[30] The Louisiana gubernatorial election of 1991 generated intense national attention because Republican state legislator David Duke, a former leader of the Ku Klux Klan who had offended many people by his admiring references to Adolf Hitler, emerged as one of the successful candidates. After an intense campaign that generated widespread national publicity, Edwin Edwards, a former governor, won the runoff election.

Timing and Frequency of Elections States also determine the timing of most elections. Federal law sets the date of the presidential election as "the Tuesday next after the first Monday in November, in every fourth year,"[31] with similar language applying to elections for the House and Senate.[32] States are free to determine the dates of all other elections, but for ease of administration they have consolidated gubernatorial and state general elections on the first Tuesday after the first Monday in November. Three states that elect their governor every two years instead of every four years hold gubernatorial elections on the same schedule as elections for the U.S. House. Thirty-four have chosen to conduct their elections (primary and general) for governor, other state officials, and the state legislature in odd-numbered years, leaving the even-numbered years for federal elections. Separating these elections permits voters to focus more on state issues than if they had to vote for state and federal candidates at the same time. Separating elections also means that state and local officials are not as likely to be hurt by an unpopular presidential candidate at the top of the ticket.

There is great variability in the timing of state and local primary elections and local general elections. Some states hold their primaries in late spring, others in early fall; some states, like Washington, hold their primary as late as mid-September. Primary elections are exclusively under the control of state law. Some states have two primaries in presidential years, one for the presidency in the spring and one for other contests in the fall. Other states have no primaries at all, but instead use a convention or caucus system.

State law also establishes the rules for local elections, but often allows cities and towns some discretion in setting the precise dates. Many municipal elections are held in the spring of odd-numbered years, again to avoid any positive or negative carryover from the candidates running for federal or statewide office. Counties usually conduct their elections at the same time state officials are elected.

State and local governments can call special elections to vote on a ballot initiative, a statewide constitutional change—or even a whole new constitution—or to replace a U.S. senator who has died or resigned. Participation in special elections varies greatly, depending on what is being decided, but turnout is generally lower than in midterm general elections. Before states hold special elections to fill a vacated U.S. Senate seat, they often have a special primary election to determine the party nominees for that election. In these primaries turnout is even lower than in the special general election.

Americans vote more often and for more different offices than do the citizens of any other democracy. The frequency of elections and the range of choices are remarkable. Yet only political activists have the inclination to follow this much politics with enough attention to be able to vote in an informed way. For this reason some have proposed election consolidation to foster more widespread participation and concentrate the task of voting to once or twice every couple of years. Such reformers say why not vote for local officers at the same time we choose the president? Others fear the resulting ballot would be too long.

PARTICIPATION: WHO VOTES?

What are the consequences of holding so many elections at so many different times? One is that Americans pick and choose which elections, if any, to participate in. Turnout varies by type of election:

- Turnout is higher in general elections than in primary or special elections.
- Turnout is highest in presidential general elections.
- Turnout is higher in general elections for president and members of Congress than in elections held solely for state officials.
- Turnout is higher in state elections than in local elections.
- Primary election turnout is generally low, but it declines from presidential primary to state officials primary to local primary.

States vary significantly in their rate of **turnout,** the proportion of the voting-age public that votes. Note that we do not calculate turnout on the basis of voter registration because there is such variability in the states' registration rules that it is unfair to compare the turnout in a state with difficult registration laws with the turnout in another state whose laws make voting much more accessible. Figure 4-4 breaks down the country into five groups on the basis of their turnout rates in state general elections between 1980 and 1990.

Turnout in primaries varies even more dramatically than turnout in general elections. In some primaries in which a U.S. Senate seat or governorship is at stake and the races are contested in both parties, turnout can approach two-

FIGURE 4-4   Turnout in State General Elections, 1980–1990

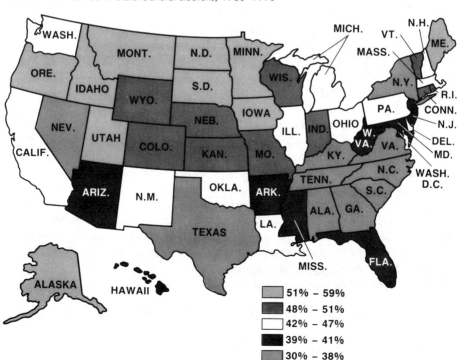

51% – 59%
48% – 51%
42% – 47%
39% – 41%
30% – 38%

Source: Statistical Abstract of the United States, 1991 (U.S. Government Printing Office, 1992).

STATE AND LOCAL CAMPAIGN FINANCE PROVISIONS

- 23 states limit the size of individual contributions.

- 22 states prohibit and 13 states limit corporate contributions; 9 states prohibit and 17 states limit labor union contributions.

- 17 states limit PAC contributions; one (Montana) limits the aggregate money candidates can receive from all PACs.

- 17 states limit or prohibit transfers; one (Wisconsin) limits the aggregate money candidates can receive from political parties and/or legislative caucuses.

- 2 states (Minnesota and Texas) limit off-election year contributions.

- 11 states offer limited public financing from the government; 3 states give financing directly to legislative candidates, and the other states give it to statewide candidates or to the political parties.

- 4 states offer partial or total tax credits to encourage small contributions.

- 5 states impose expenditure ceilings on candidates who accept partial public financing.

- 17 states raise campaign money through their income tax systems.

Source: California Commission on Campaign Financing, *The New Gold Rush: Financing California's Legislative Campaigns* (Center for Responsible Government, 1985), p. 12.

thirds that of general elections. But in primaries for less visible races, the turnout is generally much lower. When states call special elections to vote on a constitutional revision, decide a ballot proposition, or replace a U.S. senator, the turnout is almost always lower than in a regular general election, and sometimes it is much lower.

CAMPAIGN FINANCE

After the Watergate scandal in the mid-1970s many states enacted disclosure laws on campaign finance, a few instituted partial public financing of elections, and others provided partial underwriting of the costs of parties. A common element of campaign finance legislation at the state and local level is disclosure. Candidates are typically asked to file disclosure statements on where the money came from to finance their campaign, and interest groups are often required to file separate reports on how they distributed their campaign contributions. Once elected, most officials at state and local levels are required to file a different kind of disclosure form, one that indicates their personal wealth, investments, and other financial matters that may reveal conflicts of interest.

Voting Behavior in State and Local Elections

Voting choice in state and local elections is structured much the same as the voting choice at the federal level. Voters tend to vote their party identification. But candidates and issues are also important, and at the local level voters are more likely to have some personal contact with the candidates. In nonpartisan settings candidate appeal and issues are more likely to be important.

Local campaigns rely less on television and radio than national and state campaigns, but there has been a general professionalization of politics at all levels. Negative advertising, a major feature of recent presidential elections, is now more of a factor in state and local campaigns. While the cost of running for the city council, county commission, or other local office is much lower than running for Congress or the governorship, campaigns are becoming increasingly expensive at all levels.

The voting choice on ballot issue questions is also heavily influenced by campaign spending. Presumably, greater expenditures make the most difference when there is a low level of information, as is the case with many ballot propositions. And opinions in ballot propositions are more volatile because voters' views on such matters are not deeply rooted in party affiliation, feelings toward an incumbent, or party appeal. Given these factors, it is not surprising that the side that spends the most money—especially if it is the "no" side of a measure—wins most of the time.[33] Because many initiatives are supported by well-funded interests and because a vote in one state can be interpreted as perhaps the start of a national movement on that issue, initiative campaigns can attract large sums of money. Some recent examples of heavy spending include a 1988 election in Maryland in which the National Rifle Association and other groups spent a record $6.8 million in an unsuccessful attempt to defeat a hand gun registration referendum. The tobacco industry spent over $21 million in California in 1988 to defeat an initiative raising the cigarette tax.[34]

Voting on ballot questions is different from voting for candidates. Typically, a much smaller percentage skips voting on ballot initiatives. As many as 20 percent of those who go to the polls may skip voting on a particular constitutional revision, bond authorization, or advisory vote.

There are other predictable voting tendencies: Voters who are confused about ballot measures tend to vote no for those measures. "Ballot fatigue" also makes people more likely to vote no.[35] Finally, early support for a measure as determined by public opinion polls sometimes turns into strong opposition on election day. Apparently, people tend to think of an initiative as a good idea until they hear arguments against it; then they often vote no.[36]

The Future of "Grass-Roots" Democracy

The big show in American politics is clearly the presidential election. Voters, the media, and foreign observers all gravitate to the spectacle of the Iowa caucuses and the New Hampshire primary. Later we watch thousands of adults wear funny hats and behave as if they were at a birthday party as they go about formally nominating their party's choice for president. During the general election we follow the nominees as they campaign, debate, and exploit the media in efforts to persuade us to elect them to the White House.

But there is more to democracy in America than presidential elections. Thousands of candidates enter politics every year in hundreds of different kinds of contests, and voters participate by choosing from among those candidates. Primary or caucus participants narrow the field, and then a larger number of voters actually elect the officeholders.

Political parties are vital to the operation of this large-scale democracy. Political scientists argue that one of the things most needed in our system today is stronger parties. The first step in the renewal of the parties is to change their image and persuade citizens that partisan activity is essential to a healthy constitutional democracy. The next is to give people who support parties a greater say in the candidates who run under their party's label. While our candidate-centered tradition will certainly remain, it is important to moderate it with strengthened parties that can discipline candidates, at least by witholding resources that candidates cannot easily acquire elsewhere.

We would also do well to make elections more "voter friendly." The proliferation of elections, including special elections, taxes the interest and willingness to get involved of even the most committed citizens. Why not, many reformers argue, consolidate elections so that voters might exercise their vote only once or twice, rather than three or four times, a year?

Getting good people to run for office is another challenge. The spiraling cost of campaigns and the advantages enjoyed by incumbents has deterred many good potential candidates. Others are repelled by the nasty and negative tone of recent elections. But unless a democracy produces able citizens who are willing to run for office, it loses its ability to hold incumbents accountable.

Summary

1. In the United States there are technically no national elections, only state elections. Even the presidential election, which we think of as a national election, is really a set of 51 different elections to choose electors who will, in turn, cast their ballots for president. Elections for U.S. senators and representatives are conducted largely under state law.

2. State election law is important in defining who may vote, when elections will be held, how party nominees are chosen, and which candidates will appear on the ballot. State election law also establishes a framework within which fair elections are assured.

3. State registration laws make voting more or less difficult, depending on their requirements. States may require persons to register by party to vote in primary elections; when voting is thus limited, the primaries are called closed primaries. Over the course of U.S. history states have gradually eased registration requirements. Suffrage has also been expanded by adoption of constitutional amendments that granted the right to vote to African Americans, women, Native Americans, and finally, all citizens 18 to 21 years of age. A constitutional amendment also banned the use of poll taxes.

4. Political parties are essential to the functioning of democracy at all levels, but they are principally organized around the units of competition. This makes state parties vitally important. Routinely, they are patterned after the national party organiza-

tion, to include a chair, vice-chair, and a central committee. State parties are often run by full-time administrators who are often called executive directors.

5. Political parties play important roles in candidate recruitment, fund raising, voter registration, and voter mobilization, and they provide a link between people and government. Parties are also important to the operation of most state legislatures. The governor is the head of the party in power. Governors consider party loyalty when appointing people to many executive and judicial openings.

6. Voters usually vote along party lines in state and local elections, although candidate appeal and issues can also be important. Many of the same concerns about campaigns at the national level are evident at the state and local level: their escalating cost, their increasingly negative nature, and media obsession with the "character" of candidates.

7. Political parties were once strong and well organized at the local level; in some cities these organizations were called machines and were led by party bosses. Reaction to the abuses of these machines led to efforts to reform urban politics. One of these reforms was to make local politics officially nonpartisan.

8. The health of a constitutional democracy may be most in evidence at the grass roots —that is, the state and local levels. American democracy remains strong, but there are important issues which, if not addressed, could diminish its vitality.

For Further Reading

PAUL S. HERRNSON, *Party Campaigning in the 1980s* (Harvard University Press, 1988).

MALCOLM E. JEWELL and DAVID M. OLSON, *Political Parties and Elections in American States*, 3d ed. (The Dorsey Press, 1988).

V. O. KEY, JR., *American State Politics: An Introduction* (Knopf, 1956).

DAVID B. MAGLEBY, *Direct Legislation: Voting on Ballot Propositions in the United States* (Johns Hopkins University Press, 1984).

L. SANDY MAISEL, *Parties and Elections in America* (Random House, 1987).

A. JAMES REICHLEY (ed.), *Elections American Style* (Brookings Institution, 1987).

ALAN ROSENTHAL, *Governors and Legislators: Contending Powers* (CQ Press, 1990).

ALAN ROSENTHAL, *Legislative Life: People, Process, and Performance in the States* (Harper and Row, 1981).

Notes

1. Bill Berkeley, *Liberia: A Promise Betrayed* (Lawyers Committee for Human Rights, 1986), p. 108.

2. Ibid., p. 116.

3. "A Senate Panel's Report," *The Wall Street Journal*, February 11, 1991, p. A1.

4. Jane Perlez, "African Dilemma: Food Aid May Prolong War and Famine," *The New York Times*, May 12, 1991, sec. 4, p. 3.

5. John Bibby, *Politics, Parties, and Elections in America* (Nelson Hall, 1987), pp. 94–95.

6. See Cornelius P. Cotter, James L. Gibson, John F. Bibby, and Robert J. Huckshorn, *Party Organizations in America* (Praeger, 1984).

7. William Crotty, *The Party Game* (W. H. Freeman, 1985), pp. 105–06.

8. Norman J. Ornstein, Thomas E. Mann, and Michael J. Malbin, *Vital Statistics on Congress, 1991–1992* (CQ Press, 1991), p. 74.

9. Linda L. Fowler and Robert D. McClure, *Political Ambition: Who Decides to Run for Congress* (Yale University Press, 1989), p. 197.

10. Ibid., pp. 196–97.

11. Federal Election Commission, *Technical Report 2: Fast Facts on State Registration Election Procedures* (National Clearinghouse on Election Administration, 1992).

12. See A. James Reichley, "The Rise of National Parties," in *The New Directions in American Politics*, ed. John E. Chubb and Paul E. Peterson (Brookings Institution, 1985), pp. 193–94.

13. Federal Election Commission, *Technical Report*

1: Federal Election Statistics (National Clearinghouse on Election Administration, 1992).

14. For a discussion of coordinated campaigns, see Paul Herrnson, "National Party Organizations and the Postreform Congress," in *The Postreform Congress,* ed. Roger Davidson (St. Martins Press, 1992), pp. 65–67.

15. See Cotter et al., *Party Organizations in America.*

16. See Bruce E. Keith, David B. Magleby, Candice J. Nelson, Elizabeth Orr, Mark C. Westlye, and Raymond E. Wolfinger, *The Myth of the Independent Voter* (University of California Press, 1992), p. 52.

17. William H. Flanigan and Nancy H. Zingale, *Political Behavior of the American Electorate,* 7th ed. (CQ Press, 1991), p. 114.

18. See Eugene C. Lee, *The Politics of Nonpartisanship* (University of California Press, 1960); and Willis D. Hawley, *Nonpartisan Elections and the Case for Party Politics* (John Wiley and Sons, 1973).

19. See Alexander B. Callow, Jr., *The Tweed Ring* (Oxford University Press, 1976); and William Riordon (ed.), *Plunkitt of Tammany Hall* (Dutton, 1963).

20. Ernest S. Griffith, *A History of American City Government: The Conspicuous Failure, 1870–1900* (Praeger, 1974), pp. 75–76, 261–62.

21. Clarence N. Stone, *Regime Politics: Governing Atlanta 1946–1988* (University Press of Kansas, 1989).

22. U.S. Constitution, Article II, Section 1.

23. David B. Magleby, "Participation in Mail Ballot Elections," *The Western Political Quarterly* 40 (March 1987), pp. 79–91.

24. Carole Lynn Corbin, *Issues in American History: The Right to Vote* (Franklin Watts, 1985), pp. 92–93.

25. Peverill Squire, Raymond E. Wolfinger, and David P. Glass, "Residential Mobility and Voter Turnout," *American Political Science Review* 81 (March 1987), pp. 45–65. See also Thad A. Brown, *Migration and Politics* (University of North Carolina Press, 1988).

26. Raymond E. Wolfinger and Steven J. Rosenstone, *Who Votes?* (Yale University Press, 1980), p. 130.

27. James I. Lengle, *Representation and Presidential Primaries: The Democratic Party in the Postreform Era* (Greenwood Press, 1981). For more on primary elections, see Larry M. Bartles, *Presidential Primaries and the Dynamics of Public Choice* (Princeton University Press, 1988); Jeane J. Kirkpatrick, *The New Presidential Elite: Men and Women in National Politics* (Basic Books, 1976); Barbara Norander, "Ideological Representativeness of Presidential Primary Voters," *Journal of Politics* 51 (November 1989), pp. 977–92.

28. Malcolm E. Jewell and David M. Olson, *Political Parties and Elections in American States,* 3d ed. (The Dorsey Press, 1988), p. 121.

29. Flanigan and Zingale, *Political Behavior of the American Electorate,* p. 137.

30. The number would be 40 percent, except that in 1989 one candidate withdrew after the primary, alleviating the need for a runoff.

31. 3 U.S.C. 1.

32. See 2 U.S.C. 7 for the language pertaining to House elections and 2 U.S.C. 1 for that pertaining to Senate elections.

33. David B. Magleby, *The Effects of Disproportionate Campaign Spending in Ballot Propositions and Candidate Elections.* Paper presented at annual meeting of the American Political Science Association, Washington, D.C., August 1986.

34. Ibid.

35. David B. Magleby, *Direct Legislation: Voting on Ballot Propositions in the United States* (Johns Hopkins University Press, 1984), Chaps. 7–9.

36. David B. Magleby, "Opinion Formation and Opinion Change in Ballot Proposition Campaigns," in *Manipulating Public Opinion,* ed. Michael Margolis and Gary Mauser (Brooks/Cole, 1989), pp. 17–18.

5

State Legislatures

Colorado state representative Jerry Kopel of Denver has been a veteran door-to-door campaigner. He invariably asks constituents if he can help them in any way. In one recent campaign, one woman told him, "Yeah, you can water my petunias." Kopel said, "Sure," went outside, turned on the hose, and watered the petunias.[1]

As state representative Kopel found out, U.S. citizens have a pragmatic approach to their state legislators. They want them to be honest and responsive. They want them to keep taxes down. They want them to provide services. And they want them to do errands for constituents, even watering their petunias. Yet few voters actually know the names of their legislators, and fewer still contact them or attend their "meet-the-candidate" or informational town hall forums.

Many legislators and authorities on state legislatures say that voters are more hostile in the 1990s than they have been in recent decades. Some legislators blame the press and governors for too often portraying state legislatures as villains in most policy disputes. A few other legislators admit, "We're to blame," and add, "People just don't trust politicians." For example, Pennsylvania state senator Robert Jubelirer explains, "A lot of this has been done by us to us. So many campaigns are nothing but 30-second spots making the opponent out to be less than slime."[2]

Alan Rosenthal, a noted scholar of state legislatures, says there has been an increase in voter frustration toward legislatures. Support for term limits on state legislators is one example of this hostility. "The irony," he notes," is that legislatures are doing a better job of handling bigger issues than ever, but getting less and less credit for it."[3]

State legislatures are the oldest part of our government. State legislatures existed before we had the U.S. Constitution; the Massachusetts legislature, for example, is in its fourth century. These legislatures were the most powerful governing institution in the country during the Revolutionary period. Indeed, the coming of the Constitution was in part a reaction to the excessive power of the state legislatures and an attempt to limit them.

The Constitution worked. It diminished the influence of state legislatures. They are not as powerful today as they were in 1787—at least when compared to other governmental institutions. Yet they are not as secondary as they were even thirty years ago. While they used to be among the public's favorite punching bags, their inept antics winning easy laughs from comedians, journalists, and governors; such joking is less warranted today. State legislatures are important. They play a vital role in state politics and state policy making. Heeding their constituents, state legislators strive to solve problems and provide services—and do so, whenever possible, without raising taxes and creating larger bureaucracies. Legislators these days seek to make the legislature a counterbalance to governors and state bureaucracies.

Although there are influential and even charismatic state legislators in many states, such as Assembly Speaker Willie Brown in California, strong governors generally overshadow the legislative body. By its very nature, a legislature made up of many diverse individuals from different parties, speaking with many voices, cannot provide unified, swift policy leadership. Legislators cer-

---

LEGISLATIVE HUMOR

Everyone has committed verbal gaffes at one time or another, but what separates legislators from others is that their job requires so much speechmaking and other public presentations. These are real quotes; legislators really said these things. The ever-diligent media were on hand to record such misstatements for posterity:

These are not my figures I'm quoting. They're the figures of someone who knows what he's talking about.

I think I know more about this bill than I understand.

It takes real courage to vote against your convictions.

There comes a time to put principles aside and do what's right.

It's time to swallow the bullet.

From now on I'm watching everything you do with a fine-tooth comb.

Before I give you the benefit of my remarks, I'd like to know what we're talking about.

I wish some of these ideas were left to stand on their own bottoms.

I'm in favor of letting the status quo stay as it is.

This body is becoming entirely too laxative about some matters.

Source: Veteran state lobbyist Charles Henning, quoted in Malcolm Kushner, "The Serious Use of Humor," *State Legislatures,* May 1985, p. 27.

tainly cannot compete with governors for the public's attention. Moreover, in the smaller states many legislators are still part-timers, do not stay in the legislature long (three or four terms is the average), lack adequate staffs, and are generally unable to compete with the better informed governors, bureaucrats, and interest-group leaders. But even in states with well-paid and well-staffed legislative bodies, they are not likely to be the dominant policy-making branch.

A legislature's *political* functions, however, may be as important now as its law-making or policy-making functions. Legislatures are constantly reconciling pressures among competing interest groups. Representing local views at the state level, they dramatize issues and bring them into the open. In effect, the state legislature serves as a lightning rod to which most of the conflicting pressures of American society are drawn, and, says Frank Smallwood, a college professor who served in the Vermont state senate, "its primary job is to defuse these pressures so that the political system can function intact without blowing wide apart."[4]

You and your family probably know someone who is or has tried to become a state legislator, for about 12,000 to 15,000 people seek this job every two years. Sometimes there is no real contest; able incumbents are often unopposed. Nearly 80 percent of incumbents run for reelection, and they have a nearly 90 percent chance of winning renomination and reelection. An incumbent seeking reelection has many advantages over a challenger. These include name recognition, better access to campaign funds, experience in running campaigns, and many opportunities to provide constituent services. Still, few of them feel politically secure, even when they have not been opposed in the last election. "They are always wary of potentially strong opponents and work hard to build a record at the polls and in office that will discourage such persons from running."[5]

Why do so many people seek this office? For many reasons—"the excitement, power and deference, personal gain, a chance to advertise themselves, a need for self-esteem, the challenge of making good public policy, or a sense of loyalty to their political party."[6] Often the reason is a mixture of these factors, as well as a desire to be where the action is. Once elected, state legislators translate diverse public wants and aspirations into practical laws and regulations.

State legislators today are better educated, have more professional staffs, and have better committee systems and better leadership than they did a generation or two ago. They put in far more time on their work than did their predecessors thirty years ago. Most state legislators concentrate on being *lawmakers* when meeting in their state capitols. Yet they also try to be *representatives*—to listen, learn, and find out what the people like and do not like—when they are at home in their legislative districts. Invariably, too, state legislators wind up doing a lot of favors—getting a merchant a license to sell lottery tickets, persuading some state agency to look into safety standards at the local hospital, pushing for funds to repair county roads, arranging for a campaign supporter to be appointed to the state labor commission, and so on. State legislators are accessible. Citizens and students can nearly always contact their legislators and talk with them on the telephone or in person.

The Legislative Branch

All states except Nebraska have a two-house, or **bicameral legislature.** The larger chamber is generally called the house of representatives. It contains from as few as 40 members in Alaska to as many as 400 members in New Hampshire; the typical number is around 100. In all but four states the representatives serve two-year terms. The smaller chamber, known as the senate, is composed of about 40 members. State senators have four-year terms in most states.

Most state legislatures meet every year from January through May or June. Legislatures in about a dozen mostly less populous states meet only every other year. Some state constitutions limit their legislatures to regular sessions of a fixed number of days, usually sixty or ninety. Several means, such as the "special session," have been developed to get around this limitation. Such restrictions reflect the old distrust of government, the feeling that "the faster we get it over with, the better." The governor has the power to call the legislature into special session—and in some states to determine the issues that may be discussed in the special session—a power governors frequently use.

The organization and procedures of the state legislatures are similar to those of the United States Congress. A speaker, usually chosen by the majority party, presides over the lower house. In many states speakers have more power to control proceedings than their national counterpart has. For example, most speakers have the right to appoint committees and thus possess a key role in determining policy. In less than half of the states lieutenant governors preside over the senate, though usually they are mere figureheads; in other states the presiding officer is chosen by the majority party in the senate. The committee system prevails, as in Congress. In several states, such as Massachusetts, **joint committees** are used to speed up legislative action. However, state legislative committees usually do not have the same power over bills as do their national counterparts; they often lack adequate professional assistance; the seniority system is not as closely followed as in Congress; and membership turnover is somewhat higher.

Although the formal structures and procedures of the legislatures are similar from state to state, their actual operations are not. Several states, like New York and Ohio, have strong political parties that take an active part in policy making. In these states, the party caucus is an important part of the legislative machinery; in others, the parties assume little or no responsibility for the actions of their legislative members. In some states, governors lead the way; in others they are relatively unimportant.

Striking differences exist among state legislatures. Often these differences stem from historical or ethnic traditions. Sometimes they arise because of

WHAT MAKES A GOOD LEGISLATOR?

There are many ways to be an effective legislator. Many legislators specialize in issues, others in procedures or helping their districts through casework, and still others become chamber or party leaders. Nearly everyone learns that there is more to the job than making a lot of speeches or trying to get more bills passed than your colleagues do.

Legislators themselves say they admire colleagues who are confident but not arrogant, cooperative but not spineless, principled but flexible, and humorous but not silly. Retired lawmakers suggest these rules:

• Learn to count.

• Keep your word.
• Be patient.
• Be honest.
• Don't promise too soon.
• Make friends with the staff.
• Never surprise a politician.
• Learn how to build alliances.
• Learn the procedures.
• Think beyond party labels.
• Know that timing is often the key.
• Don't hog the credit.

urban-rural or east-west factional splits, and sometimes because of notable regional differences—as is the case with the "Hill people" versus the "Delta people" in Mississippi. Here is how one expert on state politics sees some of the more distinctive characteristics shaping state politics in the United States.

> In New York professional politics, political wheeling and dealing, and frantic activity are characteristic. In Virginia, one gets a sense of tradition, conservatism, and gentility. . . . Louisiana's politics are wild and flamboyant. By contrast, moderation and caution are features of Iowa. A strong disposition of compromise pervades Oregon, with politicians disposed to act as brokers and deal pragmatically rather than dogmatically. In Kansas hard work, respect for authority, fiscal prudence, and a general conservatism and resistance to rapid social change are pervasive features of the state environment. Indiana is intensely partisan. Wyoming is mainly individualistic and Ohio is fundamentally conservative. In Hawaii the relatively recent political dominance of Japanese, and the secondary status of Chinese, native Hawaiians, Hawaiians, and Haoles (whites) makes for tough ethnic politics. Yankee Republicans used to run Massachusetts, but now the Irish dominate. Their personalized style, which blends gregariousness and political loyalty, results in a politics of the clan. Mormonism of course dominates Utah.[7]

Still, legislatures have much in common, and it is important to know: (1) what they are supposed to do; (2) what their members' backgrounds are; and (3) what influences their behavior and their vote.

WHAT CAN STATE LEGISLATORS DO—AND NOT DO?

What do the 7,424 state legislators do? Among other things, they enact the laws that create state parks, specify the salaries for state officials, draw up the rules governing state elections, fix the state tax rates, determine the quantity and quality of state correctional, mental health, and educational institutions, and much more. State legislators in most of the states are more and more involved in overseeing the administration of public policy. Although they do not administer programs directly, through hearings, investigations, audits, and increased involvement in the budgetary process, legislators can and do determine whether programs are being carried out according to legislative intentions.

State legislatures have various functions within the larger federal system, such as ratifying proposed amendments to the U.S. Constitution, exercising the right to petition Congress to call for a constitutional convention to propose an amendment to the U.S. Constitution, and approving interstate compacts on matters affecting state policies and their implementation.

State legislatures have all the powers that are not given to some other agency. The Tenth Amendment to the U.S. Constitution makes it clear that power not given to the national government or denied to the states lies with the states or with the people. The state constitutions, in turn, give some of this reserved power exclusively to *non*legislative agencies and specifically deny some to the legislature. What is left is inherited by the state legislatures.

Despite all these restrictions, the legislatures still have a powerful voice in deciding crucial political questions in their states. For example, they levy state taxes, appropriate money, create agencies to carry out the tasks of government, and investigate these agencies to make sure they are doing what the lawmakers intended them to do. State legislators also have to decide on appropriate policies and spending levels for public schools, kindergarten through high school,

---

STATE LEGISLATORS: THEIR MANY ROLES

- Studying the problems of their districts and states.

- Helping enact legislative programs.

- Developing support for priority programs.

- Keeping informed on all bills and amendments.

- Attending sessions, taking part in debate, and voting on business before the legislative chambers.

- Attending committee meetings and hearings.

- Responding to calls and letters from constituents.

- Exercising legislative oversight over the administrations and the state budgets

through hearings, personal visits, inspections, and so on.

- Participating in the confirmation and impeachment processes involving various state officials.

- Serving as connecting links between local officials and state officials, and between state officials and national officials.

- Maintaining their own campaign organizations and perhaps playing active roles in their county and state political party organizations.

- Taking part in ceremonial functions.

- Voting on proposed amendments to U.S. Constitution and on various interstate compacts with other states.

and for state-supported higher education, transportation systems, public safety, prisons, and environmental regulations. State legislators, like their national counterparts, also participate in amending constitutions, have authority to impeach and try state officials, and exercise some appointive powers.

Each state's constitution prescribes the procedures its legislators must follow in order to make laws. In addition, limits on the rate of taxation, the kinds of taxes, the subjects that may be taxed, and the purposes of taxation are often spelled out in the state constitution.

With the growth of state functions, legislators are spending increasing amounts of time on casework or constituency services. Constituent relations are often the most time-consuming aspect of a legislator's job. Concerns of constituents usually arise during campaign time. Local city and school officials always need the help of legislators, and dozens of interest groups from back home are always pressing their views on legislators. Legislators usually work hard to attract constituency casework and recognize its political value. The more help they give to their home district citizens and businesses, they reason, the more they will probably be respected and reelected.

WHO ARE THE STATE LEGISLATORS?

The typical American state legislator is a 43-year-old white, male, Protestant businessman or lawyer of Anglo-Saxon origin who has had previous political experience—usually elective—at the city or county level. About 40 percent are Republicans. Lawyers continue to be the largest occupational group in most state legislatures. Many young attorneys, in fact, enter the legislature to perform a public service, secure a reputation, and build up a practice. But there has been a decline in the number of lawyers in state legislatures in recent years and an increase in the number of teachers.

Real estate and insurance dealers and salespeople are also found in legislatures in significant numbers. The number of farmers is decreasing as a result of reapportionment, the decline in the overall number of farmers, and the longer sessions of the legislatures. When legislatures used to meet for just a few winter months, farmers were able to fit their schedules to the legislative cycle.

More women and blacks are winning election to state legislatures, but both groups are still notably in the minority. Out of 7,424 state legislators, nearly 20 percent, or about 1,400, are women, more than 430 are blacks, and at least 130 are Hispanics. Women and minority groups are increasingly organized to achieve a greater voice in state governments.[8]

Because legislators must have flexible schedules, the job often attracts young people, retired people, and those whose businesses or law practices have been so successful that they can afford to take the time off. In the more populous and wealthy states, the trend is toward annual legislative sessions with reasonable salaries. New York legislators earn $57,500 a year plus $89 per day for expenses. Pennsylvania pays its legislators $47,000 annually plus $88 per day for expenses. A few other states pay at least $40,000. Other states, such as Maryland and Wisconsin, provide "living wages." But in most states legislators receive modest salaries. Thus, Texas pays $7,200; Florida pays $22,560; and Nebraska and Idaho pay their legislators $12,000 a year. In some states, legislators go to the capital for only a few months a year and are paid so little that many are able to serve only if they are independently wealthy, if they can live off their parents or spouses, or if they have other jobs that can be readily combined with legislative service (see Figure 5-1). The 400 members of the New Hampshire House earn only $100 a year.

State legislators are better educated and have better jobs than the average person. They also come more from middle-and upper-income groups. They are usually hard-working, public-spirited citizens who believe being in the legislature is a good opportunity for service.

State legislators enjoy less prestige than do members of Congress, especially in states that have large legislatures. Discouraged by modest salaries and long hours, many serve a few terms and then either retire voluntarily or run for higher office. About 20 percent of all legislators are newcomers, but there has been a gradual increase in the number of legislators seeking reelection. Some state legislators probably leave after just a couple of terms because they get bored listening to matters that frankly do not interest them. As one one-termer advised: "In short, a great deal in the political process does not—repeat does not—involve the glamorous policy issues. Most of the work is sheer routine and hardly awe-inspiring."[9] Some states now limit their legislators to a few terms in office, and these term limits will force more turnover. (We discuss the term-limit movement and its politics later in this chapter.)

Percentage of state legislators
holding other jobs.

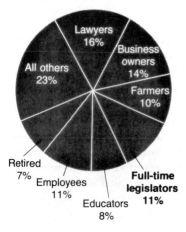

FIGURE 5-1

The Statehouse as a Second Job

Source: National Conference of State Legislatures, from a survey in 1986. New York Times, June 4, 1989, p. Y13. Copyright © 1989 by The New York Times Company. Reprinted by permission.

WHAT INFLUENCES STATE LEGISLATORS?

Political Parties Except in Nebraska, where legislators are elected on a *nonpartisan ballot* (one without party labels), all candidates for state legislatures are nominated by political parties in primaries and are elected as party members. Although the official party organization is often not a dominant force in recruiting state legislative candidates, a candidate nonetheless has to go through the party to gain the nomination. Candidates sense that parties are weaker than they used to be. Candidates welcome what help they can get from the parties, yet they usually get little money. They almost always have to form their own personal organization, separate from the local party apparatus, to wage a winning campaign.

The role of the political parties in the management of legislatures and in policy making varies widely from state to state. In nearly half the states—especially in the urban, industrialized states and the Northeast—the political party is the most important factor in decision making. In other states—in the Southwest, for example—parties appear to be somewhat less significant. Instead, rural-urban splits, conservative-liberal coalitions, or regional blocs serve as the major sources of conflict.

In nearly every state where there are two substantial parties, the political party is the device for the selection of legislative leaders and the assignment of members to committees. Party leaders in many states distribute sought-after perks, ranging from committee assignments to parking spaces. **Legislative caucuses**—meetings of all the members of one party in the chamber—sometimes also distribute campaign funds to their members and to specifically targeted districts.

Party discipline on policy matters is more likely to be found in states with a highly competitive two-party system. Here party caucuses are likely to be the place where party positions are developed, and members of a party are expected to support its policies within their legislative chambers. In fact, in a few states binding votes in party caucuses virtually force party members to vote as a unified bloc on the floor of their chamber. Such binding caucus votes, however, are taken on relatively few issues.

The party caucus is a principal instrument for legislative decision making in about half the states, including Colorado, Delaware, Idaho, Montana, California, and Utah. In several states, such as Illinois, New York, New Jersey, Pennsylvania, and Minnesota, parties play an even more prominent role than they do in Congress.

In states where one political party is so large that it dominates the legislature, the party caucus is usually not likely to play a central role in policy making. Of course it is hard to generalize about the precise role parties play in legislatures, especially in states where there is neither a highly competitive two-party system nor a one-party system but something in between. In such states you may find that both parties are highly organized and influence both the procedures and the substantive outcomes inside the state legislatures. Yet in

HOW A BILL BECOMES LAW: THE MASSACHUSETTS MODEL

1. Petitions are filled in the office of the House or Senate Clerk.
2. Clerk assigns a number to the petition and refers it to a committee.
3. Joint Committee holds public hearing before making report.
4. An unfavorable report, if accepted by the House or Senate, kills the bill. A favorable report is considered the first reading.
5. If the bill relates to state finances, it is referred to the Ways and Means Committee. When the Ways and Means Committee makes its recommendations, the bill is put on the next day's calendar for a second reading.
6. Before voting on "ordering the bill a third reading," a bill is subject to debate and amendment. If favorable action is taken and the bill is ordered a third reading, it is then referred to the Committee on Bills in the Third Reading.
7. Following a third reading, a vote is taken on "passing the bill to be engrossed." A favorable vote sends the bill to the other branch, where it follows the same procedure.
8. If a bill passes the second branch in an amended version, it is sent back to the originating branch for concurrence. If concurrence is rejected, the bill may go to a conference committee.
9. When agreement is reached by both branches, the bill is prepared for final passage.
10. Vote on enactment is taken in the House and then the Senate.
11. The bill is sent to the governor.
12. The governor, during the ten-day period allotted him by the constitution, may:

    Sign the bill into law
    Let it become law by taking no action
    Send it back with amendments
    Veto it. A two-thirds vote of both branches is required to override a veto.
    Let it die by taking no action within ten days after the session ends. This is called a *pocket veto*.

Source: Prepared and published as part of the pamphlet *Inside the State House* by the Massachusetts Legislature and the League of Women Voters of Massachusetts.

some states only the major political party plays this role. In still other such states, the parties may not be important in deciding what gets done in the legislatures.

In legislatures in which a single party has had a long-standing dominance or even overwhelming control, as in some southern states, parties are generally, less important in conducting and shaping legislative business. Because of the rise of the Republican party in the South and Southwest, however, parties and partisanship are gradually increasing in strength in such states as Florida, Texas, and North Carolina. A rebirth of partisanship and growing attention to elections of legislators are apparently making the parties more important than they have been in over half of the states (see Figure 5-2). Voting regularly with the party and being a members of the majority party can help legislators win discretionary grants or other favors for their districts.[10]

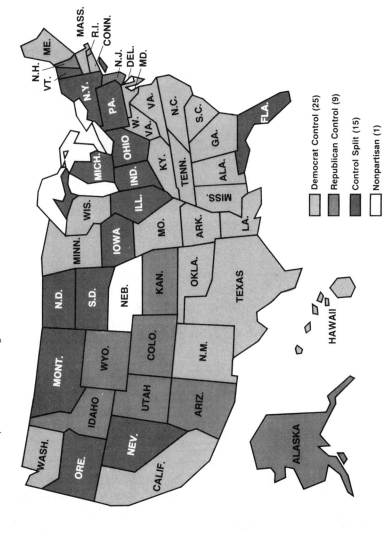

FIGURE 5-2 Party Control of State Legislatures

Democrat Control (25)

Republican Control (9)

Control Split (15)

Nonpartisan (1)

"It's true, Dave, that I have an un-savory past, but if elected to public office I hope to hold myself to a higher standard."

Drawing by Dana Fradon; © 1987 The New Yorker Magazine, Inc.

Lobbyists   Those who dislike the laws that are passed, or who like the laws that are defeated often claim that the fault lies in the integrity of the legislators. Although state legislatures do have their share of dishonest people, their number is probably no greater than in business, sports, or entertainment. Many people who may be affected by decisions seek to bend those decisions to their advantage. Anyone who reads state newspapers learns that certain bankers, insurance companies, road builders, developers, and large landholders have, on occasion, sought contracts or special rulings by illegal means.

A larger problem has long challenged the integrity of representative government in the United States. "If there is any safe axiom in American politics," writes David Broder, "it is that our legislators get the funds with which they run from the very people who have the greatest direct stake in the legislation they will pass." Broder describes the problem well:

> The arrangements are not subtle. Fund-raising dinners are held during the legislative sessions, and the distribution of campaign contributions is often done personally by the same lobbyists who are negotiating with those legislators on provisions of specific bills. The cynical remark of a Florida lobbyist, who had been "invited" to one of those mid-session "appreciation dinners" given by and for a key legislator, was that "you've got to appreciate someone for their past service—or their future service." At that point, the difference between a contribution and a bribe becomes so blurred as to be almost invisible.[11]

To **lobby** is to try to influence public officials, especially members of legislative bodies, to shape the policies they enact. The right to lobby is, of course, secured by the First Amendment to the Constitution, which expresses the right of people to petition the government for redress of grievances. State constitutions provide similar protections.

Illegal use of lobbying techniques, primarily bribery, can still be found in a few states, and major scandals were exposed in Arizona and South Carolina in the early 1990s. But direct, illegal bribery is not a widespread problem in most states. Writing about his own experiences in the Vermont state senate, Frank Smallwood observes that as a general rule, most of the lobbyists "were articulate, hard-working, and extremely well informed in their particular areas of expertise. This last attribute—information—represented their chief weapon and gave them real clout. As far as I could find out, the lobbyists didn't offer legislators any money or other direct inducements, at least, they never offered me anything, not even a sociable drink. Instead they relied on information."[12]

Effective **lobbyists** are specialists in both subject matter and legislative procedure. In fact, some of the most effective lobbyists are former state legislators. Lobbyists for organized interests know the schedule of general hearings, committee meetings, floor debates, and social events. They also know as much as possible about the legislators, their electoral support, their values, their hobbies, and who has their "ear." They are present and prepared when their interests are affected. Veteran lobbyists know how to win friends and influence legislators. One of their rules of thumb is, "It's a hell of a lot easier to kill a bill than to pass it." "If a bill hits the floor [of the Senate or the House] you don't have the foggiest idea how the vote will go unless you do an awful lot of homework. . . . To kill a bill all you need is a majority of a committee, but to pass it you need a majority of the House."[13]

How important are interest groups and state political action committees as a source of influence on state legislatures? Teacher organizations, trade associations, labor groups, and insurance, mining, real estate, and banking interests are often the most visible single-interest groups—varying, of course, from state to state. In states with an obvious major economic interest, legislators pay close attention to the needs of that interest regardless of whether the group employs lobbyists. "Agricultural interests in Iowa, the oil companies in Oklahoma, the automobile industry in Michigan, or the lumbering industry in Oregon do not need to engage much in lobbying the state legislature."[14] The legislatures in these states are not likely to pass legislation hostile to their own state's principal economic interests.

Hundreds of lobbyists openly ply their trade in the committee rooms and corridors of the state capitols. The more populated states register thousands of lobbyists. As of 1990, even less populated Vermont had nearly 650 lobbyists registered with the secretary of state's office. Much of the most effective lobbying requires generating grass-roots mail and arranging for face-to-face constituent persuasion.

On balance, probably too much is made of the negative aspects of lobbying. Even the occasional corrupt practices, however, have done much to damage Americans' faith in their state governments. Most state legislators would like to improve the image of the state legislature. In recent years most states have sought to solve the problems of conflict of interest, regulation of lobbyists, and the financing of political campaigns. Common Cause, the League of Women Voters, and other groups helped to encourage better financial disclosure, open meetings, and campaign finance reforms.

Not all of these reforms have been easy to enforce, nor have they all worked according to the original intentions. In many states attempts have been made to control lobbying and to regulate how much persons may spend to influence either elections or the legislative process. Such laws are often difficult to enforce. Further, it is sometimes unclear whether they infringe on the constitutional right of persons to petition their government or to spend their funds for political purposes. These problems will not be easily solved. "The fight for good campaign finance laws is complicated and potentially frustrating," says John D. Feerick, chair of the New York State Commission on Government and Integrity. "But it is a good and important fight, vital to the health of our democracy."[15]

Legislative Committees   Committee recommendations also influence legislative decision making. Committees vary in power and influence depending on the state; however, in general, the influence of committees has increased in the past decade or two. They used to be pale shadows of their counterparts in Congress. They often still are in the less populous states, because of short sessions, limited staffing, and turnover of both staff and legislators.

Still, legislative committees process and shape hundreds or even thousands of bills and resolutions. Here are some of the functions expected of a standing committee and, to a lesser extent, of interim committees created for assignments between sessions:

- Studying pending legislation carefully
- Conducting public hearings on proposed bills and resolutions
- Debating and modifying initial proposals
- Screening, eliminating, or burying undesirable legislation
- Grading legislation in terms of desirability
- Confirming key administrative personnel
- Monitoring or overseeing administrative practices and regulations

Legislative committees do the homework of the legislature. Some division of labor is absolutely essential. Committees weed out the weakest bills, provide citizens and interest groups an opportunity to testify before their hearings, and enable the better bills to move from one stage of the legislative process to the next. Above all, a committee system allows members to concentrate their energies on particular areas of governmental operations. Over time, legislative committees and their members develop extensive knowledge about these activities and provide useful information to their colleagues. It's impossible these days for everybody to be an expert on all aspects of state government. Committees, properly staffed and run, can evaluate the merits and faults of a proposed law more effectively than can any individual legislator.

"If you don't get committee support, your legislative program is in jeopardy," says a Michigan state legislator. "There's kind of an unwritten rule that you follow the recommendation of the committee. You may debate the committee suggestions. You may try to alter some of their suggestions. But you generally accept—unless you're opposed to the idea completely."[16]

INFLUENCES ON LEGISLATORS' VOTING

- Personal political philosophies
- Legislative colleagues
- Legislative staff specialists
- Committee recommendations
- Interest group lobbyists
- The governor
- Cabinet and agency heads

- Party leaders and party splits
- Constituent mail and opinion
- Urban and rural splits in the state
- Regional blocs within the state
- National trends
- Programs that have worked in other states

A few states appoint citizens to play a special role in legislative policy deci-sion making. Wisconsin, for example, is one of the handful of states whose leg-islatures appoint public members to interim study committees. Citizen members of these between-session legislative committees in Wisconsin are se-lected for their special knowledge of or interest in the issues under study. Often as many as 250 citizens serve on these interim legislative committees; they thus equal or even outnumber the legislators on them in a given period. These mem-bers draft reports and prepare legislative proposals for submission at the next session. They receive no salary but are reimbursed for their expenses.[17]

Other Influences Plainly, the influences that are significant in determining how state legislators cast their votes vary from issue to issue. *Political party leaders* are likely to be most influential on matters such as legislative redistrict-ing, selecting the legislature's leaders, and other issues relating to institutional interests. On issues concerning matters such as new highways, *interest groups* such as contractors and environmental groups are likely to be more significant. *Constituents* are likely to have more influence on tax issues. *Governors* and their cabinets often take the lead on economic development matters. As always, in trying to generalize about the politics of fifty different states, one must be cautious.[18]

Although state legislators are elected to represent the people and their views at the statehouse, few lawmakers think they should merely mirror or *re-present* the views of constituents. Most legislators consider themselves **trustees** of their constituents, claiming to rely on their own consciences or on their con-sidered judgments of the facts before them. Legislators who considered them-selves **delegates,** on the other hand, adhere more closely to instructions from their district's constituents. Not surprisingly, the trustee role is not only the most popular but also the easiest and most realistic to practice. Given the com-plexity of government and the difficulty of finding out where citizens stand on a wide variety of issues, the trustee role is more practical in the day-to-day deci-sion making of a legislator during legislative sessions.

On most issues that arise during the session, the explicit needs of the legislative district are not usually a major factor. On those that are important to the district, a legislator generally behaves according to implicit instructions. Thus, state lawmakers in effect act as trustees on some issues and delegates on others. Yet "conscience" is seldom the only or even the most important guide. Colleagues, committee recommendations, party leadership advice, staff counsel, lobbying by the affected interests, and a variety of similar factors are ordinarily the guides.

New legislators soon learn that it makes sense to depend on colleagues to inform them about issues assigned to their committees. "Very early in the session, you try to find other representatives who sit on other committees and who are similar to you in their outlook politically." According to a Pennsylvania legislator, "When a bill comes to the floor for a vote, you have to look to that person, you have to trust him."[19] In a sense you must follow such advice unless you know the subject well enough to have your own informed opinion.

Another aspect of state politics that often fuels legislation is the action taken by other states. Legislators frequently ask their staffs, "What is Florida or Arizona or Oregon doing on this problem?" Sometimes another state's policy affects the legislator's state, such as in the area of diesel fuel rates or college tuitions. Legislators are always on the lookout, too, for innovative tax, educational, or prison policies implemented in another state. The National Conference of State Legislatures acts as an effective clearinghouse for new ideas and shares its studies with legislators all across the country. Legislators are keenly interested in how their state ranks in a certain area, for example, on sales taxes, high school dropouts, or clean air. The press often uses such rankings in their headlines or in their assessments of the legislature. Of course, actions taken by the federal government also influence state laws and regulations. President Ronald Reagan's cutbacks and George Bush's antidrug programs are examples.

In sum, most state legislators are influenced by their colleagues and legislative leaders and by a variety of forces outside the legislature itself. These may include leaders and opinion makers in their legislative districts, the governor, state and local party leaders, interest group spokespeople, experts in the bureaucracy, and new ideas that have been implemented elsewhere.

Legislative Reform Politics

Criticisms of some state legislatures are much like those of Congress: legislative business is not conducted efficiently; committee work is not well planned, careful records are not kept; expert information is not systematically sought; introducing special and private legislation is too easy in state legislatures, and parliamentary rules prevent action and play into the hands of those who engage in favoritism. In recent years there has also been criticism that too many legislators stay in the legislature too long and are becoming career politicians rather

LEGISLATIVE FOLKWAYS

The terms *legislative folkways* or *legislative norms* refer to the shared standards of members' individual conduct, especially to what is regarded as appropriate behavior or what is expected of a member in that particular legislature. Most of these norms are also commonly found in business and other professional groups and are by no means unique to a legislature. Political scientists are not exactly sure why these norms are more important in some states than in others; we do know, however, that most of the norms listed here are honored as part of the professionalism in nearly every state legislature. Occasional mavericks violate the "rules of the game," but most newcomers to a legislature soon discover these and similar norms and abide by them.

- Treat your colleagues with respect; don't make personal attacks on them or harass them.

- Serve an apprenticeship; take some time to do your homework and go through a learning process before charging around acting like a "know-it-all."

- Don't be a publicity hound; stay away from the microphone unless you really have something to say.

- Don't conceal the real purpose of a bill or purposely overlook some portion of it in order to assure its passage.

- Don't make a commitment on a vote until you are ready to be bound by it; keep your word, be reliable when you have made a commitment.

- Committee work is your punishment for getting elected; effective legislators specialize enough in their subject areas to be able to advise their colleagues—specially those not on their committees.

- Reciprocate when you can; support your friends and colleagues whenever possible so that they will support you whenever they can.

- Defend the legislature when it comes under attack from the press, the governor, or other critics—institutional patriotism is much admired by your colleagues.

- Don't burn your bridges; learn to get along with others. Remember, today's foe may be tomorrow's ally in a crucially close vote on some new matter. A policy of "No Permanent Enemies" usually works best.

than citizen-legislators. Other alleged weaknesses are peculiar to certain states: The length of sessions is unnecessarily restricted; salaries in many states are low; the speaker is too powerful; and many legislatures lack the staff resources needed for policy making in today's complex society.

Such structural or procedural inadequacies may, in fact, make state legislatures less efficient. For example, low pay and short sessions are thought to inhibit deliberation on major issues, and lack of professional staff produces an amateur committee system or an overreliance on lobbyists, the governor, or the executive bureaucracy. State legislatures cannot perform efficiently if: (1) they are restricted by outmoded constitutions; (2) their structures are inflexible; (3) they are unable to induce outstanding citizens to run for office; (4) they are not given powers commensurate with their responsibilities; (5) they are run by factions that cannot be held accountable for their actions; (6) they cannot act unless prodded by the governor; and (7)—in general—they cannot harness their powers to transform majority preferences in the electorate, when they exist, into the public policy of the legislature.

IMPROVING STATE LEGISLATURES

Various groups and experts have tried to evaluate state legislatures. It is relatively easy to measure legislatures against certain proclaimed standards in terms of procedures and processes, yet to do so in terms of what they enact and fund is impossible except in political terms. Most evaluations of legislatures, like evaluations of legislators, tell us more about the values of the evaluator than the performance of what is being measured. Of course, the fact that there are no objective standards to determine which policies are "best" is why we have democratically elected legislatures in the first place.

Following are some specific recommendations made by one group of experts to improve legislative procedures in the states:

1. Constitutions should leave legislatures as unhampered as possible to encourage the development of their own self-reliance. Limitations on a legislature's power to appropriate public funds and to address itself to public questions should be eliminated.

2. Enactment of private bills, bills affecting few persons, and local and special bills should be minimized.

3. Legislatures should be small enough to make the position of legislator more important and visible.

4. To develop more responsibility in legislative performance, and more independence, legislatures should either have longer sessions or be continuing bodies meeting in annual sessions, without limitation of time or subject.

5. Competent professional staff should be provided, including staff for the leadership, both majority and minority.

6. State legislatures should utilize a strong system of standing committees, few in number, with broad, well-defined jurisdictions.

7. Codes of ethics should be adopted that apply to career, appointed, and elected officials in all branches of state government.[20]

Many of these recommendations have been adopted. Many legislatures now have longer sessions, professional staffs, streamlined rules and procedures, fewer and more responsible committees, and increased salaries. About half the states now employ joint legislative committees. Legislative attempts to control federal funds, legislative review of administrative regulations, and legislative efforts in the area of program evaluation and **sunset processes** (consideration of agency termination) were all intended to improve legislative effectiveness. The largely amateur, part-time state legislatures of thirty years ago are now being professionalized. This new professionalism reflects a growing determination on the part of legislators—especially state legislative leaders— to be the bosses in their own branch.

As so often is the case with so-called "reforms," soon after they are in place for a few years they generate "counter-reforms." Thus the movement to encourage full-time professional legislators with large staffs is being challenged in the 1990s by those who now believe we were better off when we had part-time amateur legislators who came to the state capitol for just a few months every two years. One of the counter-reforms earlier in the twentieth century was the movement for *unicameral legislatures*, which we will turn to next. A more recent counter-reform is the call for term limits of legislators.

TWO HOUSES OR ONE?

One of the oldest legislative reform debates in the U.S. revolves around whether there should be one or two houses in state legislatures. Although two-chamber legislatures became the established pattern in the United States early in our history, Georgia, Pennsylvania, and Vermont experimented with one-house legislatures. During colonial days the two chambers represented distinct interests; the senates stood for royal authority, the assemblies for the colonial cause. The desire to balance the aristocratic against the popular interest, and the belief in a government of checks and balances, led to the retention of bicameral legislatures after independence. During the first decades of our republic, the requirements to vote for senator and the qualifications to serve in the state senate were stricter than those for the house. By the middle of the nineteenth century, however, the same electorate was choosing the members of both houses. Today the two houses represent the same people (but in districts of different sizes). Why do we retain the two-house system?

Defenders of bicameralism insist that two chambers check hasty or ill-considered legislation. Yet even in some states with two chambers, legislation is rushed through, especially in the closing days of a session. Sometimes the second chamber discovers errors in bills enacted by the other house and makes the necessary corrective amendments. Some bills proposed by one chamber are defeated by the other, but it is impossible to develop objective standards to determine whether the defeated legislation was poor to begin with. Critics of bicameralism are persuaded that the governor's veto, the courts, and the electorate are better checks. The case for a **unicameral legislature** has been:

1. A one-house legislature would be more efficient, avoid needless delays and duplication, and permit higher salaries.

2. A one-house legislature would permit the voters more knowledge about whom to blame and whom to credit and would thereby increase accountability.

3. One strong, well-staffed house would be a more efficient counterbalance to the governor.

4. The one-chamber arrangement has worked well in Nebraska, in all our cities, and in the Canadian provinces. Further, it works well in our state constitutional conventions, just as it did in our 1787 national Constitutional Convention.

The case for the two-house legislature rests on the following claims as well as on tradition:

1. A two-house legislature permits greater scrutiny of all new laws, making it more difficult for rash, arbitrary, or emotional legislation to be enacted.

2. A two-house legislature provides for more access, more debate, and more representation of diverse points of view.

3. A two-house legislature makes it more difficult for any one person or interest to dominate state decision making; the chances are good that one of the houses will offer effective resistance.

Although there are merits on both sides, the adoption of unicameralism is still viewed as a radical step. Moreover, it is a pretty safe bet that few, if any, state legislators will be attracted to a proposal that would put the majority of them out of office. In Nebraska, for example, before the unicameral plan won at the polls in 1934 there were thirty-three senators and one hundred house members. Afterward there were just forty-nine senators.

TERM LIMITS OR NOT?

One of the more talked about legislative reforms of the 1990s calls for term limits of from six to twelve years for state legislators (and usually for other statewide elected officials, such as governors). Oklahoma, Colorado, California, and several other states have approved term-limit provisions for their constitutions. In each case they were enacted as a result of initiative petition campaigns by voters. (See the discussion of initiatives later in this chapter.)

Polls indicate strong support for the passage of similar measures throughout the country. Term-limit ballot measures have been considered in many legislatures and will be on the ballot in several states in the next few years.

Proponents of term limits contend the principle of rotation is an old and cherished one in the United States and that we should encourage citizen-legislators and discourage career politicians. Supporters also say incumbents have voted too many perks and advantages for themselves and that term limits may be the only way to restore real competition to legislative races. They argue that *permanent incumbency*—legislators and state officials staying on for multiple terms, sometimes decades—is creating a kind of "professional ruling class" that is out of touch with ordinary citizens. The term-limits movement has been called a primal scream for change in the political system and a manifestation of the frustration the public has with what is viewed as a failure of government.

Support for term limits comes from both Republicans and Democrats, yet organized support and financial aid have generally come from antitax and conservative antigovernment groups. *The Wall Street Journal* has regularly editorialized in support of the measure, but consumer activist Ralph Nader has also been among the most vocal supporters. He and like-minded populists on the left believe only the bludgeon of term limits will motivate enough legislators to give reforms such as public funding of campaigns a serious chance.

State legislators and their friends have been the main opponents of this reform. They contend term limits are a solution in search of a problem that does not exist. Most state legislators, they note, only stay in the legislature for three or four terms anyway. Indeed, most states have more of a problem acquiring experienced leadership, stability, and knowledge than they have in bringing in new blood.

Critics of term limits think that this reform is likely to have the unintended consequence of increasing the power of various unelected officials, such as lobbyists, legislative staffers, and executive branch bureaucrats. "Their expertise will become even more influential when the elected officials are all short-timers, and their arrogance will grow," writes David Broder, a respected national journalist.[21]

Critics also contend term limits will not help draft better laws or write better tax measures. Nor are they likely to take special interest money out of politics, or promote political competition in the redistricting process. Also, says Neal R. Peirce, "they're not likely to prop up our decaying political parties."[22]

Voters, of course, can dispatch legislators from office by voting for challengers, as they did with a vengeance in New Jersey in 1991 in a protest against taxes approved by the governor and the legislature. But voters seem to want the added constitutional device of doing for them what most voters do not regularly do—to roust out the incumbents.

Term limits probably will not have all of the major consequences claimed by their supporters or detractors. Laws will still be passed; budgets will be adopted and balanced; government operations will proceed pretty much as they have in the past. States with term limits may lose some excellent legislators prematurely, yet they may also lose others that nobody will much notice or miss.

All the hoopla about term limits probably diverts attention from other serious problems such as decaying parties, *gerrymandered* (uncompetitive) legislative districts, and the challenges of improving educational opportunities and economic development in the states.

Term limits, most critics contend, are an illusory "quick-fix" attempt for a symptom rather than a cure for fundamental problems in our democracy. Real solutions will take much longer, are much harder to understand, and are probably more expensive than the more simplistic term-limit approach to reforming state government.[23] But stay tuned. We are likely to see this reform put into effect in more states and cities around the nation. More than thirty states already have term limit provisions for governor and, of course, we now limit U.S. presidents to two terms.

The Politics of Drawing Legislative District Lines

When fists flew in the Illinois legislature back in 1981, it was not over policy. It was about politics—the politics of redrawing legislative boundaries. "That's no surprise," observed a writer for *The Washington Post*. "Redistricting is the political equivalent of moving in the left-field fence for a right-handed pull hitter. By changing the boundaries, redistricting helps some, hurts others—and leaves just about everyone else scrambling."[24]

State legislatures have the key responsibility for reapportionment—drawing legislative district boundaries for both their own and their state's U.S. House of Representative districts. Legislatures are reapportioned after each census, most recently after the census of 1990. Nine states delegate these responsibilities to redistricting or reapportionment commissions; most legislatures, however, consider these once-a-decade responsibilities so important as to be unwilling to turn control over this task to anybody else. Yet they sometimes turn into the most political, crass, selfish, and agonizing acts that legislators engage in.

The drawing of legislative district boundaries has long been a subject of some controversy. **Gerrymander** means the drawing of district boundaries to benefit one party, group, or incumbent. The term was first used to describe a strange salamander-shaped district drawn in northeastern Massachusetts while Elbridge Gerry was governor; however, a district does not need to be odd in shape to be gerrymandered.

The politics and debate about redistricting is most intense in the years immediately after the census is taken. The 1990 census resulted in the redistricting of the state legislatures in all fifty states.

A major redistricting battle took place in the 1950s and 1960s when state legislatures gave rural and small-town voters more votes in the legislature than they would have been entitled to on the basis of their declining population. In Georgia, for instance, the 1960 reapportionment gave the largest county with 556,326 inhabitants no more representation than the three smallest counties, whose combined population was 6,980.[25] City officials complained bitterly that the small-town and farm-dominated legislators were unsympathetic to their problems and were forcing rural notions of right and wrong upon them.

The battle over reapportionment, however, was more complex than just a rural versus city struggle. As the century proceeded, the suburbs—not the central cities—came to be most underrepresented in many states. Even more to the point, many who live and do business within the city or live in its suburbs feel closer politically to those who live on farms and small towns than they do to other city dwellers. Thus, some conservative business interests located in cities or close-in suburbs favored rural domination of the state legislatures because they thought "cow-country legislators" would be more responsive to their demands and less responsive to the social welfare schemes championed by many urban legislators.

ENTER—THE FEDERAL COURTS

But no matter how much they protested, people who were underrepresented in the state legislatures made little progress. Legislators from small towns and farm areas naturally did not wish to reapportion themselves out of jobs, and their constituents did not wish to lose their influence. Even though the failure of state legislatures to reapportion often violated express provisions of state constitutions and raised serious questions under the U.S. Constitution, state and federal judges took the position that issues having to do with legislative districting were "political" and outside the scope of judicial authority.

Finally, the U.S. Supreme Court stepped in. In 1962, in the famous case of *Baker v. Carr,* the Court held that voters do have standing to challenge legislative apportionment and that such questions should be considered by the federal courts. Arbitrary and capriciously drawn districts do deprive people of their constitutional rights, and federal judges may take jurisdiction over such cases.[26] *Baker v. Carr* started a small tidal wave.

ONE PERSON, ONE VOTE

In *Wesberry v. Sanders* (1964) the Supreme Court announced that as far as *congressional* representation is concerned, "as nearly as practicable one man's vote in a congressional election is to be worth as much as another's."[27] And in the same term the Court extended this principle to representation in the *state legislatures,* although subsequently it has slightly modified this decision.

In *Reynolds v. Sims* (1964) the Court held that "the fundamental principle of representative government in this country is one of equal representation for equal numbers of people, without regard to race, sex, economic status, or place of residence within a state." In the Court's view, this principle applied not only to the more numerous house of the state legislature, which was usually based on population, but also to the state senate, where representation was often based on area, such as the county or some other governmental unit. Defenders of this pattern had argued that as long as the house or more numerous chamber represented population, the senate could represent geographical units. Look at the federal system embodied in the U.S. Constitution, they said. Isn't representation in the U.S. Senate based on area? Although many thought this to be a compelling argument, a majority of the Court did not. Chief Justice Earl Warren explained: "Legislators represent people, not trees or acres. Legislators are elected by voters, not farms or cities or economic interests. . . . The right to elect legislators in a free unimpaired fashion is a bedrock of our political system."[28] The federal analogy, in short, does not hold; political subdivisions are not and never have been sovereign entities.

The Supreme Court has been especially rigid about how states draw congressional districts. A state legislature must justify any variance from strict mathematical equality among such districts by showing that it made a good-faith effort to come as close as possible to this standard. The Supreme Court is, however, less insistent upon absolute equality for state legislative districts. Thus the Court, in 1983, upheld a Wyoming plan that allocated at least one state legislative seat per county, saying that Wyoming's policy was rational and appropriate to the special needs of that sparsely populated state. "This holding, however, represents the exception to the general rule of a 10 percent maximum permissible deviation between state legislative districts."[29] But the requirement that the districts be established in accordance with the *one-person, one-vote* principle still remains.

NEW RULES FOR REDRAWING THE DISTRICTS

Even though the one-person, one-vote principle is firmly established, many issues affecting the nature of legislative representation continue to be hotly debated. In northern metropolitan areas, for instance, the general pattern is for the core city to be Democratic and the surrounding suburbs Republican. If legislative district lines are drawn like spokes from the central city to the suburbs, fewer Republicans will thus be elected than if the district lines are drawn in concentric circles. Although partisan gerrymandering is permissible, *Davis v. Bandemer* (1986) established some constitutional constraints.[30]

There has been an increasing attack of past redistricting efforts on the part of minorities, who contend that redistricting has resulted in violations of the Voting Rights Act of 1965 and the dilution of minority influence at the polls. Can racial or ethnic considerations be used in drawing up legislative districts? Racial considerations are not automatically unconstitutional. If district lines are drawn in order to protect the voting strength of blacks, and if they do not force white voters out of the process or unfairly minimize their voting strength, there is no constitutional violation. However, the Constitution does forbid, says the Supreme Court, the deliberate attempt to draw district lines in order to "impose a racial slur or stigma, or minimize the voting strength of particular races or religions."[31]

In its 1986 *Thornburg v. Gingles* (478 U.S.30) ruling, the U.S. Supreme Court said that the Voting Rights Act of 1965, as amended in 1982, requires states to avoid diluting the voting strength of minorities, and where possible to draw districts composed of a majority of minority voters. This ruling has raised many questions concerning 1990s redistricting efforts. Must majority African American and Hispanic districts be created where they have not previously existed merely because it may be possible to create them? Must minority communities live in a relatively compact geographic region to warrant a legislative district? Or must redistricters go to great lengths to create a majority black or Hispanic district in a state? And how large a majority of blacks or other minorities does a district need in order to be acceptable?

Recent court decisions and the rise of ethnic and racial consciousness in the United States almost guarantee that numerous groups will make claims before the courts throughout the 1990s that redistricting has violated their constitutional rights and prevented them from effective participation and representation in their state's political processes. Most observers agree that the process of drawing new districts must actively reach out to those who were historically shut out from representation. The end product should respect cohesive geographic, ethnic and racial communities of interest. Yet districts should be designed, wherever possible, to encourage competition between the parties and candidates. Such competition leads to a vigorous public dialogue and encourages voters to become informed and involved. It also helps make elected officials accountable for their views and actions.

In the past the courts declared redistricting schemes that hurt racial minorities to be unconstitutional[32] but avoided ruling on gerrymandering that helped or hurt political parties. In a potentially very important decision (Davis v. Bandemer), the Supreme Court asserted the power to strike down election district lines if the majority party in a legislature had manipulated them so severely as to "considerably degrade" the voting strength of another party.[33] While theoretically possible, such a partisan gerrymander has yet to be identified by the court.

One possible indicator of partisan bias in redistricting is the ratio of seats a party receives for its votes. In Indiana the Republicans captured 57 of the 100 state house seats with less than half of the statewide vote. In 1984 California Democrats won 60 percent of the U.S. House of Representatives seats with just 48 percent of the vote. Yet the courts said that these cases did not have effects severe enough to violate the constitutional rights of the victimized party.

Redistricting that gives the appearance of being blatantly partisan or exclusionary doubtless undermines confidence in our representative institutions, and this again raises the whole question of who should be charged with the responsibility for drawing legislative boundaries.

WHO SHOULD REDRAW LEGISLATIVE BOUNDARIES?

Critics of the current system of districts being drawn by the incumbent legislators say one-person, one-vote and fairness principles are often violated when the party in power juggles district lines to its own advantage. A spokesperson for Common Cause says: "The present system stinks. . . . Legislators who set the boundaries for their own districts have a basic conflict of interests. . . . [It's] a crummy system of backscratching."[34] Hence Common Cause, the League of Women Voters, and the National Civic League call for the establishment of an independent nonpartisan commission to draw district lines. Such a commission would be prohibited from using information about incumbent legislators, the political affiliations of registered voters, or previous election results to draw boundary lines that favor any group or person or that dilute the influence of racial or minority interests. A handful of states, including Ohio and Montana, currently use such a system. Legislators, not surprisingly, generally oppose this idea, claiming that it is like trying to take politics out of politics. They say the legislature, because it represents all interests in a state and is regularly accountable to the public, is the single best institution to resolve reapportionment issues.[35]

A fundamental question in any democracy, of course, is how the people are to be represented in the legislative branch of government. This is unavoidably a *political* issue, in the highest sense of the word. Repeated attempts have been made to find a body of "experts" who know how to do these things better than the people through the political process. One might argue, for example, that the dominant party will draw up tax legislation or spending programs to reward its supporters and punish its opponents, whereas a body of experts could doubtless design a more "rational" and "fair" system of taxation. But people who believe in democracy might be skeptical. Independent nonpartisan commissions are likely to reflect middle-class and upper-class values and might, in fact, emphasize only these values under the guise of nonpartisanship.

In the early 1990s, some states are looking seriously at their redistricting methods. The more extravagant promises made by independent commissions will probably prove difficult to realize. Still, no one doubts that political controversy will continue to surround reapportionment arrangements no matter what form they take. And no one doubts the ability of incumbents in the majority to "rig" elections through reapportionment. In the words of the old-time politicians: "You tell me the results you want, and I'll draw the district map to do it."

Direct Legislation: Policy Making by the People

Does "We the People" mean the people themselves should govern directly? Around the turn of the century, the **Populists** and **Progressives** fought to "return the government to the people" through the initiative, referendum, and recall. Give the voters the power to make or veto laws and to recall officials, they said, and the political machines will be destroyed and the special interests beaten. In fact, some of our states have given the people the power to make their own laws.

Populists and Progressives had good reason between 1890 and 1912 to want to bypass their legislatures, for in several states the legislatures were indeed either incompetent or under the domination of the political machines. (The Southern Pacific Railroad's political machine in California had dominated the selection of state legislators, governors, and U.S. senators for years.) The Progressives placed enormous trust in the wisdom of the individual and in the notion that voters would inform themselves about issues and make responsible decisions on a variety of policy questions put before them.

Americans vote on all kinds of state and local ballot issues. About 250 citizen-initiated issues were placed on state ballots in the 1980s. Another one thousand issues were referred to voters by state legislators. Citizens have turned to the initiative process to try to regulate handguns in California, to protect the moose in Maine, to encourage the death penalty in Massachusetts, to approve the sale of wine in local grocery stores in Colorado, to abolish daylight saving time in North Dakota, and in many states to pressure the national government for some type of nuclear freeze, to enact English as the official language, and to ban nuclear power.

Critics lament the rise in what they call "public policy making by bumper-sticker." But legislators themselves are in various ways responsible for many of the issues that get placed on the ballot:

> Legislators have developed something of a "multiple personality" relationship with ballot measures. On the one hand, many legislators and staffers recognize that an initiated measure is a form of rejection of representative democracy and a subtle kind of no confidence vote toward the legislatures. On the other hand, many legislatures have "referred" tough policy issues to the public vote. In many instances, the same person who condemns the power of big spending on ballot questions will initiate a petition drive when his or her key issue dies in the legislature.[36]

INITIATIVE

The **initiative petition** procedure permits a designated minimum number of voters to propose a law that will be enacted if approved by a majority of the voters at a subsequent election. Twenty-three states, mostly in the West, authorize the making of laws by means of the initiative petition (see Figure 5-3). In states such as California, Oregon, Washington, North Dakota, Arizona, and Colorado, the initiative has become almost a regular feature of state political life.

In some states the *direct initiative* applies to constitutional amendments and to legislation; in others it can be used only for one or the other. In a state that permits the direct initiative, any individual or interest group may draft a proposed law and file it with a designated state official—usually the secretary of state. Supporters have only to secure a certain number of signatures (between 5 to 15 percent of those who voted in the last election) to ensure that the measure is placed on the ballot at the next election for approval or disapproval.

The *indirect initiative* is used in a few states such as Massachusetts. After a certain number of petition signatures have been collected, the state legislature is given an opportunity to act on the measure without alteration; if they approve it, the law simply goes into effect. If they do not approve it, the proposed legislation is then placed on the ballot, although in some states additional signatures are required before the proposal can be placed before the voters.

FIGURE 5-3   Citizen-Initiated Initiative, Referendum, and Recall at the State Level

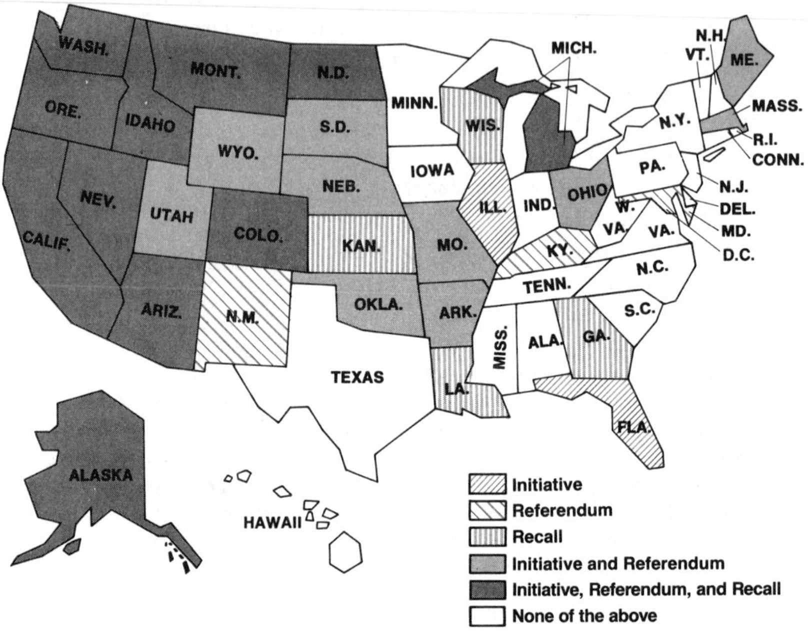

Initiative

Referendum

Recall

Initiative and Referendum

Initiative, Referendum, and Recall

None of the above

NOTE: The initiative can be used for constitutional amendments only in Florida and in Illinois.
Initiative petitions can only be used for statutory changes in Alaska, Idaho, Maine, Utah, Washington, Wyoming, and the District of Columbia.
The initiative can be used for both constitutional and statutory changes in all the other states noted here as having the initiative.
About 36 states permit recall of various local and elected officials.

REFERENDUM

The *popular* **referendum** permits a majority of the voters to veto legislation or reject constitutional amendments. In 1988, for example, Massachusetts voters voted to repeal their legislature's recently adopted pay raise by the referendum process. The referendum is simply a way of letting the people vote on recently passed laws or proposed amendments to a state's constitution. It is required in every state except Delaware for the ratification of constitutional amendments. Legislation may be subject to mandatory or optional referendums. The *mandatory referendum* calls for a waiting period, usually sixty to ninety days, before legislation goes into effect. If during this period a prescribed number of voters sign a referendum petition requesting that the act be referred to the voters, the law does not go into effect unless a majority of the voters give their approval at the next election. The *optional referendum* permits the legislature at its discretion, to provide that a measure shall not become law until it has been approved by the voters at an election. This second kind is the most common.

Although in several states referendums are often held statewide, referendum democracy also flourishes at the local level. The annual volume of referendums presented to voters in school districts, cities, and counties runs to several thousand, and many of these are on topics of considerable importance and controversy—bonds for school buildings, fluoridation of water, banning of bottles, restrictions on nuclear power facilities, and approval or rejection of convention facilities or dome stadiums.

RECALL

Recall is the means by which voters may remove elected public officials before the end of a term. Fifteen states, mostly in the West, provide for recall of state officers, but many others permit the recall of local officials. Recall also requires a petition, but it needs more signatures (typically 25 percent of voters in the last election for the position of the official to be recalled) than the initiative and referendum. There are various kinds of recall election. In some the official must stand on his or her record; in others candidates are permitted to file and run against the incumbent.

In effect, recall is like impeachment by the public. But unlike impeachment, formal charges of wrongdoing against the incumbent are not required. Rather, recall permits throwing people out of office merely because of policy differences. For recall, voters need only circulate petitions and obtain the required number of signatures. Recall is seldom used at the state level, although one governor and several state legislators have been recalled, including two Michigan state senators and one Oregon lawmaker in the 1980s. In Arizona, a recall campaign against Governor Evan Mecham in 1987 obtained far more than the needed signatures and forced the close scrutiny of Mecham that led to his impeachment and ouster by the Arizona state legislature.

Perhaps as many as two thousand county and municipal officeholders have been discharged around the country since Los Angeles became the first local government to adopt the recall in 1903. Mayors have been recalled from Seattle to Atlantic City. Mayor Mike Boyle of Omaha, for example, was turned out of office in a 1987 recall election that brought 56 percent of the eligible voters to the polls—a city election record. Three city council members were ousted by recall in Honolulu in 1985. Six Grand Junction, Colorado city officials were recalled in 1986.

While critics of the recall say it is an unruly process that deters good people from running and discourages leaders from taking decisive actions, the recall helps to lessen incumbent arrogance. The recall is a helpful, if crude, safety valve, permitting "citizens to eject those officials who violate the public trust. It has not, in any essential way, lessened the independence of well-intentioned public officials."[37]

THE DEBATE OVER DIRECT DEMOCRACY

Political scientists differ over the desirability of direct legislation. Early opponents argued that such measures would undermine the legitimacy of representative government and open the way for radical or special interest legislation.

Critics of the initiative and referendum believe the Progressives who advocated direct legislation were overly idealistic and that these mechanisms are likely to be used less by citizens than by special interests. According to these critics, only well-organized interests could gather the appropriate number of signatures and mount the required media campaigns to gain victory.

What have been the results of these populist devices? Historically, direct legislation by initiative has typically resulted in progressive victories on consumer and economic issues, and conservative victories on social issues. Direct democracy has not weakened our legislatures. Seats in state legislatures are still valued, sought after, and competed for by able citizens. Nor has unwise legislation been enacted, as a general rule. The overall record suggests that the voters reject most unsound ideas that get on the ballot.

Viewed from another perspective, most of the perceived flaws of the populist processes are in many ways also the flaws of democracy. We often wish we had more information about issues and candidates—especially those running for state and county offices. Delegates at constitutional conventions or national party conventions frequently have similar misgivings when they are forced to render yes and no votes on complicated issues. So, too, members of state legislatures—especially in those frantic days near the end of their sessions—yearn for more information, more clarity about consequences, and more discussion and compromise than time will permit.

Critics of direct legislation fear the very fabric of legislative processes and representative government is at stake. To be sure, lack of faith in legislative bodies prompts the use of direct legislation devices. But it is an illusion, they say, to believe that the voter has the proper information to decide on complex, technical matters.[38] The critics also suggest that the best way to restore faith in the legislature is not to bypass it but to elect better people to it. Supporters of populist democracy say they have not given up on the legislative process. Rather, they wish to use direct legislation only when legislatures prove unresponsive. If our legislature will not act, they say, give us the opportunity to debate our proposals in the open arena of election politics. Supporters further contend the people *can* make decisions on complex and controversial matters.

A new problem is the number of issues on the ballot. California voters often have had to decide on a dozen or more ballot issues, some initiated by interest groups and the rest placed on the ballot by the legislature. Most Californians complain there are too many and that "the process had gotten out of hand." On the other hand, a majority of Coloradans indicated in 1990 that they wanted to vote on more issues, not less.

Voters in California and throughout the country insist that citizens ought to occasionally have the right to vote directly on issues. They especially say this when their representatives seem afraid of offending certain interest groups. Further, every survey on direct democracy finds that both voters and nonvoters say they would be more likely to vote and more likely to become interested in politics if some issues appeared along with candidates on their ballots.

Another serious problem has arisen in California. Political consulting

AN INITIATIVE AND REFERENDUM FOR NEW JERSEY?

In early 1986 Republican Governor Thomas Kean of New Jersey urged passage of a measure that would allow voters to vote on policy issues. His reasoning: "We have good government in New Jersey, but we can make it better—more responsive— more efficient. The people of most states have the right to directly change their laws. People in New Jersey deserve the same right. We should not be afraid of the people who elected us. I ask you to pass . . . legislation to give the people the right of initiative and referendum."

The plan won the support of the United Taxpayers of New Jersey, Common Cause, the League of Women Voters, and the state's Public Interest Research Group.

Opposed to the adoption were the state's leading business and industry associations, labor unions, and some former governors. One former governor called the proposal costly and cumbersome and said it would detract from the ability of the legislature to weigh state problems and address them after careful study. Dr. Alan Rosenthal of the Eagleton Institute of Politics at Rutgers University said the direct legislation system "shifts power from the people, through their elected representatives, to zealots, power groups and fringe groups."

In 1992 Democratic Governor James Florio came out in favor of the initiative and referendum for New Jersey. Florio, who had pushed a massive tax increase through the legislature in 1990, was the target of a vehement public backlash as a result of his tax policies. Perhaps this embrace of the initiative and referendum was a gesture of acknowledgment that public officials should respect the voters and their views. Again, however, this proposal was defeated in New Jersey.

firms, for a price, will gather signatures and put nearly anything you want on the ballot. Deceptive pitches are made trying to get enough people to sign petitions. It takes a small fortune to do this, and only the well-organized, well-financed single-interest groups can afford it.

Critics of ballot democracy sometimes have a view of state legislators that borders on the mythical: highly intelligent; extremely well-informed; rational, virtuous, wise, and deliberative; as managerially competent as a corporate executive and as substantively informed as an expert professor. These same critics, however, tend to view the people as a "mob" unworthy of being trusted. Yet the people are the voters who elect legislators. Experience suggests that on most issues, especially the well publicized ones, voters grasp the meaning of the issue on which they are asked to vote, and they cast an informed vote. Most studies indicate that voters who vote on ballot measures do so more responsibly than we have any right to expect.

The legislative process is never perfect. Even with larger staffs, hearings, bicameralism, and other distinctive features of constitutional democracy, mistakes are made and defective bills are enacted into law by our legislatures. The Supreme Court has overturned hundreds of state measures as unconstitutional, and state legislatures often spend much of their time amending or otherwise improving measures passed the previous year that did not quite work out. As a practical matter, the competence and rationality of both the legislative and the direct ballot processes can stand improvement. The charge, however, that voters are not competent enough to decide on occasional issues put before them is usually exaggerated.[39]

Experience suggests that neither the best hopes of the Progressives nor the worst worries of their critics have been realized. Yet, whatever the merits of the initiative, referendum, and recall, it is clear that these mechanisms have notable limits; in no way could they even begin to replace a legislature.

Summary

1. Although Americans greatly value the state legislature as a vital institution in our constitutional form of government, we are quick to criticize its imperfections. Perhaps we overestimate the possibilities for responsive and representative legislatures. Or perhaps we make legislatures the target of our complaints when the imperfections and the imperfectibility of people are really at the heart of the matter.

2. The nation's 7,424 state legislators are called upon to represent our diverse views, help formulate state public policy, oversee the administration of state laws, and help mediate political conflicts that arise in the state.

3. What are the main influences on a state legislator's voting decisions? Colleagues, committee recommendations, district considerations, party leaders, staff reports, the governor's urgings, lobbyists, constituent mail, visits, and phone calls can all be influential depending on the type of issue.

4. State legislators are asked to represent all the people in chambers that are constantly subjected to intense lobbying by organized interests. Lobbyists and interest group representatives are important sources of information, but often the elected state legislator is the only effective representative and voice for the unorganized citizen.

5. Legislative reform efforts are part of political life in most states. Most states now have open-meeting laws, and staff available to assist with committee work. Many also have conflict-of-interest and financial disclosure laws. Some states have recently limited the number of terms legislators can serve.

6. The politics of reapportionment, or redrawing legislative boundaries, heat up every ten years after the census is taken. Redistricting is never easy. Political careers can be ruined by redrawn boundaries. Major controversies have arisen over partisan and exclusionary drawing of legislative district lines, and the federal courts are increasingly asked to establish guidelines that will shape redistricting in the states.

7. Direct legislative procedures, especially the initiative petition, are a prominent part of the legislative process, particularly in the West. Other direct mechanisms, such as the referendum and the recall, are also available to voters in many states.

For Further Reading

GERALD BENJAMIN and MICHAEL J. MALBIN, eds. *Limiting Legislative Terms* (Congressional Quarterly Press, 1992).

DIANE D. BLAIR. *Arkansas Politics and Government: Do the People Rule?* (University of Nebraska Press, 1988).

BRUCE E. CAIN. *The Reapportionment Puzzle* (University of California Press, 1984).

THOMAS E. CRONIN. *Direct Democracy: The Politics of the Initiative, Referendum, and Recall* (Harvard University Press, 1989).

VIRGINIA GRAY, HERBERT JACOB, and KENNETH N. VINES. *Politics in the American States,* 5th ed. (Scott, Foresman, 1990).

BERNARD GROFMAN. *Political Gerrymandering and the Courts* (Agathon, 1990).

MALCOLM JEWELL and PENNY MILLER. *The Kentucky Legislature: Two Decades of Change* (University Press of Kentucky, 1988).

MALCOLM JEWELL and SAMUEL C. PATTERSON. *The Legislative Process in the United States* (Random House, 1986).

WILLIAM J. KEEFE and MORRIS S. OGUL. *The American Legislative Process,* 8th ed. (Prentice Hall, 1993).

DAVID MAGLEBY. *Direct Legislation* (Johns Hopkins University Press, 1984).

ALBERT J. NELSON. *Emerging Influentials in State Legislatures: Women, Blacks and Hispanics* (Praeger, 1991).

ALAN ROSENTHAL. *Governors and Legislatures: Contending Powers* (Congressional Quarterly Press, 1990).

ALAN ROSENTHAL. *Legislative Life: People, Process and Performance in the States* (Harper and Row, 1981).

ALAN ROSENTHAL. *The Third House: Lobbyists and Lobbying in the States* (Congressional Quarterly Press, 1992).

FRANK SMALLWOOD. *Free and Independent: The Initiation of a College Professor into State Politics* (Stephen Greene Press, 1976).

See the journal *State Legislatures,* published ten times a year by the National Conference of State Legislatures. *Legislative Studies Quarterly* often has articles on state legislatures; it is published by the Legislative Studies Section of the American Political Science Association. Also, *Governing,* published monthly by Congressional Quarterly, Inc., regularly covers state politics and state legislative issues.

Notes

1. Jerry Kopel, quoted in John Sanko, "Campaign Trail Is No Primrose Path," *Rocky Mountain News,* August 5, 1990, p. 28.
2. Robert Jubelirer, quoted in David S. Broder, "Legislatures under Siege," *State Legislatures,* July 1991, p. 21.
3. Alan Rosenthal, quoted in ibid.
4. Frank Smallwood, *Free and Independent: The Initiation of a College Professor into State Politics* (Stephen Greene Press, 1976), p. 218.
5. Malcolm Jewell, *Representation in State Legislatures* (University of Kentucky Press, 1982), p. 47. See also Keith E. Hamm and David M. Olson, "The Value of Incumbency in State Legislative Elections," paper presented to the American Political Science Association annual meeting, September 1987. See also Malcolm Jewell and David Breaux, "The Effect of Incumbency on State Legislative Elections," *Legislative Studies Quarterly* (November 1988), pp. 495–514.
6. Samuel C. Patterson, "Legislators and Legislatures in the American States," in *Politics in the American States,* 4th ed., ed. Virginia Gray et al. (Little, Brown, 1983), p. 174. See also Alan Rosenthal, *Legislative Life: People, Process and Performance in the States* (Harper and Row, 1981), chap. 2.
7. Rosenthal, *Legislative Life,* pp. 112–13.
8. On women in elections, see Susan J. Carroll, *Women as Candidates in American Politics* (Indiana University Press, 1985); Ronna Romney and Beppie Harrison, *Momentum: Women in American Politics Now* (Crown, 1988).
9. Smallwood, *Free and Independent,* p. 223. See also Alan Rosenthal, "Turnover in State Legislatures," *American Journal of Political Science* (August 1978), pp. 609–16.
10. See Joel A. Thompson and Gary F. Moncrief, "Pursuing the Pork in a State Legislature," *Legislative Studies Quarterly* (August 1988), pp. 393–401.
11. David Broder, in *Campaign Money: Reform and Reality in the States,* ed. Herbert E. Alexander (Free Press, 1976), p. 313. See also Michael Johnston, *Political Corruption and Public Pol-*

icy in America (Brooks/Cole, 1982); Ruth Jones, "Financing State Elections," in *Money and Politics in the United States,* ed. Michael Malbin (American Enterprise Institute, 1984).

12. Smallwood, *Free and Independent,* p. 165.

13. Quoted in ibid., p. 164.

14. Patterson, "Legislators and Legislatures in the American States," p. 170.

15. John D. Ferrick, "Effective Campaign Finance Law: It's a Three-Way Street," *Governing,* January 1989, p. 82. See also Karen Hansen, "Walking the Ethical Tightrope," *State Legislatures,* July 1988, pp. 14–17.

16. Quoted in Gerald Stollman, *Michigan: State Legislators and Their World* (University Press of America, 1979), p. 56.

17. Lucinda Simon, "Wisconsin Legislature Mobilizes Citizen Input," *State Legislatures,* April 1985, p. 35.

18. Donald R. Songer, Sonja G. Dillon, Darla W. Kite, Patricia E. Jameson, James M. Underwood, and William D. Underwood, "The Influence of Issues on Choices of Voting Cues Utilized in State Legislatures," *Western Political Quarterly* (March 1986), p. 118.

19. Quoted in David Ray, "The Sources of Voting Cues in Three State Legislatures," *Journal of Politics* (November 1982), p. 1081.

20. Adapted from Alexander Heard, ed., *State Legislatures in American Government* (Prentice Hall, 1966). See also Donald G. Herzberg and Alan Rosenthal, eds., *Strengthening the States: Essays on Legislative Reform* (Doubleday Anchor, 1972).

21. David S. Broder, "Worse Than the Disease," *The Washington Post National Weekly Edition,* September 24–30, 1990, p. 4.

22. Neal R. Peirce, "A Primal Scream for Change in the Political System," *The Sun,* November 4, 1991, op ed. page.

23. Adapted in part from Thomas E. Cronin, "Term Limits: A Symptom, Not a Cure," *The New York Times,* December 23, 1990, p. E11.

24. Jack Quinn et al., "Redrawing the Districts, Changing the Rules," *The Washington Post National Weekly Edition,* April 1–7, 1991, p. 23.

25. Gordon E. Baker, *The Reapportionment Revolution* (Random House, 1966), p. 47.

26. 369 U.S. 186 (1962).

27. 376 U.S. 1 (1964).

28. 377 U.S. 533 (1964).

29. Jeffrey M. Wice, "Drawing the Lines," *State Legislatures,* July 1988, p. 31.

30. 478 U.S. 109 (1986).

31. *United Jewish Organizational of Williamsburg, Inc. v. Hugh L. Carey,* 430 U.S. 144 (1977).

32. *Mobile v. Bolden* 446 U.S. 55 (1980).

33. *Davis v. Bandemer* 478 U.S. 109 (1986).

34. Bruce Adams, quoted in Janet Simons, "Reapportionment Here It Comes Again." *State Legislatures,* November/December 1979, p. 15. See also National Civic League press release, "National Civic League Announces Release of Redistricting Principles," February 25, 1991.

35. This position is presented in Bruce E. Cain, *The Reapportionment Puzzle* (University of California Press, 1984). For related studies, see Bernard Grofman et al., eds. *Representation and Redistricting Issues in the 1980s* (D.C. Heath, 1982).

36. M. Glenn Newkirk, "Initiatives and Referenda: What Did the Voters Say?" *State Legislatures,* January 1983, p. 16.

37. Thomas E. Cronin, *Direct Democracy: The Politics of the Initiative, Referendum, and Recall* (Harvard University Press, 1989), p. 156.

38. See David Magleby, *Direct Legislation* (Johns Hopkins University Press, 1984).

39. Cronin, *Direct Democracy,* chaps. 4, 8.

6

State Governors

Governor Mario Cuomo of New York says he is always running into people who want him to increase spending. For example, someone will come up to him and say her daughter is in a state institution and it's awful. "They only change the sheets twice a day. Can't you do something—can't you have them change the sheets at least three times a day?" Cuomo says sure, he can have them changed three times a day. But then he looks the woman in the eye and says: "Now what are you going to give me so that I can pay for it? Do you want to wait longer in line at the Motor Vehicle office to get your license renewed? Do we stop paving the road in front of your home? Do you mind if we plow the snow less often?" Typically, of course, he hears that the people requesting the additional new spending don't want to forgo any of those things, which prompts the governor to say, "Well, then, I don't understand. Where do I get what I need to do what you want?" His point is simple. Given limited resources, choices must be made by elected officials. They cannot afford to do everything everyone would like to have provided by the state. Politicians are elected to negotiate the tradeoffs. You must "give to get."[1]

The job of governor is one of the most important and exacting challenges in American political life.[2] Because the Reagan and Bush administrations have succeeded in decentralizing to the states many of the responsibilities once considered national priorities, governors now have to be more than effective managers. They also have to ask the right questions, consider long-term implications and side effects of their policies, and recruit large numbers of able advisers and specialists to help them.

In this chapter, we'll look at how governors come into—and keep—office, the typical governor's power and influence, efforts to bring modern management techniques to the governor's office, how the governor interacts with other elected state officials, and the rewards of being governor. But first, we examine our rising expectations of state governors.

Rising Expectations of State Governors

How do we evaluate governors? Pretty much as we assess and rate presidents, although the constitutional powers of governors vary from state to state, and their existing formal powers are not necessarily constant.[3] Governors have to be leaders who can devise new initiatives, realize increased savings and efficiency, and inspire people to believe in them and their programs. An effective governor also has to perform countless symbolic and ceremonial functions and win the respect of the people and the legislature in order to exercise fully the executive functions of the office.

Today a governor is expected to be, among other things, the state's chief policy maker, architect of the state budget, a savvy political party leader, chief recruiter of the best available advisers and administrators, and an inspiring renewer of confidence in state programs. The governor must also champion the state's interests against the encroachments of federal or local governments and be the state's chief booster to attract business and tourism. Effective governors must have their own foreign policy—making trips to foreign nations to encourage foreign investment in their states and promote their local products abroad. Whether they want to or not, governors must also propose investment taxes to the legislature and the voters for such programs as education and economic development. A governor in the 1990s also plays an increasingly subtle role as a ecrucial link among states and between the local and the national governments.

We expect governors to be excellent judges of people and to be able to make tough decisions and assume responsibility—especially in crisis situations. We want them to have a zest for combat, when this is needed, and an overall ability to inspire confidence. They must also be able to withstand unfair criticism and have a sense of proportion, compassion, and humor. We also ask: Are their appointments good? Do they formulate policy effectively? Do they grasp the important realities of their states' budgetary and economic development requirements? Do they communicate their views forcefully? Are they able to get programs through the state legislature? Do they run honest and efficient administrations? Can they meet crises such as state prison revolts? What of the tone and style of their leadership and their relations with the people? Do they know what needs doing and get it done? In short, are they effective?

As Table 6-1 shows, a number of twentieth-century governors have won respect for their effectiveness. Of course, governors have always been a major source of national leadership. In many ways, in fact, the governorship is a train-

TABLE 6-1   Twentieth-Century Governors Hall of Fame

Term	Governor	State
1901–06	Robert LaFollette	Wisconsin
1911–13	Woodrow Wilson	New Jersey
1919–21	Alfred Smith	New York
1923–28	Alfred Smith	New York
1928–32	Huey Long	Louisiana
1943–54	Earl Warren	California
1943–54	Thomas Dewey	New York
1959–73	Nelson Rockefeller	New York
1961–65	Terry Sanford	North Carolina
1965–77	Daniel Evans	Washington
1971–79	Reubin Askew	Florida

Source: George Weeks, "A Statehouse Hall of Fame," *State Government*, 55, no. 2 (1982), pp. 67–73. © 1992 The Council of State Governments. Reprinted with permisson from *Journal of State Government*.

This list was drawn up by a veteran aide to Governor Milliken of Michigan. He sought advice and nominations from many of the experts in the field. Others might nominate Franklin Delano Roosevelt of New York, Adlai Stevenson of Illinois, Edmund G. Brown of California, John Connally of Texas, William Scranton of Pennsylvania, Richard Hughes of New Jersey, Harold Hughes and Robert Ray of Iowa, Tom McCall of Oregon, Lamar Alexander of Tennessee, or Robert Graham of Florida. Doubtless others among the more than one thousand who have served deserve consideration.

ing ground for important national political positions. Since 1900, about 125 former governors have become U.S. senators. A number of former governors have also served in the president's cabinet. Sixteen governors became presidents—including William McKinley, Theodore Roosevelt, Woodrow Wilson, Calvin Coolidge, Franklin Roosevelt, Jimmy Carter, Ronald Reagan, and Bill Clinton—in this century alone.

Becoming and Remaining Governor

Each state's constitution and laws spell out the rules of eligibility, tenure, and salary for its governor. In most states, to run for the office a person must be at least 30 years of age, a citizen of the United States, and a state resident for at least five years immediately preceding the election. In theory, then, any qualified voter of the state who is at least 30 years of age is eligible for the office of governor. In practice, however, there are well-traveled career paths to the governor's office. Most of our governors in the past generation have been white male attorneys who have first won election to city or state legislative positions. (Women are still a distinct minority in the governor's office.) A large number were state legislators or held statewide elective office. In one recent year, for example, thirty-one governors were attorneys, two were farmers, one was a dentist, and most of the others were businesspeople. The most common path is

We The People

Women Governors

Nellie Taylor Ross, Wyoming	1925–27
"Ma" Ferguson, Texas	1925–27, 1933–35
Lurleen Wallace, Alabama	1967–68
Ella Grasso, Connecticut	1975–80
Dixie Lee Ray, Washington	1977–81
Martha L. Collins, Kentucky	1983–87
Madeleine Kunin, Vermont	1985–91
Kay Orr, Nebraska	1987–91
Rose Mofford, Arizona	1988–91
Joan Finney, Kansas	1991–
Ann Richards, Texas	1991–
Barbara Roberts, Oregon	1991–

election to the state legislature, followed by election to a statewide office such as attorney general, lieutenant governor, or secretary of state.

Members of Congress have run for governor in several states recently; thus former U.S. Senators Pete Wilson, Lawton Chiles, and Lowell Weicker won election in California, Florida, and Connecticut in 1990. Members of the U.S. House of Representatives have won election as governors in states such as New Jersey and South Carolina. A few mayors of big cities have gone on to become governors, as happened in Ohio and Maryland in recent years.

Sometimes a person who has not held any elective office will win a governorship, although such individuals typically have been active in political life. Ronald Reagan, for example, had been known primarily as an actor and television personality, yet he had also served several terms as president of the Screen Actors Guild, a powerful union, and had been an effective speaker and fundraiser for the Republican party prior to his successful run for California governor. William Weld served as a highly visible U.S. attorney and later as a top U.S. Justice Department official before being elected governor of Massachusetts. Occasionally, too, a prominent business leader who is involved in a state's economic development program can parlay that leadership role into a viable governor's race.

GOVERNORS ON THE SPOT

Once elected, governors enjoy high visibility in their states. Governors earn over $100,000 in several states, such as New York, Michigan, and North Carolina; the average is now about $85,000. In addition, most governors receive an expense allowance, and all but four are provided an executive mansion.

But just as governors have become increasingly important in recent years, they have also had to work with the twin problems of rising aspirations and scarcity of resources. People want better schools, highways that do not require any land or spoil the environment, adequate welfare programs, aid to local school districts, civil rights, safe streets, and clean air and streams. But they do not want higher taxes. Recent years have been a period of fiscal stress for most states, and governors are often caught in the middle. "We can dream dreams," governors often say, "but if we can't pay the bill, we can't have new programs."

Many governors complain—sometimes bitterly—that federal mandates, grant-in-aid programs, guidelines, and formulas shape so much of their activities that there is little left for them to decide. They want the federal government to give more dollars to the states but without strings. The governors want federal dollars given to agencies they control rather than directly to mayors, city councils, school boards, or welfare agencies. In short, most governors complain they are faced with a whole range of problems, all of which they are expected to solve, yet few of which are within their authority. A governor is expected to fight on all fronts—and emerge victorious—to decrease the rate of unemployment, revitalize the state's economy, and keep taxes from rising.

REELECTION AND RAISING TAXES

One asset of being a governor today is likely reelection. At least in recent years about two-thirds of the governors who sought reelection have won, even when they faced serious economic problems. Most elections for governor are now scheduled for nonpresidential election years (for example, 1993 or 1994). Reformers have successfully argued that presidential and gubernatorial elections should be separated so that governors are not subject to the tides of national politics.

But not everyone is reelected; incumbents often believe that to run after four years of making tough and often controversial decisions and thereby gaining opponents is no advantage at all. Occasionally a governor who loses reelection blames the defeat on an increase in state taxes or a depressed state economy.

Because voters do reward frugality and sometimes punish elected officials for tax increases, most governors will go to great lengths to avoid having to raise taxes. Indeed, most politicians believe that a governor who proposes new taxes will face defeat in the next election, although studies cast doubt on this mentality. Circumstances often dictate what a governor can or cannot do. The health of the state's economy and the public's attitude toward the need for new programs and new revenues are critical factors in determining what a governor must do. A governor who does not propose new initiatives to improve the state's transportation or educational systems may face opponents in the next election who can win precisely because the governor failed to lead in these areas.

An examination of governors throughout the last decade makes it clear that a gubernatorial call for tax increases *in general* is not likely to be successful. Yet voters and the legislature will often go along with governors who can make a compelling case for new revenues and new investments. When governors request a tax increase targeted for a specific worthy cause (for example, improving the schools), voters often will support them. This is especially true if "political leaders are candid about why they need the money, sensible and fair in how they intend to spend it and courageous enough to lead the fight themselves." Governors in Indiana, Virginia, Tennessee, and Arkansas in recent years proposed and campaigned for "investment taxes" and generally became more popular because of their efforts. "Americans are neither selfish nor shortsighted on taxes—they just want assurance that their money will be spent wisely."[4]

Two hundred years ago most states had one- or two-year terms for their governors. Nowadays all states but three have four-year terms, and virtually all states allow governors to run for more than one term. Some recent governors, such as James Thompson in Illinois, Richard Lamm in Colorado, and Mario Cuomo in New York, have been elected for three or four terms as governors of their states. But at least 30 states have imposed a two-term limit on governors, and the term-limitation movement is growing. California, Oklahoma, and Colorado, for example, all imposed a two-term limit on governors as a result of citizen-initiated ballot measures in 1990.

A Governor's Formal Powers and Influence

Before the American Revolution royal governors, appointed by the British Crown and responsible to it, had broad powers, including extensive veto power over the actions of the voter-elected colonial legislatures. As anti-British sentiment increased, royal governors became more and more unpopular. Thus the position of state governor in the new republic was born in an atmosphere of distrust. Initially, most state legislatures elected state governors, a method that ensured the governors would remain under the control of the people's representatives. The early state constitutions also gave the governors few powers and terms of just a year or two.

Gradually, however, the office of governor grew in importance. In New York the position of chief executive was sufficiently formidable by 1787 that it became one of the main models for the proposed American presidency. Yet, if we look at the formal sources of authority in the U.S. Constitution and in a typical state constitution, we can see significant differences. "The executive

Power," says the Constitution, "shall be vested in a President of the United States of America." Compare this statement with its counterpart in a typical state constitution: "The executive department shall consist of a Governor, Lieutenant Governor, Secretary of State, Treasurer, Attorney General," and perhaps other officials. Unlike the president, the Governor *shares* executive power with other elected officials. Most state constitutions go on to say that "the supreme executive power shall be vested in the Governor, who shall take care that the laws be faithfully executed." Thus it is the governor to whom the public looks for law enforcement and the management of sprawling bureaucracies.

Governor Samuel W. Pennypacker, Pennsylvania's chief executive from 1903 to 1907, once told how he had come to office eager to be sure the laws of the state were faithfully executed. Looking around to see what tools he had to carry out this responsibility, he discovered that the only people to whom he could look for help were his secretary, the janitor, and his chauffeur. The prosecutors and police, locally elected and locally controlled, were subject to little or no gubernatorial supervision. The attorney general was elected independently by the voters and was not responsible to the governor. Of course, the governor could call out the National Guard, but this is a clumsy way to enforce the law. "So," said Governor Pennypacker, "I created the state police." Today all states have a police organization. In some states the governor has been given authority to supervise the activities of local prosecutors.

Still, in 1950 about half the states had just two-year terms for governors— an extremely short time for evaluating and devising meaningful solutions to complex state problems. Now all but New Hampshire, Rhode Island, and Vermont have four-year terms. Until recently many states forbade a governor to seek immediate reelection; today only two states, Kentucky and Virginia, do so. Nearly half of the states have also strengthened the governorship by making the lieutenant governor run with the governor as a team, so that the chief executive is less likely to be faced with a hostile lieutenant governor. Most important, in almost all states the governor presents the state budget to the legislature and controls spending after the budget has been approved. This means state officials look to the governor as well as the legislature for funds.

It is difficult to specify exactly the powers of a typical governor because they vary widely from state to state (see Table 6-2). In most states constitutional changes have centralized more formal constitutional authority in governors. But governors' actual power and influence depend on their ability to persuade. This power, in turn, usually depends on their reputation, popularity, knowledge of what should be done, and, of course, their ability to communicate. They must have political skills as well as constitutional authority if they are to provide leadership. To supplement their formal powers, most governors hold town meeting forums around their state, appear monthly on radio and television talk shows, and invite legislators and other influential party and policy leaders to the executive mansion for lobbying and consultation sessions.

Remember, however, that not all states have powerful governors, and the

TABLE 6-2   Rankings of States According to the Formal Powers of the Governor

Strong	Moderate			Weak
Arkansas	Alaska	Mississippi		Alabama
Connecticut	Arizona	Missouri		Maine
Hawaii	California	Montana		Nevada
Kansas	Colorado	North Dakota		New Hampshire
Maryland	Delaware	Ohio		New Mexico
Massachusetts	Florida	Pennsylvania		North Carolina
Minnesota	Georgia	South Dakota		Oklahoma
Nebraska	Idaho	Virginia		Rhode Island
New Jersey	Illinois	Washington		South Carolina
New York	Indiana	Wisconsin		Texas
Oregon	Iowa	Wyoming		Vermont
Tennessee	Kentucky			
Utah	Louisiana			
West Virginia	Michigan			

Source: Adapted from Thad L. Beyle, "Governors," in Politics in the American States, ed. Virginia Gray et al., 5th ed. (Scott, Foresman and Company, 1990), p. 228.

Note: Rankings are based on budget powers, appointive and organizational powers, tenure potential, and veto powers.

powers of a governor are not necessarily constant; they may be decreased. On occasion, in fact, they are decreased by capable state legislatures.

Most governors have the following powers:

• Appointive powers
• The power to prepare the state budget
• The right to veto legislation and item-veto appropriations measures
• Ordinance-making power or executive order powers
• The power to command the state National Guard
• The power to pardon or grant clemency
• The opportunity to help establish the legislature's agenda

Let us look briefly at some of these powers.

APPOINTIVE POWERS

Perhaps a governor's most important job is to recruit talented leaders and managers to head the state's departments, commissions, and agencies. Governors also appoint a cabinet of advisers and senior administrators. Through recruitment of effective people and prudent delegation to them, a governor can provide direction for the state government.

Some governors can appoint hundreds of key officials; others, such as those in Mississippi, South Carolina, and Texas, have severe restrictions on their appointive powers. In most states the governor is one executive among many, with only limited authority over *elected* officials, whom the governor can neither appoint nor dismiss. And if these officials are political enemies of the governor, they will not accept the governor's leadership. Governors have greater, yet still limited, power over *appointed* administrative officials. Further, in most states governors must share appointive power with the state senate, and may remove people only when they have violated the law or failed in their legal duties. The growing professionalism of state administrators whose programs are supported in part by federal funds is giving them a measure of independence from the governor as well as greater loyalty toward their counterparts at the national level than toward other state officials.

Governors face other problems as well. First, administrative salaries are modest in many states, especially in the smaller ones, and it is often hard to get people to leave much better paying jobs in private industry. The situation is even worse when the state capital is in a remote or rural section of the state. Second, leaders in some state legislatures often demand that their friends be appointed to certain top posts in the state's executive branch, and they will threaten to be uncooperative if the governor does not go along with some of their "suggested" nominees. Finally, relatively high turnover in many state positions often hampers a governor's efforts to carry out programs.

FISCAL AND BUDGETARY POWERS

A governor's fiscal and budgetary powers are usually a key weapon in getting programs passed. In most states the governor now has nearly full responsibility to prepare the budget and present it to the state legislature. The art of budget making involves assessing requests from various departments and agencies and balancing them against scarce resources. Governors and their staffs have to calculate the costs of existing and newly proposed programs and weigh those costs against estimated revenues or income for the state. The final budget document is presented to the legislature for adoption as an appropriations measure. State monies cannot be spent without legislative appropriations.

Legislators can, and usually do, make a number of alterations in a governor's budget. In theory, a legislature controls all state activities and the overall budget process because it has the final say in approving the budget. In practice, however, most legislatures do not review every budgetary item; they merely trim or make additions at the margins. Hence, budgets usually reflect the policy views of those responsible for their preparation—namely, the governor and the governor's budget office.

Plainly, a governor who has control over the budget and uses this power effectively has an important asset. This is somewhat more true where governors have the power of the **item veto,** a provision that permits governors to veto individual items in an appropriations bill while signing the remainder of the bill into law.[5] Here they can influence the flow of funds to the executive departments and thus shape the latter's activities. However, this is less true for agencies headed by elected officials. Purchase, fiscal, and personnel matters, moreover, are frequently centralized under the governor. When implemented by a strong staff and backed by a strong political base, a governor's fiscal powers are extremely important.

The governor's political power to enforce budget recommendations varies from state to state and from time to time. Taxpayer revolts—almost rebellions in states such as Connecticut and New Jersey—are often intense. Taxpayers have made it clear they do not want to pay more in taxes, but they also do not want a reduction of state services. At the same time, federal funds have been cut. This has probably been one of the most pressing problems governors have had to face in the 1990s.

Most states spend at least 40 percent of their state's budget on education. Social assistance, transportation, prisons and criminal justice programs, health and rehabilitation efforts, and state parks and recreation consume other large portions of the budget. Fifty percent of the state's revenue usually comes from taxes; another 20–25 percent comes from federal sources. Charges for goods and services or users' fees account for perhaps 15 percent of the revenues. When state revenues don't match expenses, governors have to strike some kind of balance.

VETO POWERS

In all states except North Carolina, governors have relatively strong veto powers. To override a governor's veto, both chambers of state legislatures have to obtain a two-thirds majority vote. In all but seven states the governor has, in addition to the regular veto of entire bills, the power to veto individual items in appropriations measures. In a few states the governor can even reduce a particular appropriation. Both the *item veto* and the **reduction veto,** like all vetoes, can be overridden by the legislature (the former usually by a two-thirds or three-fifths vote in both chambers; the latter by a majority vote). In some

"I had a horrible nightmare last night. I dreamed I was re-elected!"

Bob Englehart, *The Hartford Courant.*

states, however, many new laws and appropriations measures are sent to the governor after the legislature has adjourned. To reassert their roles in relation to the governor, several state legislatures have adopted measures to allow the legislature to call itself into special session to reconsider a governor's vetoes. Certain states have even established a veto session—a short session following adjournment so that the legislature can reconsider all measures vetoed by the governor.

Amendatory or **conditional vetoes** (found in about seventeen states) allow governors to return a bill to the legislature with suggested changes or amendments. The legislators must decide whether to accept the governor's recommendations or attempt to pass the bill in its original form over the veto.

EXECUTIVE ORDERS

One long-standing power of governors is their authority to issue executive orders that have the force of law. Even though these executive orders differ from statutes or formal acts passed by the legislature, they have almost the same binding effect.

Governors can issue executive orders as a result of specific constitutional grants, laws passed by their legislatures, or their implied powers as chief executive of the state. Governors have been given this quasi-legislative power because state legislatures often pass very general—some would say vague—laws. Sometimes the executive ordinances supplementing a law are both more detailed and more important than the general guidelines contained in legislation. Recent governors have issued executive orders during such emergencies as natural disasters or energy crises, in compliance with federal rules and regulations, or to create advisory or coordinating commissions.[6]

But just as Congress has become more assertive in recent years, state legislatures have also increased their supervision over the rules and regulations issued by executive agencies. They want to ensure that what is done is actually what they intended.

COMMANDER IN CHIEF OF THE NATIONAL GUARD

Emergencies add to the authority of an executive because they call for decisive action. As commander in chief of the state's National Guard when it is not in federal service, the governor may use this force when local authorities are inadequate—in case of riots, floods, and other catastrophes, for example. Hardly a year goes by in which the National Guard of some state does not see emergency duty. In most states the state police are also available for emergencies.

These days Congress puts up most of the money to operate the National Guard. That fact, along with the supremacy clause of the U.S. Constitution, gives Congress, and the president, the power to take charge of a state's National Guard even against the wishes of a governor. A unanimous Supreme Court ruled that Congress can authorize the president to call state guards into active duty and send them outside the United States despite the objections of the governors, several of whom had tried to keep President Ronald Reagan from calling their respective guards into training exercises in Honduras.[7] States could if they wish (but none has done so) provide and maintain from their own funds a defense force exempt from being drafted into the armed forces of the United States.

THE PARDON POWER

In half the states, governors may pardon violators of state law; in the other states, they share this duty with a pardoning board. The governor may—except in cases of certain specified crimes or in cases of impeachment—pardon the offender, commute a sentence by reducing it, or grant a reprieve by delaying the punishment. The governor is normally assisted by pardon attorneys or pardon boards that hold hearings and sift the evidence to determine whether there are reasons for a pardon. A Tennessee governor caused considerable controversy and sparked federal investigation because he pardoned or paroled several dozen convicts just before leaving office in early 1979. Critics charged that some allegedly "purchased" their releases. Seldom, however, is the pardon power the subject of such controversy, presumably because it is generally administered with appropriate care.

In the 1988 presidential election, a Massachusetts policy permitting convicted rapists and others to be furloughed became an issue in the election. Many states permitted criminals to be released for limited periods of time before their prison terms were up, but Massachusetts was the only state that furloughed prisoners sentenced to life terms without the possibility of parole—a policy that had been endorsed by Governor Dukakis. Willie Horton, a convicted rapist, escaped while on furlough and was later caught, after beating a couple and committing rape in Maryland. Supporters of Bush for president played up this violent act in television ads. Bush critics said his campaign was subtly (or not so subtly) appealing to a racist bias because Horton was black.

POLICY-MAKING INFLUENCE

How much policy-making influence do governors have? Although their constitutional authority varies from state to state, their actual ability to influence legislation varies even more widely than a reading of the state constitutions might suggest.

Obviously, governors can send messages to their legislatures and argue for their programs. In some states they can trade appointive jobs for legislative support. They can also use their veto powers to trade for votes. They can usually attract more public attention to their views than any single legislator. Yet being the spokesperson for a policy does not guarantee success. Much depends on a governor's ability, political base, and personal popularity, as well as on the political situation in which he or she operates. Some states have a long tradition of strong executive leadership. When governors have the support of powerful political organizations, they can guide policy. The governors of New York, for example, have strong constitutional positions, and they are also likely to have party organizations behind them as well as close ties with followers in their respective legislatures.

But even in states in which they are less likely to be national figures, governors may derive power from a large popular following or strong party organization. The governor of Nevada has much less formal power than the governor of New York and carries less weight on the national political scene, yet within the state the Nevada governor's control over minor jobs, contracts, and patronage may make this governor an important figure. And the governors of Nevada or similar rural and smaller states generally have few other institutions or interests to compete with in exercising what policy influence they have. "Powerful governors in large urbanized states have many others with whom they must compete—heads of major industries, media personalities, mayors of large cities, and even presidents of prestigious universities," comments political scientist Thad Beyle. "There are lots of big fish in a larger pond, which can mean that a governor may not be as powerful as it might first appear."[8]

Balanced against all these formal powers are great obstacles, which may include a hostile legislature, cutbacks in federal funding, a depressed state economy, corrupt party or administrative officials, regional tensions in the state (downstate versus upstate, east versus west, or urban versus rural), special interests and lobbyists, a cynical press, an indifferent or apathetic public, the sheer inertia of what critics call "the vast immovable inherited bureaucracy of government," antique civil service systems, and the reluctance of most citizens to get involved.

Some governors claim they are handicapped and that their programs are sacrificed because the opposition party is in control of the legislature. Others blame what they allege to be narrow-minded state lobbyists or an unfair press. One western governor complained that many of his state's problems—and many of the natural resource and social problems in western states—are caused by out-of-state, absentee landlord businesses or the national government, who together control much land in the West. The federal government owns at least half of the land in the West, a landmass, in fact, larger than Western Europe. The land is managed, regulated, and overseen by a score of federal agencies, such as the National Park Service, the Forest Service, the Bureau of Land Management, the Fish and Wildlife Service, and the Department of Defense.

Still, governors are the most important policy leaders in the states. Observers differ, however, over how much these officials can actually do. Some claim that social and economic conditions really determine both how much money is available and how it is spent. In fact, they say governors have little leeway in budget and policy determination. Even though governors often come into office hoping to begin new programs, they may spend most of their time

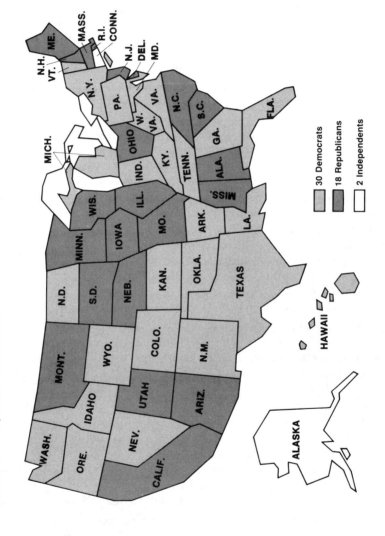

FIGURE 6-1 Party Control of the Governor's Office

30 Democrats

18 Republicans

2 Independents

raising money just to keep things going; hence they are viewed by some observers as merely budget balancers rather than public policy leaders or shapers of a state's future. Some leading scholars, however, dispute this. Their research shows that a governor's ability to provide political leadership does affect the quality and implementation of public policy. The governor's role as leader of his or her political party also has an important impact on policy. The coalitions that governors form within their political parties help them put into effect the policies that they desire.[9] A governor's role increases in a state that has a competitive two-party system. In such a state, legislators of the governor's party are likely to work more closely with the governor to produce a successful legislative record.

In recent years, we have witnessed the election of a new breed of well-educated and able governors who have been effective in enlarging their policy-making roles. They are able to appoint more and better state officials; most states now have some kind of cabinet system. Many contemporary governors come to office with impressive legislative and administrative experience. They are more likely to be real executive heads of government—not just figureheads. In short, many of the institutional barriers have been greatly diminished. The new governors are in a position to use their appreciable talents and to work to reshape public policy priorities in their states.[10] Because states will be playing a larger role in planning and administering a wide range of social and economic programs, the managerial and planning ability of each governor is clearly important.

Managing the State

Some governors, however, come to office with no broad philosophy of management. Others are practicing attorneys or former state or national legislators and are used to handling each issue as it comes up, deciding it on its merits, and then delegating the administrative responsibilities to staff or department heads. Together, governors and their senior staffs must perform a variety of functions including the following:

- Changing or initiating policy
- Maintaining a policy or a position under pressure
- Settling disputes among different agencies or factions within agencies
- Promoting the state (attracting tourism, exports, investment)
- Recruiting top state administrative and judicial officials
- Proposing budget priorities
- Improving the quality of services rendered to the taxpayers
- Settling disputes with the federal government and with nearby states

Even though management duties occupy a fair amount of time (see Table 6-3), many governors consider them the least glamorous of their responsibilities. Yet they can hardly ignore their functions as their states' chief executive. Voters expect governors to make programs run more efficiently, modernize the governmental structure, and be responsible for the performance of their many state employees. Of course, style and quality of leadership vary from governor to governor and from state to state. Management can also vary greatly from one agency to another; in addition, different kinds of programs demand different kinds of management.

Governors have also had to become more involved in "grantsmanship" and in the planning and coordinating of federal grant-in-aid programs. The national government has passed much legislation that specifically designates the governor as the chief planning and administrative officer in the state. This role has led both to more flexibility *and* to more headaches for governors. On the one hand, to the extent these federal funds are still available, governors now have a form of patronage—services and programs for influential professional and local communities. On the other, this new intergovernmental relations role requires more time, more staff, and constant negotiations both with the "feds" and with local and interest group leaders vying for the money or services involved.

INFLUENCING STATE AGENCIES

Understandably, senior public servants in a state usually look upon governors as important managerial and policy-making influences on their agencies. But state legislatures also have significant power. Plainly, some agencies are not very responsive to their governors. Public agencies exist in a political climate; sometimes they are more responsive to interest groups, the legislature, or their own definitions of the public interest. Some reformers have long thought that all agencies should be accountable to the governor all the time. Others believe we should examine the given tasks of an agency and ask: "How far should it be removed from having to respond instantly to public opinion or to a governor's perception of public opinion? What questions should be left in the hands of the political system, the electorate, and the governor to be 'managed,' and which ones should be delegated to professional managers who are not directly accountable to any part of the political system?"[11]

A study of the Massachusetts governor's office differentiated four kinds of state agencies according to the ways in which a governor deals with them:

1. Those agencies requiring constant scrutiny, such as departments of corrections and public welfare

2. Those agencies that receive constant scrutiny because of the governor's personal preferences, such as the department of mental health

TABLE 6-3
How Governors Say They Spend
Their Time

Activity	Percent of Time Spent[1]
Managing state government	29%
Working with the legislature	16
Meeting the general public	14
Performing ceremonial functions	14
Working with press and media	9
Working with federal government	7
Working with local governments	7
Carrying out political activities[2]	6
Recruiting and appointing	6
Doing miscellaneous activities (staff, interstate, reading, phoning)	16

Source: Thad L. Beyle, "The Governor as Chief Legislator," State Government (Council of State Governments) (Winter 1978), p. 3.

[1] Totals do not add to 100 percent but are averages of the governors' estimates of the time they devoted to the particular activities. Percentages based on responses from those scheduling gubernatorial time in forty states.

[2] Plainly, some governors understate time spent campaigning for reelection.

3. Those agencies that receive gubernatorial attention because of a single crisis, such as the department of community affairs

4. Those agencies the governor leaves alone, such as housing and finance agencies[12]

MODERNIZING STATE GOVERNMENT

Another key development giving the governor more control over state government is the application to state administration of modern management techniques, such as strategic planning, systems analysis, and sophisticated computer and budgeting systems. In fact, the modern system of professional management is gradually replacing the old back-scratching or buddy system.[13]

There has been a trend toward increasing governors' involvement and control of the administration and streamlining of executive departments. In urban states with competitive party systems—such as New York, Illinois, New Jersey, Pennsylvania, Washington, and California—governors have considerable formal constitutional authority to organize their administrations as they see fit. Even in more rural states, such as South Dakota, hundreds of agencies have been consolidated into a few comprehensive units as the result of executive orders from the governors.

The wave of state reorganizations that followed World War I and was repeated after World War II has continued. Attempts to reorganize state governments have not received universal praise, however. In some states reorganization commissions submit reports that are filed away and forgotten. Groups that profit from the existing structure—for example, those who have a pet bureau under their influence—can be counted upon to resist changes. So, too, can officials who fear loss of job or prestige. Also, legislators are often reluctant to approve recommendations that might make the governor too powerful.

Other critics oppose not so much the idea of reorganization as the basic principle of *strengthening executive power and responsibility*, which has dominated the reorganization movement. During the past several decades reorganizers have urged that the governor be made the true manager of the executive branch. The following principles of reorganization have been suggested:

1. Agencies should be consolidated and integrated into as few departments as possible, so that similar functions will be grouped together and the governor will be able to exercise real control.

2. Lines of responsibility should be fixed and definite.

3. Single executives are preferable to boards and commissions.

4. The governor should have power to appoint and remove subordinates, including officers now elected, with the possible exception of the auditor.

5. The governor should have control over budgeting, accounting, reporting, purchasing, personnel, and planning, and should have the staff necessary to do these jobs.

Although they agree that centralized budgeting, purchasing, and the like are all good objectives, critics contend that conditions differ in each state and that no one pattern will fit all conditions. Often, they say, there is little evidence to support the adoption of these reforms. What evidence do we have that the people will hold the governor accountable and that the governor will devote time and energy to administrative matters? Most governors are interested chiefly in legislative problems and public relations, and often they are not judged on their executive abilities. There is thus a real danger that the reorganizers are overlooking basic values in their concern with saving money. Intent on efficiency and economy, reformers often fail, some critics say, to warn their clients of the risk involved in creating a powerful chief executive where no effective party or legislative opposition exists to keep a strong governor in check.

Reorganizers agree it is wrong to make changes without regard to local conditions and problems. However, they maintain that the basic ideas—integrated authority, centralized direction, simplified structure, clear responsibility —are sound. In fact, it is more likely that narrow special interests not responsible to the voters will take over government when the administrative structure is cumbersome, confusing, and too spread out. The legislature can more effectively supervise an administration integrated under the governor's control than one in which responsibility is split.

EFFECTS OF REORGANIZATION

Some observers say a half century of strengthening the governors has not given us more efficient or democratic state government. Others say it has. Still others say there is little evidence one way or another. Often the reorganizations change only organizational charts, with little impact on actual operations. Although large savings have been realized through centralized purchasing and the adoption of modern money-management practices, it is difficult to measure the results of consolidating departments, creating a governor's cabinet, strengthening the governor's control over the executive branch or establishing the office of **ombudsman** to handle citizen complaints. At the same time, the best-governed states do seem to be those in which the administrative structure has been closely integrated under the governor.

The reorganization of state administrative procedures is almost always justified in terms of efficiency and economy. Although few would deny the importance of saving money, it is doubtful that the costs of operating state governments can be substantially reduced except by reducing their functions. Thus, we must ask, reorganization for what?

Overall formal reorganization is not the only way states modify and modernize their governmental structures. Often they change in stages, copying innovations from other states. Certain states, in fact, serve as exporters of innovations. So does the federal government. When the federal government creates a department of housing and urban development, states often respond by creating departments of community affairs; when the federal government establishes a department of transportation, so do several of the states; and when the federal government creates a special White House–level office for trade, many governors set up their own offices for trade and export responsibilities.[14]

Other Statewide Elected Officers

In many states other executive officials elected by the people include the lieutenant governor, secretary of state, attorney general, treasurer, and auditor (see Table 6-4).

The job of the *lieutenant governor*, like that of the vice-president, depends very much on the mood of the governor (except in Texas, where the lieutenant governor is sometimes as politically powerful as the governor). In a few states a

TABLE 6-4
Elected Executive Officials
in the States

Governor	50
Attorney general	43
Lieutenant governor	42*
State treasurer	38
Secretary of state	36
State auditor	25
Superintendent of education	16
Agriculture commissioner	12
Controller	10
Insurance commissioner	8

Source: *The Book of the States, 1990–91* (Council of State Governments, 1990). Copyright by the Council of State Governments. Reprinted with permission.

* In the state of Utah one elected official serves as both lieutenant governor and secretary of state.

lieutenant governor presides over the senate and acts as a cabinet officer or even as a coordinator of several departments and agencies.[15] In almost every case the lieutenant governor becomes governor or acting governor in case of the death, disability, or absence of the governor from the state. Doubtless for this reason, more governors have sprung from this office than from any other.

Because the lieutenant governor sometimes leads a party faction different from that of the governor—and is occasionally even a member of the opposition party—he or she may become a thorn in the side of the chief executive. Thus twenty-three states now provide for the election of the governor and lieutenant governor as a team—the same way candidates for president and vice-president run in national elections. "The advent of team election, coupled with the assignment of weighty administrative tasks and larger salaries and budgets, has considerably strengthened the oft-maligned office of lieutenant governor."[16] Still, many lieutenant governors have no statutory duties. In several smaller states, being lieutenant governor is a part-time job. A recent Nevada lieutenant governor, for example, practiced law nearly full time in Las Vegas and was paid $8,000 a year. He joked: "Heck, [presiding over the State Senate when it is] in session is the only thing I do—and check on the obituaries to see if I should be in Carson City [the capital]."

Are lieutenant governors really necessary? Eight states are doing without one. If the job they perform best is assuming the governor's job in case of death, resignation, or impeachment, critics think, the job is not needed. The succession or replacement function could be performed by a state's attorney general, secretary of state, or the ranking member of the governor's party in the legislature. Some have suggested that replacing a governor would be important enough to call a special election so that the people of the state could truly participate in the selection of their governor. An interim governor could be designated by a state legislature for the sixty or ninety days leading up to the special election.

Although the position of lieutenant governor has worked out well in some states, the view persists that lieutenant governors are often in search of both a job definition and assignments that make them look important. The staffs and cabinets that are growing up nowadays around governors make the governor's chief of staff more of a deputy governor than most lieutenant governors. Then, too, many candidates for lieutenant governor appear to seek the post only for the name recognition and "the credential" to advance their political careers as they await forthcoming elections. In sum, the value to the state of the obscure office of lieutenant governor is debatable.

The *attorney general*—or state's chief lawyer—gives advice to state officials, represents the state before the courts, and in some states supervises local prosecutors. Some attorneys general have real authority over local prosecutors and may prosecute cases on their own initiative, although in most states prosecution of criminals remains under the control of the local county prosecutor.

The attorney general is becoming an increasingly prominent state office, and in more and more states, attorneys general have taken the lead as champions of the consumer and protectors of the environment. They have launched major investigations into the insurance industry and into business practices. The office is often a stepping-stone to the governorship.

Disputes between attorneys general and governors can be partisan (different parties or conflicting ambitions), but they also can be issue oriented. Thus governors in many states have their own staff lawyers to represent them in fights with the states' attorneys general.

The *secretary of state* publishes the laws, supervises elections, and issues certificates of incorporation. In some states the secretary issues automobile licenses and registers corporate securities. This office is sometimes the dumping ground for jobs that do not seem to belong to any other office and are not important enough to justify setting up a new agency. Yet several secretaries of state in recent years have begun modernization efforts in voter registration processes or have sponsored campaign finance and disclosure reforms. For example, former Illinois Secretary of State Jim Edgar (whose office regulated motor vehicles) used a campaign against drunk driving to help propel himself into the governor's office.

The *treasurer* is the guardian of the state's money. Although in some states the job is largely ministerial, state treasurers generally have the vital responsibility of ensuring that cash is available to meet the obligations of the state and that all available funds are invested to maximize interest return.

The *auditor* in most states has two major jobs: (1) to authorize payments from the state treasury, and (2) to make periodic audits of officials who handle state money. Before money can be spent, the auditor must sign a warrant certifying that the expenditure is authorized by law and that the money is available in the treasury. This job is more accurately called the *preaudit* and is increasingly being assigned to a comptroller appointed by and responsible to the governor. The auditing *after* the money has been spent, however, is a job that most believe should be given to an officer responsible to the legislature. Even the most extreme advocates of centralized administration believe the auditor should not be responsible to the governor.

Other elected statewide officials may include superintendent of public education, agriculture commissioner, public utilities commissioner, controller, and insurance commissioner. Positions like these are placed on the ballot in fewer states than positions like treasurer or auditor. Putting positions like these on the ballot results in a longer ballot and voter fatigue; in one instance as many as 50 percent of those who went to the polls failed to vote for superintendent of public instruction.[17] Proliferation of elected statewide officials also makes it more difficult for governors to manage and lead state government. Think of the kinds of challenges a president of the United States would face if the secretary of defense or the head of the Environmental Protection Agency were elected rather than appointed!

As part of the trend toward integrated administration, the duties of elected state officials have generally been limited to the functions specified in the constitution and the more important functions given to officials appointed by the governor. In many states the budget directors and agency chiefs under the governor have more important roles than the state treasurer or the secretary of state. Yet elected officers can often control patronage, attract a following, and thus develop a political base from which they can attack the governor's program and administration.

Sometimes progressive and controversial initiatives in state governments come from these elected officials. An attorney general in Texas helped design and pass the Texas Open Records Act, one of the broadest and most strictly enforced freedom-of-information statutes in the country. A secretary of state in Massachusetts modernized election laws, helped enact campaign finance laws, and championed conflict-of-interest reforms. A state treasurer in Colorado battled to transfer some of his state's revenue deposits from a few large Denver banks to smaller banks around the state and devised incentives for these banks to stimulate lending for student and small business loans and for low-income housing and family farms.

The Rewards of Being a Governor

Can anyone really succeed as governor? Some do not. Yet some, like Robert Ray of Iowa, Bob Graham of Florida, Thomas Kean of New Jersey, Dan Evans of Washington, Bill Clinton of Arkansas, and Richard Riley of South Carolina, became popular despite the political "heat" and the need to make tough decisions. In a sense governors don't have accomplishments; the people do. "A governor achieves his personal best by being honest and by staying in touch

BEING GOVERNOR: THE MOST DIFFICULT ASPECTS

1. Coping with less time for one's family

2. Working with legislature

3. Performing ceremonial duties

4. Keeping long hours

5. Making tough decisions

6. Accepting loss of privacy

7. Dealing with squabbles among government agencies

8. Working with federal government

9. Building and keeping staff

10. Working with the press

Source: Adapted from Thad Beyle, "Governors' Views on Being Governor," in *Being Governor: Views from the Office,* ed. Thad L. Beyle and Lynn R. Muchmore (Duke University Press, 1983), p. 25.

---

with the people who elected him to serve them," says former Governor Lamar Alexander of Tennessee.[18] Former Governor Tom Kean of New Jersey echoed similar thoughts when he reflected, "When our common values are tapped and their energy released, we can do anything." Kean added, "I have tried to show during my political career, and especially my years as governor, that responsible government can meet people's needs and bring them together, that government can made a difference in the way we live."[19]

Who are the best governors? A popular former governor of Utah, Scott Matheson, once wrote that they have been the men and women who have the right combination of values "for quality service, the courage to stick to their convictions, even when in the minority, integrity by instinct, compassion by nature, leadership by perception, and the character to admit wrong, and when necessary, to accept defeat."[20]

Governors are elected and are supposed to be responsive to the electorate. To the extent that they are able to persuade the public and maintain support, governors are effective. To the extent that they lose the support of the voters, they are not. That's how democracy generally works.

Summary

1. One of the strengths of the federal system is that the states can act as laboratories of democracy, testing ideas that—if successful—can be copied on the national level. The states are also the testing place for many of our national leaders.

2. The job of governor is one of the most difficult tasks in American politics. Governors are usually male lawyers in their 40s or 50s. Their chances for reelection are good, but their chances for accomplishing what they set out to do are nearly always overestimated by everyone—themselves included.

3. Today a governor is expected to be the state's chief policy maker, the architect of the state budget, the chief manager of the state administration, and the political and symbolic leader in the state. The governor also plays an increasingly complex role as

the crucial link between the national and local governments. In short, governors are asked to accomplish miracles in this era of scarce resources and rising demands.

4. Governors have many formal powers. The most important are their budgetary and appointive powers. But a governor's formal powers mean little if he or she is not a persuasive communicator with good judgment and the capacity to think clearly. Governors, as a general rule, have more responsibility than power.

For Further Reading

GLENN ABNEY and THOMAS P. LAUTH, *The Politics of State and City Administration* (State University of New York Press, 1986).

LAMAR ALEXANDER, *Steps Along the Way: A Governor's Scrapbook* (Thomas Nelson Publishers, 1986).

ROBERT D. BEHN, ed., *Governors on Governing* (University Press of America, 1991).

THAD L. BEYLE and LYNN R. MUCHMORE, eds., *Being Governor: Views from the Office* (Duke University Press, 1983).

THAD L. BEYLE, ed., *Governors and Hard Times* (Congressional Quarterly Press, 1992).

THOMAS H. KEAN, *The Politics of Inclusion* (Free Press, 1988).

ROBERT S. MCELVAINE, *Mario Cuomo: A Biography* (Scribner's, 1988).

CELIA MORRIS, *Storming the Statehouse: Running for Governor—with Ann Richards and Diane Feinstein* (Scribners, 1992).

DAVID OSBORNE, *Laboratories of Democracy: A New Breed of Governor Creates Models for National Growth* (Harvard Business School Press, 1988).

ALAN ROSENTHAL, *Governors and Legislatures: Contending Powers* (CQ Press, 1990).

LYNNE M. ROSS, ed., *State Attorneys General: Powers and Responsibilities* (Bureau of National Affairs, 1990).

LARRY SABATO, *Goodbye to Good-Time Charlie: The American Governor Transformed,* 2d ed. (Congressional Quarterly Press, 1983).

ROBERT VAUGHAN et al. *The Wealth of States: Policies for a Dynamic Economy* (Council of State Planning Advisers, 1984).

See also various special issues of the quarterly *State Government.*

The National Governors' Association publishes a variety of surveys, reports, and studies including a weekly *Governors' Bulletin* and the *Proceedings of the National Governors' Association* annual meetings. These and related documents can be purchased by writing to the National Governors' Association, 444 N. Capitol Street, NW, Washington, D.C. 20001.

Notes

1. This story is adapted from Robert S. McElvaine, *Mario Cuomo: A Biography* (Scribner's, 1988), pp. 337–38. See also the assessment of Governor Pete Wilson's turbulent first years as governor of California in Robert Reinhold, "The Curse of the Statehouse," *The New York Times Magazine,* May 3, 1992, pp. 27–28, 54, and 58–59.

2. Three of the best general treatments of governors are Thad Beyle and Lynn Muchmore, eds., *Being Governor: Views from the Office* (Duke University Press, 1983); Coleman Ransone, Jr., *The American Governorship* (Greenwood,

1982); and Larry Sabato, *Goodbye to Good-Time Charlie: The American Governor Transformed,* 2d ed. (Congressional Quarterly Press, 1983).

3. See Keith J. Mueller, "Explaining Variation and Change in Gubernatorial Powers, 1960–1982," *Western Political Quarterly* (September 1985), pp. 424–31.

4. Fred Branfman and Nancy Stefanik, "Who Says Raising Taxes Is Political Suicide?" *Washington Post National Weekly Edition,* February 13–19, 1989, p. 24. See also the excellent case studies of governors in Michigan, Massachusetts, Penn-

sylvania, Arizona, and elsewhere who pushed through economic development programs in the 1980s in David Osborne, *Laboratories of Democracy: A New Breed of Governor Creates Models for National Growth* (Harvard Business School Press, 1988).

5. See G. Abney and T. P. Lauth, "The Line-Item Veto in the States; An Instrument for Fiscal Restraint or an Instrument for Partisanship?" *Public Administration Review* (May/June 1985), pp. 372–77. See also David C. Nice, "The Item Veto and Expenditure Restraint," *Journal of Politics* (May 1988), pp. 487–99.

6. E. Lee Bernick, "Discovering a Governor's Powers: The Executive Order," *State Government* (Summer 1984), pp. 97–101.

7. *Perpich et al. v. Department of Defense,* 110 L Ed 312 (1990).

8. Thad Beyle, "Governors" in Virginia Gray, et al., eds., *Politics in the American States: A Comparative Analysis* (Scott Foresman, 1990), p. 230.

9. Sara McCally Morehouse, *State Politics, Parties and Policy* (Holt, Rinehart and Winston, 1981); Osborne, *Laboratories of Democracy.*

10. Sabato, *Goodbye to Good-Time Charlie;* McElvaine, *Mario Cuomo.*

11. Martha W. Weinberg, *Managing the State* (MIT Press, 1977), p. 24.

12. Ibid, p. 227. For a study of a charismatic state bureaucrat who achieved notable independence from several governors as well as from the state legislature in New York, see Robert A. Caro, *The Power Broker: Robert Moses and the Fall of New York* (Knopf, 1974). See also *Governing*

the *American States: A Handbook for New Governors* (National Governors' Association, 1978).

13. See, for example, Lynn Muchmore and Harley Duncan, "The Kansas Balanced Base Budget System," *State Government* (Summer 1982), pp. 106–09.

14. For some general observations on the patterns of state reorganization, see James L. Garnett, *Reorganizing State Government: The Executive Branch* (Westview, 1980). See also Donald C. Stone, "Orchestrating Governor's Executive Management," *State Government* (Spring 1985), pp. 33–39, for a look at the growing staffs that work with governors.

15. Gail B. Manning and Edward F. Feigenbaum, eds., *The Lieutenant Governor: The Office and Its Powers* (Council of State Governments, 1987). See also Kathleen Sylvester, "Lieutenant Governors: Giving up Real Power for Real Opportunity," *Governing* (February 1989), pp. 44–50.

16. Sabato, *Goodbye to Good-Time Charlie,* p. 74. See also Eugene Declerq and John Kaminski, "A New Look at the Office of Lieutenant Governor," *Public Administration Review* (May/June 1978), pp. 256–61.

17. David B. Magleby, *Direct Legislation: Voting on Ballot Propositions in the United States* (Johns Hopkins University Press, 1984), p. 85.

18. Alexander, *Steps along the Way,* p. 141.

19. Thomas H. Kean, *The Politics of Inclusion* (Free Press, 1988), p. 248.

20. Scott Matheson with James Edwin Kee, *Out of Balance* (Peregrine Smith Books, 1986), p. 186.

Judges and Justice in the States

D o you know the name of the chief justice of your state supreme court? Probably not. You should, but you are not alone—about 99 percent of your fellow citizens don't either. Although you hear more about the activities of federal judges than about their state counterparts, the 28,000 state and municipal judges conduct most of the nation's judicial business. They preside over most criminal trials, settle most lawsuits between individuals, and administer most estates. Further, they interpret state laws and play a vital role in determining who gets what, where, when, and how. Thus they have a crucial role in making public policy.

State judges have the final say—most of the time. Through **writs of habeas corpus**—petitions to federal courts alleging that petitioners are being held by a state as the result of a proceeding that denies them due process of law in violation of the U.S. Constitution—criminal defendants may occasionally get federal district judges to review the actions of state courts. And if, in disposing of a case, state judges have to interpret the meaning of the U.S. Constitution, a national law, or a national treaty—that is, if the case raises a *federal question*—the losing party may request the U.S. Supreme Court to review the decision of the highest state court to which it may be taken under state law. Of the hundreds of thousands of decisions decided by state judges each year, however, only a handful reach the Supreme Court.

In recent decades state courts have become even more prominent in the political life of their state. In addition to the **new judicial federalism**, in which state judges have started to apply their own state constitution more rigorously, especially the provisions of the bill of rights in that constitution, there also has been a revolution in state **tort law,** the law relating to noncontractual injuries to person, reputation, or property. This revolution has opened state courts to more people to sue more often about more disputes: product liability suits, for example, brought by people who believe they have been injured as the result of faulty products, and malpractice suits brought by people who believe they have been injured as the result of faulty action by doctors, hospitals, lawyers, and other professionals. As state courts have become more active, state judges have become embroiled in controversial issues and have antagonized substantial interests. And as the public has grown sophisticated about the importance of judges as policy makers, judicial politics have become a significant feature of the political landscape.

The Structure of State Courts

Each state has its own court system. Because the fifty systems vary, it is difficult to generalize about them.[1] For convenience we categorize and discuss state courts as follows: minor courts of limited jurisdiction, trial courts of general jurisdiction, and appellate courts (see Figure 7-1).

MINOR COURTS

Minor courts handle misdemeanors, the less serious violations of state and local laws, traffic cases, and civil suits involving relatively small amounts of money. In some places they also hold preliminary hearings and set bail for more serious charges. Decisions of these courts may be appealed and in most instances tried *de novo*, that is, tried all over again without reference to what happened in the minor court. In most places these courts are financed and administered by the local unit of government: the township, the city, or the county.

In cities, these minor courts are known as municipal courts and are often divided into traffic courts, domestic relations courts, small claims courts, and police courts. Paid magistrates trained in the law preside over most of these courts.

In a few states, especially in rural areas, the justice of the peace system still survives. Justices of the peace are elected for short terms. They need not be trained in the law, and they usually serve from two to six years. Their authority is limited to performing marriages, notarizing papers, handling traffic violations, and hearing misdemeanors—usually those involving fines of less than $200. They also hear minor civil disputes. Because plaintiffs often can choose among several justices of the peace in a county, they may pick the one most likely to decide in their favor. Thus it has been said that JP stands for "Judgment for the Plaintiff."

The traditional justice of peace courts are being phased out. Since 1974 in

FIGURE 7-1   The Structure of State Courts

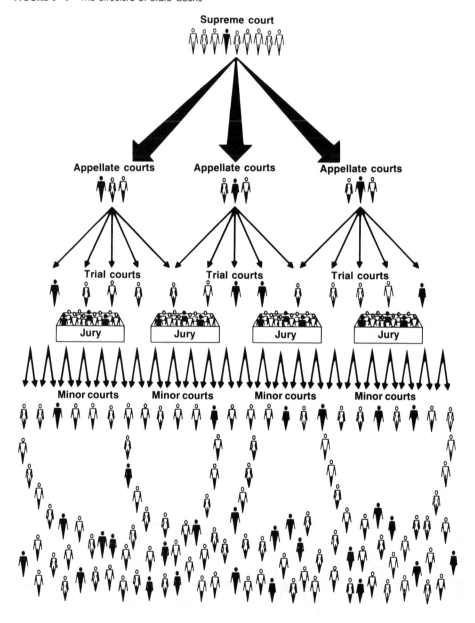

California, for example, all judges of these courts have had to be lawyers. Beginning in 1990 they have had to cease practicing law and to become "certified" by the chief justice of the California Supreme Court. Their courts are now *courts of record* (in contrast to courts where proceedings are ignored in case of appeals) whose orders are entitled to the same recognition as any other court. Almost all of the justices of the peace work on assignment in municipal courts, and the number of justice courts has dropped from 360 in 1974 to 53.[2]

Courts handling "minor crimes"—night courts, police courts—are often so crowded that cases are "processed" with little time for individual attention. While many critics of the legal system contend that judges are too lenient and those accused of crime are "back on the streets" too quickly, others charge that poor and ignorant defendants often spend days in jail waiting for their cases to come to trial.

A new and apparently effective reform is the establishment of "court-watching" groups. In some cities these groups are sponsored by organizations concerned with seeing that the courts treat those charged with crimes fairly. In other cities the groups are sponsored by organizations concerned that judges may be too easy on defendants. Prosecutors, public defenders, and judges, it is alleged, too often become a comfortable work group, with little or no public scrutiny. Court watchers make these professionals more sensitive to the views of the general public.

TRIAL COURTS OF GENERAL JURISDICTION

Trial courts where cases first appear *(original jurisdiction)* are called county courts, circuit courts, superior courts, district courts, and common pleas courts. They administer common, criminal, equity, and statutory law. Some states maintain separate courts for criminal and civil matters. States generally also have special probate courts to administer estates and handle related matters. These courts are courts of record in which trials take place, witnesses are heard, and often juries render verdicts, although most cases are heard and decided by a judge. Decisions of the general trial courts may be reviewed by appellate courts; most decisions of trial judges are not reviewed, however, and become final.

APPELLATE COURTS

In a few states—Mississippi, Montana, Nebraska, Nevada, North Dakota, Rhode Island, West Virginia, and Vermont—appeals from trial courts are carried directly to the state supreme court. Most states, however, have intermediate appeals courts that fit into the system in much the same way that the United States courts of appeals fit into the federal structure.

All states have a court of last resort, a court usually called the supreme court. (In Maine the court of last resort is called the Supreme Judicial Court; in Maryland and New York this court is called the Court of Appeals. And, if that is not confusing enough, in New York the trial courts are called Supreme Courts. Texas has two courts of last resort—a Supreme Court that handles civil matters and a Court of Criminal Appeals; so does Oklahoma.) Unless a federal question is involved, these state supreme courts are the highest tribunal to which a case may be carried. State courts of last resort have from three to nine judges; most have seven. Each state court has developed its own method of operating, with the pattern and practices varying widely among the states. "Also noteworthy is the fact that the rules used in the U.S. Supreme Court have not been adopted by the states."[3]

All state judges of all state courts, trial as well as appellate, take an oath to uphold the supremacy of the U.S. Constitution, and all state judges have the power of judicial review. They may refuse to enforce, and may restrain state and local officials from enforcing, state laws or regulations or actions of any local official or government if they conclude that such laws or regulations or actions conflict with the state constitution or the U.S. Constitution. State judges may also declare actions of federal officials or federal laws or regulations to be in conflict with the U.S. Constitution, subject to final review by the U.S. Supreme Court.

STATE COURTS AND STATE POLITICS

Judges are a much more prominent part of the American political scene than are judges in any other democracy. This is true at both the national and state levels. But state courts play a role somewhat different from that of national courts. Here are the differences:

1. State courts are more deeply and more often involved in the affairs of their legislative and executive branches than the Supreme Court is involved in congressional and presidential matters.[4]

2. State judges are unconstrained by the doctrine of federalism in dealing with local units of government.

3. State judges are much less constrained than federal courts from hearing cases brought by taxpayers. (In federal courts persons lack *standing to sue* —the legal right to sue—if they are objecting to the actions of a government merely because they are taxpayers. They must show some more immediate injury.) In fact, in nine states the state supreme court can set aside the case or controversy requirement and give **advisory opinions** at the request of the governor or state legislature. An advisory opinion is an opinion unrelated to a particular case that gives a court's view about a constitutional or legal issue.

4. State judges feel much less need than do most federal judges to exercise restraint or to argue that they are doing so. Unlike federal judges, most state judges are subject to direct political accountability. In most states judges

serve for limited terms and stand for election, so they too can claim to be representatives of the people. "As elected representatives, like legislators, they feel less hesitant to offer their policy views than do appointed judges."[5] In addition, if there is dissatisfaction with a decision of a state supreme court, it can be more readily set aside than can a decision of the U.S. Supreme Court. Most state constitutions are much easier to amend than the U.S. Constitution.[6]

What all this amounts to is that "state supreme courts rarely have the last word on state law. The people can always claim that prerogative by tossing out the judges, passing a new law, or amending the state constitution to correct a judicial misstep."[7] "A California judge once said that he never forgot there was a crocodile in our baththub."[8]

How Judges Are Chosen

Judges are selected in four different ways (see Figure 7-2):

1. Appointment by the governor
2. Election by the legislature
3. Popular election
4. Modified appointment plan, known as the *Missouri Plan.*

Appointment by the governor, with confirmation by the state senate, is used in Delaware, Maine, and New Jersey, and with confirmation by a council in Massachusetts and New Hampshire. In Delaware and Massachusetts governors have chosen to restrict their appointments to those whose names are submitted to them by judicial nominating commissions. Election by the legislature is the constitutional practice in Connecticut (nominated by the governor from merit selected panel), Rhode Island, South Carolina, and Virginia.

POPULAR ELECTION

Judges are chosen by popular election in nearly half the states, some of which, mostly in the West and upper Midwest, hold nonpartisan primaries for nominating judicial candidates and elect them on nonpartisan ballots. That a nonpartisan ballot is used does not necessarily mean that political parties are unimportant. In at least half the states holding nonpartisan elections, parties actively campaign on behalf of candidates.[9] Some states try to isolate judicial elections from partisanship by holding them on separate days from other elections. The U.S. Supreme Court sidestepped ruling on a provision of the California constitution forbidding political parties from endorsing or opposing

FIGURE 7-2   Method for Selection of Judges of the Court of Last Resort

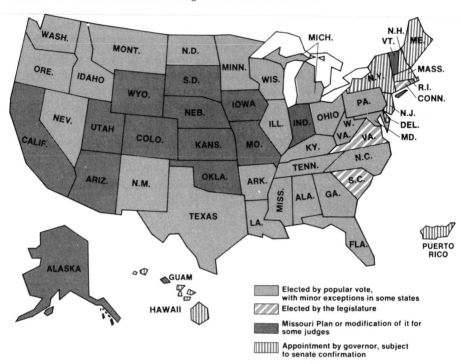

judicial candidates in nonpartisan elections.[10] Such a provision raises First and Fourteenth Amendment issues that the Supreme Court will have to resolve sooner or later.

Most states have adopted provisions similar to the American Bar Association's code of judicial conduct that ban judicial candidates from telling the electorate anything about their views on legal and political matters—whether they are in favor, for example, of harshly punishing criminals or of expanding privacy rights. These provisions are designed to keep future judges from making promises on how they will decide cases. Candidates are beginning to challenge these laws as limiting their constitutional right to speak and restricting the voters' rights to know how candidates stand on legal and political questions.[11]

It is interesting to note that "a majority of the judges serving in states utilizing an elective judiciary . . . are in fact initially appointed by the governor to fill mid-term vacancies, usually occasioned by the retirement or death of sitting judges . . . and these appointed judges are overwhelmingly favored in their first electoral bids following appointment."[12]

Until recently, there was little interest in judicial elections, and voter turnout tended to be low. This lack of attention to judicial politics is beginning to change, and judicial elections are becoming increasingly contested. "More than half the state judges in the United States now face some form of election to either win or retain a seat on the bench."[13] Moreover, the costs of judicial elections are beginning to escalate, and these costs are raising concerns in some states—Texas is a leading example—that judges are put in a compromised position because of the need to raise funds for their campaigns.

Still, most judicial elections attract little attention. Judges have little voter recognition and, especially at the trial level, few voters even know who judicial candidates are and even fewer know what the candidates stand for or how they have performed.[14] Voter interest tends to be higher when judges are part of contested elections on the same partisan ballots as presidents, governors, or senators.

The one-person, one-vote rule (see Chapter 5) that applies to legislative elections does not apply to judicial elections.[15] States may create judicial districts so that one judge "represents" many more voters than another judge. However, although there is no requirement that states elect judges, if they choose to do so, the federal Voting Rights Act of 1965 applies to these judicial elections.[16]

The Voting Rights Act of 1965 forbids any practice or procedure that dilutes the voting power of minorities. When judges are elected *at-large* for a city or a state, African-American and Hispanic candidates sometimes find it difficult to get elected. Because the African-American and Hispanic voters on whom they depend for votes tend to be concentrated in the inner cities or in certain geographic areas, their votes become diluted in citywide or statewide elections. For example, in a state in which the population consists of 20 percent black voters, 20 percent Hispanic voters, and 60 percent white voters, if there are five judges to be elected and all five are elected on a statewide basis, it is unlikely that any black judges or Hispanic judges will be elected. Thus, spokespersons for Hispanics and African Americans argue that the solution is to divide such a state into five districts with one judge elected in each district, and draw the district lines in such a way that African Americans and Hispanics make up a majority of the voters in as many districts as possible, giving them a chance to elect at least one of their own.

Although the Supreme Court has not yet ruled directly on the issue of at-large judicial districts, it did hold in a 1991 case that the Voting Rights Act applies to judicial elections and thereby called into question the use of at-large elections for the selection of judges. As a result, more African-American and Hispanic judges will likely be serving on state benches in the future.

MERIT SELECTION: THE MISSOURI PLAN

Many lawyers and political scientists have argued in favor of some kind of selection process in which there is a prescreening process before judges are appointed or elected to ensure that only candidates of merit will be considered. One such merit plan is the **Missouri Plan**.[17] The Missouri Plan, as used in most states, provides that whenever a vacancy occurs in a court to which the plan applies, a special nominating commission (usually composed of three lawyers elected by the bar, three citizens appointed by the governor, and the chief justice) nominates three candidates.[18] The governor selects one, who then serves as a judge for at least a year. At the next general election the voters are asked: "Shall Judge X be retained in office?" If a majority of the voters agree, the judge serves a full new term (typically six to twelve years); if not, another person is selected by the same procedure. At the end of his or her term, the judge certifies a wish to have his or her name placed on the ballot, and the voters are again asked whether they want to retain that judge in office.[19] These uncontested elections, in which a judge runs against his or her own record, are called *retention elections.*

In California the governor makes the initial selection with the approval of a commission instead of choosing among names submitted by a special nominating commission. After a period of service the judge runs in the next general election against his or her own record. Because of this modification of the Missouri Plan (in fact, California adopted its system first), some observers classify the California Plan as a separate entity.

Even more of a hybrid is the system used in New Mexico, where a judicial nominating commission sends names to the governor, who selects a judge. Then at the next general election the judge so selected may be challenged in a partisan election by an opponent nominated in the other party's primary. If no opponent is nominated, the incumbent gets a "free ride." Whoever wins that election then serves one term and thereafter runs against his or her own record in a retention election.[20]

Most voters know very little about judges, and what information they get comes from interested parties, especially those who dislike what the judges have done. To provide a more balanced picture, a few states have tried to supply more neutral information about judicial performance. In Colorado an evaluation committee in each judicial district disseminates information through newspaper supplements. In Alaska a Judicial Council, composed of three lawyers, three nonlawyers, and the chief justice, provides information that is widely publicized.[21]

Retention elections usually generate little interest and low voter turnout.[22] In all, less than one hundred judges out of more than two thousand have been removed as the result of retention elections. Occasionally state supreme court judges are vigorously challenged in retention elections, especially when their decisions vary appreciably from the mainstream of public opinion and arouse the hostility of significant special interests. In 1985 Justice Hans A. Linde of the Oregon Supreme Court, advocate for an active role for state supreme courts in applying state constitutions to protect civil liberties, retained his seat in a close election against a vigorous challenge that he was "soft on crime." As one observer commented, "You can take the opposing candidate out of elections, but you can't take the elections out of the political arena."[23]

The 1986 retention election for Chief Justice Rose Elizabeth Bird and two of her associate justices of the California Supreme Court rivaled the gubernatorial election in terms of public interest and dollars spent. In fact, the Bird retention election was very much an issue in the gubernatorial contest between Republican George Deukmejian and Democrat Tom Bradley. Under Bird's leadership, it was alleged, the California Supreme Court had failed to apply the death penalty provisions of the California constitution; it was also alleged that Bird had allowed her own personal values to override her obligations as a judge. Her defenders argued that the attack upon her undermined the integrity of the courts, compromised judicial independence, and made judges too responsive to public opinion. She and two associate justices were defeated.[24] As a result, the governor appointed more conservative justices, and the California Supreme Court has taken a more conservative stance.

THE APPOINTIVE VERSUS THE ELECTIVE SYSTEM

For two hundred years people have debated the merits of an appointive versus an elective system for the selection of judges. Those who favor the appointive method contend voters are uninformed about candidates and are not competent to assess legal learning and judicial abilities. Popular election, they assert, puts a premium on personality, requires judges to enter the political arena, and discourages many able lawyers from running for office. Finding the entire system irrational, one candidate for judicial office wrote, "I got used to people saying they would vote for me because 'you look like a judge.' " He stated: "There are ordinarily almost no issues in a judicial campaign upon which one can take a stand, and fewer still that strike any real sparks." In a community of any size, "there is no way for a judicial candidate to communicate relevantly with the electorate. This circumstance alone renders fraudulent the suggestions that judges are popularly elected: substitute 'blindly' for 'popularly.' "[25] Because of the lack of issues in some states, what counts is a popular name. In Ohio, for example, "Browns have run against Browns (in one Supreme Court race three Browns were running) and O'Neills against O'Neills."[26] Most voters, they say, have so little information about the merits of the candidates that judges who have names that get mixed up with popular radio or television personalities or with some prominent public official often get elected.

Proponents of the appointive system also contend that the elective process conceals what is really going on. Absent name recognition, voters go for party labels, which are increasingly less significant as indicators of ideology.[27] In fact, because many vacancies are created when a sitting judge retires or dies, it is often the governor who selects the judges. The governor makes an interim appointment who serves until the next election, and this individual usually wins the election.

What are the arguments of those who oppose the appointive system and favor the elective method? Judges, they argue, should be directly accountable to the people; when judges are appointed they are apt to lose touch with the general currents of opinion of the electorate. Moreover, the appointive process gives governors too much power over judges. And even if judicial elections do not result in the defeat of many sitting judges, the elections serve to foster accountability because judges do not want to be defeated and will try to maintain popular support.

Interest in reforming the system for selection of state judges is once again heating up. Recent Texas elections for supreme court justices have triggered debate over the propriety of judicial candidates taking so much money from so few people. In 1988 more than $7 million was spent by judicial candidates for six of the nine seats on the state supreme court; most of it was contributed by a small group of lawyers.[28] Pennsylvania is another state in which allegations of special interests buying favoritism through campaign donations to judicial candidates have stirred up pressures for adoption of the Missouri Plan.[29] In general, bar associations, corporate law firms, and judges tend to favor some kind of merit selection system, while plaintiffs, attorneys, women's associations, minority associations, and labor groups are skeptical or opposed. In many states that continue to elect judges, it is increasingly clear that judicial candidates are dependent on a small number of law firms or special interests for their campaign funds. This situation encourages pressure for "reforming" the judicial selection process in those states.

Which system produces better judges?[30] The first problem is to define a "good judge." Most people define a good judge as one who makes decisions they like. Even when we describe desirable features more precisely—the ability to maintain neutrality between parties, a knowledge of the law, writing ability, personal integrity, physical and mental health, and the ability to handle judicial power sensibly—we are naming factors that are hard to measure.[31]

Are judges selected by one method more likely to make decisions of a certain kind than are judges chosen by other methods? Are judges of greater legal knowledge and probity more likely to be selected by one method rather than by another? These are difficult questions to answer. We do have some studies, but most of them cover a relatively brief period in only a few states.[32] Nevertheless, several tentative conclusions are emerging.

1. Despite the debate about methods, says one scholar, "elected and appointed judicial systems do not differ ... much in their results."[33]

2. Other studies point to judicial elections as working against women and minorities. One study found: "Judicial elections ... have a built-in bias for men. ... Quite simply, few women, blacks, Hispanics, or Asians have the political connections, financial resources, and campaign sophistication to overcome the stereotype that has the blindfolded woman holding the scales of justice, but a white man sitting at the bench dispensing it."[34] Other studies show that "more women are chosen by gubernatorial appointment and merit methods, but that blacks fare as well in judicial elections and nearly as well in legislative." Another study found that "merit systems

tend to produce higher proportions of Protestant judges" in contrast to Catholic and Jewish judges.[35] Variations between the two systems are extremely small, however (see Figure 7-3), and "there is some question whether these variations are statistically significant."[36]

3. The Missouri Plan has not eliminated partisan politics in the selection of judges, but it has altered the nature of such politics. It has "taken the partisan aspects of judicial selection out of . . . local [politics] . . . and projected them into the political world of the highest public official in the state."[37]

4. There appears to be no difference between the kinds of decisions made by judges selected through merit selection plans such as the Missouri Plan and those made by judges elected to office.

5. Democratic judges tend to make more liberal decisions than their Republican colleagues do.[38]

6. Courts to which judges are nominated and elected on a nonpartisan ballot show less partisan division than those whose judges are nominated by party conventions and elected in partisan elections.

7. State court judges, compared with those of the U.S. Supreme Court, tend to reach unanimous decisions. This phenomenon appears to be unrelated to the matter of judicial selection, although there is a slight tendency for elective judiciaries to have a larger number of dissents than appointive ones.[39]

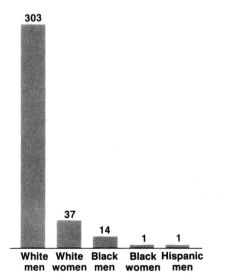

FIGURE 7-3
Race and Sex of the 356 Judges Who Sit on the Highest Courts of the 50 States
Source: National Center for State Courts, Williamsburg, Virginia.

HOW JUDGES ARE JUDGED

Unlike federal judges, who hold office during "good behavior," most state judges are selected for fixed terms, typically six to twelve years. In Massachusetts, New Hampshire, and Puerto Rico, judges serve to age 70; in Rhode Island they serve for life. But it is the states—rather than the national government—that have taken the lead in establishing procedures to judge the judges.

Because impeachment has proved to be an ineffective means to remove judges, today each of the 50 states has a board, commission, or court to handle allegations of judicial misbehavior. Despite the objections of many judges, these commissions are most often composed both of nonlawyers and lawyers. The commissions investigate complaints and hold hearings for judges who have been charged with improper performance of their duties or unethical or unfair conduct. Establishment of these commissions appears to have helped restore public confidence in the state judicial systems.[40]

The Judicial Reform Movement

In 1906, at a meeting of the American Bar Association in St. Paul, Minnesota, Roscoe Pound, a distinguished figure in the legal profession, made a now-famous speech titled "The Cause of Popular Dissatisfaction with the Administration of Justice." Pound spoke about waste, delay, and obsolete procedures, and he inaugurated almost a century of judicial reform.

Many of the reforms Pound proposed—court unification, centralized management, state financing, merit selection—have been adopted, but many of the problems he outlined—waste and delay—continue to plague our courts. The "tort revolution" has encouraged our increasing tendency to sue one another as well as the government. We are, many charge, a "litigious society." Dockets are crowded, relief is costly, and inordinate delays are common. A group of experts trying to predict the future of state court systems recently concluded, "An all-

"We all make mistakes, as Your Honor knows, having been twice reprimanded by the New York State Commission on Judicial Conduct."

Drawing by Stevenson; © 1981 The New Yorker Magazine, Inc.

pervasive preoccupation with drug and criminal case overload dulls optimism about the courts' ability to plan their futures," and "Access to the courts is narrowing for most Americans."[41]

Although there is a "dissolution of the scholarly consensus about their efficacy,"[42] some of the reforms frequently urged by those concerned with improving the administration of justice include:

1. Judges should be selected by some kind of system, such as the Missouri Plan, that screens candidates in terms of their qualifications.

2. Judges should be paid adequately so that they have the financial independence to concentrate on their work and so that successful lawyers will be willing to serve on the bench. In most states judges' salaries are considerably less than the average incomes of the practicing attorneys of the same age and experience. Judges are unable to earn anything beyond their salaries. They must be cautious about investments in order to avoid conflicts of interest.

3. Judges should serve for long terms. The arguments here are much the same as those for tenure for college professors: Judges should be able to make decisions without fear of losing their jobs. Although only a few constitutional changes have extended judicial terms, actual tenure for judges is often longer than it might appear from looking at constitutional provisions. Incumbent judges are ordinarily reelected. And some state constitutions have been amended to ensure that sitting judges merely run against their own records, which in effect gives them longer terms.

4. Alternative methods to decide disputes—such as neighborhood justice centers and arbitration and mediation forums—should be established. Through the Dispute Resolution Act of 1979, Congress has encouraged states and localities to develop *alternative dispute resolution mechanisms* (ADRs) especially for domestic relations issues. Half the states are operating arbitration programs as part of their court system. Mediation, pretrial settlements, and medical malpractice panels are available in many states. And despite the trendy nickname of "rent-a-judge," the rather old practice of hiring private decision makers is being revived. These decision makers are paid by the parties to the dispute, who agree in advance to abide by the outcome. In some states these decisions can be reviewed by appeals courts.[43]

5. Rule-making powers should be given to the state supreme court or its chief justice. More and more states are permitting judges to adopt rules relating to procedural matters and codes of professional conduct. Some rules even require lawyers to continue their education by taking refresher courses.

6. Although no person should be appointed or elected to a court solely because of race or sex or ethnic background, our courts need to be more representative of the communities they serve.[44]

The judicial reform movement has been successful, but, like most reform movements, it has its critics and skeptics. Some observers suggest that court delay is not as serious a problem as has been charged and that the remedies adopted may undercut our checks and balances system.[45] However one feels about the merits of the proposed reforms, clearly the problems at which they are aimed will require more than procedural changes. Delay, for example, often works to the advantage of defendants and their attorneys who wish to postpone trials. At other times prosecutors want delays in order to put pressure on defendants to accept guilty pleas. Lawyers may seek delays so that they can accept more clients and make more money. Further, no matter how modernized the management of court business, the flow of legal business grows continuously. And this increase leads to another, somewhat more controversial, recommendation.

Some people propose that traffic violations, automobile injury cases, and so-called "victimless crimes" should be handled by some procedure other than court trial. New York has led the way in removing from the courts minor traffic offenses that do not involve serious moving violations; other states are following this lead. No-fault insurance programs could reduce the large number of cases stemming from automobile accidents. As half the people in prison, as well as half the trials that are held, involve victimless crimes such as using marijuana, "decriminalization" would substantially reduce the load on the courts. Six states, for example, have already repealed statutes on public drunkenness and now consider alcoholism a disease rather than a crime.

The reform of state judicial systems is enmeshed in partisan, ideological, and issue politics. Moreover, judges are but one part of the total justice system. Their operations are best studied in the context of the entire system.

The Justice System

Justice is handled in the United States by a whole series of institutions that are only loosely connected to each other. In addition to judges there are juries, prosecutors, defense counsel and public defenders, victims and defendants. Parole, probation, and prison officials are also part of the justice system and a variety of means have been developed for managing those who plead guilty or are judged guilty.

THE JURY

Although most of us will never be judges or serve as professionals in the administration of justice, all adult citizens have an opportunity—even an obligation—to be jurors. Trial by jury in civil disputes is used less often these days; people either make settlements prior to trial or elect to have their cases decided by a judge alone or referred to a mediator or arbitrator. Furthermore, only a small fraction of criminal cases are actually disposed of by a trial before a jury.

WHAT YOU SEE DEPENDS ON WHERE YOU SIT,
OR THINGS ARE ALWAYS MORE COMPLICATED THAN THEY LOOK

Consider this chilling story:

A twenty-two year old male is arrested for burglary and assault with a deadly weapon, both felony offenses carrying maximum penalties of ten or more years. At arraignment the judge notes that the accused has a prior record. . . . He sets bail at $10,000. Unable to afford a bondsman's fee, the accused is sent to the county jail. Two months later the judge reduces the bond to $2500, and relatives of the accused scrape together the money. Three months and six court appearances later, he pleads guilty to a single count of criminal trespass . . . and receives a five-month sentence with two months credited for time served in pretrial custody.

Everyone involved agrees that this case is troubling.

The arresting officer . . . will point to the reduced bail and light sentence as evidence that the courts do not care.

The public defender . . . will point out that his client, presumed to be innocent until proven guilty, spent two months in jail solely because he is poor. . . .

The defendant's family is distraught because of the financial hardship. . . .

The prosecutor . . . is frustrated because she could not locate one key witness.

The judge is irritated because the case appeared on his calendar eight times before it was . . . resolved. . . .

After several trips to court, the proprietor of the burglarized store feels twice victimized—not only did he lose money during the robbery, but he has now lost money every time he left his store in order to appear in court.

The one available witness . . . is indignant at the lack of respect accorded her by the prosecutor. . . .

The defendant claims that, finding the door to the drugstore open, he entered to see if anything was wrong. He might conclude that he got off easy or that [the public defender] had sold him down the river.

A first-time observer in the courtroom would not have understood what was going on. But, noting that the accused was black and that all those in a position to affect his fate were white, he might have drawn a conclusion of race discrimination.

No one is satisfied.

Let us again consider the case. Although the accused was charged with possession of a deadly weapon, the police were not able to produce a gun. The only *evidence* about the gun is the statement by the (witness) who claimed to have seen and been hit by it when she encountered the accused in the doorway to the drugstore. . . . The police report . . . states that the [witness] . . . refused medical treatment and "seemed intoxicated." [Furthermore,] some details changed each time she recounted the incident. . . . Although the proprietor . . . reported the loss of several cameras and transistor radios, in addition to cash, the accused was quickly caught based on the witness's identification. One of the items listed was never recorded, and the money involved was not large or identifiable. . . .

Was the court lenient? Although the defendant had a history of prior arrest, he had only two convictions, both on breach of peace, and had never done time. . . .

Five months is above average for trespass cases. Harsh? Frustrated by reports of the failure of probation, drug and alcohol treatment programs, the judge feels he has no option other than to put the offender behind bars. But aware that violence and sexual abuse were commonplace in state prisons and impressed that the offender's family had stood beside him, the judge hopes that he will be safer in the local jail and that he will be better able to maintain ties with his family. Still, the judge, ambivalent about the sentence, expresses hope that the offender may be eligible for daytime work release after a month or so, unaware that this program has been eliminated in recent budget cuts.

Source: Condensed from Malcolm M. Feeley, *Court Reform on Trial* (Twentieth Century Fund, 1983). Copyright © 1983 Twentieth Century Fund, Inc. Reprinted by permission.

Still, jury trials, and the threat of them, remain a key feature of our justice system.[46]

We have moved from a jury system in which service was restricted to white male property owners to one in which jury duty is the responsibility of all adult citizens. Today more time and energy are spent in trying to persuade (or coerce) people to serve on juries than in trying to exclude them. Because jury service is time consuming and burdensome, many middle-class professionals and other busy people do their best to avoid serving. Judges are often willing to excuse doctors, nurses, teachers, executives, and other highly skilled persons who plead that their services are needed outside the jury room. As a result, juries are often selected from panels consisting in large part of older people, those who are unemployed or employed in relatively low-paying jobs, single people, and others who are unable to be excused from jury service. Some states have reacted to these problems by making it more difficult to be excused.

Trials by jury take more time than *bench trials* (trials before judges). They also cost more. As a result, some states are using juries of fewer than twelve for many crimes, and a few are permitting verdicts by less than a unanimous vote. The Supreme Court has approved these practices for states, provided the juries consist of at least six persons.[47]

THE PROSECUTOR

As noted, only a handful of those accused of committing a crime actually stand trial. And only 10 to 15 percent of those who are convicted are declared guilty as the result of a formal trial before either a judge or a jury. Most people who go to prison or who have to pay a criminal fine do so because they plead guilty.

"Presiding" over this out-of-courtroom process is the prosecutor. The eighteen thousand prosecutors in the United States are usually county officials, locally elected and subject to little, if any, supervision by state authorities. In Connecticut they are appointed by judges, in the Virgin Islands by the attorney general, and in New Jersey by the governor, with the consent of the state senate. A prosecutor has "more control over life, liberty, and reputation than any other person in America."[48] (Incidentally, the prosecutor is largely an American invention, one of the few governmental positions we did not inherit from England. To this day, the administration of criminal justice in Britain is based on the theory of private prosecution of criminals.)

When presented with a case by the police, the prosecutor must decide first whether to file formal charges. He or she may: (1) divert the matter out of the criminal justice system and turn it over to a social welfare agency; (2) dismiss the charges; (3) take the matter before a grand jury, which almost always follows the prosecutor's recommendation; (4) in most jurisdictions file an **information affidavit,** which serves the same function as a grand jury indictment.

The decision to charge or not to charge is "well nigh unreviewable in theory and even less reviewed in practice."[49] Of course, there may be political consequences. A prosecutor who decides not to charge a person accused of some notorious crime is likely to be subject to political pressure and public criticism. But for routine crimes the prosecutor is politically in a better position to dismiss a charge than are the police. Police are supposed to enforce every law all the time. Of course, it is impossible for them to do so, and they must exercise discretion. But officers who fail to arrest a person alleged to have committed a crime could well be charged with failing in their duty. The prosecutor, however, has more leeway. In fact, the prosecutor is less likely to be criticized for dropping a case because of insufficient evidence than for filing a charge and failing to get a conviction.

DEFENSE COUNSEL, PUBLIC DEFENDERS, AND OTHERS

Many defendants cannot afford the legal counsel to which they are constitutionally entitled. The **assigned counsel system** is the oldest system to provide such defendants with counsel, and it continues to be used, especially in rural areas. Judges appoint attorneys to help defendants who cannot afford them. Sometimes such attorneys are paid from the public treasury, but other times they are not. They are expected instead to do the work *pro bono*—for the public good. Seldom are they given funds to do any investigatory work on behalf of their clients. Often judges pick young lawyers just beginning their careers or old ones about to retire. Some less scrupulous lawyers make their living as assigned counsel and are quick to plead their clients guilty. They are known contemptuously as members of the "copout bar."[50] After looking at the assigned counsel system, one writer concluded, "It results in incompetence being more the rule than the exception."[51]

Dissatisfaction with the assigned counsel system has led to the creation of the **public defender** system, first started in Los Angeles in 1914 and now used in most big cities. Under this system the government provides a staff of lawyers whose full-time job is to defend those who cannot pay. The system provides experienced counsel and relieves the bar of an onerous duty. Critics—including some defendants—protest that because public defenders are paid employees of the state, they are not likely to work as diligently on behalf of their clients as they would if they were specifically assigned to them. But most observers consider the defender system superior to the assigned counsel method. Steps are being taken to increase the pay of public defenders, protect their independence, and see that they win the confidence of those they represent. Washington, D.C.; Seattle, Washington; and Contra Costa County, California, have especially strong public defender programs.

VICTIMS AND DEFENDANTS

When we talk about our criminal justice system, we sometimes get so carried away with abstractions that we forget that the two most important parties in any criminal case are not the prosecutor and the defense attorney but the victim of the crime and those accused of it.

We The People

Equal Justice?

• In the late 1980s, blacks (about 12 percent of the U.S. population) made up:

28 percent of all those arrested for crimes

47 percent of all prisoners in state correctional facilities

31 percent of all prisoners in federal correctional facilities.

• Since the 1930s, more than half of the 3,800 prisoners executed in the United States have been black, including nearly 90 percent of those executed for rape.

Perceptions of Justice

	Percent Agreeing	
	Black	White
Blacks are treated less than equally by the justice system	80%	35%
Blacks are treated less than equally in:		
Arresting	72	44
Setting bail	52	24
Charging	71	36
Plea bargaining	53	28
Conviction	68	32
Sentencing	67	31
Granting parole	53	25

Victims of Crime

	Black	White
Rates per 1,000 persons age 12 and over		
Robbery	8.6	4.6
Assault	23.6	22.2
Rape	1.2	0.6
Rates per 1,000 households		
Burglary	91.6	57.5
Larceny	101.7	92.5
Motor vehicle theft	23.7	13.9

Source: Joe R. Feagin and Clairece Booher Feagin, *Social Problems: A Critical Power-Conflict Perspective*, 3d ed. (Prentice Hall, 1990), pp. 282–85. © 1990. Adapted by permission of Prentice Hall, Englewood Cliffs, New Jersey.

In general terms, defendants are likely to be "younger, predominantly male, disproportionately black, less educated, seldom fully employed, and typically unmarried. By the time the sorting process has ended, those sent to prison will consist of an even higher proportion of young, illiterate, black males."[52]

Victims, too—compared to the rest of the population—tend to be young, black or another minority, and uneducated. A substantial number of victims, either because of lack of knowledge or what to do or fear of doing it, never report crimes to police and prosecutors.

Our system puts the responsibility for prosecuting criminals on the government. In most instances victims have no role, perhaps, other than as witnesses. They are not consulted about what the charge should be or asked what they think might be an appropriate penalty. The matter is strictly between the state, represented by the prosecutor, and the accused, represented by an attorney.

Around 1980 the crime victim movement started. Initiated originally by liberals (chiefly feminists concerned about the difficulty of winning prosecutions for rape and about the harsh treatment of women witnesses) the crime victim movement quickly gained the support of conservatives who consider the present system unfair to victims. In the 1984 Victims of Crime Act, Congress authorized federal funds to support state programs compensating victims and provide funds to some victims of federal crimes as well.

More and more states are adopting a "victim's bill of rights." These bills of rights make it easier for victims to recover their stolen property held in police custody. They also give victims a chance to be heard when prosecutors file formal charges, when judges set bail and impose sentences, and when parole boards consider releasing prisoners. These victim's bills of rights are not without their constitutional problems. Yet the U.S. Supreme Court, after first holding to the contrary, has upheld the right of a prosecutor to make statements to a capital sentencing jury regarding the personal qualities of the victim and to allow such a jury to consider "victim impact" evidence relating to the personal characteristics of a murder victim and the emotional impact of the crime on the victim's family.[53]

Almost all states now compensate victims or have strengthened the laws permitting victims and their families to sue for civil damages or have done both.[54] Winning these suits is easier than obtaining convictions. In a civil suit

---

VICTIM'S BILL OF RIGHTS

- Right to return of stolen property held in police custody
- Right to be heard when prosecutors file charges, when judges set bail and impose sentences, and when parole boards consider releasing prisoners
- Right to receive information about one's case
- Right to protection from intimidation
- Right to monetary compensation
- Right to be notified before release of attacker
- Right to participate in plea bargaining
- Right to sue for civil damages

STATE'S ACTION ON VICTIM'S RIGHTS

- 44 states provide victims with information about their cases and protection from intimidation
- 39 states provide monetary compensation for crime victims
- 39 states notify felony victims of the release of their attackers
- 35 states permit victims to offer the judge their opinion about sentencing
- 23 states allow victims to participate in plea bargaining negotiations
- 5 states have ballot proposals for a state constitutional amendment granting rights for victims

one merely has to prove that the accused *more probably than not* committed the act, not that he or she did so *beyond a reasonable doubt*, as in a criminal trial. The problem is that defendants seldom have resources. Even if victims win the right to collect damages from the defendants, they often are unable to do so. As a result, under the stimulus of federal matching funds, most states now provide a victims' compensation program.

PLEA BARGAINING

A common practice is for the prosecution to offer to reduce the seriousness of the charge if a defendant will enter a plea of guilty to a lesser crime. This practice is called **plea bargaining.** In many places "between 95 and 99 percent of felony convictions are by plea."[55] At one time this practice was universally condemned. Many people still feel that there is something "dirty" about it, like bartering away justice, and that it leads to "condemnation without adjudication."[56]

Critics argue that plea bargaining forces people to give up their rights; moreover, defendants often do not get off much more leniently for pleading guilty to lesser offenses than if they stood trial.[57] Defenders of plea bargaining contend it works, producing "a result approximating closely, but informally and more swiftly, the results which ought to ensue from a trial, while avoiding most of the undesirable aspects of that ordeal."[58] Many—but not all—of the several commissions of experts and investigators who have recently looked into the matter have endorsed plea bargaining.

Plea bargaining offers something to all those involved. Prosecutors are able to dispose of cases quickly, avoid long and drawn-out trials, eliminate the risk of losing cases, and build up better "election-worthy" conviction records. Those who are accused, by pleading guilty to lesser offenses, avoid the danger of being sentenced for more serious charges. Defense attorneys avoid "the dilemma of either incurring the expense of going to trial with a losing case or appearing to provide no service whatever to their clients."[59] By being able to handle more clients, they can also make more money. Judges are able to dispose of cases on their dockets more easily.

Once the bargain between the prosecutor and the defendant's attorney has been accepted, the matter is taken before a judge. The judge goes through a series of questions to the defendant: "Are you pleading guilty because you are guilty? Are you aware of the maximum sentence for the crime to which you are entering a guilty plea? Were you coerced into pleading guilty or offered anything in return for it? Are you satisfied with the representation afforded by your attorney?" Following appropriate responses, the plea is accepted.[60] As long as defendants know what they are doing and enter into the bargain intelligently, by pleading guilty they waive their constitutional rights to trial and may not subsequently back out of the arrangement. Prosecutors also must live up to their side of the bargain.[61]

TRADITIONAL JUSTIFICATIONS FOR IMPRISONMENT

1. *Retribution.* Society is entitled to punish those who commit crimes, and if the state does not do so, people will be tempted to take the matter into their own hands.

2. *Deterrence.* Putting those who commit crimes in prison warns others and keeps some who might otherwise violate the law from doing so.

3. *Protection of society through incapacitation.* Some persons are so dangerous to the life and property of others that the only thing to do with them is to lock them in prison.

4. *Rehabilitation.* By placing convicted persons in a protected and controlled environment, we can work to rehabilitate them so that they will eventually become law-abiding and productive citizens.

SENTENCING

Due process must be observed in sentencing, which takes place in open court. The prisoner must be present and represented by counsel. In many places, social workers are assigned to help the judge determine the proper sentence. The judge also receives recommendations from the prosecution (and in some jurisdictions from the victim as well), hears the arguments of the defense, and then sets the sentence within the limits prescribed by the state.

The judge sets the sentence, but concerns about sentencing permeate the judicial system. One writer has put it this way:

> Because police and prosecutors screen out a large proportion of the doubtful cases, most left to be dealt with by the courts are those in which there is no serious dispute over the guilt or innocence of the defendant. . . . This fact sets the tone for the process. . . . Everyone concerned—the defense lawyers, the prosecutor, the judge, the probation officer—becomes aware of the fact that he or she is involved in a process where the primary focus is on deciding what to do with the people who are in fact guilty.[62]

Early in our national history, retribution, deterrence, and protection of society were the primary purposes of sentencing. Then rehabilitation became the major goal and many thought it was a more humane approach. The indefinite sentence became popular, motivated by the idea that each prisoner should be considered an individual suffering from an "illness." Each prisoner should be diagnosed; a course of treatment should be prescribed; and if and when a "cure" is certified by such experts as psychologists and social workers, the prisoner should be released.

Recently most political leaders and many scholars have become disillusioned about our ability to effect "cures."[63] Others are also disillusioned about the deterrent effect of imprisonment. A comprehensive study of rehabilitative efforts inside prisons, although rejecting the conclusion that "nothing works," nonetheless stated: "We do not know of any program or method of rehabilitation that could be guaranteed to reduce the criminal activity of released offenders."[64]

This disillusionment with rehabilitation, combined with growing concerns about "crime in the streets" and mounting criticism about alleged judicial leniency, has fueled legislative action for mandatory minimum sentencing requirements and for narrowing judicial discretion.[65] State after state has adopted mandatory prison-term statutes for more and more crimes.

Judicial discretion remains broad, however. Penal codes do not set very specific terms of punishment. Different judges issue different sentences to defendants convicted of the same crime.[66] To reduce such disparities, several reforms have been suggested, including establishing more precise legislative standards, creating advisory sentencing councils, and adopting the British practice of allowing appellate courts to modify sentences.

PROBATION AND PRISONS

Prison populations in the United States are skyrocketing. Today 435,237 guards, probation officials, and parole officers keep custody over close to 2 million persons on probation and over 710,054 people in 800 prisons. Add to this number, those who are serving shorter jail sentences and it numbers millions. (*Prisons* are for committed criminals serving long sentences; *jails* are for short-term stays.) Although the prison population of the United States actually declined during the 1960s, public demands for tougher sentences caused it to climb once again after 1967. It has doubled since 1970 and continues to increase at a rate of 7 percent a year. An expert group estimates that during the five-year period ending in 1994 inmate populations will increase by nearly another 70 percent.[67] It costs $75,000–$100,000 to build each cell, and on average $23,000 a year must be spent to guard and feed each prisoner.[68]

The increase in the prison population has resulted in serious overcrowding. In most states conditions are so bad that in recent years federal judges have issued orders calling for either immediate improvement or the release of persons being held in situations that violate the Eighth Amendment prohibition against cruel and unusual punishment.

Prisoners have very little political clout. Even so, because the overcrowding is so severe and the prison population is growing so fast, most states are responding to judicial intervention by spending millions to build new prisons and renovate old ones. The federal Civil Rights of Institutionalized Persons Act (1980) authorizes the Department of Justice to bring suits in behalf of persons being held under conditions that violate the Constitution, and the department has done so.

Relatively few people commit most of the violent crimes. One out of every three persons let out of prison returns in three years. If we could identify these "career criminals" (**recidivists**) and keep them in prison, while at the same time releasing those offenders who are not likely to commit other crimes, we might be able to cut down on the overcrowding in the prisons and better protect the public. The trouble with this "throw-the-career-criminals-in-jail-for-a-long-time" theory is that it is not easy to determine in advance who are career criminals and who are not. For this reason some argue that requiring every criminal convicted of a second offense to stay in prison for five years would cut down the crime rate by 16 percent. To do this, however, would triple the present prison population and would require billions to build new prisons plus $12 billion more each year to keep the additional prisoners.[69] Some cities and counties have even resorted to "privatization," turning over the responsibility for operating jails to private firms on a contractual basis. More than five thousand prison beds in five states, including two state prisons in Texas, are presently being so managed.[70]

The high cost of corrections, in fact, may lead some states to rethink the wisdom of indiscriminate mandatory minimum sentence statutes and to reconsider the need to create for nonviolent offenders such alternatives as halfway houses, intensive probation, work release programs, and other community corrections facilities, even home confinement, first pioneered in New Mexico in 1983, where prisoners are subject to a variety of monitoring devices.[71] The problem is that these alternative solutions are subject to political attack for being "soft on criminals." Even so, the pressures to find places to hold prisoners is so great that correctional officials believe that these alternative procedures, including home confinement, will become an increasingly important part of the criminal justice system.[72]

Courts in Crisis

The effectiveness of George Bush's attack on Michael Dukakis in the 1988 presidential campaign for his allegedly being "soft on crime" reflects the concern of many Americans that "there has been a breakdown in the criminal justice system in America." A U.S. senator and a former federal prosecutor echo this view. They charge that because courts are "overwhelmed by the huge volume of cases," "career criminals beat the system," defense attorneys "shop" for judges known for lenient sentences, prosecutors are "blackmailed" into accepting lenient plea bargains, and many career criminals "are given only a few months punishment."[73]

Critics agree that the system is in crisis but disagree on what the crisis is. There are at least two general models for thinking about our criminal justice system. The crime control model considers criminals to be "inputs" into the system. If it worked properly, the system would "process" these inputs and produce results. Those who use this model are disturbed when they discover that the elements of the criminal justice system operate with little relation to one another—that it is a "system" more in word than in fact. They are alarmed that the system is "jammed." The due process model, on the other hand, con-

FIGURE 7-4   Crime and Punishment: It Seldom Works That Way

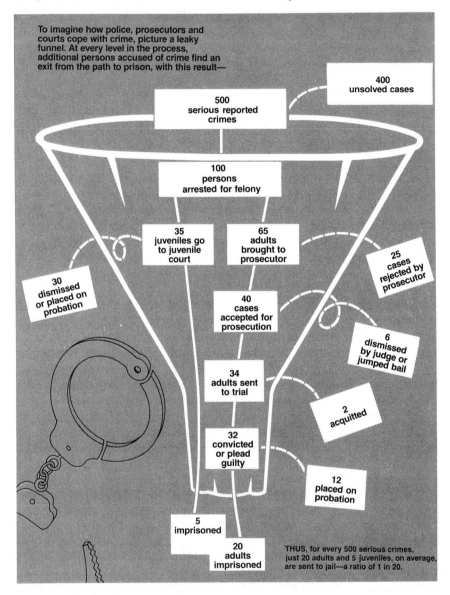

To imagine how police, prosecutors and courts cope with crime, picture a leaky funnel. At every level in the process, additional persons accused of crime find an exit from the path to prison, with this result—

400 unsolved cases

500 serious reported crimes

100 persons arrested for felony

35 juveniles go to juvenile court

65 adults brought to prosecutor

30 dismissed or placed on probation

25 cases rejected by prosecutor

40 cases accepted for prosecution

6 dismissed by judge or jumped bail

34 adults sent to trial

2 acquitted

32 convicted or plead guilty

12 placed on probation

5 imprisoned

20 adults imprisoned

THUS, for every 500 serious crimes, just 20 adults and 5 juveniles, on average, are sent to jail—a ratio of 1 in 20.

siders police, prosecutors, defense attorneys, judges, and correctional officials to be adversaries. Those who use this model tend to be more worried about an innocent person's being convicted or about unfair treatment of the poor and minorities than about the system's not working efficiently. That it takes a long time to dispose of cases is of less concern than that the system might not be just.[74]

Summary

1. State and local judges, prosecutors, juries, and correctional officials, along with the police, are key participants in our system for the administration of justice.

2. State and local courts are also important arenas for the making and carrying out of public policy.

3. For many years state and local courts operated with little public attention and not much public concern. Today, both as agencies for the making of public policy and as instruments for the administration of justice, they are the objects of many studies and the recipients of large sums of money. But the problems are difficult, especially because there is no agreement about what the problems are. As in every other field in which actions have important consequences, change is likely to be made incrementally, and it will come about as the result of the push and pull of political pressure.

4. Judges, together with jurors, prosecutors, and correctional officials, make up a loosely interrelated justice system. Many believe that this system is not properly dispensing justice to individual defendants or protecting the public from career criminals.

For Further Reading

AMERICAN BAR ASSOCIATION, Special Committee on Criminal Justice in a Free Society, *Criminal Justice in Crisis* (American Bar Association, 1988).

AMERICAN JUDICATURE SOCIETY, *Judicature, the Journal of the American Judicature Society*, published monthly.

STEVEN BRILL, *Trial by Jury* (Simon & Schuster, 1989).

GEORGE F. COLE, *The American System of Criminal Justice*, 5th ed. (Brooks/Cole, 1989).

PHILIP J. DUBOIS, *From Bench to Ballot: Judicial Elections and the Quest for Accountability* (University of Texas Press, 1980).

SUSAN P. FINO, *The Role of State Supreme Courts in the New Judicial Federalism* (Greenwood Press, 1987).

HENRY R. GLICK, *Courts, Politics, and Justice* (McGraw-Hill, 1988).

JOSEPH R. GRODIN, *In Pursuit of Justice: Reflections of a State Supreme Court Justice* (University of California Press, 1989).

JOHN GUINTHER, *The Jury in America* (Facts on File Publications, 1988).

RICHARD HAWKINS and GEOFFREY P. ALPERT, *American Prison Systems* (1989).

DAVID HEILBRONE, *Rough Justice: Days and Nights of a Young D.A.* (Pantheon Books, 1990).

HERBERT JACOB, *Justice in America: Courts, Lawyers, and the Judicial Process*, 4th ed. (Little, Brown, 1984).

WALTER K. OLSON, *The Litigation Explosion: What Happened When America Unleashed the Lawsuit* (Dutton, 1991).

G. ALAN TARR and MARY CORNELIA ALDIS PORTER, *State Supreme Courts in State and Nation* (Yale University Press, 1988).

Notes

1. Thomas A. Henderson, Randall Guynes, Carl Baar, and Neal Miller, *The Structural Characteristics of State Judiciaries* (Institute for Economic and Policy Studies, 1981).

2. Jean Guccione, "Justice Court Judges Adjust to New Status," *Los Angeles Daily Journal*, May 6, 1991, p. 1.

3. Melinda Gann Hall, "Opinion Assignment Procedures and Conference Practices in State Supreme Courts," *Judicature* 73 (December 1989/January 1990), p. 209.

4. Robert F. Williams, "In the Supreme Court's Shadow: Legitimacy of State Rejection of Supreme Court Reasoning and Results," *South Carolina Law Review* (Spring 1984), p. 353.

5. Hans A. Linde, "Observations of a State Court Judge," in *Judges and Legislators: Toward Institutional Comity*, ed. Robert A. Katzmann (The Brookings Institution), 1988, p. 118

6. Pete J. Galie, "The Other Supreme Courts: Judicial Activism among State Supreme Courts," *Syracuse Law Review* 33 (1982), pp. 731–93.

7. Elder Witt, "State Supreme Courts: Tilting the Balance toward Change," *Governing*, August 1988, p. 38.

8. Ibid. For similar thoughts of the Chief Justice of the Connecticut Supreme Court, see Ellen A. Peters, "State Supreme Courts in our Evolving Federal System," *Intergovernmental Perspective* 17 (Fall 1991), p. 22.

9. Herbert Jacob, *Justice in America: Courts, Lawyers, and the Judicial Process*, 4th ed. (Little, Brown, 1984).

10. *Renne v. Geary*, 115 L. Ed 2d 288 (1991).

11. Milo Geyelin and Allanna Sullivan, "Limitations on Judicial Campaigns Challenged," *Wall Street Journal*, March 21, 1991, p. B8.

12. Philip L. Dubois, "Sate Trial Court Appointments: Does the Governor Make a Difference?" *Judicature* (June/July 1985), pp. 20–21.

13. Edwin Chen, "For Judges, the Stakes Are Rising," *Los Angeles Times*, March 4, 1988, p. 1.

14. Anthony Champagne and Great Thielemann, "Awareness of Trial Court Judges," *Judicature* 74 (February/March 1991), p. 276.

15. *Wells v. Edwards*, 409 U.S. 1095 (1973).

16. *Chisom v. Roemer*, 115 L. Ed 2d 348 (1991); *Houston Lawyer's Assn. v. Texas Attorney General*, 115 L. Ed 2d 379 (1991). Tracy Thompson,

"The New Front in the Battle for Civil Rights: Judgeships," *Washington Post National Weekly Edition*, December 18–24, 1989, p. 34.

17. J. W. Peltason, *The Missouri Plan for the Selection of Judges* (University of Missouri Studies, 1945). The plan was previously known as the Nonpartisan Plan for the Selection of Judges or the Kales Plan until called the Missouri Plan by this monograph.

18. Beth M. Henschen, Robert Moog, and Steven Davis, "Judicial Nominating Commissioners: A National Profile," *Judicature* 73 (April/May 1990), pp. 328–34.

19. Philip L. Dubois, "The Politics of Innovation in State Courts: The Merit Plan of Judicial Selection," *Publius* 20 (Winter 1990), p. 40.

20. Eric D. Dixon, "A Short History of Judicial Reform in New Mexico," *Judicature* 73 (June/July 1989), pp. 48–50.

21. "The Need for Judicial Performance Evaluations for Retention Elections," *Judicature* 75 (October/November 1991), p. 124.

22. William K. Hall and Larry T. Aspin, "What Twenty Years of Judicial Retention Elections Have Told Us," *Judicature* 70 (April/May 1987), pp. 340–47; also Susan B. Caron and Larry C. Berkson, *Judicial Retention Elections in the United States* (American Judicature Society, 1980).

23. Robert D. Raven, "Does the Bar Have an Obligation to Help Ensure the Independence of the Judiciary?" *Judicature* (August/September 1985), p. 67.

24. John T. Wold and John H. Culver, "The Defeat of the California Justices: The Campaign, the Electorate, and the Issue of Judicial Accountability," *Judicature* 70 (April/May 1987), pp. 324–39.

25. Jon R. Waltz, "Some Firsthand Observations on the Election of Judges," *Judicature* (October 1979), pp. 186–87.

26. G. Alan Tarr and Mary Cornelia Aldis Porter, *State Supreme Courts in State and Nation* (Yale University Press, 1988), p. 170.

27. Champagne and Thielemann, "Awareness of Trial Court Judges," p. 276.

28. Peter Applebome, "Rubber Stamp Is Gone in Texas Judicial Elections," *New York Times*, October 21, 1988, p. B12; Anthony Champagne,

"Judicial Reform in Texas," *Judicature* 72 (October/November 1988), pp. 146-68.

29. Paul M. Barrett, "Campaign Practices in Judges' Elections Spark Drive for Merit Appointments in Pennsylvania," *Wall Street Journal*, December 9, 1988, p. A16.

30. Philip L. Dubois, *From Ballot to Bench: Judicial Elections and the Quest for Accountability* (University of Texas Press, 1980), pp. 27-28.

31. Sheldon Goldman, "Judicial Selection and the Qualities of a 'Good Judge,' " *The Annals of the American Academy of Political and Social Science* (July 1982), pp. 113-14.

32. Mary L. Volcansek, "The Effects of Judicial Selection Reform: What We Know and What We Do Not," in *The Analysis of Judicial Reform*, ed. Philip L. Dubois (Lexington Books, 1982), pp. 78-79.

33. Stuart S. Nagel, *Comparing Elected and Appointed Judicial Systems* (Sage Publications, 1973), p. 36. See also Susan P. Fino, *The Role of State Supreme Courts in the New Judicial Federalism* (Greenwood Press, 1987), p. 114; David W. Allen, "Voting Blocks and the Freshman Justice on State Supreme Courts," *Western Political Quarterly* 44 (September 1991), pp. 726-47.

34. John H. Culver, "Politics and the California Plan for Choosing Appellate Judges," *Judicature* (September/October, 1982), p. 158. See also Henry R. Glick and Craig F. Emmert, "Selection Systems and Judicial Characteristics: The Recruitment of State Supreme Court Judges," *Judicature* 70 (December 1986/January 1987), p. 235.

35. Glick and Emmert, "Selection Systems," p. 235.

36. Ibid., p. 230, summarizing *The Success of Women and Minorities in Achieving Judicial Office: The Selection Process* (Fund for Modern Courts, 1985). See also Nicholas P. Lovrich, Jr., Charles H. Sheldon, and Erick Wasmann, "The Racial Factor in Nonpartisan Judicial Elections," *Western Political Quarterly* 41, (December 1988), pp. 807-11.

37. Richard A. Watson and Rondal G. Downing, *The Politics of the Bench and the Bar: Judicial Selection under the Missouri Nonpartisan Court Plan* (Wiley, 1969), p. 353.

38. See Sheldon Goldman, "Voting Behavior on the U.S. Courts of Appeals Revised," *American Political Science Review* (June 1975), pp. 491-506, for a review of articles on the relationship between partisanship and judicial behavior.

39. Melinda Gann Hall and Paul Brack, "Order in the Courts: A Neo-Institutional Approach to Judicial Consensus," *Western Political Quarterly* 42 (September 1989), p. 403.

40. Jolanta Juskiewicz Peristein and Nathan Goldman, "Judicial Disciplinary Commissions: A New Approach to the Discipline and Removal

of State Judges," in *Analysis of Judical Reform*, ed. Dubois, pp. 93-106.

41. Franklin M. Zweig et al., "Securing the Future for America's State Courts," *Judicature* 73 (April/May 1990), pp. 297-98.

42. Tarr and Porter, *State Supreme Courts*, p. 61.

43. Dixie K. Knoebel, "The State of the Judiciary," *The Book of the States* (Council of State Governments, 1990), p. 197.

44. Beverly Blair Cook, "Women Judges in the Opportunity Structure," in *Women, The Courts and Equality*, ed. Laura L. Crites and Winfred L. Hepperle (Sage Publications, 1987), pp. 143-71.

45. Geoff Gallas, "Court Reform: Has It Been Built on an Adequate Foundation?" *Judicature* (June/July 1979), pp. 29-30; Raymond T. Nimmer, *The Nature of System Change: Reform Impact in the Criminal Courts* (American Bar Foundation, 1978).

46. John Guinther, *The Jury in America* (Facts on File Publications, 1988).

47. *Burch v. Louisiana*, 441 U.S. 130 (1979); *Ballew v. Georgia*, 435 U.S. 223 (1978). See Reid Hastie, Steven D. Penrod, and Nancy Pennington, *Inside the Jury* (Harvard University Press, 1983), for a study showing that nonunanimous verdicts are more likely to bring in convictions than those requiring unanimity. Federal courts often use juries of less than twelve for civil cases. For federal criminal trials the Supreme Court still requires both the common law jury of twelve and unanimous verdicts.

48. Robert H. Jackson, *Journal of the American Judicature Society* (1940), p. 28, quoted in Jack M. Kress, "Progress and Prosecution," *The Annals of the American Academy of Political and Social Science* (January 1976), p. 100.

49. Kress, "Progress and Prosecution," p. 109.

50. Charles E. Silberman, *Criminal Violence, Criminal Justice* (Random House, 1978), p. 303.

51. Ibid.

52. Ibid., p. 218.

53. *Payne v. Tennessee*, 115 L Ed 2d 720 (1991), overruling *Booth v. Maryland*, 482 U.S. 496 (1987) and *South Carolina v. Gathers*, 490 U.S. 805 (1989).

54. Robert Elias, *Victims of the System: Crime Victims and Compensation in American Politics and Criminal Justice* (Transaction Books, 1983); John R. Anderson and Paul L. Woodward, "Victim and Witness Assistance; New State Laws and the System's Response," *Judicature* (December 1984-January 1985), p. 221; Peter Finn, "Collaboration between the Judiciary and Victim-Witness Assistance Programs," *Judicature* (December 1985-January 1986), p. 192.

55. John H. Langbein, "Torture and Plea Bargaining," *Public Interest* (Winter 1980), p. 48. See

also Malcolm M. Feeley, *The Process Is the Punishment* (Russell Sage, 1979).

56. Langbein, "Torture and Plea Bargaining," p. 51.

57. Thomas M. Uhlman and N. Darlene Walker, "A Plea Is No Bargain: The Impact of Case Disposition on Sentencing," *Social Science Quarterly* (September 1979), pp. 218–34.

58. Thomas Church, Jr., "Plea Bargains, Concessions and the Courts: Analysis of a Quasi-Experiment," *Law and Society Review* (Spring 1976), p. 400. For a contrary view, see National Advisory Commission on Criminal Justice Standards and Goals, *Report of the Task Force* (U.S. Government Printing Office, 1979).

59. Church, "Plea Bargains, Concessions and the Courts," p. 400.

60. Jonathan D. Casper, *American Criminal Justice: The Defendant's Perspective* (Prentice Hall, 1972), pp. 52–53. Abraham S. Goldstein, *The Passive Judiciary: Prosecutorial Discretion and the Guilty Plea* (Louisiana State University Press, 1981), is critical of judges for not supervising plea bargains more actively.

61. *Santobello v. New York*, 404 U.S. 257 (1971).

62. Edward Barrett, "The Adversary Proceeding and the Judicial Process," lectures to the National College of State Trial Judges, quoted in Lynn M. Mather, "Some Determinants of the Method of Case Disposition: Decision-Making by Public Defenders in Los Angeles," *Law and Society Review 12* (Winter 1974), pp. 187–88.

63. Henry N. Pontell, *A Capacity to Punish* (Indiana University Press, 1985).

64. Lee Sechrest, Susan O. White, and Elizabeth D. Brown, eds., *The Rehabilitation of Criminal Offenders: Problems and Prospects*, Panel on Research on Rehabilitative Techniques of the National Research Council (National Academy of Sciences, 1979), pp. 3–6.

65. William B. Eldridge, "Shifting Views of the Sentencing Functions," *The Annals of the American Academy of Political and Social Sciences* (July 1982), pp. 104–11.

66. John Hagan and Kristin Bumiler, "Making Sense of Sentencing: A Review and Critique of Sentencing Research," in *Research on Sentencing*, vol. 2, eds. Alfred Blumstein et al. (National Academy Press, 1983); Susan Welch, Michael Combs, John Gruhl, "Do Black Judges Make a Difference?" *American Journal of Political Science* (February 1988), pp. 126–35.

67. National Council on Crime and Delinquency, based in San Francisco, cited in Gary Enos, "Prison Crisis Shackles Governments," *City and State,* May 21, 1990, p. 11.

68. Gail S. Funke, "How Much Justice Can States Afford?" *State Legislatures,* July 1984, pp. 26–27.

69. Edna McConnell Clark Foundation, *Time to Build? The Realities of Prison Construction* (New York, 1985).

70. Gary Enos, "Fortress Mentality Straps Privately Operated Jails," *City and State,* May 21, 1990, p. 11.

71. Barbara Fink, "Opening the Door on Community Corrections," *State Legislatures,* September 1984.

72. Gary Enos, "Despite New Technology, Home Confinement Faces Risks, Public Opposition," *City and State,* May 21, 1990, p. 14.

73. Arlan Specter and Paul R. Michel, "The Need for a New Federalism in Criminal Justice," *The Annals of the American Academy of Political and Social Sciences* (July 1982), pp. 67–69.

74. Herbert Packer, "Two Models of the Criminal Process," *University of Pennsylvania Law Review* (November 1964), pp. 1–60.

8

Local Government and Metropolitics

There are more than 87,000 units of local government in the United States. Illinois alone has over 6,400, Pennsylvania has over 5,300, Texas has nearly 4,200, Rhode Island has 125, and Hawaii has only 19. The average number of units per state is around 1,700 (see Table 8-1). Counties, cities, school districts, townships, water control districts, park districts—all are crowded together and piled on top of one another. The Chicago metropolitan area alone has about 1,000 units of local government. Average citizens live under five or six layers of government. They pay taxes to all of them—federal, state, county, municipal, and others—and they are supposed to help select all of their leaders.

Why do we have such a patchwork of government in this country? The basic pattern was imported from England, as were so many of our governmental forms. As time passed, new governments were created to take on new jobs when the existing units proved either too small or unequal to the task. Also, people kept moving to, or at least near, the large cities, and urbanization began to take hold. Decades of compromise and struggle among conflicting groups have given us our present system. It creaks and groans. It costs a lot of money. It is inefficient. But it is here to stay.

Local governments vary in their structure, size, power, and relation to one another. But in a constitutional sense they are all the same because they all live on power "borrowed" from the states. The states are basically unitary governments; constitutionally, all power is vested in the state governments, and local units exist only as agents of the states and exercise only those powers expressly given to them by their respective state governments.

TABLE 8-1   Number of Governments in the United States

Type of Government	1972	1982	1992
Total	78,269	81,831	86,743
U.S. government	1	1	1
State governments	50	50	50
Local governments	78,218	81,780	86,692
County	3,044	3,041	3,043
Municipal	18,517	19,076	19,296
Township	16,991	16,734	16,666
School district	15,781	14,851	14,556
Special district	23,885	25,078	33,131

Source: U.S. Department of Commerce, Bureau of the Census, 1992 Census of Governments.

Overview of State and Local Relations

How does the *unitary* nature of state-local relations contrast with the *federal* nature of nation-state relations? The slicing up of governmental power among the various local units and the state government leads to many of the same problems we noted in the chapter on federalism. There is the same conflict between groups that want the state to do something and groups that fear an invasion of local rights. There is the same need to share functions among the various units of government as economic and social conditions change. And there are the same disputes over whether a local majority or a statewide majority is to have its way. Yet there is also a crucial difference.

In the beginning state legislatures were given almost unlimited constitutional authority over their local governments, and they ran them pretty much as they wished. They granted, amended, and repealed city charters, established counties, determined city and county structure, set debt limits, and passed laws for the local units. But by the end of the nineteenth century many state constitutions had been amended to forbid their legislatures to pass laws dealing with particular local governments. In place of legislative enactments, constitutional provisions determined the structure, and in some cases even the process, of local governments.

Because local governments are created by the state legislatures and have no constitutional authority in their own right, there are fewer obstacles to state interference in local matters than there are to national interference in state matters. State officers participate in local government to a much greater extent than federal officers do in state politics. When doubts have arisen about the authority of local governments, the courts have generally decided against them.

As in so many areas of politics, the difference between state-local and nation-state relations is one of degree rather than of kind. Moreover, during the past several decades home-rule amendments have been added to about half the state constitutions. These amendments authorize many cities and some counties to run their own affairs, and they limit the power of state officials to interfere in local matters. Thus **constitutional home rule** in a small way introduces the federal principle into *state* constitutions.

Restricting the legislature's power did not, however, end the enormous state influence over local governments, for while the legislature's authority was being curtailed, the power of state administrative officials was being expanded. Problems once thought to be local came to be viewed as statewide. Many local governments lacked the money to do essential jobs. They could not afford specialists, and their administrative standards were notoriously low. Sometimes the states just took over a job previously handled by local people; at other times the states offered local governments financial assistance, with certain strings attached. Gradually state officials were given more and more authority to supervise local officials. This tendency became especially evident in law enforcement, finance, health, highways, welfare, and election procedures.

The extent of state control over local units varies from state to state and also among the different kinds of local government within each state. At one extreme, local officials merely have to file reports with specified state officials. At the other extreme, some state officials have the authority to appoint and remove some local officials, thus exerting considerable control over local affairs.

At present we are witnessing an acceleration of state grants of general authority to counties and cities, or what is known as **legislative home rule.** In Alaska, Montana, and Pennsylvania general grants have been made to nearly all local jurisdictions.

Trends affecting state-local relations over the past 25 years can be summarized as follows:

- States have loosened the constraints on and broadened the authority of county and city governments.
- Counties in particular have acquired more authority.
- States have encouraged the reform of state and local fiscal systems, and many states have granted local governments broader taxing authority.
- State reforms in school financing have reduced fiscal disparities among school districts within states.
- Local governments have become more dependent on state and federal financial aid.
- Most states have established state departments of community affairs or state-local relations commissions to increase consultation between state and local governments.[1]

State officials are genuinely conscious of local problems. This heightened concern is acknowledged by mayors and city managers, who regularly work with both state and federal officials. As noted in our discussion of federalism, the direct ties in recent years between national and local officials, especially in the larger urban areas—ties that used to ally them against state officials—have been weakened as the result of severe cutbacks in federal assistance. Many, perhaps most, city managers today report they have better working relations with state than with federal officials.

Counties in the United States

Counties are the largest jurisdiction within a state, yet they are often overlooked or invisible. Only a few counties are better known than the major cities or local municipalities within them. Thus Westchester County, New York; Montgomery County, Maryland; Bucks County, Pennsylvania; Marin County, California; Orange County, California; Dade County, Florida (which includes Miami), and Cook County, Illinois (which includes Chicago), are nationally known celebrity counties. Then, too, some cities, such as Denver, Philadelphia, and San Francisco, are simultaneously cities and counties. Although cities are not alternatives to county governments but rather additional layers of government, city residents tend to look to city hall as the place where community affairs are managed. Where there is no city hall, however, the county courthouse is often the center of politics.

States are divided into counties (in Louisiana they are called parishes, and in Alaska they are known as boroughs). With a few exceptions (such as Connecticut and Rhode Island, where counties have lost their governmental function), county governments exist everywhere in the United States. There are more than 3,000 of them, and they vary in size, population, and functions. Loving County, Texas, for example, has fewer than 150 inhabitants; Los Angeles County, California, has about 8.8 million (see Table 8-2).

There are two major types of counties: large urban ones like Los Angeles County, Cook County, and Dade County; and nearly 2,400 rural ones. The urban counties have many of the same structures as their rural counterparts, but they are more intertwined with their urban centers. Our discussion centers primarily on county governments outside the large urban centers.

County governments are least active in New England states, where the county is little more than a judicial district; county officials do some road building, yet not much else. Elsewhere the traditional functions of counties are law enforcement, highway construction and maintenance, tax collection and property assessment, recording of legal papers, and welfare. Until recently, counties in many states acted almost exclusively as functionaries for the state government, performing various state-mandated duties. Counties were convenient subdivisions; they spent most of their time merely carrying out policies established elsewhere.

Despite the perception that the counties are dying governments, they have within recent years taken on more tasks than they have lost. Counties in a few states have given up some of their responsibilities, but in most other states, especially in the South, they are taking over from the states such urban functions as transportation, water and sewer operation, and land-use planning.[2]

TABLE 8-2
Population Distribution of County Governments

Population Group	Total
500,000 and over	80
250,000 to 499,999	94
100,000 to 249,999	244
50,000 to 99,999	377
25,000 to 49,999	612
10,000 to 24,999	908
9,999 and below	730
Total	3,045

Source: U.S. Bureau of the Census, 1990.

Elsewhere, cities are contracting with counties to provide such joint services as personnel training, law enforcement, and correctional facilities. Although people continue to move to the suburbs, rural areas, and new cities, they still want the services to which they grew accustomed in the old traditional cities. They expect suburban counties to provide urban functions and to fight for state and federal funds to help support these functions.

COUNTY GOVERNMENT

How are counties organized to do their jobs? Counties, even more than municipalities, exist to enforce state laws and to serve as administrative units of state governments. Most counties have little legislative power. The typical county has a group of officials who act as the central governing body. They have various titles, but most frequently they are called a "board of commissioners" or "supervisors." They vary in size from a "board" of one in one county in Georgia to a 46-member board in one Wisconsin county, but the majority have from three to seven members, with a median size of six. They administer state laws, levy taxes, appropriate money, issue bonds, sign contracts on behalf of the county, and handle whatever jobs the state laws and constitution assign to them. Many states, in response to the growing awareness that problems such as waste disposal and transportation cannot be solved except on a regional basis, have given countywide agencies major policy-making responsibilities.

   County boards, as we shall call these agencies, are of two types. The larger boards are usually composed of township supervisors or other township officials; the smaller boards are usually, though not always, elected from the county in at-large elections (see Figures 8-1 and 8-2). At-large elections are under attack for making it difficult for minorities to be elected to office. Minorities, especially when they are concentrated in a few areas, can usually win more seats in a district rather than in an at-large election system.

   County board members are often key political leaders, and in some states

FIGURE 8-1
County Council-Elected Executive Form

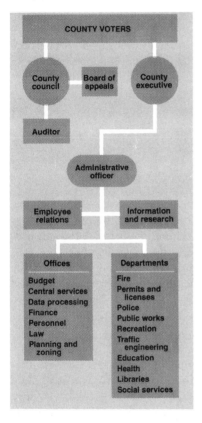

FIGURE 8-2
The Commission Form of County Government

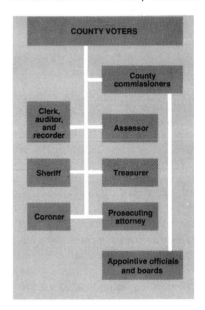

they control local affairs through their power over state patronage. They are much more important than a mere listing of their formal powers might suggest. Solving road problems and granting contracts to road contractors are frequently the major business conducted at board meetings.

The county board shares its powers with a number of other officials, most commonly the sheriff, the county prosecutor or district attorney, the county clerk, the coroner, and the auditor. These are generally elected officials. Sometimes county treasurers, health officers, and surveyors are also found on the ballot. In general, counties are administered by an unwieldy collection of relatively independent agencies, and until recently there was seldom a single administrator or executive responsible for coordinating activities. However, today about 800 counties appoint a chief administrative officer who serves at the pleasure of the county commissioners. Approximately 400 counties now elect a county executive who is responsible for most administrative functions.

WHO GOVERNS THE COUNTY?

County governments are not always as headless as they might appear. There is a politically active tier of individuals, elective officers (such as sheriff, district attorney, and sometimes county clerk), and people who lobby or do business with county officials. In some rural areas a "courthouse gang" can still be found. This may be an informal group who occasionally breakfast or lunch together or who belong to the local Rotary or Kiwanis Club and regularly run such civic events as the county fair or rodeo, as well as Fourth of July and Memorial Day observances. The makeup of these networks varies from county to county, but they usually include a few of the county commissioners, the county executive, the local publisher, local lawyers involved in criminal and probate work, road contractors, a few developers, representatives of the home builders and real estate interests, and party and political officials who know how the system works and how to get things done.

Some urban and suburban counties (of which there are an increasing number) still have political machines, often dominated by one political party. Democrats, for example, still control Cook County, Chicago, and the sprawling borough of Queens in New York City, while Republicans are very much in control of Nassau County, Long Island, in suburban New York. These counties offer considerable patronage to those who win office; indeed, as investigations in the New York area have disclosed, illegal kickbacks to party and elected officials are not uncommon.

The county is also an electoral district, and members of the state legislature are often graduates of county courthouse politics. Effective county politicians often run for higher office. U.S. Senator Alfonse D'Amato of New York served as a county executive in Nassau County before winning his senate seat. County executives in New Jersey, New York, and Michigan have recently run for governor. Moreover, the local chair of the Democratic or Republican county political organization may be a major influence on county and state politics.

In the recent past a member of the courthouse elite was often recognized as the county boss, or simply as the boss around the county seat. This is less true today, yet there still are people who can influence county decisions on certain issues—for example, the editor or owner of the local paper or television station, the president of the chamber of commerce or economic development board, the president of a local bank, the executive director of the farm bureau, or the leader of a union or civic organization. Occasionally, certain county officials—sometimes the presiding officer of the county board or commission—exercise considerable political influence over what issues are even discussed.

In general, however, the same types of interest and civic groups that organize to influence state legislatures and city halls are also found in and around county governments. Politics may be less publicized at the county level, but if some nuclear waste site or community college controversy erupts, we suddenly see which people are in positions of power and influence in the county. Although counties are frequently our least visible layer of government, they are vitally important, and county governments are embroiled in highly political decisions about who gets what, when, and at what price.

COUNTY PERFORMANCE

How well do counties do their job? It's a mixed picture. First, there are too many of them. It is not uncommon to have a county of 5,000,000 people next to a county of only 50,000 or even 20,000 people. Counties were originally organized on the idea that the county seat should be no more than a day's journey for everyone within the county's borders. Farm families could pile into their wagons and head for the county seat. While the farmers were attending to business, their families could shop and pick up the local gossip. Then they could all get home in time to do the evening chores. Today, of course, a farmer can drive across a whole state in a day.

Second, the small area and population of many counties inevitably leads to inefficiencies. Study after study has shown that money could be saved and services improved by consolidating counties. Although there is much talk about such action, few consolidations take place. Rural residents take pride in their counties and do not like to see them lose their identities. County officeholders, their families, and their friends do not want county jobs to disappear. Businesses depend on officers, employees, and others drawn to the county seat for much of their patronage.

Finally, although counties have often been the forgotten stepchildren of the state, their jurisdictional boundaries give them great potential for solving complex problems that are impossible to solve at the city level. In more and more states this fact is being recognized. County government, once thought to be a dying level of government, is well suited for certain types of policy and administrative leadership.

Town Hall Democracy, New England Style

Settlers in New England in the 1660s adopted a community-meeting style of participative government as they made common cause to survive in the new land. Doubtless they adapted certain practices from community meetings then popular in England. The town is still the principal kind of rural or noncity government in New England. It is sometimes difficult for outsiders to understand that a New England town is a unit of government that includes whatever villages there may be, plus the open country. Except where a municipality has been incorporated, the town performs most of the functions a county does elsewhere. Connecticut, in fact, has abolished counties except for sheriff services. Maine has 22 cities and about 400 towns that use the town meeting system of democracy; Vermont has 8 cities and over 200 towns using the town meeting process. About 1,300 New England towns (especially those with populations under 20,000) still hold annual town meetings open to all voters.

The assemblies at town meetings usually choose a board of executive officers, historically called *selectmen*. These boards, which generally have three to five members, carry on the business of the town between meetings. The selectmen are in charge of town property, grant licenses, supervise other town officials, and call special town meetings. A town clerk, treasurer, assessor, constable, and the school board, as well as numerous other persons, are elected by the voters or appointed by the selectmen.

The New England town meeting has long been a celebrated institution. The picture of sturdy, independent citizens coming together to talk over public affairs and speak their minds is a stirring one. The New England town is sometimes pointed to as the one place in the United States where there is no elite and where participatory democracy really exists. And the town meeting is the most obvious example of direct democracy. The voters participate directly in making rules, passing new laws, levying taxes, and appropriating money. Despite this idealized picture, it is generally a veteran group of activists that provides political and policy-making leadership.

In its heyday the New Hampshire town meeting was an all-day event combining community business and neighborly socializing. When New England communities grew too large for the "y'all come" type of town meeting to be feasible, they often modified the process to make it a representative town meeting. At representative town meetings, 200 or more people from the various town precincts are elected to serve staggered three-year terms (one-third of the members are selected each year).

Some state and local officials in New England say the town meeting system is on the decline.[3] Derry, New Hampshire, for example, held its last town meeting in 1985, when it switched to a mayor-council system. The town meeting had served Derry well for most of its 158-year history, but it proved unable to deal with rapid growth and an influx of people who commute long distances to work.

The Suburbs

Since the 1940s the areas around the cities have been the fastest-growing places in the United States. Roughly 50 percent of Americans now live in suburban communities. The suburbs grew at the expense of the cities for a variety of reasons: inexpensive land, lower taxes, better air, more open space for recreational purposes, better services, less crime, better highways, and the changing character of the inner cities. In the post–World War II years massive numbers of the poor and dispossessed—both black and white—migrated from rural areas to the central cities, especially in the northeast and north-central regions (see Figure 8-3). Three out of every five blacks in the United States now live in the cen-

FIGURE 8-3   Moving to the Suburbs

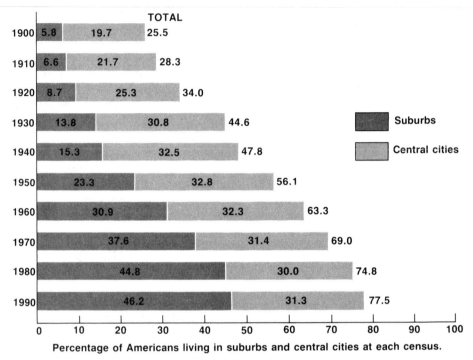

Percentage of Americans living in suburbs and central cities at each census.

Data through 1940 exclude Alaska and Hawaii. 1960 total is larger than the sum of suburbs and cities because of rounding.

Source: U.S. Census Bureau, as reported in *The New York Times*, June 1, 1992, p. A11.

tral city of a major metropolitan area. Middle- and upper-middle-income whites have fled from many of these metropolitan areas to the suburbs in search of more homogeneous communities.

Young families who could afford it left the crowded and blighted cities in search of more pleasant living quarters. Industries moved from the central cities in search of cheaper land, lower taxes, and an escape from city building and health codes. Business followed both the people and the industries, and a myriad of shopping centers grew in outlying communities. Much of this exodus was instigated by one or more federal policies, such as mandatory busing or the construction of public housing.[4]

About 125 million Americans are now suburbanites—that is, they live outside the central cities in the 280 regions designated by the Bureau of the Census as **Standard Metropolitan Statistical Areas (SMSAs)**. Demographers predict that the suburban population will increase 10 percent by the year 2000, and that most of the new jobs created in the United States will continue to be located in the suburbs or newer cities on the fringe of the central cities.

The sheer complexity and fragmentation of government administrations in suburbia often create confusion, if not frustration. Each suburban city has its own government, fire and police departments, school system, street-cleaning equipment, and building and health codes. *Special-district* governments piled on top of one another further complicate the situation (see the box on special districts). Also, all the major tasks of suburban government are bound together with those of the metropolis. The central city usually maintains an elaborate police department with detective bureaus, crime-detection laboratories, and communications networks, but its jurisdiction stops at the city line. However, criminals do not stop at the city line. Suburbs have fewer police, and they are often untrained in criminology, so they call on urban police expertise. Or consider traffic problems. Superhighways run through suburbia, and they all have a number of access roads. In matters of health, too, there are often wide differences in standards between parts of a metropolis. But germs, pollution, and smog do not notice city signposts.

What of government and politics in the suburbs? It is dangerous to generalize, because individual suburbs vary so greatly. Some, like Paradise Valley, Arizona; Woodside, California; Potomac, Maryland; Dover, Massachusetts; Cherry Hills Village, Colorado; and Laguna Beach, California are the residences of the rich, and as such are governed by an efficient cluster of specialists. Others are lower-middle-class neighborhoods of blue-collar workers. Some, like Compton and East Palo Alto, California, or Glen Arden and Seat Pleasant, Maryland, are predominantly African American. Still others are populated with

---

SPECIAL DISTRICTS

Special districts are units of government typically established to provide one or more specific services, such as sewage disposal, fire protection, water supply, or pollution control for a local or regional area. They are often created to enable an existing unit of government to evade established tax and debt limits or to spread the tax burden over a wider area than individual municipalities or counties. Many smaller special districts are formed in suburban areas to obtain urban services without having to create a city government or be annexed by one.

Special districts usually have governing boards appointed by officials of other governments or elected by the general public. Special districts are useful for dealing with urgent problems that overlap boundaries of existing units of government.

Some critics say that the rapid increase in special districts in the past 30 years has prevented comprehensive planning. Critics also lament that few citizens know who runs these special districts and even fewer know how these officials make decisions. Doubtless special districts are a "shadow government" to the average citizen, and it is undeniable that these bodies add to the layering of governments in metro regions. Still, special districts are here to stay, and we will probably see more of them formed in the next generation. Many urban and regional problems defy city and county boundaries, and regional special districts for transit authorities, recreation, water, and a number of other matters offer an economies-of-scale approach that will continue to make sense to government officials at the grass roots.

young professional families or baby boomers who are more interested in their next promotions than in their communities. Some suburbanites consider local government basically a device to protect their property, schools, and homes from "invasion" by minority groups. Occasionally suburban dwellers become aroused about major problems like educational policy or taxation, but in the absence of explosive issues, local suburban politics is often low-key.

CITIES VERSUS SUBURBS: HOW BIG IS THE CONTRAST?

Many of us grew up thinking of a suburb as a place of single-family houses that all look alike, where husbands travel to the city to work, and where the life-style revolves around children, barbecues, and well-kept lawns. These stereotypes still have a basis in reality in some suburbs, but for the most part, they are myths that greatly distort the fast-changing character of our suburban areas. In fact, there are all kinds of housing patterns in suburbia; an increasingly large number of suburban residents of both sexes work in their own communities or in other nearby suburbs; and many suburbs provide the services and economic opportunities once found only in the central cities. Older suburbs increasingly face growth and aging problems. And although tax levels and rates generally remain higher in central cities, suburbs have experienced increases in taxes and expenditures similar to those borne by the central cities. Moreover, as noted, not all suburbs are the same, and many people who live in the central cities have the same life-styles and values as suburban residents. Still, many central cities find that their principal antagonists in the state legislature and in Congress are not representatives of rural areas but rather legislators from the suburbs. The longstanding cleavage between city and suburbs persists as a major feature of political life in many metropolitan areas.

Nonetheless, we must not draw too sharp a contrast between suburban and central-city problems. Many suburbanites have discovered that the lower land prices and taxes are deceptive, for they often have to pay higher fire insurance rates than city dwellers, pay more for garbage collection, and are required to build and maintain their own septic tanks. Moreover, as suburban real estate becomes more valuable and the suburbs grow in size, many new and expensive facilities are needed. Suburbanites are also beginning to suffer from the nagging problems of crime, traffic congestion, pollution, troubled schools, and racial hostility once thought of as the marks of city life. "There's no constituency for serious long-term planning, and few localities put serious dollars into it," writes Neal R. Peirce, a veteran observer of local government in the United States. "Suburbanites often distrust their local councils—and not without reason, because developers contribute the biggest campaign dollars."[5]

Further, few of the fastest-growing suburbs care about housing for the poor or even for the lower-paid employees of the giant firms that relocate to them. To ask typical suburban government officials to think creatively or compassionately about housing for lower-income groups or minorities is simply unrealistic. Whether intentionally or not, many suburban zoning and related

LAYERS OF GOVERNANCE IN A TYPICAL SMALL TOWN

17. United States of America

16. Commonwealth of Pennsylvania

15. Air Quality Control Region

14. Southwestern Pennsylvania Regional Planning Commission

13. Western Pennsylvania Water Company

12. Allegheny County

11. Allegheny County Port Authority

10. Allegheny County Criminal Justice Commission

9. Allegheny County Soil and Water Conservation District

8. Allegheny County Sanitary Authority

7. City of Pittsburgh

6. South Hills Area Council of Governments

5. South Hills Regional Planning Commission

4. Pleasant Hills Sanitary Authority

3. Baldwin-Whitehall Schools Authority

2. Baldwin-Whitehall School District

1. Borough of Whitehall

ordinances in effect exclude low- and moderate-income people. A resegregation of America is often the result.

The American City

Although several cities existed when the U.S. Constitution was written, the nation was overwhelmingly rural in 1787, and seven out of ten people worked on farms. People clustered together mainly in villages and small towns scattered throughout the 13 states and neighboring territories. The United States is now a nation of over 19,000 cities, and although some cities have just a few hundred people, others have millions. Three American supercities have populations larger than the total population of the Republic in the 1780s.

The villages and cities of the 1760s and 1770s were the indispensable workshops of democracy, the places where democratic skills were developed, where grand issues were debated, and, above all, where the people resolved their commitment to fight the British to secure their fundamental rights.

What does the word *city* call to mind today? Bright lights, crowded streets, museums, slums, skyscrapers, malls, and lots of people. To some, the city is Main Street, Courthouse Square, the old cannon down by the harbor or riverfront, and farm families shopping and talking on Saturdays. A city is not merely improved real estate. It is also people: men and women living and working together. Aristotle observed that people came together in the cities for security, but they stayed there for the good life. The "good life" is defined differently by different people, yet it often includes these attractions:

- Employment opportunities
- Cultural centers, museums, performing arts centers, theaters
- Diverse educational institutions
- Entertainment and night life
- Professional sports teams
- Good restaurants
- Diversity of people and life-styles

Every municipality has two major purposes. One is to provide government within its boundaries: to maintain law and order, keep streets clean, educate children, purify water, create parks, and in other ways make the area a good place in which to live. And as an instrument of the state, the city has a second major purpose: to carry out state functions. Cities are distinguished from counties in the greater amount of discretion given to local officials and the greater emphasis placed on local functions. A county is supposed to operate primarily as an administrative unit of the state. A city has its own character. This distinction, of course, is one of degrees.

Each city has its own *charter*. The charter is to the city what a constitution is to the national or the state government. The charter, however, is not necessarily a single document. A city's charter outlines the structure of the government, defines the authority of the various officials, and provides for their selection.

LOCAL HOME RULE

European cities can do anything that is not expressly forbidden by the national government. American cities have only those powers expressly conferred on them by the state governments. State legislatures still exercise a great deal of control over city affairs. In addition to drawing up charters for the cities, the legislature allots functions to local officials and withdraws them at will. Where state and local laws conflict, the state law is almost always enforced.

About 40 states have some form of home-rule provision for their cities and towns. Some states have **legislative home rule,** meaning the state legislature delegates authority with regard to certain functions so the cities do not have to ask permission continually to deal with them. In about half the states, however, the state *constitution*, not the state legislature, delegates to citizens of certain-sized cities (a few extend the power to all municipalities) authority that they may exercise *without the concurrence of the state legislature.* These are the *home-rule states.* The people of the city may elect a group of citizens to draw up a charter. After the charter has been approved by local voters (in some states it must also be approved by the legislature or the governor or both to ensure that it does not conflict with the state constitution), it becomes the city's basic instrument of government and may be amended by local citizens. Further, home-rule cities have the general power to dispose of matters of local concern without having to seek special authorization from the legislature. Most cities of over 200,000 people, and about 40 percent of cities of 5,000 or more, have some measure of home rule.

The independence from state legislature control of home-rule cities, especially the smaller and medium-sized ones, should not be exaggerated.[6] These cities have some freedom in determining the general structure of their city governments, but home rule often only slightly increases their substantive powers. For when all is said and done, the state legislature and governor usually control most of the assets and much of the political clout. Still, some cities, such as those in Michigan, Texas, Connecticut, and North Carolina, have acquired significant substantive powers through home-rule provisions.

Is home rule worth the political struggle required to get it? Despite the rather small increase in local autonomy home rule represents, and despite the fact that constitutional home rule introduces an element of rigidity into state-local relations and enhances the authority of state judges (who often have to determine which laws prevail), most reform groups favor it. It frees the state legislature from having to deal with some local matters and it permits administrative flexibility (depending on how the flexibility is used and what side you are on, you may see this as desirable or undesirable). Perhaps home rule's chief importance is symbolic. It may have the effect of discouraging state legislatures from interfering in local affairs and of encouraging greater responsibility at the grass-roots level of government. It also gives the voters of a particular city the power to decide for themselves the general structure of their municipal government.

Although formal charters are good sources of information for learning how the people in our 19,000 cities are governed, city charters can be misleading. Real government—in the sense of the rules by which our cities are run, in contrast to the provisions of their legal charters—ranges from the narrowest participation to the widest participation. Note that the different structures are not neutral in their impact, for different forms encourage different kinds of participation and responsiveness. In short, power and clout and who gets what, where, and how can definitely be shaped, at least in part, by a city's structural arrangements.

THE MAYOR-COUNCIL CHARTER

The **mayor-council charter** is the oldest and most popular charter in the smallest and the largest cities (see Figure 8-4). Under this type of charter, the city coun-

FIGURE 8-4   The Strong Mayor-City Council Form

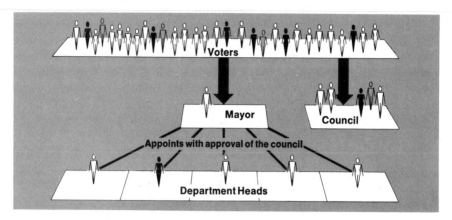

cil is usually a single chamber. The size of the council varies from as few as two members to as many as 50, though seven is the median size in cities with over 5,000 people. Many methods are used to select the council members: nonpartisan and partisan elections, elections by large and small wards, or elections from the city at large. Sometimes special local parties participate in local elections— for example, the Citizens party or the Taxpayers party. How council members are chosen is an important fact in determining how power is distributed in a city. Large cities that elect members in partisan elections generally choose them by small districts or wards rather than at-large. This tends to support strong party organizations. Nonpartisan at-large elections make party organization difficult. The larger the election districts, the more likely citywide considerations will be brought to bear in the selection of council members and the greater the influence of citywide institutions such as the local newspapers.

The difference between at-large or large-district elections and elections based on small, single-number districts can be significant for racial and ethnic representation on the city council. The at-large system tends to produce councils made up of the city's elite and middle classes. The single-member district and ward systems give minorities and the less advantaged a better chance for representation.

Under the Voting Rights Act of 1965, the United States attorney general may prevent certain cities, subject to the limitations of the act, from adopting the at-large system if the effect would be to dilute the voting strength of African Americans, Chicanos, and other protected groups. But what of cities or counties that have long had such systems? Can they be forced to give them up because such elections virtually ensure that blacks will never be elected? The mere fact that no black is elected under a certain system does not by itself constitute a violation of the Fourteenth or Fifteenth Amendment. The Constitution forbids only practices adopted or maintained with the purposeful intent to discriminate.

When Congress debated the extension of the Voting Rights Act in 1982, civil rights advocates urged it to outlaw at-large systems in all areas covered by the act. They contended it is impossible to show a discriminatory purpose because not many city officials are so foolish as to admit that they favor the at-large system just to keep blacks from being elected. Others argued that cities should be free to adopt whatever election system they wished; after all, the Constitution guarantees that no person will be denied the right to vote because of race, not that candidates of the voter's own race will win an election. Congress, after specifically stating that the Voting Rights Act does not require proportional representation, said the following: In trying to determine whether or not an election procedure—including an at-large system—violates the Civil Rights act, federal judges should look into the totality of the circumstances, including the results.

Moreover, the Supreme Court has made it easier in recent years to prove that at-large systems violate both the Constitution and the Voting Rights Act. Discriminatory intent need not be proved by direct evidence; it may be inferred from the following facts: (1) a city or county has a past history of discrimination designed to keep blacks from voting; (2) blacks make up a large majority of the population; and (3) no black has ever been elected to office under an at-large system.[7]

STRONG MAYOR/WEAK MAYOR COUNCILS

The powers of the mayor vary from charter to charter (and even more widely from city to city and mayor to mayor). There are, however, two basic variations of the mayor-council form: **strong mayor-council** and **weak mayor-council**. Under the strong mayor-council form, the mayor is elected directly by the people and given fairly broad appointment powers. The mayor, often with the help of his or her own staff, prepares and administers the budget, enjoys almost total administrative authority, and has the power to appoint and dismiss department heads. This system obviously calls for a mayor to be both a good political leader and an effective administrator, qualities not always found in the same person.

In weak mayor-council cities mayors are often elected from among the membership of the elected city council rather than directly by the people. The mayor's appointive powers are usually restricted, and the city council as a whole generally possesses both legislative and executive authority. The mayor in the weak mayor-council form usually must obtain the council's consent for all major administrative decisions. Often weak mayor-council cities permit direct election by the voters of a number of department heads, such as police chief or controller. In weak mayor-council cities there is no single administrative head for the city, and power is fragmented. The weak mayor-council plan was designed for an earlier era, when cities were smaller and government simpler. It is especially ill suited to large cities where political and administrative leadership is vital.

Tracing the office of mayor over the years and through various charters, we

REFLECTIONS OF MAYOR BARBARA ACKERMANN OF CAMBRIDGE, MASSACHUSETTS

"I wanted to be a link between citizens and city government and to help the bureaucracy see their responsibilities in human terms. Among my special goals were better schools, better police work, better public housing.

Always an underlying goal had to do with the welfare and growth of the children. People say it's the job of parents to raise them. No doubt, but it's a rare parent who does that totally alone. The city has an effect on each child, for good or bad. Helping the children grow—grow healthy and useful and free—is a key part of the overwhelming job we hand to the amateurs who guide our troubled cities."

Mayor Ackermann's advice to those who enter city politics:

1. Remember what Archimedes said of the lever: If I stand in the right place, I can move the earth. One politician, one employee, one citizen who keeps pushing can make a difference.

2. Be sure you're moving it the right way.

3. Once you've got your goals clear, stick to them. . . .

4. Watch out for the clever professionals whose policies are not the city's.

5. Remember it's easy to agree that a problem exists, hard to agree on the part of the problem you want to attack, hardest of all to agree on a solution.

6. Once there is agreement that something will happen, follow up to make sure it does.

7. Be sure you're right. Watch out for the people who think they are the good guys. Including yourself.

Source: Adapted from Barbara Ackermann, "You the Mayor?" *The Education of a City Politician* (Auburn House, 1989), pp. 266–67.

---

find a general trend toward an increase in mayoral authority. Like the presidency and the governorship, the office of mayor has grown in importance. Most cities have altered their charters to give their mayors power to appoint and remove heads of departments and investigate departmental activities, send legislative messages to the city councils, prepare the budgets, and veto council ordinances. In other words, the mayors have been given a share in policy making, and city administration has been centralized under the mayor's direction.

Many people believe the strong mayor-council system is the best form of government for large cities because it gives the cities strong political leaders and makes efficient administration possible. Further, by centering authority in the hands of a few individuals, it makes less likely the growth of "invisible government" by people who have power but are not publicly accountable for its use.

THE COMMISSION CHARTER

In 1900 the city of Galveston, Texas, was flooded by storm-driven tides. Over 6,000 people lost their lives, and property worth millions was destroyed. When the mayor and aldermen showed themselves incapable of acting in the emergency, power fell into the hands of a group of businesspeople who had been discussing methods of improving the harbor. After studying the charters of several cities, they went to the legislature with what was then a somewhat novel proposal for a new charter. They asked that control of the city be vested in five commissioners. The legislature approved.

The idea of placing all governmental powers in the hands of five people flew in the face of the traditional doctrine of separation of powers. Many thought it was too dangerous to give a small group control over both administration and legislation. For this reason, another charter system, known as the Des Moines Plan, included the initiative, referendum, recall, and nonpartisan ballots for primaries and elections.

The commissioners, usually five, collectively constitute the city council; individually, they are the heads of the departments of city administration. Most commissioners work full time at their city jobs and actively administer the affairs of their particular departments. One of the commissioners is selected by the commission as mayor, but in most cities the mayor has little more power than the other commissioners (see Figure 8-5).

The **commission charter** was widely heralded as introducing safe and sane business methods to city affairs. But after a brief spurt of popularity, the new idea lost much of its glamor; the party bosses were suspicious of it and the city reformers disappointed in it. Although it provided for more integrated control than the old mayor-council system, the commission charter left the city without a single responsible administrative head; in effect, a commission city has five mayors.

By 1917 over 500 cities were governed by the commission form. By 1993, however, only about 170 cities still had this kind of charter. Many cities have turned away from the commission form to a system that provides for a strong mayor or to the council-manager form. "Use of the plan is slowly disappearing today."[8] Larger cities usually shift to the strong mayor-council plan. Salt Lake

FIGURE 8-5 The Commission Form for Cities

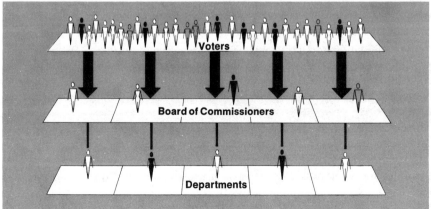

City, for example, did so in early 1980, and Lawrence, Massachusetts, did so in 1986. And Galveston, too, has shifted to the council-manager plan.

THE COUNCIL-MANAGER CHARTER

The **council-manager plan,** also known as the city-manager plan, was acclaimed at the turn of the century as the latest word in municipal reform. It is indeed one of this nation's significant governmental innovations. In 1908 the small city of Staunton, Virginia, appointed a general manager to direct the city's work. Little note was taken of the step, but Richard Childs, an advertising man active in the short-ballot movement, became interested in the plan.

Childs was enthusiastic about the commission plan because it applied two basic ideas, *unification of power* and a *short ballot,* to city affairs. But it did not go far enough. Childs reasoned that if a chief administrative officer were added to the commission plan, the results should be even better. The city manager plan soon became the darling of both reformers and the business elite. They liked the idea that the council would serve as a sort of "board of directors" in the business sense of setting broad policies, while a professional executive would see that these policies were carried out with businesslike efficiency.

Today about 2,700 cities, located in virtually every state, operate under a council-manager charter. It has, in fact, become the most popular form of local government in medium-sized cities of more than 10,000 citizens. It is especially popular in California, where about 98 percent of the cities now use it. The largest cities operating under a city manager are Dallas and San Antonio; other large cities using the plan are San Diego, Phoenix, Kansas City, Cincinnati, Oakland, Rochester, and Fort Worth.

Under the council-manager charter the council is usually elected in nonpartisan primaries and elections, either on a citywide basis or by election districts much larger than the wards in mayor-council cities. The council appoints a city manager and supervises the manager's activities (see Figure 8-6). It makes the laws, approves the budget, and, although it is not supposed to interfere in administration, the council often supervises city government through the manager. A mayor is expected to preside over the council and represent the city on ceremonial occasions, but many mayors in fact do a good deal more than this (see box on the job of the mayor in council-manager cities). Contrary to what some textbooks imply, the mayor in council-manager cities can sometimes be a strong policy and political leader as well as a dominant influence in exercising political power.[9]

The city manager advises the council on policy and supervises the administration of city business. Because council-manager cities try to attract the best available persons, few of their charters require the councils to select managers from among local citizens nor do they prescribe detailed qualifications. Although city-manager charters seem to call for a nonpolitical city manager who merely carries out policies adopted by the council and for council members

FIGURE 8-6   The City Council-Manager Form

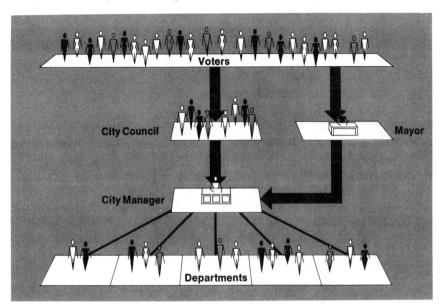

who refrain from interfering with the administration of city affairs, in practice it is often difficult to distinguish clearly between making and applying policy.[10]

How has the city manager plan worked? In cities characterized by low social diversity and high consensus about community goals, the council-manager form has met with considerable success. Such cities have generally enjoyed improved standards of public employment, reduced costs, and better services. But some observers say it has also weakened political leadership in these cities and has confused citizens as to who really provides policy leadership.

Do structural reforms make any difference? That is, do council-manager cities with at-large, nonpartisan elections produce different kinds of policies because of their structural arrangements? One student of urban politics concludes that political structures do have an impact on public policies: "Reformed cities respond more pronouncedly to those pressures that tend to reduce spending; unreformed [meaning mayor-council or commission] cities respond more to those pressures that increase spending. If reformers wished to impose a middle-class efficiency ethos on city government, they were successful."[11] Exactly how and why these policy differences arise is not wholly clear. The fact that council-manager and nonpartisan election systems have been adopted mainly in cities whose residents have higher-than-average incomes may be a factor.

But there is too much variation in American cities to label cities and their forms and predict policy outcomes. The more scholars examine the relation-

---

THE JOB OF THE MAYOR IN COUNCIL-MANAGER CITIES

- Ceremonial leader
- Spokesperson for council
- Presiding officer
- Educator: performs informational and educational tasks
- Promotes informal exchange between the council and the manager and staff.
- Team leader: builds consensus and enhances group performance.
- Goal setter: sets goals and objectives for council and manager; identifies problems.

- Organizer: guides the council in recognizing its roles and responsibilities.
- Policy advocate: develops programs; lines up support for or opposition to proposals.
- Promoter: promotes and defends the city; seeks investment; handles external relationships.

Source: Adapted from James H. Svara, "Understanding the Mayor's Office in Council-Manager Cities," *Popular Government*, Fall 1985, p. 7.

---

ship between political attitudes or orientations and the structures of city government, the less they are convinced there are clear-cut cause-and-effect linkages.[12]

THE RISE OF "EDGE CITIES"

First there were towns and cities with their downtowns. Then there were suburbs. Next came the malls. Most recently, Americans have built cities on the edge of cities, or on the fringes of the metropolitan area. Writer Joel Garreau calls these "edge cities" and suggests that every American city that is growing grows in the fashion of Los Angeles, with multiple urban cores. Thus we have Tyson's Corner, outside of Washington, D.C.; the Perimeter Center at the northern tip of Atlanta's Beltway; the Galleria area west of downtown Houston; and the Schamburg area west of O'Hare Airport outside of downtown Chicago—and hundreds more edge cities across the country.

Edge cities are places with 5 million or more square feet of office space, 600,000 or more square feet of retail space, and more jobs than bedrooms. More often than not, these edge cities were empty spaces or farmland just 30 years ago. First came some freeways, then a mall or two, and then industrial parks. Edge city is a creation of the marketplace that is encouraged by American values. Land is cheaper beyond the city limits. And more and more Americans prefer commuting to a campuslike workplace in the country rather than taking a bus, train, or subway into the old inner cities.

Two-thirds of all American office facilities are now located in these edge cities. Edge cities are still works-in-progress, yet they are the crucible of America's urban future. "Having become the place in which the majority of Americans now live, learn, work, shop, play, pray, and die, Edge City will be the forge of the fabled American way of life well into the twenty-first century."[13]

But now that they have mushroomed in size and the nearby malls are aging, some of the problems of the inner city have caught up with the edge cities: traffic congestion, parking problems, crime, pollution, and urban blight. Political problems have cropped up as well. Edge cities are often run by "shadow governments"—private owners who set the fees for policing, transportation arrangements, and various other services that are financed by taxes in a normally run community. There is not much room for democracy, or government by the people, in many of these edge city operations. They are essentially a business, and if you don't like what you are offered, your main alternative is to get out and go somewhere else.

Like it or not, these edge cities have transformed urban and metropolitan America. They have offered a great escape from the inner-central cities—for those who could afford to move their businesses and shops to these new locations. But they have left behind some of America's greatest community challenges. Affluent firms and populations leave the center cities to solve their economic and social problems with less money—and in many cases, less civic leadership—than they had before the rise of the edge city.

The rise of the edge city has contributed, along with suburbs and special districts, to the further dispersal of political power and authority in the metropolitan areas of America.

Who Influences Local Policy Making?

Americans like to believe that every citizen is at least potentially equal in having a say in local government. We know, however, that people like mayors or prominent local business leaders have more influence than the rest of us. Nursing home residents, the unemployed, migratory workers, young drifters, and the indigent are unlikely to have much influence. In fact, neither the very poor nor the very rich have much influence over local city halls. Participation in community affairs is far more often a middle-class and upper middle-class practice.

Most Americans, most of the time, leave the responsibility of running the cities and counties to local officials and those few hundred people willing and able to serve on boards and in local civic organizations. The traditionally important people in city government are still the mayor, other elected representatives, senior public administrative officials, the district attorney, local judges, and state and national representatives. But if most people do not choose to be leaders in their communities, it does not mean they do not care about tax rates, the quality of life, and the availability of services in those communities. Hundreds of local people can be quickly mobilized if city hall mishandles local affairs and makes unpopular decisions.

Indeed, activism has increased in recent years. It is now common for people to form groups to protect their communities from waste landfills, toxic dumps, shopping malls, and highways (see Table 8-3). With dogged persever-

TABLE 8-3
Groups with Clout in City Councils

Neighborhood associations	95%*
Businesses	95
Elderly	88
Realtors/developers	79
Environmentalists	79
Municipal employees	77
Labor unions	60

Source: National League of Cities, Survey of America's City Councils, 1991.

* Percent of city council/members who said a group has some or considerable influence on council decisions

ance and shoestring budgets, middle-class protest groups have often successfully taken on city hall or won victories for their neighborhoods in the courts. Typical interest groups active in local government are:

- Neighborhood associations
- Chambers of commerce
- Local trade and manufacturing associations
- Business leaders of major local concerns (bankers, department store owners, publishers, managers of local high-tech or steel companies)
- Small merchants' associations (downtown merchants' groups, Main Street associates, shopping mall owners)
- Taxpayers' associations
- Civic associations
- Utilities (power, electricity, and fuel companies)
- Real estate and home builders' associations
- Local contractors
- Local unions
- League of Women Voters
- Public employee groups (teachers, police, and fire fighters)
- Civil and human rights groups (Urban League, NAACP, Hispanic and Asian-American groups)
- Parents' groups (PTA, Mothers Against Drunk Driving)
- Environmental groups (Sierra Club)
- Farmers' groups (Farm Bureau, Farmers Union)

- Religious organizations
- Ethnic and fraternal organizations
- Single-interest groups (NIMBY—Not In My Back Yard; PUKE—People United for a Klean Environment; CARE; WATCHDOG; TRIM; SWAT)

Not all of these groups are equally important. And other groups could be added for specific communities, depending on their special problems and ethnic, class, and commercial makeup. Ask yourself about your home community. Which groups or individuals appear to enjoy access to and special influence at city hall? Can groups successfully fight city hall and get decisions modified or reversed? What groups have done this in recent years? Do minorities and the less privileged have to acquiesce to unfair or unreasonable decisions made by the city elites, or is there considerable political equality in your home area?

A sure way to involve people in city government is to propose a new policy that threatens the values and safety of the homes of middle- or upper-middle-class taxpayers. The slightest hint that a correctional facility, a freeway, a garbage dump, or a toxic disposal site is coming to their neighborhood will swiftly mobilize citizens who are otherwise happy to be passive spectators in local government. Likewise, the firing of a popular school principal, the closing of a neighborhood school, or a major increase in the property tax will produce a volley of citizen protest that can change the policy-making process at city hall.

Above all, voters and the mildly active or attentive citizens in a community help set the general tone of their community government. Elected and appointed officials regularly try to sense the mood of the local citizenry. They want to avert marches on city hall, recall elections, and citizen dissatisfaction. Their desire to be reelected keeps them reasonably accountable.

This does not mean that Americans rave about the quality of services received from local governments. Although they generally respond favorably to the services they get from city government and local public transportation agencies, they rate them less favorably than they do the services provided by commercial organizations that are in the consumer services business.

Despite low turnouts at city government hearings, town meetings, and local elections, and despite considerable public indifference to the decisions made at city hall, probably more people are involved in more local government activities today than ever before. In general, the middle class, the middle-aged, and the homeowners in a community are most likely to participate. Also, people usually have more influence through a group than they do as individuals, and a coalition of groups can often exercise considerable clout in city policy-making processes.

GRASS-ROOTS SELF-HELP MOVEMENTS

Apart from political participation within the formal structures of city or community government, countless people are coming together in their own neighborhoods to tackle common problems or to form neighborhood cooperatives. Some of these self-help groups simply handle collective baby-sitting arrangements or organize charity events or golf tournaments. But others are involved in neighborhood crime watches, or bike path or Little League field construction. Local nonprofit groups in New York have built award-winning apartment complexes amid burned-out inner-city tenements. Other groups have mobilized to bring about storefront revitalization, street improvement, and area beautification programs by initiating farmers' markets, miniparks, and gardens.

The contemporary grass-roots self-help movement is rooted in America's past. In former times the whole community often rallied when a neighbor's farm burned down; volunteer fire departments emerged out of this tradition. Local Grange and consumer cooperatives also reflect this impulse. But since Americans have become a highly mobile and increasingly impersonal society, we have drifted away from these traditions. Today, most Americans shop at shopping malls rather than on Main Street or in the old village or downtown area. At the same time, they resent the fact that public institutions designed to serve them have become remote and perhaps overly professionalized. Thus people across the country sometimes join together to do in an informal and decentralized way what extended families or small villages of the past used to do. Simply, they come together and embark upon community improvements.

Just as most business innovations in America take place in small firms, so are most social experiments and innovations generated in small neighborhood or community entities rather than in the large, cumbersome, traditional government bureaucracies. In a way, these efforts are part of the "small is beautiful" trend in recent decades. Yet they have also occurred because formal local governments have sometimes become remote from problems and overly cautious about dealing with them. Many local groups seeking help from city hall or from county officialdom give up after running into the forest of building codes, zoning rules, and countless other regulations that inhibit innovation in local government. The alternative to despair is to do it yourself. And this is exactly what is happening in grass-roots America right now. The more successful experiments are watched carefully by the professionals at city hall, and some of the "innovations" will be absorbed either by those in office or by new candidates. Some of these new candidates, indeed, will be products of these neighborhood groups and will win election on the basis of these innovations.

The Central City and Its Politics

Today the metropolis, not the farm or the small town so beloved in American fact and fiction, is where most Americans live. About 75 percent of the American people live on about 5 percent of the land. Almost 80 percent live in metropolitan areas. Fifty-five percent live within 60 miles of coastal shoreline

(Atlantic, Pacific, Gulf of Mexico, or along the Great Lakes or the St. Lawrence River). Thirty percent live in central cities.

The political, economic, and legal problems of our metropolitan regions are obviously interconnected. Policy makers at all levels of government constantly seek better ways to govern our metro areas, to achieve sensible economic growth and equity, and to ensure environmentally safe metro regions. There are no easy answers.

Some observers consider the jumble of civic jurisdictions the main impediment to sound government in the sprawling supercities of America. They say the vast dispersal of power leads to fragmentation that discourages coherent policy planning. However, those people who want to control their local schools and determine how the land around them is used believe fragmented power prevents their urban government from becoming coercive—just as separation of power and divisions between state and national governments check and balance power in the larger jurisdictions.

Others say our inner cities are plagued by racial and ethnic tensions, not just white/black rivalry, but Latinos, Koreans, and a host of other racial and ethnic rivalries. The 1992 Los Angeles riots, looting, and fires were an extreme case. Gangs, poverty, broken families, drive-by-shootings, and drug-related crimes make life miserable for millions who live in the inner cities.

Today's giant cities unquestionably face problems: congestion, slums, smog, tension, rootlessness, loss of community, unsafe streets, neglected children, and unrestrained sprawl and visual pollution. Yet is this new? Writers and critics since Thomas Jefferson have projected an unflattering image of the city as a cold, impersonal, and often brutal environment in which crime flourishes and people lose their dignity.

Supporters, on the other hand, contend the big city is not just a place of smog and sprawl; it is the center of innovation, excitement, and vitality. The city offers social diversity and puts less community pressure on the individual to conform. The large community is a meeting place for talent from all over the nation and the world: dancers, musicians, writers, actors, and business leaders. Traditionally, big cities have provided jobs and opportunities. New York City, for example, is called the Big Apple—the land of opportunity. People who like living in the city point out that fairly homogeneous smaller communities that retain some identity often exist within metropolitan areas. Some of the best known are Greenwich Village and Soho in lower Manhattan, Georgetown and Cleveland Park in Washington, D.C., the Russian Hill and Chinatown sections of San Francisco, and the North End and South Boston areas in Boston.

Some dismiss the notion that there is an urban crisis in America. They contend most city dwellers, except perhaps those in the inner city, live more comfortably and conveniently than ever before, with more and better housing, schools, and transportation. By any conceivable measure of material welfare the present generation of urban Americans is on the whole, better off than other large groups of people have ever been anywhere at any time. There is con-

FIGURE 8-7   Metro Areas in the United States

A METRO AREA IS . . .
... in the minds of most people, a big city and its suburbs. But the Census Bureau, which counts 284 metro areas, uses a more formal definition:

■ A metro area is built around one or more central counties containing an urban area of at least 50,000 people. It also includes outlying counties with close ties – economic and social – to the central counties. To be considered part of the metro area, the outlying counties must meet certain criteria, including numbers of commuters, population density and growth, and urban population.
■ In New England, metro areas are composed of cities and towns rather than whole counties.

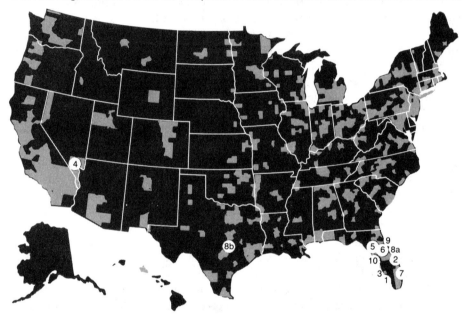

**THE FASTEST-GROWING
METRO AREAS ...**

1. Naples, Fla., 77%
2. Fort Pierce, Fla., 66%
3. Fort Myers, Fla., 63%
4. Las Vegas, 60%
5. Ocala, Fla., 53%
6. Orlando, Fla., 53%
7. West Palm Beach, Fla., 50%
8a. Melbourne-Titusville, Fla., 46%
8b. Austin, Tex., 46%
9. Daytona Beach, Fla., 43%
10. Bradentown, Fla., 43%

Source: The Washington Post National Weekly Edition, August 10–16, 1992, p. 32.

gestion in our cities, to be sure, yet many people find advantages as well as disadvantages. Many cities, especially in the West and South, are in good shape, and Boston, Pittsburgh, Baltimore, and Indianapolis are now viewed as revived, not decaying.

Cities survive. Throughout history cities have been threatened by political, social, and environmental catastrophes. Urban decay, in one form or another, has always been with us. Cities thrive because they are able to respond effectively to crises. Today the differences are mainly those of scale, consequences, and speed of change. One difference today, perhaps, is the enormous extent of drugs and drug-related crime in the inner city, which, along with racism, are our greatest domestic challenges. How well cities will survive, and with what mix of people, will depend on the tides of the national economy, the way our regions are organized, the way our social and economic policies are designed, and the vision and leadership individual cities muster to build their future.

INTEREST GROUPS IN BIG CITIES

The stakes and prizes of big-city politics are considerable: appointments to city offices; tax considerations; regulation of businesses, professions, and other activities; and city contracts to provide such city services as education and sanitation. These—and a general interest in honest, efficient, and coordinated metropolitan government—encourage interest groups to mobilize as much influence as they can to deal with the urban government. City politicians must deal with the kind of interest groups found anywhere in an industrial society: organized workers, business leaders, neighborhood associations, professional associations, good government associations, home builders and developers, consumers, taxpayers, environmentalists, and various racial and ethnic groups. Typically, their concerns are more the concerns of city officials than of a governor or a president. The mayor of a big city constantly operates in the eye of a political hurricane.

The most powerful groups in most large cities are typically various business groups. It is only a modest oversimplification to equate the interests of big cities with the interests of business employers who provide the economic base for taxes and for jobs. Mayors realize this and know they will be judged on how well they promote the local economy. But today business groups have to share power and influence with others, and on most issues they cannot dominate politics without allies.[14]

Cities also have so-called problem groups, composed of people who share a concern about a particular city problem even though they have different economic interests. Groups concerned with halting highway construction, curbing the size of large office buildings, fighting toxic waste dumps, or developing parks or bicycle trails can put a great deal of pressure on city hall, especially when supported by the local media. Once the problem is solved or somehow disappears, however, the group may disappear with it.

Another special interest group is the good government or reform group. In some cities these groups have enjoyed such strong leadership and wide support that they have operated almost like political parties. But in most big cities re-form groups are simply one more pressure on city hall, and they are often di-vided among themselves. Their activities range from trying to improve an entire metropolitan area, as the Citizens Leagues in Minneapolis-St. Paul and Baltimore have done, to simply collecting facts and figures.

Also important are the unions of city employees. Police, firefighters, street cleaners, teachers, and other public employees have organized into unions, many of which are affiliated with the national AFL-CIO. These groups say they are concerned about the city as a whole, yet they are especially interested in specific matters that affect them, such as pay, working conditions, and job se-curity. Although in most states strikes by city employees providing vital serv-ices are prohibited by law, enforcement is difficult. Teachers and municipal workers use the strike, or the threat of a strike, to force cities to increase wages and provide better benefits. Such unions are often a major influence in larger cities. Mayors, both liberals and conservatives, complain that public-employee unions are sometimes so powerful they make the old-fashioned political ma-chine look tame.

INTEREST-GROUP TACTICS

Ordinarily, groups in a metropolis pursue the same activities as pressure groups anywhere. They put out press releases, hold meetings, write letters to the mayor and council, and generate all the pressure they can. Occasionally a local interest group is extremely effective. A few years ago, for example, the Kellogg Company threatened to halt its plans to build an expensive new headquarters building and even to move its 700-person office staff to some other city unless Battle Creek city (population 35,724) merged with nearby Battle Creek town-ship (population 20,615). The famous cereal company, with long roots in the community, viewed a merger as the best means to cure the political division that was splintering the area's economic development efforts. Its bold plan worked; the two communities put aside differences and approved a city annex-ation of the township. Local residents in both communities feared the stagger-ing economic consequences a Kellogg pullout would bring to their already depressed economy.

Community organizations sometimes use the *initiative, referendum,* and *recall* (the tools of populism discussed earlier). Although the recall is employed only occasionally—usually in such western states as Oregon, Colorado, and California—there have been some notable recalls: mayors in Omaha and Atlan-tic City and three city council members in Honolulu in 1985. Mayors of three larger cities—San Francisco, Seattle, and Cleveland—faced recall elections in the past decade, but all three mayors beat the recall. Although the recall is still an uncommon event in urban politics, the initiative is now considered more routine.

In a growing number of communities across the nation, zoning and land-use regulations are sometimes being written not at city hall but by grass-roots citizen movements concerned about the quality of life in their neighborhoods. "No-growth" or "slow-growth" advocates are behind many of these initiative drives. But "ballot-box planning" also involves efforts to slash property taxes and defeat school and highway bonds. Occasionally even the developers or a union will bypass normal legislative channels and put measures on the ballot. Residents in the suburbs are especially watchful in guarding against parking problems, high-density housing, traffic gridlock, and other woes they fled the city to escape.

An interest group confronts many different centers of power and decision making. Bargaining exists between interests and city leaders, and between interests and the bureaucracy. The interest-group arrangements of the central city are in many ways similar to those of the national electorate. Within many central cities the electorate is made up of the foreign born, African Americans, Hispanics, Asian Americans, and blue-collar workers. In national elections these groups generally support the Democratic party, and the same partisan ties usually hold for local politics. But to gain control of the central city, politicians must also appeal to the middle classes in the "outer wards," whose interests are much like those of suburbanites, and to upper-income apartment or townhouse dwellers.

THE CHALLENGE OF GROWTH AND ECONOMIC DEVELOPMENT

Until recently everybody, or at least almost everybody in most cities, wanted to see his or her city grow bigger. Everybody was a city booster. The local newspaper, the television stations, the radio stations, the chamber of commerce, the union leaders, the business community, the developers, the teachers, and proud citizens worked together to attract new industries. Such industries would bring, they hoped, new jobs, more amenities, increased land values, and more opportunities for the young. The consensus was that a city with a growing population was a healthy one; one with a losing population a sick one.

Local politicians find it difficult to oppose economic development and economic growth. Those who do sometimes find it hard to secure campaign funds. However, beginning in the early 1980s an anti-growth movement developed. There had always been such feelings, centered primarily in the wealthy suburbs surrounding central cities. In fact, many suburbs were created to escape the growth taking place in central cities. They adopted building and zoning codes and land-use regulations making it difficult, if not impossible, for any new industries to be located in their suburb and to keep out any persons who could not afford large houses on large lots. They carefully planned their new suburbs to ensure they would not become too crowded. These zoning regulations were attacked in the courts as designed to keep the poor and the blacks out of the neighborhood, but as long as they were racially neutral on their face, the courts left them undisturbed.

By the 1980s environmental concerns began to spread from a few suburbs into most suburbs, especially in the Sunbelt. Around the city, and in areas undergoing development, coalitions began forming to fight this growth. Individuals disturbed by noise, pollution, and traffic jams and fearful that developers would build too many houses too close together, bringing in too many people for the infrastructure of roads and sewage disposal in the community, joined together. Toxic leakage at Love Canal in New York, dioxin-tainted soil at Times Beach, Missouri, and hazardous waste at the Rocky Flats nuclear plant near Denver sensitized the nation to the dangers from industrial plants. Environmentalism is now a major political force countering growth.

The issue of growth, slow growth, or no growth is being hotly debated in most regions, and it has brought together new coalitions and stimulated new policy fights. The battles in the 1990s tend to be fought over environmental impact statements. These government-mandated reviews of the potential environmental and ecological impact of new buildings and projects came into being in 1969 as a result of a federal government requirement that stipulated that an environmental assessment must be filed and approved for large projects funded even in part by federal funds. These reports must specify the benefits and costs of the projects and provide an open process for public reactions to be registered and heard.

Most states now have such requirements. This has been a boon for local consulting firms that often win the contract to prepare these reviews. During the 1970s and early 1980s these environmental reviews tended to be neither as much bother or as costly as their opponents claimed, nor as helpful as their proponents had hoped.

But by the 1990s these reviews became a new and controversial part of the local politics. They prompted prolonged litigation and cost millions of dollars. They are used mostly by anti-growth groups to kill or slow up projects. Critics in California claim that environmental impact reviews are driving businesses to other states and have contributed to the prolonged recession of the early 1990s. Thus the debate now takes the form of whether the economic costs—in terms of lost jobs, lost local revenues, and stalled economic growth—are worth the trade-off of protecting the environment. This will continue to be a haunting policy question, and, of course, like in most urban dilemmas, there is seldom a simple answer. But the sides are sharply drawn and the days of easy arbitration or reconciliation are over.

SPECIAL PROBLEMS OF THE CENTRAL CITY

One persistent problem facing most core cities is the exodus of many businesses that take with them important jobs and revenues while low-income groups remain in the city. At the same time the need for city services has greatly expanded. In the last century masses of new immigrants arrived from Europe. In this century migrants have come from the rural areas, especially from the South. More recently this country has welcomed waves of newcomers from Puerto Rico, Cuba, Korea, Vietnam, the Philippines, Nicaragua, Haiti, and Mexico. The number of immigrants from other Latin American countries is also on the rise. The majority of migrants settle first in the inner cities— usually in the poorest, most decaying sections. Invariably, these new arrivals put great stress on the schools and on community safety. Overcrowding and substandard housing in these areas increase health and fire hazards. And despite city-renewal efforts, central cities, in contrast to the middle and outer rings of suburbs, have:

1. More older persons
2. More substandard housing
3. More students from non-English-speaking backgrounds
4. More unemployment
5. Older buildings
6. Higher crime rates
7. Higher population densities
8. Higher percentages of African Americans and most other minorities
9. Higher costs for city services per resident
10. More children living in poverty

Why do problems accumulate in the core city? The migration of persons lacking the job skills needed for an automated and complicated economy puts heavy demands on welfare agencies. Crowding in segregated districts intensifies urban decay and slum conditions. To meet the stepped-up housing needs of people who cannot pay high rents, the city provides housing programs. But this creates tension both among those who are forced to move out of these areas and among those who are forced to move into the housing. People who live in congested areas require more police protection, but police problems grow when different racial and ethnic groups live close together in inner city areas. Also problematic are the movement of thousands of people into the core city in the morning and out to the suburbs or edge cities in the evening, the congestion of the streets, the traffic jams and the pollution of the air. Faced with all these problems, big cities need money, and this is precisely the resource they usually lack.

The sad reality of racism is yet another persisting problem in the central cities. Racial and ethnic discrimination and outright violence between antagonistic groups has become a nightmare for those trying to govern the nation's major cities.

Any picture of central cities as composed exclusively of huddled starving, homeless youth gangs and unemployed masses, however, is misleading. Nor is it fair to say simply that central cities have all the problems and suburbs all the resources. Central cities do, to be sure, have more "high-cost-citizens" (truly needy, handicapped, and senior citizens). And most aging cities are losing population. Yet the decline in population is not a major cause of higher per capita costs in the old central cities, and the spreading of costs among fewer taxpayers is not the sole cause of financial stress in the inner cities. Rather, higher operating costs in the cities result from aging public works, reduced proportions of middle-class homeowners, and increased populations requiring government services. Then, too, land, rents utilities, and taxes are less expensive in the outer suburbs and in some of the newer edge cities, and service companies that can easily move are doing so to lower their operating costs. Many workers in the inner cities are left behind as these companies flock to cheaper locations on the metro outskirts.

Central-city mayors find it difficult to increase revenues or to force suburbanites to pay a larger share of the bill for the city services they use. From the perspective of a mayor, the lack of politically available tax resources is an ever-present reality. This is the economic problem. The legal problem is that most of the states have not permitted their cities to get at wealth in any meaningful way with a local income tax. One result has been the increased organization of cities to lobby for fiscal relief in state capitals and especially in Washington, D.C. In an effort to recapture part of the tax base that escapes to the suburbs in the evenings, some cities have imposed local payroll or other types of commuter taxes to obtain revenue from people who work in the central cities and make frequent use of their facilities yet live in the suburbs. Some city officials say the payroll or commuter tax is an effective way to shift some of the burden to those who benefit from the city but live beyond its borders. But others say it is unlikely to provide significant long-term revenue growth, and they think it encourages even more businesses to leave the city.

Mayors and Leadership in Central Cities

Two hundred years ago the notion of a strong mayor providing vigorous leadership was nonexistent. The need for strong mayoral leadership developed a hundred years ago in the late nineteenth century. It was seen as a means to deal with the social revolution brought on by urbanization, massive waves of immi-

"I dreamed that I was mayor of a large American city."

Drawing by Stevenson. © 1990 The New Yorker Magazine.

gration, and mounting economic problems of growing cities. In the larger cities, gradually and often grudgingly, the office of mayor became a key position for political leadership. In 1899 the reform-minded National Municipal League adopted the "strong mayor system" as part of its first model city charter in an attempt to lead cities out of the "dark ages" of municipal government. Confidence in the strong mayor system has waxed and waned over time, and its adoption in cities varies considerably depending on both partisan and ideological considerations.

BIG-CITY MAYORS

The typical mayor is a college graduate, an experienced grass-roots politician, usually has a business or a legal background, and is forty to fifty years old. Although most mayors are male, several of the nation's largest cities have recently had women mayors, including Pittsburgh, Houston, Dallas, San Diego, San Antonio, and Washington, D.C. In fact, nearly 20 percent of municipal governments with a population of 30,000 or more in the United States are headed by women, and the number is growing. Many of these women worked their way up through service on school boards and city councils and in the League of Women Voters. An increasing number of blacks also serve as mayors. Currently African-American mayors serve in over 300 cities, including Atlanta, Baltimore, Los Angeles, Denver, Philadelphia, Detroit, Oakland, New York, Seattle, Newark, Richmond, and Washington, D.C.

Today mayors head large urban bureaucracies. Most put in long hours and six-day weeks. They are frequently caught in the middle of public-employee strikes, tax controversies, and city-suburb clashes. They make endless trips "with hat in hand" to state and national legislatures. Central-city mayors in the largest cities earn $80,000 to $150,000, and in middle-sized cities between $40,000 and $80,000. City managers, chief city administrators, and top appointees sometimes make more than the mayors.

Mayors of large cities have the same basic functions as any major executive. As chief of state, they issue proclamations, receive important visitors, appear at endless breakfasts, luncheons, and dinners, and launch community and charity drives. As chief executives, they appoint heads of agencies, draw up budgets, check up on administration, deal with sudden emergencies, mediate among warring department chiefs, and try to get rid of incompetents or misfits. Although partisan politics is waning as a feature of city government, mayors as chief of their party still usually dominate the party's city organizations. Mayors help recruit candidates for office, deal with revolts and opposition within their parties, and represent their parties in Washington or the state capitals. As chief legislators, mayors draw up proposed legislation and also make many specific policies. As chief fundraisers, mayors bargain for more money for their cities before state and national legislatures. Indeed, the only presidential powers metropolitan mayors do not hold at the city level are commander in chief and chief of foreign relations. Yet many mayors, such as those in New York, San Francisco, Atlanta, and Miami, do have their own "foreign policies" as they travel abroad seeking foreign investments and singing the praises of the local exportable goods.

Mayors share legislative power with the city council. Typically, mayors have extensive power to recommend legislation and to participate in the legislative process; for example, most have a broad veto power over policy measures and appropriations. But the balance of power varies from city to city. Much depends on the basis by which the council is elected—for example, whether its members are elected by the same party organization that supports the mayor or by a personal organization of their own. A mayor's relations with the city's legislative branch are essentially political, much as they are for the president and governor. Sometimes the mayor must depend on control of the party organization to ensure support in the council, as in Chicago, because the city council (called the Board of Aldermen there) consists of 50 members elected in relatively small districts or wards. Other cities may have more streamlined executive-legislative relationships, yet their mayors are likely to be weak officials unless they have enough political and personal influence to encourage considerable council or board cooperation.[15]

MAYORS AS INNOVATORS

One of the mayor's roles in a major city is to help revitalize the economy and attract new investments, sports teams, conventions, and tourists. Sometimes it takes an almost missionary zeal to overcome the pessimism and despair that beset some inner cities in America. Recent mayors in Indianapolis, San Antonio, and Baltimore have won high praise for their leadership and renewal efforts. They have been model renewers.

It used to be said that Indianapolis was the city you drove through or flew over on your way to somewhere else. But Indianapolis has become the Cinderella city of the Snow- and Rustbelts. More than $1 billion in downtown developments changed the landscape of the inner city. A 61,000-seat Hoosier Dome was constructed; the Baltimore Colts were lured to town; countless major restaurants sprang up; a world-class zoo was opened in a 260-acre state park just west of the downtown area; and the old Union Station was renovated.

Indianapolis Mayor William H. Hudnut III was reelected by landslide margins. "Cities are," he says, "the laboratory in which the experiment that is American democracy is being conducted." Preaching a bit, he says cities are the training ground for civilization. "If we do not succeed there, we will not succeed anywhere. If we can't make the city work, we can't make the country work—or the world either, for that matter. But we can." What did Hudnut do? He instilled a can-do, entrepreneurial attitude about what Indianapolis could become. He bucked the trend of suburban investment and urban disinvestment, emphasizing that you cannot be a suburb of nothing. He persuaded banks, local foundations, and universities, as well as state and federal officials, to participate in his downtown renewal programs. Realizing Indianapolis needed to diversify its economy, he worked to attract high-tech, mid-tech, low-tech, and some non-tech companies—whatever would create jobs.

Mayor Hudnut claims five principles guided the leadership style he used to help Indianapolis gain population and revitalize its economy.

1. *The entrepreneurial city creates partnerships with the private sector.* Public- and private-sector joint ventures are key. "The for-profit and not-for-profit segments of the private sector get together with some government to make things happen. Sometimes one sector takes the initiative, sometimes another, but they are all involved in creative leveraging of each other; they cooperate, establish a consensus, and move ahead."[16]

2. *The entrepreneurial city takes risks.* Hudnut puts it bluntly: The really good local public officials are not afraid to share power, risks, and rewards with the private sector. Cities, he says, are investors too; in return for tangible support for a project, they earn a share of the profit by participating in revenues, rents, and cash flow.

3. *The entrepreneurial city looks for better methods of management.* When it makes sense, a city should contract operations out—for example, trash collection, snow removal, even parts of its transportation system. Although a city is not exactly the same as a business, it has distinctive social, moral, and civic responsibilities too.

4. *The entrepreneurial city treats amenities as economic assets.* Hudnut suggests there is a profitable connection between a commitment to culture, the arts, and preservation projects on the one hand, and job generation and economic-development opportunities on the other. He claims that many businesses are coming into Indianapolis because of the city's commitment to the arts as well as to the theme of fitness. These quality-of-life projects make the central core of the city more attractive, enhancing business growth and helping reverse the negative trend of a declining industrial base.

5. *The entrepreneurial city combats urban decline and attracts urban reinvestment, not by going to Washington and asking for more money, but by creatively using nontraditional resources at home.* Hudnut, who was not only mayor of Indianapolis but also served as president of the National League of Cities, notes that venture capital funds are being set up in cities all around the nation. Business incubator programs for new and existing companies are being established. Home-grown economic-development projects are springing up and producing results, encouraging investment, creating new jobs, and expanding the revenues of the inner cities.

Four-term Mayor Henry Cisneros, who stepped down in 1989 as the chief executive of San Antonio, the tenth largest city in the country, was an effective leader-renewer. Born in a Hispanic barrio in the "across the tracks" west side of San Antonio, Cisneros earned degrees from Texas A & M, Harvard, and George Washington University. After serving on the city council for several years, he narrowly won election as mayor in 1981. He won reelection by landslides. Although San Antonio still has plenty of problems, Mayor Cisneros was able to attract scores of new companies and was partially responsible for helping to launch a major biotech research park, a $125 million world amusement area, and a domed-sports complex.

Cisneros says providing successful urban leadership requires working 12- to 14-hour days, a strategy he followed. He maintained personal relationships with the plant managers and company leaders he lured to and involved in the life of San Antonio. The real answers, he observes, are not found in confrontation, obstruction, or denial of access, but rather in cooperation and inclusion in the fashioning of a common stake in the future.

What was his strategy for leadership? First, to be better in delivering services, to be more financially responsible, to be leaner, tougher, better than anybody. Second, to work with equal intensity to make the system work for people who have been outside the economic mainstream.

Baltimore Mayor William Schaefer was another recent take-charge, entrepreneurial modern mayor who did so well as mayor that he became governor of Maryland. Along with business, civic, and architectural leaders, he capitalized on Baltimore's splendid harbor and transformed a bleak scene of deteriorating warehouses into a visually exciting center for retail, residential, cultural, and waterfront activity. Although he was called the best mayor in America, "the genius mayor," and the like, Schaefer had more than his share of problems in the city rated by the U.S. Census Bureau as the nation's eighth poorest. He (and Baltimore) also lost their football team to Indianapolis.

Undaunted, this several-term mayor set out to improve things. He rebuilt City Hall. He built five interstate highways, got a solid subway system going, helped build one of the nation's foremost aquariums, and launched a world trade center. He fought for the Harborplace that has been an enormous boost to civic pride and economic revitalization. He provided the leadership for a new symphony hall and for a new stadium that helped keep Baltimore's major league baseball team in the city. The list goes on and on.

MAYORS AS CHIEF EXECUTIVES

The main job of the mayor is administrative in the broadest sense of the term. Mayors supervise the big "line" agencies—police, fire, public safety, traffic, health, sanitation—as well as a host of special agencies, such as the board of elections, the city planning agency, and commissions that regulate particular occupations and professions. Big-city mayors usually have staffs that carry out typical executive office functions such as personnel, management, budgeting, scheduling, and public relations. In this respect mayors face the same tasks as corporate executives: coordinating a variety of different activities, assigning responsibilities, checking that projects are carried out, finding the ablest people to take charge, and allotting money through control of the budget.

As noted, many of the nation's better mayors are especially adept at forging economic partnerships with corporate and private-sector leaders. Together they have initiated some significant revitalization projects: the Quincy Market–Faneuil Hall in Boston, the Nicollet Mall area in downtown Minneapolis, the smoke control and Golden Triangle projects in Pittsburgh, and countless similar enterprises resulted from the joint efforts of creative mayors and civic entrepreneurs (often bankers, architects, and corporate officers) to beautify their cities.

Usually mayors become involved with the private sector in economic-development activities in an effort to help promote economic activity and economic opportunities. They try to secure additional jobs, increase a specific tax base, make the city more attractive to certain kinds of businesses, or coordinate future public-service expansion with private-sector requirements and projected uses. The private sector becomes involved in city economic-development projects because its economic success depends upon having a solid labor base with appropriate skills, a constant consumer population, stable communities as measured by housing and school indicators, and stable or increasing property values, which prevent erosion of private assets.

Mayors also have to deal with public or special authorities. Essentially like such public corporations as the Tennessee Valley Authority, these authorities

---

THE "MAYOR JONES" STORY

We hear more about politicians who are indicted or convicted of crime than we do about the thousands of good men and women who work hard, often for very little in return. One is reminded of the fellow who decided to visit an old college buddy in a small town in another state. He had heard his chum had become the town's mayor. It being Saturday afternoon, he asked at the local service station where he might find Mayor Jones and was told: "That no good so-and-so? He's probably off fishing, just like every other day." At the local drug store on Main Street, he heard: "That jerk? I wouldn't tell you if I knew."

After similar repeated attempts, he decided to go by City Hall on the chance someone there might be able to direct him to his friend's house. The building was almost deserted, but there in the mayor's office, hard at work, was his old friend. After a few pleasantries, the out-of-towner asked why his friend wanted a job that kept him working on a beautiful Saturday afternoon. Was it the high salary? "Oh no," the mayor replied, "there is no pay at all." Well, then, was it for the bribes—contractors' graft and the like? No, the mayor said, all city contracts were let by competitive bidding. Perhaps the mayor controlled a lot of patronage jobs? No, all the jobs were now treated under a civil service system. "Why in the world, then," demanded the out-of-towner, "do you take a job like this?" Replied the mayor, "For the prestige, of course."

have been set up to undertake important yet specialized functions in the big cities. (Examples are the Metropolitan Water District of Southern California and the Port Authority of New York.) These agencies oversee functions lying outside as well as inside the boundaries of the city. They have a legal mandate granted to them by the state (or states) to raise money, hire experts, and take over some city services, such as transportation, water, and housing. Why public authorities? In part because state legislatures are sometimes hostile to mayors and prefer to place important functions outside the reach of mayors and political "machines," and in part because the authorities have financial flexibility (for example, they might be able to incur debt outside the limits imposed on the city by the state). But most important, many problems are simply too big or cover too wide a geographic area to be handled properly by the city itself.

Public authorities pose a special problem for central-city mayors. Not only are many of the vital functions of metropolitan government placed beyond the mayor's direct control, but even worse, a mosaic of special authorities and special districts constantly comes into contact—and conflict—with "line" agencies dealing with the same problems in the city. But if public authorities are a problem for mayors, they are also a temptation. By helping to sponsor these independent agencies, mayors can sometimes cut down on their direct administrative loads. They can tap other sources of funds and keep their own cities' tax rates lower than they would otherwise be. If things go wrong, they can say they did not have authority over a certain function and hence cannot be held responsible. However, this may adversely affect the city's welfare and the capacity of its residents to govern themselves effectively.

Ways to Govern Metro Regions

The division between central city and suburbia; the rise of the edge cities; the growth of countless special districts; the existence of divided executive authority, fragmented legislative power, splintered and noncompetitive political parties; the absence of strong central governments for whole metropolitan regions; and the necessity that mayors and other city leaders bargain with so many national, state, and local officials—all these factors suggest that metro regions are shapeless giants with nobody in charge.

At the turn of the century reformers were afraid of boss domination. But in the modern metropolis the mayor of the central city lacks authority even over agencies within the city. Political machines don't run the central city, let alone the whole metropolis. Urban bureaucracies may wield a lot of power over a few areas, but they do not offer metropolitan leadership. "Special interests" seldom really control the metropolis, nor usually does a "business elite" or any other kind of "they." And even if "they" did control politics, that is not the same as governing. Who, then, governs the metropolis? Does anybody provide coherent leadership?

REFORM STRATEGIES

The growing fragmentation of governments in large metropolitan areas has brought about a variety of metropolitan reform movements and structural inventions aimed at improving performance and reducing corruption. Political scientists and public administration specialists have not been bashful about proposing remedies. We look here at some of the better-known ideas, all of which have been tried somewhere, but none of which has been adopted nationwide.

Annexation In the growing cities of the South, West, and Southwest, the large central cities have absorbed adjacent territories. Oklahoma City, for example, added almost 600 square miles. Houston, Phoenix, and Kansas City, Missouri, San Antonio, El Paso, and Colorado Springs have also expanded their boundaries. In these and several other cities the now extended city serves almost as a de facto regional government. Annexation has not proved helpful, however, to most cities in the Northeast and Midwest because these cities are ringed by entrenched suburban communities that do not want to be annexed, and state laws make it difficult for the central city to do so against the wishes of the suburbs. Even in such places as the Houston metropolitan area, the annexation option is plagued by legal obstacles, political jealousies, and additional complications.

Agreements to Furnish Services The most common solution to the problems of overlapping and duplicating jurisdictions is for the units of government to contract services. This "reform" is applauded by many economists. They say it comes close to providing a market that operates according to laws of supply and demand. Most agreements involve just a few cities and a single activity. For example, a city may provide hospital services to its neighbors, or contract with the county for law enforcement. Especially popular in the Los Angeles area, the contract system is also used in other parts of the country.

Regional Coordinating and Planning Councils Just about all metro regions have some kind of council of government (COG). These began in the 1950s and were encouraged by the national government during the 1960s and 1970s. Congress, in fact, mandated that certain federal grants be reviewed by this kind of body. In essence, these councils are forums established to bring locally elected officials together. They have devoted most of their time and resources to physical planning and noncontroversial activities that do not touch on the urban problems of race and poverty. Councils are set up, moreover, in such a way as to give suburbs a veto over any project that would threaten their autonomy. In a few regions the councils do assume operating responsibilities over such regional activities as garbage collection, transportation, and water supply. Critics say the councils rarely provide for creative areawide governance, yet they have provided an important common ground for elected officials to talk about mutual problems and they have helped to solve some problems in many of the regions.

City-County Consolidations   One traditional means of overcoming the fragmentation of metro regions is to merge the central city with the larger county. This is a pet reform of business elites, the League of Women Voters, and chambers of commerce. It is viewed as a rational, efficient way to simplify administration, cut costs for taxpayers, and eliminate duplication.

At least 25 city-county mergers have taken place. They can usually be brought about only by a public referendum that the citizens of the region must approve. Although efforts have been made to consolidate cities with counties —Boston, New York, Philadelphia, for example—few such efforts have been successful. In addition to St. Louis, Nashville, Jacksonville, and Indianapolis, consolidations have occurred in only a handful of smaller urban areas. What happened in Indianapolis is typical of these consolidations, most of which are in the South and West. In 1970 Indianapolis combined with Marion County to create UNIGOV. This required special permission by the legislature. UNIGOV provides many services, but the school systems remain separate, as do the police and sheriff departments.

The era of city-county consolidation appears to be over. Only two such consolidations took place in the 1980s. These proposed mergers are usually defeated by county voters. But it is no longer unusual to find counties running what used to be city jails, zoos, libraries, and similar services. Formal and informal agreements abound as cities and counties deal with "the problems of overlap and fragmentation by shifting responsibilities for providing specific services among themselves."[17]

Federated Government   A strategy that attempts to take into account political realities advocates building on existing governments. Backers of this strategy conclude that it is both undesirable and impossible to create a single giant metropolitan government for a large area. To do so would be to eliminate all of the "us" governments and substitute a distant "them" government. Instead, they advocate keeping the units with which people identify but assigning some crucial functions to an areawide metro government.

One of the few attempts—and there have been only a few—to create a federated government is the Twin Cities Metropolitan Council for the Minneapolis-St. Paul region. This regional organization, established by the legislature in 1967, consists of a 17-member council. Sixteen members are appointed by the governor to represent equal population districts, and the seventeenth is a full-time chairperson-executive who serves at the pleasure of the governor. A staff conducts research, planning, and coordination for the 140 cities, 7 counties, and about 36 special districts in the region. In matters defined as regional, this council can and does veto local actions or prevent actions by local governments. Prior to 1967 the Twin Cities region had been plagued for years by governmental fragmentation, tax inequities, and inconsistent provision of services.

"We love the view. It helps to remind us that we're part of a larger
community."

Drawing by Weber; © 1986 The New Yorker Magazine, Inc.

Because the central cities were tightly ringed by established suburban communities, the idea of a city-county merger was not appropriate. Today the Metropolitan Council, in essence a new layer of government superimposed on top of
existing units, serves as a metropolitan planning and policy-making, as well as
policy-coordinating, agency. It reviews applications for federal funds from the
region. It guides regional planning and development and opposes local actions
that would endanger the overall welfare of the region. The Twin Cities model
would appear to be a ready candidate for transfer elsewhere, yet this has not
happened.

THE POLITICS OF METROPOLITAN REORGANIZATION

Nearly every metropolitan area today has or wants regional bodies that can integrate and coordinate the maze of governmental structures. There is already a
degree of cooperation, although much of it is informal, voluntary, or contrac-
tual. Progress in designing areawide, multipurpose, integrated metropolitan
governing bodies has been slow and will remain that way. Why? In part because
different cities and jurisdictions have differing political needs. They depend on
specific needs and changes in the physical and political context. For example,
city-county consolidation has been an effective solution for Nashville, but it
could not get beyond the proposal stage in Pittsburgh or beyond the electorate
in Memphis. Annexation has worked well in Phoenix and Oklahoma City, but
would be of little help in cities ringed by incorporated suburbs, such as Boston,
Denver, and Miami. Similarly, although the urban county approach serves the

Los Angeles area reasonably well, it would be less effective in New England's traditionally weak counties.

In most metropolitan regions, to combine city and suburbs would be to shift political power to the suburbs. In most northern centers, this would give Republicans more control of city affairs. In other cases it would enable Democrats to threaten the present one-party Republican systems in the suburbs. Under these circumstances neither Democratic leaders in the central cities nor Republicans in control of the suburbs show much enthusiasm for metropolitan schemes. African Americans usually oppose area consolidation or similar reform proposals because they dilute their political power, often rather severely.

In general, although residents of the metropolis want better services, they hope to achieve them by negotiation and other traditional or innovative devices. Although there is no rebellion against the existing structure, a notable increase in interlocal and regional collaboration has occurred. It was generally done on an issue-by-issue basis and reflects an incremental pattern of evolution. Through patchwork, piecemeal, and pragmatic arrangements, the public receives the services it wants—and is willing to pay for.[18]

SOLUTIONS OUTSIDE THE METROPOLIS

Some people believe solutions to metropolitan problems are beyond the capacity of the metropolis itself. They favor a strengthened role for the national government, with special emphasis on ensuring "equity" or on relating services directly to needs. Some advocate reviving federal revenue sharing, yet they would give back revenue only on the condition that local governments rationalize the governmental machinery of the whole metropolis. Others believe the job must be done by the states, which hold the fundamental constitutional power. Still others put forward bold proposals to establish regional governments that would rule huge regions embracing many metropolitan areas.

Big-city mayors have made it clear that, in their judgment, the urban condition is acute, and that we must, especially in this post–Cold War era, rearrange our national priorities and allocate billions of dollars for massive aid to large cities. The cities themselves lack the resources and political jurisdiction necessary to attack the basic causes of urban pathology. "We surrender," some mayors have been saying, in effect, to Washington. "Treat us like a conquered and occupied nation. Give us the kind of aid you gave Germany and Japan after the Second World War."

In the matter of federal aid, however, the Reagan and Bush administrations were seldom sympathetic to big-city mayors. Fiscal constraints are limiting federal programs. In the 1990s states have had to cut services and raise taxes. States are also unable to deal easily with the problem of giant cities that stretch over state lines. New regional governments? A bold idea, but one that appears beyond the capacity of the American people to engineer without threatening local home-rule values.

Summary

1. Governmental forms at the grass roots in the United States come in a great variety of shapes and structures and perform various functions. However, since constitutional power is vested in the states, all counties, cities, and towns have in common the fact that they act as agents of the state.

2. The most common governmental form at the county level is a board of county commissioners, although larger urban counties are moving to council-administrator or council-elected executive plans.

3. There is no typical suburb. Although many suburbs are homogeneous, suburban America is highly heterogeneous. Suburbs are confronting urban problems, and the inner rings of older suburbs often look very much like the central cities.

4. The most common governmental forms at the city level are the mayor-council and the council-manager (city-manager) plans. Mayor-council governments generally have a strong mayor as well as partisan city elections. They operate with a ward system and have reasonably short and simultaneous council terms. Council-manager cities generally select the mayor from the council, operate with at-large and nonpartisan elections, and have overlapping terms for council members. In general, city-manager cities are found in medium to large cities and in western, especially Sunbelt, cities.

5. Americans live in a metropolitan nation, with most of us residing in central cities or in outlying communities known as suburbs. There is considerable fragmentation of governmental units in our metropolitan areas, and this fragmentation tends to undermine citizen involvement in the problems of the metropolis.

6. The standard of living in the central cities of the United States may be much better than it was 50 years ago, but the inequalities between many central cities and their middle and outer rings of affluent suburbs are increasing. Central cities are often faced with economic hardships, intense racism and drug-related gangs and criminals. Fragmentation and dispersal of political authority in the metro areas and even in many of the central cities themselves often make it not only difficult to govern the big cities, but also to respond with adequate policies and funds to treat the problems of the metropolis.

7. For a generation or more, reformers thought the answer to the problems of metropolitan government was to elect a strong central-city mayor or to establish a regional government for the whole area. Both solutions have been difficult to achieve and have some drawbacks. And resistance to regional government continues to be great. The structure of many of our largest cities seems designed to undermine effective governance yet a lot of collaboration nonetheless takes place.

For Further Reading

BARBARA ACKERMAN, *"You the Mayor!" The Education of a City Politician* (Auburn House, 1989).

JAMES M. BANOVETZ, ed., *Small Cities and Counties: A Guide to Managing Services* (International City Manager Association, 1985).

GEORGE S. BLAIR, *Government at the Grass Roots* (Palisades Publishers, 1981).

MATTHEW CRENSON, *Neighborhood Politics* (Harvard University Press, 1983).

BARBARA FERMAN, *Governing the Ungovernable City* (Temple University Press, 1985).

JOEL GARREAU, *Edge City* (Doubleday, 1991).

JOHN J. HARRIGAN, *Political Change in the Metropolis*, 4th ed, (Scott Foresman, 1989).

GERALD L. HOUSEMAN, *State and Local Government: The New Battlefield* (Prentice Hall, 1986).

KENNETH T. JACKSON, *Crabgrass Frontier: The Suburbanization of the United States* (Oxford University Press, 1985).

CHRISTOPHER JENCKS and PAUL E. PETERSON, eds., *The Urban Underclass* (Brookings Institution, 1991).

DENNIS R. JUDD, *The Politics of American Cities*, 3d ed. (Scott Foresman, 1988).

DAVID R. MORGAN, *Managing Urban America*, 3d ed. (Brooks-Cole, 1989).

JACK NEWFIELD and WAYNE BARRETT, *City for Sale: Ed Koch and the Betrayal of New York* (Harper and Row, 1989).

GARY RIVLIN, *Fire on the Prairie: Chicago's Harold Washington and the Politics of Race* (Holt, 1992).

MICHAEL SMITH, *City, State and Market: The Political Economy of Urban Society* (Blackwell, 1988).

CLARENCE N. STONE, *Regime Politics: Governing Atlanta* (University Press of Kansas, 1989).

JAMES H. SVARA, *Official Leadership in the City: Patterns of Conflict and Cooperation* (Oxford University Press, 1989).

WILLIAM JULIUS WILSON, *The Truly Disadvantaged: The Inner City, the Underclass and Public Policy* (University of Chicago Press, 1987).

See also *Governing: The Magazine of States and Localities*, published monthly by Congressional Quarterly, Inc.; *The National Civic Review*, published by the National Civic League; and *The Municipal Yearbook*, published annually by the International City Management Association.

Notes

1. These and related trends are documented in Chapter 14, ACIR, Commission Report, *The Question of State Government Capability* (Government Printing Office, 1985).

2. On the role of counties, see Donald C. Menzel et al., "Setting a Research Agenda for the Study of the American County," *Public Administration Review*, March–April 1992, pp. 173–82; Vincent Marando and Mavis Reeves, "Counties as Local Governments," *Journal of Urban Affairs* 13 (1991), pp. 45–53. A standard work is Herbert S. Duncombe, *Modern County Government* (National Association of Counties, 1977).

3. But see the celebration of town meetings in Shirley Elder, "Running a Town the 17th-Century Way," *Governing*, March 1992, pp. 29–30.

4. Kenneth T. Jackson, *Crabgrass Frontier: The Suburbanization of the United States* (Oxford University Press, 1985).

5. Neal Peirce, "The New Suburbia Is Transforming Open Lands to Urban Village Ghettos," *Today Journal*, September 6, 1985, pp. 6–7.

6. James M. Banovetz and Thomas W. Kelty, "Home Rule in Illinois: Image and Reality," in *Illinois Issues* (Sangomon State University, 1987).

7. *Rogers v. Lodge*, 458 U.S. 613 (1982); and *Thornburg v. Gingles*, 478 U.S. 30 (1986).

8. Charles R. Adrian, "Forms of City Government in American History," in *The Municipal Year Book, 1988* (International City Management Association, 1988), p. 9.

9. For the experience of one mayor in a council manager city, see the memoir by Cambridge, Massachusetts, Mayor Barbara Ackermann, *"You the Mayor!" The Education of a City Politician* (Auburn House, 1989).

10. Harmon Zeigler et al., *City Managers and School Superintendents* (Prager, 1984). For earlier studies, see Richard J. Stillman, *The Rise of the City Manager* (University of New Mexico Press, 1974); and Ronald O. Loveridge, *City Managers in Legislative Politics* (Bobbs-Merrill, 1970).

11. William Lyons, "Reform and Response in American Cities: Structure and Policy Reconsidered," *Social Science Quarterly*, June 1978, p. 130.

12. Bryan Jones, *Governing Urban America* (Little, Brown, 1983).

13. Joel Garreau, *Edge City* (Doubleday, 1991), p. 8.

14. See, for example, the analysis of other groups such as the African Americans in Atlanta in

Clarence Stone's *Regime Politics: Governing Atlanta* (University of Kansas Press, 1988).

15. For studies of recent mayors in New York City and Chicago, see Sam Roberts, "Mayor Dinkins: Every Day a Test," *New York Times Magazine,* April 7, 1991, pp. 27–29 and 46–50; and Gary Rivlin, *Fire on the Prairie: Chicago's Harold Washington and the Politics of Race* (Holt, 1992).

16. Former Mayor William H. Hudnut III, Woodrow Wilson Address, Princeton University, February 1986.

17. John Herbers, "17th-Century Counties Struggle to Cope with 20th Century Problems," *Governing,* May 1989, p. 46.

18. Eileen Shanahan, "Going It Jointly: Regional Solutions for Local Problems," *Governing,* August 1991, pp. 70–76.

9

Staffing and Financing State and Local Governments

On an early spring day in 1992 the residents of Montpelier, Vermont, faced an unexpected flood. An ice floe acted as a dam, diverting the Winooski River, which was already near flood stage from the spring thaw. Before the ice floe could be dislodged, the river flooded the entire downtown area of Montpelier, with as much as six feet of water near the state capitol. The governor called out the national guard to rescue people stranded on top of their automobiles and to help with the evacuation of office buildings. Schools were closed, but getting the children home was difficult. Electricity was cut off because of fear of fire from downed electrical lines. Telephone service was also shut off.

During emergencies like this one faced by the citizens of Montpelier, we are reminded not only of the shared need for public safety but also of how much we rely on government for the provision of basic services. Things as simple as working traffic lights, a functioning telephone system, and electricity all come under the purview of state and local governments.

Government involves many things—legal authority, popular consent, shared values—but it is also very much a matter of people and money. People must be elected and hired, salaries must be negotiated and paid, and materials must be purchased. Over 15 million people work in state and local governments within the United States.[1] The cost and quality of government depend partly on the ability and performance of public employees and partly on the adequacy of the resources they use.

Public Employees: Essential to Government

When we talk about the state, the city, or the county government, we are simply using shorthand symbols for groups of people. When we say the government builds the roads or runs the schools, we really mean that a group of public officials or public employees performs these functions. In a sense, the individuals who work for our state and local governments *are* the state and local governments. Wages for public employees constitute more than half of the cost of state and local government.[2] How are these people chosen?

A few of them are elected. The rest are generally appointed through some kind of **merit system** in which selection and promotion depend on demonstrated performance (or merit) rather than on political patronage. The patronage system has not disappeared, and in many jurisdictions it still helps to know the right people and belong to the right party. But these practices are not as prevalent as they once were. Many jurisdictions now administer competency or "knowledge" tests to prospects and employees before hiring or promoting them. Moreover, the Supreme Court has declared it unconstitutional for most public employees to be dismissed for political reasons. Affirmative action requirements call for recruitment through open procedures. Unionization has had a negative effect on patronage.[3] See page 236 for a comparison of merit and collective bargaining systems.

STATE AND LOCAL MERIT SYSTEMS

Almost all states now use merit systems to choose their public servants. Merit systems are generally administered by a civil service commission, typically composed of three members appointed by the governor, with the consent of the state legislature, for a term of six years. The commission prepares and administers examinations, provides lists of job openings, establishes job classifications, and prepares salary schedules. It also serves as a board of appeal for those who are discharged. Civil service commissions are increasingly concerned with in-service training, collective bargaining, administering affirmative action programs, and filling top-level executive positions.

How well do these commissions do their job? Critics complain they are too slow because they are hampered by red tape and clumsy rules; since job lists are not kept up-to-date, it often takes weeks to fill vacancies. A more serious charge is that civil service commissions have deprived responsible officials of authority over their subordinates. There is so much emphasis on insulating public servants from political coercion, it is argued, that employees enjoy too much job security, and administrators cannot get rid of incompetents. It has been known to take months and several elaborate hearings to dismiss secretaries who could not type or librarians who could not read. Although merit systems are supposed to emphasize ability and minimize political favoritism, they sometimes discourage able people from seeking public-sector jobs.

TABLE 9-1   Comparison of Merit and Collective Bargaining Systems

	Collective Bargaining	Merit Systems
Management rights	Minimal or none; bilateralism	Maximal or total; unilateralism
Employee participation and rights	Union shop or maintenance of membership Exclusive recognition	Open shop (if any recognition)
Recruitment and selection	Union membership and/or occupational license Entrance at bottom only	Open competitive examination Entrance at any level
Promotion	On basis of seniority	Competitive on basis of merit (often including seniority)
Classification of positions	Negotiable as to classification plan; subject to grievance procedure as to allocation	Intrinsic as to level of responsibilities and duties on basis of objective analysis
Pay	Negotiable and subject to bargaining power of union	Based on balanced pay plan or subject to prevailing rates
Hours, leaves, conditions of work	Negotiable	Based on public interest as determined by legislature and management
Grievances	Appeal by union representation to impartial arbitrators	Appeal through management, with recourse to civil service agency

Source: Frederick C. Mosher, "Democracy and Public Service: The Collective Services," in *Classics of Public Administration*, Jay M. Shafritz and Albert C. Hyde, eds. (Brooks/Cole, 1992), p. 507.

PUBLIC-EMPLOYEE UNIONS

Public-employee unions have grown rapidly over the past generation as government workers have organized to demand better wages, hours, working conditions, and pensions. These unions now wield considerable political clout in most states and in many cities. In places such as New York City, they are viewed as one of the two or three most powerful forces in political life. State and local governments have found themselves involved in collective bargaining and voluntary or binding arbitration processes.

More than half of all state and local public employees are unionized. The American Federation of State, County, and Municipal Employees (AFSCME), representing over a million members, has been the fastest-growing union in the country in recent decades. Other large public-employee unions are the International Association of Fire Fighters, which represents over 175,000 fire personnel; the National Education Association, which represents about 1.6 million teachers; and the American Federation of Teachers, which represents another

580,000 teachers. The fire fighters' union, often considered one of the most effective political organizations among the public-employee unions, sometimes engages in door-to-door and telephone campaigning to elect city officials. Furthermore, unions raise funds for candidates and sponsor letter-writing campaigns to influence city officials. Union pressure in recent decades is a major reason the average pay of public employees has risen faster than that of workers in private industry. When benefits are added to base salaries, the average pay of public-sector employees has risen over 300 percent faster than that of people employed in private industry.[4] Hence, many people believe public employees in most areas of the country are reasonably well paid.

The failure of the civil service system to meet many of the needs of public employees encouraged the growth of public-sector unions. Growth was also spurred by the success of union collective bargaining in the private sector. But much of the success of public-employee unions has come about because government workers learned how to become a political force within cities and states. Most public employees are educated, intelligent people who can provide hard-pressed candidates with research, mailing help, and much-needed campaign contributions. The public-employee unions have succeeded in part because they can deliver two of the most valuable components of campaigns—

THE MAYOR AS COLLECTIVE BARGAINER

Mayors differ from presidents of private corporations in several ways. First, they have responsibility for the total universe of a public constituency. Second, their union constituency helped put them in their job, so, in a sense, mayors are employees of their own employees.

Public services are primarily monopolistic in character. There is no one else who supplies the services governments provide, and such services must be handled here and now. Many are so vital to public health and survival that a stoppage can be catastrophic, and this places great pressure on the bargainer. Then, too, because of the public nature of government operations, bargaining often takes place in a goldfish bowl of publicity.

The diversity of services that a city must provide results in a broad spectrum of occupational classes in public service and, therefore, often a proliferation of bargaining units. In the private sector, in contrast, a whole industry may be organized as a single industrial unit, or at most, a few. In the public sector each union may try to outdo all the others in gains, creating a "whipsaw" effect that can be very costly for governments.

Municipal chief executives are also more restricted than executives in private industry in dealing with labor matters because the results must be accepted by their legislative bodies. This is particularly true wherever the legislative body can exert a strong check on executive power. It may then look upon any substantial move by the mayor during negotiations as an usurpation of its own powers.

Source: Former Milwaukee Mayor Henry W. Maier, "Collective Bargaining and the Municipal Employer," in *Public Workers and Public Unions*, ed., Sam Zagoria (Prentice Hall, 1972).

money and labor (not to mention the votes of their members, members' families, and friends).

This success has produced a growing backlash, however. Surveys show that the general public thinks public workers not only have more job security but also as good or better wages and fringe benefits than people working in the private sector. Critics point out that public employees seem to have the best of both worlds: civil service job protection coupled with most of the bargaining power of an industrial labor union. In addition, public-employee unions in some cities are so well organized as special-interest groups that they help elect the very officials who must bargain with them. Although collective bargaining and unionization have long been generally accepted in the private sector, these rights are not so widely accepted in the public sector. One reason for this is that the government generally operates as a monopoly provider of many vital services.

Because the public sector provides services almost everyone wants and perceives as necessities, demand is relatively constant. Also, public-employee unions are organized as an effective political force, so they influence crucial decisions that affect taxation and the allocation of revenue. Some believe these two factors may lead to unfair influence, resulting in a redistribution of income in favor of public employees. Awareness of this distortion effect and of the increasing clout of the unions has stiffened the spines of some city and state officials. Today it is not uncommon for mayors in large cities to fight the unions and win support from taxpayers and business groups who think the unions have overstepped their proper bounds.

ARE PEOPLE ON THE PUBLIC PAYROLL ENTITLED TO STRIKE?

Deeply embedded in our civic ethic is the idea that civil servants should not strike, especially those (like police and fire fighters) on whom the public depends for vital services. Many state and local elected officials, and certainly many ordinary citizens, believe it is wrong and dangerous for police, fire fighters, and hospital workers to strike. In 1919 Massachusetts Governor Calvin Coolidge became famous for opposing the Boston police strike with these words: "There is no right to strike against the public safety by anybody, anywhere, anytime." At the national level, Ronald Reagan's decision to fire all air traffic controllers who engaged in an illegal strike in 1981 was supported by most of the public. When serious problems arise, like the unexpected flooding of Montpelier described earlier, no one wants to be in the middle of a public employees strike.

Strikes by all public unions are illegal in most states, and even states that permit them prohibit strikes by those who provide "vital and essential services." Nevertheless, such strikes do occur, and in most instances local and state officials are more concerned with getting people back to work than with sending them to jail for violating the law. Thus amnesty for the strikers has usually been the rule. Union organizers, for their part, refuse to consider their strikes as defying the law; instead, they believe the strike is a legitimate and useful weapon in a labor dispute. Still, the strike is generally viewed as a weapon of last resort, to be used only under intolerable conditions.

Moreover, striking has political risks for the public-workers unions. Adverse public reaction may strengthen the hand of governors, mayors, or other politicians opposed to the unions. Many union leaders now favor **compulsory arbitration** over the strike, and more than 20 states have enacted laws providing for some form of arbitration. Union leaders who favor arbitration hope that it will gain them something they might not get at the bargaining table, but without arousing the public backlash that usually accompanies strikes. **Binding arbitration** is used in several states, mostly in such public-safety areas as police and fire protection. In binding arbitration a neutral third party or mediating board hears the arguments of both sides in the dispute and devises what it considers to be a fair settlement. The arbitrator's verdict is final.

An alternative to binding arbitration is *last-best-offer arbitration*, in which the arbitrator considers the final offers of both sides and then selects one. The alleged advantage of this method is that it encourages realistic offers and voluntary settlement. Fearing that the other side's proposal may be chosen as more reasonable, both parties tend to make their offers more realistic.

Although binding arbitration does not guarantee there will be no public-employee strikes, the number of such strikes has been reduced in states where it is practiced. However, the settlements that result from binding arbitration are often expensive. Each decision in a binding arbitration case has a ripple effect on the rest of a city or state administration. A pay raise for one group sets the standard for other public workers. In cities, for example, the police or fire fighters are usually the pacesetters in the politics of winning higher pay. The director of labor-management relations for the U.S. Conference of Mayors complains that binding arbitration "is a lot like leading the mayor and the city council into a large closet, locking the door and turning the key over to a stranger who came to town to clear up a personnel problem in one department and wound up preparing a plan for fiscal chaos."[5]

PROVIDING PUBLIC SERVICES FOR A PROFIT?

In an effort to make government more efficient and curb the growing influence of public-employee unions, many communities have contracted out certain "public services" to those in the private sector who can provide the services at lower costs and still make a profit. Today virtually every service is contracted out somewhere in the United States, and this trend is expected to continue.

Gary Jensen's American Emergency Services is an example. This business employs nonunion workers to put out fires in Elk Grove Township, Illinois, and has been turning a profit. The township would have to spend about $200,000 more a year than it pays Jensen if it ran its own fire department. Jensen's principal saving comes from his lower labor costs. Although similar efforts are being tried in cities and states across the country, the idea of the **privatization** of fire and ambulance services, and even of the operation of city and state prisons, is relatively new. Bay County Jail, in Panama City, Florida, one of the few privately operated jails in the country, is being watched carefully by other public officials.

As cities and states have become hard pressed for cash, efforts to encourage entrepreneurs to provide public services at a profit have increased. Delegation of emergency and police powers to profit-making corporations, however, raises questions of liability and guarantees of individual rights. It also raises fears that private contractors will hire transient help at less pay, undermining merit systems and public-employee morale.

Privatization of various public services has been hotly debated. Advocates, including many of those who bid on contracts, some academics, and some city managers and city and state elected officials, say privatization keeps taxes down and increases public-sector productivity. Opponents, including public-employee unions, other academics, and other city and state officials, contend that privatization raises serious issues of accountability, quality, flexibility, and integrity. Public-employee groups such as AFSCME say privatization:

- Masks hidden costs to government, including the expenses of contract preparation and monitoring contractor performances
- Emphasizes the profit motive, making contracted services neither cheaper than publicly provided services nor of comparable quality
- Locks public officials into inflexible contracts that prevent responses to unforeseen circumstances
- Increases opportunities for corruption
- Diminishes government accountability to citizens[6]

What are the practical limits to privatization? Would it work in the military or in large city departments? One limit to privatization is the idea of **public goods,** which are services or commodities that individuals benefit from but cannot be separately sold or given to individuals. Things like clean air, national defense, and public safety are usually seen as public goods.[7] For successful privatization to occur, the contract between the government and the private company providing the service must define that service to the satisfaction of both parties. Because of the wide range of services provided by local police departments or by the navy, it may be difficult to word such a contract. On the other hand, garbage collection and snow removal can be easily defined and specified in a contract, making these services ripe for privatization, so the trend toward privatization of municipal services like these will continue through the 1990s.

Paying for State and Local Government

State and local governments get most of their money from taxes. Yet, unlike the federal government, they do not control the monetary machinery and often have to secure voter consent through referenda before they can levy taxes. In addition, state and local governments frequently have to run programs and meet other responsibilities mandated by higher levels of government, which do not always provide the funding to fulfill those mandates. Federal aid, which greatly increased in the 1960s and 1970s, declined about 25 percent in real dollars by the 1990s.[8]

The politics of the federal budget deficit and the antitax mood of the public in recent decades have meant that Congress and the president often enact new polices for which the state and local governments have to pick up the tab. At the same time, citizens have high expectations for services provided by their state and local governments and, when asked, indicate they would like even more services.

The combination of increasing demands on state and local governments and decreasing federal funding has made state and local governments the fiscal "stress joints" of American government. Many states have had to raise taxes, and even more have cut spending. Because states are typically unable to use deficit spending for general government programs, they have had to respond incrementally to shortfalls by strengthening and diversifying their revenue bases.[9] In addition, state and local leaders have generally done a prudent job in spending government monies.

The overlapping layers of government by which the American people regulate their lives complicate the tax picture. Tax policies at different levels of government often conflict. While the national government is reducing taxes to encourage spending, states may be raising them.[10] Indeed, when the federal government cuts both taxes and federal grants to states and local units, state and local governments often have little choice but to raise taxes. This is precisely what happened in the late 1970s and early 1980s. The passage and implementation of the Reagan income tax cut of 1981 is seen by some as the turning point when federal aid to states and localities decreased significantly and, consequently, state taxes had to be increased.[11] State and local government revenues adjusted to personal income rose by more than 25 percent between 1969 and 1989, while federal revenues adjusted to personal income actually declined over the two decades.[12] Figure 9-1 presents the shifts in total government financing for the period 1969–89.

Over the 20-year period from 1969 to 1989, total state and local government revenue in the United States rose sixfold, from $313 billion to $1,917 billion. Yet most of this increase was the result of inflation. Once inflation is accounted for, government revenue only rose from 35 percent of GNP in 1969 to 39 percent in 1989. This relative stability in total government revenue, however, hides a shift in where the money came from.

FIGURE 9-1   Changes in the Relation of Government Revenue Relative to Personal Income, 1969–1989.

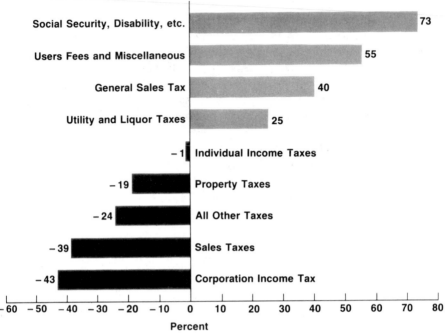

Source: Allen D. Manvel, "Shifts in Govenmental Financing—1969–1989," Tax Notes 51 (June 3, 1991), p. 1201.

State and local governments are increasingly financed by "nontax" devices like user fees, revenues from publicly owned utility companies and liquor stores, and lotteries, as well as from what is technically called "insurance trust revenue"—payroll deductions for retirement and disability programs. The Bureau of the Census lists all these as "contributions" rather than "taxes." This is not a meaningful distinction to taxpayers, however, since the government collects the money from their paychecks in the same way it collects income taxes.

Until recently, each level of government paid little attention to the tax policies of the other levels. The number of taxing authorities also makes tax gathering an expensive operation. For example, national officials, state officials, and some local officials collect taxes on gasoline, and each level of government maintains its own tax-collecting office for individual taxpayers as well. Taxpayers are allowed to deduct certain business expenses and state taxes from their federal, but not from their state, income tax. Thus changes in state laws can affect the amount of federal tax a person must pay. If a state increases its taxes, the national government receives less money. While there is little coordination in setting tax policy, there is generally good cooperation between state and federal tax administrators. Three major categories of taxes in the United States are each targeted more to one level of government than another and are administered more at one level than another (see Table 9-2).

TABLE 9-2 Taxes and Level of Government

Administered By	Income Tax	Sales Tax	Property Tax
Federal government	Yes	No[a]	No
State governments	Piggyback on federal taxes. Adjusted Gross Income for most part	Yes	State supervision and oversight
Local governments	No	No Piggyback on state taxes in most cases	Yes

[a] The federal taxes on gasoline and cigarettes are examples of excise taxes.

[b] By "piggy-back" we mean the states build their state income tax using some parts of the federal tax categories and tax forms.

No matter who collects the taxes, all the money comes out of a single economy. Although each level of government has a different tax base, and each tax hits some groups rather than others, all taxes ultimately depend on the productivity of the American people. And that productivity is affected by many of the activities of government. Through their taxes, the people buy police protection, parks and educational programs, highways, and other things they consider desirable. Table 9-3 indicates what percentage of personal income is paid in taxes in all 50 states and Washington, D.C.

WHO SHALL PAY THE TAXES?

A good tax, as an old saying has it, is one somebody else has to pay; a bad tax is one you have to pay. Who bears the cost of state and local services is decided in

TABLE 9-3 State and Local Tax Revenue as a Percentage of Personal Income, 1990

Alabama	9.57%	Illinois	10.95	Montana	12.65	Rhode Island	11.40
Alaska	19.62	Indiana	10.25	Nebraska	11.51	South Carolina	11.38
Arizona	12.53	Iowa	11.88	Nevada	10.61	South Dakota	10.29
Arkansas	9.65	Kansas	11.05	New Hampshire	6.35	Tennessee	9.40
California	11.44	Kentucky	10.76	New Jersey	10.59	Texas	10.59
Colorado	10.89	Louisiana	11.64	New Mexico	12.75	Utah	12.21
Connecticut	11.00	Maine	12.21	New York	15.54	Vermont	12.19
Delaware	11.02	Maryland	11.18	North Carolina	11.12	Virginia	10.16
Washington, D.C.	17.51	Massachusetts	10.63	North Dakota	11.19	Washington	12.30
		Michigan	11.66	Ohio	11.01	West Virginia	12.22
Florida	10.10	Minnesota	13.12	Oklahoma	10.86	Wisconsin	12.77
Georgia	11.29	Mississippi	10.58	Oregon	12.25	Wyoming	14.63
Hawaii	14.00	Missouri	9.44	Pennsylvania	10.62	**U.S. Average**	11.48
Idaho	11.31						

Source: U.S. Bureau of the Census, Government Finances: 1989–90 (Government Printing Office, 1991), p. 101.

the United States by politics. The people of any state, through their elected representatives, are free to extract whatever taxes they wish from whomever (in that state) they wish, as long as their taxing practices meet the stipulations of the federal Constitution.

The Constitution forbids states to tax exports or imports or to levy tonnage duties without the consent of Congress; to use their taxing power to interfere with federal operations; to discriminate against interstate commerce, unduly burden it, or directly tax it; to use their taxing power to deprive persons of equal protection of the law, or to deprive individuals of their property without due process. Constitutional lawyers and judges spend much of their time applying these principles to concrete situations. Out of hundreds of disputes, courts have decided that states may collect both sales taxes from interstate sales and income taxes from persons and corporations within the states, even if the income was earned from interstate business. However, states may not tax the privilege of engaging in interstate commerce or the unapportioned gross receipts from interstate transactions.

State constitutions also restrict state taxing power. Certain kinds of property, such as that used for educational, charitable, and religious purposes, are exempt from taxation. State constitutions frequently list the taxes that may be collected (all others being forbidden) and stipulate the amount of tax that may be collected from various sources.

The ability of people in a city, county, or other local unit to tax themselves is even more restricted. State and local officials can collect only those taxes, in the amount, by the procedures, and for the purposes that the state constitution or state legislature authorizes. Let us look more closely at the major types of taxes they can collect.

GENERAL PROPERTY TAX

Widely criticized as "one of the worst taxes known to the civilized world," the **general property tax** is still a chief revenue source for local governments. Thirty years ago it provided 45 percent of the revenues for state and local governments, and an even higher percentage of the revenues for local governments alone. Today it provides under one-third of total state and local government revenues. But some states remain acutely dependent on property taxes. New Hampshire, for instance, raises nearly two-thirds of its state and local revenues from the property tax. At the other end of the scale, Alabama and New Mexico raise only about one in ten of their state and local tax dollars from the property tax.[13]

The property tax is difficult to administer, leads to favoritism and inequities, and takes little account of ability to pay.[14] A hundred years ago, wealth was primarily *real* property—land and buildings—that was relatively easy to value. Assessors could guess the value of the property a person owned, and this was a good test of his or her ability to help pay for government. Today wealth takes many forms. People own varying amounts of *personal* property—both *tangible* (such as furniture, jewels, washing machines, rugs, and paintings) and *intangible* (such as stocks, bonds, and money in the bank). It is possible to concentrate a large amount of wealth, difficult to value and easy to conceal, in a small rented apartment. The nature of real property has also changed. It no longer consists mainly of barns, houses, and land, but rather of large industrial plants, great retail stores, and office buildings whose values are hard to measure. In addition, property ownership is less likely these days to reflect ability to pay taxes. An elderly couple with a large house valued at $200,000 may be living on social security payments and a small allowance provided by their children. They have to pay higher local taxes than a young couple with two healthy incomes who live in a rented apartment.

Although many communities stipulate that the general property tax be imposed on all property, this is not what actually happens. Over 20 percent of real property in cities is exempt. For example, about half of the actual property in Boston, nearly 35 percent in New York City, and 25 percent in Baltimore is tax-exempt. Intangible personal property is seldom taxed. Some communities deliberately impose a lower rate on intangible property to induce owners to announce ownership. In addition, tangible personal property such as watches, rings, and so on often escapes taxation or is grossly undervalued. In most cities an unwritten understanding develops concerning the kind of property the honest taxpayer should list. The good citizen who attempts to follow the letter of the law is kindly advised by the assessor that it is not necessary.

The general property tax is hard to adjust to changing circumstances. This tax is typically administered by an *assessor*, who attempts to place a value on property—an **assessment**. The assessment may or may not reflect the real market value of the property. In some states the assessment is legally required to be a percentage of market value—say, 25 percent. The **property tax rate** is usually a tax per $1,000 of assessed valuation or some other such measure. Local and state governments can do very little to change the assessment, but they can raise or lower the rates. To compare property taxes across communities, one must know both the policy on assessment and the property tax rate. Because these vary so much, it is often hard to make accurate comparisons. For instance, the rate in one city may be only $10 per $1,000, while in another it is $40 per $1,000. But in the second city valuation may be computed at only a tenth of "real" value. That is why claims by local politicians that they have kept down the tax rate must be carefully scrutinized.

During times of rising prices, assessed values increase much more slowly than the general price level does. Thus when governments need more money, the lagging tax bases fail to provide it. When prices fall, valuations do not drop at the same rate. When people cannot pay taxes, property may be sold on the market to cover tax delinquency, but such occurrences are rare. In some areas property taxes are already so high that to increase them may discourage businesses and lower-income families from living in the locality.

A property owner typically makes one tax payment (although many home mortgage holders now deduct a partial tax payment with each month's mortgage payment), yet that payment may include taxes charged by three, four, or more governmental units like the city, county, school board, or the water, utility, and other special districts. The lump-sum payment aspect of the property tax is one reason for its widespread unpopularity. Another is its complexity. The property tax is difficult to explain and complex to administer.

In recent years considerable controversy has been stirred up by heavy local reliance on the property tax to support public schools. As a result, the amount of money actually available to finance education varies tremendously from area to area; rich suburban areas with high property valuation per pupil are able to spend much more than poor areas, like the central cities, that need the most money. Reformers have urged states to take over the financing of public education, or at least to assume a greater share of the burden, in order to equalize differences from community to community. Although this is not a popular idea, most states do distribute funds to local districts in an attempt to ensure more equitable expenditures.

Those hoping for greater state support for the public schools have often turned to the courts, arguing that reliance on the property tax results in a denial of equal protection and violates the Constitution. Several state courts have ruled that wide differences between school districts in per pupil expenditures are inconsistent with the equal protection clause of the Fourteenth Amendment.[15] The California Supreme Court, for example, saw wide per pupil expenditure differences as violating the California Constitution (*Serrano v. Priest*, 1971).[16] However, the U.S. Supreme Court held (*San Antonio Independent School District v. Rodriguez*, 1973) that there is no federal constitutional requirement that the amount spent per pupil in each school district must be the same.[17]

The Supreme Court's 1973 decision temporarily slowed the push toward intrastate equalization of school expenditures, but the controversy and the issues raised remain. Several other state courts have now handed down rulings similar to *Serrano*. New York and Wyoming courts, for example, have held that their state constitutions require that education be financed in a way that avoids differences in funding due to differences in wealth among local school districts.

Despite its weaknesses, the general property tax remains an important source of revenue for local government. Supporters of the tax say it is a practical and suitable tax. After all, they argue, real rather than personal property is the chief beneficiary of many local services, such as fire protection. Alternative taxes are few, and each has disadvantages. Moreover, some of the bad features of the general property tax can be corrected by improving property tax assessment and administration methods.

One effort to reform the general property tax is the *circuit-breaker exemption* (sometimes called a *negative income tax*) by which most states and certain cities give a form of tax relief to lower-income families and the elderly. A circuit breaker is a property tax credit, the value of which depends on a household's property tax bill and its income. The idea is to protect family income from property tax overload in the same way an electrical circuit breaker protects a family home from an electrical current overload. "That is, when the property tax burden of an individual exceeds a predetermined percentage of personal income, the circuit breaker goes into effect to relieve the excess financial pressure."[18] The circuit-breaker property tax exemption seems to be most popular in the Great Lakes and Plains states and least popular in the Southeast, where property tax burdens are low. Economists and tax authorities have debated the merits and problems created by this reform. Until a comprehensive negative income tax or some other income-maintenance plan is established to provide cash payments to the poor, circuit-breaker exemptions will probably remain part of the tax structure in many states.

Hostility to the property tax spawned the tax revolt of the late 1970s, which continued through the 1980s and into the 1990s. The watershed event in the politics of tax cutting was passage of California's Proposition 13, which set a 1 percent limit for taxes on a property's market value based on its 1975–76 assessment and limiting increases to a maximum of two percent a year.[19] Throughout the 1970s, California property taxes had risen dramatically, and polls found that voters overwhelmingly wanted them cut. Direct citizen involvement in making fiscal policy is not uncommon in the United States, and there has been a resurgence of initiative and referendum activity generally in recent decades.[20] Passage of Proposition 13 elevated tax reduction to an important issue nationwide. Heralded as the start of a modern tax revolt, Proposition 13 triggered the approval of tax and spending limits in more than a dozen states during 1978 and 1979. It also helped to spur movements for constitutional amendments setting federal spending limits, requiring a balanced federal budget, and indexing income tax brackets. The tax issue was not limited to ballot initiatives, but spread to state legislatures. During the 1978 and 1979 legislative sessions, 37 states reduced property taxes, 28 states cut income taxes, and 13 states restricted sales tax collections; income and sales tax cuts alone surpassed $4 billion.

One provision of Proposition 13 permitted local assessors to raise property taxes on property when sold. This means that two identical houses in the same subdivision can be liable for very different property taxes. A challenge to this provision went all the way to the U.S. Supreme Court, which ruled that this difference in treatment between newer and older owners passed the "reasonableness test" required for tax classification under the equal protection clause.[21]

The importance of the California tax-cutting vote grew as Proposition 13 received national attention. Political commentators frequently observed that passage of the proposition signified a new move toward conservatism, the resurgence of the middle class, a general tendency to tax cutting, and a strong message to government. Indeed, one of the most important consequences of Proposition 13 was that it gave rise to a new conventional wisdom that the public had become more conservative and desired less government.[22] The impact of this ballot proposition was profound. Proposition 13 prompted leaders in both parties to speak in more fiscally conservative tones.

Cutting taxes, either at the state or local level, is an indirect way of attempting to limit government spending. Loss of revenue from a single tax source, however, can be made up by increasing intergovernmental transfers, by drawing on budget surpluses, or by creating new revenue sources like user fees or local income taxes. Thus tax cuts do not necessarily achieve the end of reducing or limiting government spending. Recognition of this fact has fostered a wide variety of more direct limitations on government spending. Spending limitations can be enacted without tax cuts and, unlike tax cuts, incur few political costs since no services are being reduced in the short run. In their simplest form, such limitations restrict future spending to current levels; more typically, they provide for an annual increase in spending that is either limited to a fixed percentage or tied to increases in personal income or inflation.

New Jersey was the first state to enact spending limits that applied to both the state and local governments. Passed in 1976, the New Jersey law limits the growth in state expenditures to the annual percentage increase in per capita personal income, and restricts localities to increases of no more than 5 percent without voter approval. California's successful 1979 Proposition 4 limits the growth in government spending to the percentage increase in the state or local government's population.

Because of the wave of property tax limits imposed during the 1970s and 1980s and the widespread perception by politicians that raising property taxes is unpopular, property taxes declined by nearly 20 percent relative to personal income in the period 1969–89.[23] Even with improved tax administration, the general property tax is not supplying local units of government with the money they need to render the services their citizens want. Moreover, states have tended to reserve the property tax to local units, and thus need other sources of funding for themselves. See Table 9-4 for a summary of the various revenue sources.

OTHER TAXES

Sales Taxes   Born during the Great Depression, the **sales tax** is now the most important source of revenue for states. Almost all states impose some kind of general sales tax, normally on retail sales. Local sales taxes were uncommon until after World War II, but now many larger communities also impose a general sales tax. City sales taxes are unpopular with local merchants, who fear they drive business away. In most cases, this is a minor issue that arises only along state borders where consumers can drive into another state with a lower sales tax to make their purchases. Most consumers do not pay that much attention to the sales tax on most items.

Sales taxes are easy to administer and produce large amounts of revenue. Despite their tendency to bear down hardest on lower-income groups, their popularity is increasing. Many consumers consider sales taxes relatively painless because they can avoid paying a large tax bill at one time. But labor groups

TABLE 9-4 Percentage of State and Local Tax Revenues by Source

State	Sales Tax	Licences	Income Tax	Corporate Income Tax	Other
Alabama	54%	8%	28%	5%	5%
Alaska	7	6	—	15	73
Arizona	62	7	23	4	5
Arkansas	57	6	30	6	2
California	40	5	36	13	6
Colorado	45	6	43	5	2
Connecticut	67	6	8	14	6
Delaware	14	32	37	12	5
Florida	80	6	—	5	9
Georgia	46	3	41	8	2
Hawaii	64	2	31	4	1
Idaho	54	8	32	7	0
Illinois	52	7	29	9	3
Indiana	57	3	33	5	2
Iowa	46	9	38	6	2
Kansas	46	6	34	8	6
Kentucky	46	5	28	7	15
Louisiana	55	10	15	6	14
Maine	49	6	37	6	2
Maryland	44	4	42	5	5
Massachusetts	34	3	47	13	4
Michigan	39	6	34	18	4
Minnesota	44	6	43	7	1
Mississippi	66	9	17	5	4
Missouri	52	8	34	5	1
Montana	26	10	34	7	24
Nebraska	54	7	32	6	1
Nevada	83	13	—	25	12
New Hampshire	44	14	5	25	12
New Jersey	53	6	26	12	3
New Mexico	57	7	17	3	17
New York	32	3	52	8	5
North Carolina	41	7	40	11	2
North Dakota	52	10	18	6	15
Ohio	52	8	34	6	1
Oklahoma	46	11	26	3	14
Oregon	15	14	61	8	2
Pennsylvania	51	10	24	9	6
Rhode Island	51	4	35	7	3
South Carolina	54	5	33	6	2
South Dakota	83	8	—	6	3
Tennessee	76	10	2	9	3
Texas	77	15	—	—	8
Utah	49	5	40	4	2
Vermont	49	8	33	7	3
Virginia	41	6	45	5	3
Washington	75	5	—	0	20
West Virginia	53	6	23	10	8
Wisconsin	45	5	39	8	3
Wyoming	35	11	—	—	54

Source: The Book of States, 1990–91 (Council of State Governments, 1990) pp. 298–299.

and low-income consumers remain opposed to sales taxes, favoring wider use of the more progressive income tax instead. They argue that people with small incomes spend larger percentages of their budgets on food and clothing than do the wealthy, so sales taxes fall heaviest on those least able to pay. Hence many states exempt food and drugs from the sales tax.

All states tax some services as well as goods, but none have a broad-based tax on services. Connecticut has a tax on some services like income-tax preparation, and Massachusetts has repealed its sales tax on services.

States continue to search for ways to tax services, both because they are under acute pressure to find new revenues and because the service sector of the economy continues to expand. Among the kinds of services taxed in some states are cable television, landscaping, videotape rental, and photocopying.[24] States and local officials listen with concern to talk about the federal government imposing a **value-added tax (VAT)** like that used in many Western European countries. This tax is imposed on whatever value is added to a product at each stage of production and distribution. Should the federal government impose such a tax, state and local officials fear their ability to use the sales tax will be reduced.

States and localities have long yearned for a way to collect tax revenues from yet another elusive source—the ever-expanding mail-order catalog business. An estimated $3 billion in revenues is lost to states and localities because they are largely unable to tax out-of-state mail-order merchants.[25] In 1992 the Supreme Court ruled that states could collect a sales tax on mail-order merchandise if Congress passed a statute permitting it. As a result, Congress is being pressured to pass legislation forcing catalog merchants to collect sales taxes and return them to the appropriate states and communities. States badly need this money. There is also a question of fairness, because local merchants in competition with these huge mail-order firms do have to collect sales taxes, which puts them at a disadvantage. Moreover, Americans are making more and more catalog purchases, and are likely to go on increasing their buying by phone, computers, and other high-tech devices that save them from traditional shopping. The mail-order merchants and their direct-marketing association lobbyists claim it would be an administrative nightmare to collect and reimburse all the sales taxes, and add they should not be obligated to collect taxes for a state in which they do not have a presence. Sooner or later, though, the sales tax is likely to catch up with them. A few of the larger mail-order corporations are beginning to comply, either voluntarily or because courts have ordered them to do so.

Income Taxes The state income tax has been one of the fastest-growing major revenue sources for most states, trailing the general sales tax. All but a handful of states impose a tax on personal income, and income tax revenue is higher than general sales tax revenue in nearly 20 states. Personal income taxes are generally **progressive taxes,** or graduated; that is, the rate goes up with the size of the income. State income tax rates, however, do not rise as sharply as the federal income tax and seldom go above 10 percent. Corporation incomes are frequently taxed at a flat rate. As a result of the tax reforms of the 1970s and 1980s, personal income taxes have actually declined relative to personal income. In some states exemptions are generous. Because of the importance and burden of the federal income tax, many citizens feel that states should exercise restraint in this area.

States generally do not allow local governments to levy income taxes. However, some cities—following the lead of Philadelphia and Toledo—now collect a payroll tax. In fact, every city in Ohio has an income tax. Philadelphia imposes a relatively small flat tax on salaries of all persons and net profits of unincorporated businesses and professions. The Toledo tax applies also to corporate profits. The municipal income tax enables hard-pressed cities to collect money from "daytime" citizens who use city facilities but live in the suburbs. This tax is especially popular in cities in Ohio and Pennsylvania, but it is also being collected by New York City, Detroit, and Louisville.

Special Excise Taxes   Almost all states tax gasoline, alcohol, and cigarettes. Because many cities also tax these items, the local, state, and federal levies often double the cost of these "luxury" items to the consumer. Taxes on such items are known as **excise taxes.** Gasoline taxes are sometimes combined with the funds collected from automobile and drivers' licenses and earmarked for highway purposes. Liquor taxes often consist of both license fees to manufacture or sell alcoholic beverages and levies on their sale or consumption; they are used for general government spending. Some states own their own liquor stores, with the profits going to the state treasury. High taxation of liquor is justified on the grounds that it reduces the amount of alcohol consumed, falls on an item that is not a necessity of life, and eases the task of law enforcement. Some states, like North Carolina, set aside part of their alcohol taxes for mental health programs and the rehabilitation of alcoholics. If the tax is raised too high, however, liquor purchases tend to be diverted into illegal channels and tax revenues fall off. Connecticut has the highest excise tax on cigarettes. High tobacco taxes in states like Connecticut, New Jersey, and Maine, compared with low tobacco taxes in states like the Carolinas, have led to interstate smuggling up and down the East Coast.

Severance Taxes   In several states **severance taxes** have been a key source of revenue. This is a tax on the privilege of "severing" such natural resources as coal, oil, timber, and gas from the land. In recent years the severance tax accounted for more than 20 percent of tax collections in eight states: Alaska, Louisiana, Montana, New Mexico, North Dakota, Oklahoma, Texas, and Wyoming. Although more than 30 states rely on some type of severance tax, the possibilities for this tax are highly concentrated and cannot be tapped by most states. California is the only major oil-producing state that does not have a significant severance tax.

Most of the oil- and gas-producing states were hurt financially in the mid-1980s when oil prices dropped from $28 a barrel to less than half that. Texas,

Oklahoma, and Louisiana, for example, which had long relied on severance and sales tax receipts to finance their state governments, had to cut spending on education, libraries, and human services, as well as postpone various public-works projects, until oil prices should rebound.

The state and local taxes described above do not begin to exhaust the kinds of taxes collected by state and local governments. Admission taxes, stock transfer taxes, inheritance taxes, parimutuel taxes, corporate franchise taxes, license fees, taxes on utilities, and insurance are common.

NONTAX REVENUES

In addition to taxation, states derive some revenue from fees and special service charges. At least 10 percent of the money collected by state and local governments comes from these sources. Fees are charged for inspecting buildings, recording titles, operating courts, licensing professions, disposing of garbage, and other special services. Parking meters have become an important revenue source for some cities. Municipal governments frequently operate water-supply and local transit systems. City-operated liquor stores are administered by, and turn a profit in, certain cities in Alaska, Minnesota, North Carolina, and South Dakota. Some states and cities run other business enterprises from which they make money (and sometimes lose it, too). North Dakota, for example, operates a state-owned bank. Municipally owned gas and power companies often contribute to city treasuries. In some cases, utility profits are large enough to make other city taxes unnecessary.

Over 30 states and the District of Columbia operate **lotteries** to generate revenue without raising taxes. Lotteries are not entirely new; the Continental Congress ran a lottery to help finance the Revolutionary War. Indeed, all 13 colonies used lotteries as a form of voluntary taxation in the 1780s. Lotteries also helped to establish some of the nation's earliest colleges, notably Princeton, Harvard, and Yale. In 1964 New Hampshire was the first state to revive the practice in modern times to help balance its budget.

During the 1980s state lotteries increased in popularity as more states adopted them, and gross receipts grew to $18.7 billion by 1990. However, this dramatic growth slowed in 1991 and 1992.[26] As Figure 9-2 indicates, state-run lotteries provide under 3 percent of all state tax revenues, but few states that have lotteries would want to have to increase other taxes in order to do without the lotteries. States pay out about half of their gross receipts from lotteries in prizes and roughly 6 percent in administration. The remaining revenues are used for public purposes.[27]

Most elected officials like lotteries because they raise revenue without raising taxes. Yet because they take money from many people and return it to only a few, many economists say lotteries are a form of tax, and an inequitable one at that. Furthermore, critics contend that lotteries take advantage of poor people: "You're seven times more likely to be killed by lightning than to win a million in the state lottery."[28] Lottery operations have also been criticized as

FIGURE 9-2   Selling Hope: Lotteries as a Source of Revenue

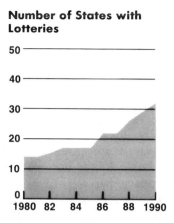

Number of States with Lotteries

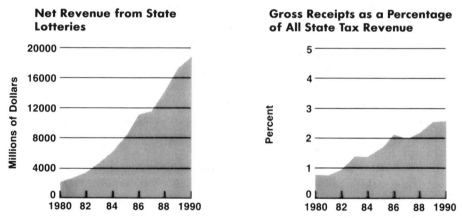

Net Revenue from State Lotteries

Gross Receipts as a Percentage of All State Tax Revenue

Source: U.S. Bureau of the Census, *State Government Finances*, various years, and Advisory Commission on Intergovernmental Relations, *Significant Features of Fiscal Federalism*, 1991.

inefficient revenue producers. Prizes and administrative costs take up roughly 60 percent of the money collected.

Americans now spend well over $12 billion each year buying lottery tickets from their state governments. Nine states took in over a billion dollars each in 1990. California had gross receipts of $2.4 billion.[29] These funds are used for a variety of purposes. Massachusetts sends its lottery money back to local governments; California distributes most of its lottery windfall to local school boards for educational purposes; Pennsylvania gives it to programs for the elderly; Colorado uses the bulk of it for capital construction projects. Other states also allocate these monies to education. The rest (for example, Oregon and Iowa) channel lottery revenues into funds to be used for any purpose.

Opposition to the lottery often comes from church groups, who contend that state lotteries are immoral because they are a form of legalized gambling. Proponents counter that churches themselves often raise funds through raffles, bingo, and other games of chance. Opponents argue that lotteries are a bad investment because they yield a poor rate of return. Proponents respond that tickets are purchased more for their entertainment value than as an invest-ment. "When all is said and done"—and everyone has had a say in this debate —"there are two inescapable facts about state lotteries: (1) they are capable of generating significant amounts of absolute revenue which can be used for pub-lic purposes, and (2) they are attractive to a willing public which is ready to play."[30]

USER FEES OR CHARGES

State and local collection of **user charges**—charges or fees paid directly by indi-viduals to use certain public services—has grown rapidly in recent years. State and local governments routinely charge fees for certain services, and a recent study found that nearly 14 percent of all expenditures came from such fees.[31] Examples of services that users pay fees for are toll roads, higher education, hospitals, airports, parks, sewerage, and solid waste management. Other serv-ices are much harder to impose fees for. For some, fees could be charged, but such charges would raise questions of fairness and access. The cost of libraries could be paid entirely by library users, for instance, but most states and locali-ties seek to encourage library use by the disadvantaged as well as everyone else by heavily subsidizing them.

It is not always easy to distinguish between individual and community benefits. Public schools obviously benefit the individual families who use them more than the families who do not. Yet education is generally thought to yield considerable benefits for the community at-large, so it is financed by taxes rather than user fees. Similarly, we would not want to pay for our fire depart-ments by charging people whose homes or businesses experienced fires in a given year. Objections are also raised to user fees when they deprive poor peo-ple of needed services.

GRANTS

Grants from state to local governments have become increasingly important during the last several decades. The national government, until the 1980s, allo-cated large sums to the states and cities. States give over $140 billion to local governments. States officials also return to local governments revenues col-lected from certain taxes, often without specifying the purposes for which the money should be used.

Borrowing Money

When all the taxes and fees are added together, state and local governments col-lect large sums of money. These funds typically go to pay for operating ex-penses—garbage collection, police protection, and social services. In order to fund longer-term projects—so-called capital expenditures—cities and states often have to borrow money. During the early years of the nineteenth century, states and cities subsidized railroad and canal builders. The money for this, as well as for financing other public improvements, came from bonds issued by the cities or states and purchased by investors. Provision for payment of debts was inadequate, and citizens were burdened with debts long after the improvements had lost their value. As a result, default on obligations was frequent.

Aroused by the legislatures' abuse of their powers, voters insisted on constitutional amendments restricting legislative discretion to borrow money. Over the years state constitutions placed elaborate restrictions on the power of state legislatures and local councils to borrow money or pledge public credit. More recently, the National Tax Reform Act of 1986 restricted the ability of states and localities to issue tax-exempt debt. The power to borrow money for the long term now routinely requires voter approval.

Short-term borrowing is less frequently used because better fiscal planning generally ensures that taxes are collected in time to cover necessary operating expenses. Even so, officials sometimes need to borrow money for a short time. This *floating debt* consists of bank loans, tax-anticipation warrants, and other notes, all of which are paid out of current revenues.

For some purposes, long-term borrowing by states and cities is necessary. The cost of building schools, constructing roads, and clearing slums is so large that it is not feasible to pay for these things out of current revenue. Moreover, because these improvements have long lives and add to the wealth of the community, it is reasonable to pay for them by spreading the cost. For this purpose, governments issue bonds, often with voter approval. The best practice—now required by many state constitutions—is to issue serial bonds, a portion of which come due each year and are retired out of current annual revenues.

State and local bonds are attractive to well-to-do investors because the interest is exempt from federal income tax. For this reason, state and local governments can borrow money at a lower interest rate than can private businesses. Although credit ratings differ sharply according to economic health, the credit of most cities and states is good. Hence they can easily find buyers for their bonds. *General obligation bonds* are backed by the credit of the issuing governments. *Revenue bonds* are backed only by the income from the particular project in which the money is invested. Because governments are often permitted to issue bonds beyond the limitations on their general indebtedness, they use them whenever possible. One of the consequences of the tax revolt has been "creative financing," including a greater reliance on the sale of bonds. However, as New York City learned in the 1970s, excessive reliance on bonds can be detrimental to the fiscal health of a state or city.

Economic Downturns and Government Retrenchment

One consequence of Reaganomics of the 1980s was the transfer of greater government responsibility to state and local levels without commensurate funds to pay for these activities. One effect, as we have seen, has been an increase in state and local government spending. But paying for this growth became more difficult as the United States entered a recession in the early 1990s and many states faced shortfalls in tax revenues. Unable to use deficit financing for operating costs, many states cut back on services, freeze employment, and even lay off workers.[32]

John Shannon, former director of the Advisory Commission on Intergovernmental Relations—an agency that gathers information on taxing and spending at all levels of government—has written that there were three "R's" that shocked state and local governments in the recent past. The first R was the *revolt* of the taxpayers, which started with California's Proposition 13 and quickly became a national phenomenon. The second R was the *recession* of the early 1980s and early 1990s, which placed demands on state and local governments to care for the unemployed and needy. And the third R was the *reduction* in federal grant-in-aid funds, which meant state and local governments were more on their own.[33]

Recession reinforced the problems raised when the federal government pulled out of more and more assistance programs. States search for ways to make ends meet and to live within their revenue projections. Here are a few ways states are attempting to put their economic houses in order:

1. Several states have imposed freezes on new state jobs. Some have even implemented public-employee layoffs to reduce expenditures.

2. States are searching for means to improve their tax collection methods. They are using more sophisticated computer systems and designing programs that deny state and local licenses and contracts to tax avoiders.

3. Several states have successfully held "tax amnesty" periods similar to local library-book amnesty weeks. A grace period is announced, during which tax avoiders can make their payments free of interest penalties. Immediately after the amnesty period, prosecution and fines or penalties for unpaid taxes are stepped up and vigorously enforced.

4. Some states have adopted a controversial new form of taxing the profits of corporations: the **unitary tax.** The unitary tax considers a corporation's domestic receipts and taxes the portion presumably earned in that state. Earlier proponents of the unitary tax had even advanced the idea that some portion of profits earned outside the country could be taxed by the state, but today it is conceded that the tax only stops "at the water's edge." Still, it is often difficult to determine how much of corporate profits were earned in a particular state. Whether they call it a unitary tax or not, most states employ a formula to determine the proportion of a company's profits that are taxable. Typically, a state "averages three factors: the percentage of total payroll in the state, the percentage of total sales in the state. This average is then multiplied by total profits to determine the amount of profits taxable in the state."[34] Corporations dislike this tax and several states, like Colorado, have repealed it in the hope of encouraging

companies, including foreign investors, to relocate to their state. Meanwhile, other states are using or considering adoption of this additional source of revenue.

Most states still rely on traditional sources of revenue as they try to balance their budgets. In addition to some reliance on the just-described strategies, states are likely to try slight increases in personal, corporate, sales, and excise taxes, and slightly greater reliance on lotteries. And whenever the public resists such tax increases, we are likely to see further cutbacks in services. Indeed, cutbacks in services are probable in any event. As every governor and state legislator learns, one of the grand paradoxes of government in the United States is that citizens simultaneously want improved and increased services *and* lower taxes. The sharp federal cutbacks of the late 1980s, combined with recession, unemployment, and depressed oil and farm prices, are forcing many states to confront and weigh these stark economic and political realities more than at any time in the past generation.

There is tremendous variability in the mix of taxes found in American states and cities. To understand public finance in the United States requires an understanding of the history and politics of the states. Nevada, for instance, has no personal income tax because it has long relied on taxing legalized gambling. Other states rely heavily on severance taxes, a few on personal property taxes. Some, like Oregon, do not impose a sales tax, and efforts to enact one have been repeatedly defeated in recent years. One of the great advantages of this tremendous variety of tax structures is that it permits states and cities to learn from one another—an important advantage of federalism.

Summary

1. One of the most controversial aspects of state and local government in recent years has been the unionization of over 50 percent of public employees at the state and local levels. Public-employee unions have been increasingly successful in recruiting new members and bargaining for better wages, hours, working conditions, and pensions. Their success has caused some public backlash.

2. State and local governments have been the fastest-growing part of government for the past 25 years. But even though state and local governments provide more services than before, the tax burdens on middle-income families are not much greater in relative terms than they were 25 years ago. States have also become the chief fount of aid to cities, replacing the federal government, which had previously been a major source of money to localities in the forms of categorical and block grants and general revenue sharing (GRS).

3. State governments also changed their taxing and spending approaches as a result of the taxpayer revolt of the late 1970s and early 1980s and the imposition of spending limits on state and local governments. Voters and legislatures also imposed tougher limitations on borrowing in many states, further limiting how states and localities can obtain money.

4. State and local governments have diversified their revenue sources by turning to such devices as lotteries, user fees, and taxes not previously used at the state and

local level. This diversification was made necessary by economic downturns and by cutbacks in federal support. Intergovernmental grants from states to cities and school districts have increased in importance as local governments have had to deal with rising costs and expectations but with limited revenues.

For Further Reading

Advisory Commission on Intergovernmental Relations, *Significant Features of Fiscal Federalism*, 1992 ed. (Government Printing Office, 1992).

TERRY N. CLARK and LORNA C. FERGUSON, *City Money: Political Processes, Fiscal Strain and Retrenchment* (Columbia University Press, 1983).

TIMOTHY CONLAN, *New Federalism: Intergovernmental Reform from Nixon to Reagan* (Brookings Institution, 1988).

CHARLES T. GOODSELL, *The Case for Bureaucracy*, 2d ed. (Chatham House, 1985).

CHARLES H. LEVINE, ed., *Managing Fiscal Stress: The Crisis in the Public Sector* (Chatham House, 1980).

MICHAEL LIPSKY, *Street-Level Bureaucracy* (Russell Sage, 1980).

JAMES A. MAXWELL and J. RICHARD ARONSON, *Financing State and Local Governments*, 4th ed. (Brookings Institution, 1986).

RICHARD A. MUSGRAVE and PEGGY B. MUSGRAVE, *Public Finance in Theory and Practice*, 5th ed. (McGraw-Hill, 1989).

National Conference on State Legislatures, *Legislative Budget Procedures in the 50 States* (National Conference of State Legislatures, 1988).

MICHAEL PAGANO and RICHARD MOORE, *Cities and Fiscal Choices* (Duke University Press, 1985).

B. GUY PETERS, *The Politics of Taxation: A Comparative Perspective* (Blackwell, 1991).

E.S. SAVAS, *Privatizing the Public Sector: How to Shrink Local Government*, 2d ed. (Chatham House, 1987).

ALBERTA M. SBRAGIA, *Municipal Money Chase: The Politics of Local Government Finance* (Westview Press, 1983).

RICHARD SCHICK and JEAN C. COUTURIER, *The Public Interest in Government Labor Relations* (Ballinger, 1977).

DAVID O. SEARS and JACK CITRIN, *Tax Revolt: Something for Nothing in California* (Harvard University Press, 1982).

THOMAS R. SWARTZ and JOHN E. PECK, eds., *The Changing Face of Fiscal Federalism* (M. E. Sharpe, 1990).

Also, the U.S. Bureau of the Census regularly publishes reports on state and municipal finances.

Notes

1. U.S. Bureau of the Census, *Public Employment: 1990* (Government Printing Office, 1991), p. 1.
2. Bureau of the Census *Statistical Abstract of the United States, 1991* (Government Printing Office, 1990), p. 284.
3. *Elrod v. Burns*, 427 U.S. 347 (1976).
4. Wendell Cox and Samuel Brunelli, *America's Protected Class: Why Excess Public Employee Compensation is Bankrupting the States* (American Legislative Exchange Council, 1992), p. 8.
5. "Compulsory Binding Arbitration," *State Legis-*latures, April–May 1977, p. 15. For additional views, see Nolan J. Argly, "The Impact of Collective Bargaining on Public School Governance," *Public Policy*, Winter 1980, pp. 115–41; and Robert E. Campbell, "Collective Bargaining: One Experience," *Public Management*, March 1980, pp. 9–11.
6. Thomas B. Darr, "Pondering Privatization May Be Good for Your Government," *Governing*, November 1987, p. 47. A provocative and controversial book advocating this option is E. S.

Savas, *Privatizing the Public Sector: How to Shrink Local Government*, 2d ed. (Chatham House, 1987).

7. Edward M. Gramlich, "The Economics of Fiscal Federalism and It's Reform," in *The Changing Face of Fiscal Federalism*, ed. Thomas R. Swartz and John E. Peck (M. E. Sharpe, 1990), p. 153.

8. Steven D. Gold and Mark Seklecki, "The Federal Budget: What's (Not) in It for the States?", *State Legislatures*, April 1986, pp. 18–20. See also Steven D. Gold, *The Unfinished Agenda for State Tax Reform* (National Conference of State Legislatures, 1988).

9. John Shannon, "The Deregulation of the American Federal System: 1789-1989," in *The Changing Face of Fiscal Federalism*, ed. Thomas R. Swartz and John E. Peck (M. E. Sharpe, 1990) pp. 17–34.

10. Norman Walzer and Glenn W. Fisher, *Cities, Suburbs and Property Taxes* (Oelgeschlager, Gunn and Hain, 1981). See also C. Lowell Harriss, ed., *The Property Tax and Local Finance* (Academy of Political Science, 1983).

11. Row W. Bahl, Jr., "Changing Federalism: Trends and Interstate Variations," in *The Changing Face of Fiscal Federalism*, ed., Thomas R. Swartz and John E. Peck (M. E. Sharpe, 1990), p. 59.

12. Allen D. Manvel, "Shifts in Governmental Financing—1969-1989," *Tax Notes* 51 (June 3, 1991), p. 1202.

13. Michael Vlaisaulievich, *State Tax Notes*, November 18, 1991, pp. 421–22.

14. For a brief history of the property tax, see Dennis Hale, "The Evolution of the Property Tax: A Study of the Relation Between Public Finance and Political Theory," *Journal of Politics*, May 1985, pp. 382–404. See also Harriss, *The Property Tax and Local Finance*.

15. See Roy Bahl, David L. Sjoquist, and W. Loren Williams, "School Finance Reform and Impact on Property Taxes," Proceding of the Eighty-third Annual National Tax Association Conference, 1990 (National Tax Association, Tax Institute of America, 1991), pp. 163–71.

16. *Serrano* v. *Priest*, 5 Cal.3d, 487 P.2d 1241, 96 Cal. Rptr. 601 (1971).

17. *San Antonio Independent School District v. Rodriquez* 411 U.S. 1 (1973).

18. James A. Maxwell and J. Richard Aronson, *Financing State and Local Governments*, 3d ed. (Brookings Institution, 1977), p. 158. See also U.S. Advisory Commission on Intergovernmental Relations, *Property Tax Circuit-Breakers: Current Status and Policy Issues* (Government Printing Office, 1975); and Steven D. Gold, "Circuit Breakers and Other Relief Measures," in Harriss, ed., *The Property Tax and Local Finance*.

19. Proposition 13 made news not only in the United States but abroad as well. Reporting on the California campaign, *The Economist*, a British newsweekly, titled its editorial on Proposition 13 "Taxes Overboard" and concluded that "California's vote, like most things Californian, was just bolder, better, more innovative—in short a harbinger of things to come."

20. David B. Magleby, *Direct Legislation: Voting on Ballot Propositions in the United States* (Johns Hopkins University Press, 1984), pp. 61–76.

21. *Nordlinger v. Hahn*, 60 U.S. *Law Weekly* 4563 (June 18, 1992).

22. See "Is There a Parade?", *The Nation* 227 (October 14, 1978), pp. 363–64; "Conservatism," *U.S. News and World Report* 84 (January 23, 1978), pp. 24–25. Not all commentators agreed that the country was turning conservative, however, or that Proposition 13 was evidence of a fundamental shift in voter attitudes. For examples of this disagreement, see Everett Carl Ladd, "What the Voters Really Want," *Fortune*, December 18, 1978, pp. 40–44, 46, 48; Curtis B. Gans, "Conservatism by Default," *The Nation*, 227 (October 14, 1978), pp. 372–74; and Tom Bethell, "The Changing Fashions of Liberalism," *Public Opinion* 2 (January–February 1979), pp. 41–46.

23. Allen D. Manvel, "Shifts in Governmental Financing—1969-89," *Tax Notes*, June 3, 1991, p. 1202.

24. "Tips for Taxing Services," *State Legislatures*, vol. 16, no. 9 (October 1990), p. 9.

25. Dick Kirschten, "Division in Mail-Order Tax Collection," *National Journal*, May 13, 1989, p. 1195. See also Paul M. Barrett, "Justices Rebuff States on Taxing Mail-Order Sales," *Wall Street Journal*, May 27, 1992, p. A3.

26. Ronald Smothers, "Many State Lotteries Feel the Pinch of Recession, and Perhaps Monotony," *The New York Times*, February 2, 1992, sec. 1, p. 16.

27. For a discussion of lotteries, see Alan J. Karcher, *Lotteries* (Transactions, 1989); also Charles T. Clotfelter and Philip J. Cook, *Selling Hope: State Lotteries in America* (Harvard University Press, 1989).

28. Susannah Calkins, "State Lotteries: Has a Growth Industry Faltered?" *Tax Notes* 54 (March 23, 1992), p. 1563.

29. Curt Suplee, "Lotto Baloney," *Harper's*, July 1983, p. 15. See also Elder Witt, "States Place their Bets on a Game of Diminishing Returns," *Governing*, November 1987, pp. 52–57.

30. Marcia L. Whicker et al., "Lotteries as a Source of Revenue for State Government," *Public Affairs Bulletin*, Bureau of Governmental Research and Service, University of South Carolina, no. 29 (July 1985).

31. Allen D. Manvel, "The Government-Financing Role of Current Charges," *Tax Notes* 52 (July 1, 1991), p. 118.

32. Ronald Brownstein, "More Conflicts Likely in Era of Empty Pockets," *Los Angeles Times*, July 18, 1991, sec. A, p. 5; and Martin Tolchin, "Despite Billions in Tax Raises, States Slash Services," *The New York Times*, October 30, 1991, sec. A, p. 16.

33. Quoted in Thad L. Beyle, "From Governor to Governors," in *The State of the States*, ed. Carl E. Van Horn (CQ Press, 1989), p. 54.

34. Steven Gold, "Unitary Tax: Wave of the Future?", *State Legislatures*, January 1984, p. 14. See also Martin Tolchin, "With Lobbies in Full Cry, California Debates Repealing Multinational Tax," *The New York Times*, February 18, 1986, sec. B, p. 12.

10

State and Local Policy Making

For a few days in May of 1992 the eyes of the nation watched as thousands of rioters took to the streets of Los Angeles and other cities to protest the not guilty verdict handed down in the police brutality case against four Los Angeles policemen. The police had been accused of using unnecessary force and violating other laws in the arrest of Rodney King. A videotape repeatedly played on television showed the officers hitting King 56 times in 81 seconds with their night sticks.[1] In the days and weeks that followed, a national debate ensued about the jury verdict, which more than three-quarters of whites and 95 percent of African Americans disagreed with.[2]

Within minutes of the jury's announcement of its not guilty verdict in the King case, large numbers of rioters took to the streets in a rampage that destroyed $1 billion worth of property and resulted in the deaths of 55 persons. The Los Angeles Police Department, unable to control the rioting, left some sections of the city to mob rule, and shop owners in those sections resorted to guns to protect their property and themselves. Los Angeles Mayor Tom Bradley, who had been feuding with Police Chief Darryl Gates for a long time, called upon Governor Pete Wilson for help. Wilson responded by calling up the national guard. But even the National Guard and the imposition of a dusk-to-dawn curfew failed to stop the looting and burning. Finally, after two days of rioting, President Bush sent 5,000 federal troops to restore order.

In the days and weeks after the Los Angeles riot there were questions about why it took so long to restore order and also about the underlying racism in America and the desperate conditions African Americans face in large cities like Los Angeles. We can learn a lot about policy making by thinking about the Los Angeles riot. Maintaining the peace, long a local government function, was insufficient here; it required the concerted efforts of federal, state, and local authorities to restore order. The welfare system, jointly funded by federal and state governments, but administered at the local level, has come under increasing attack from all sides.

Welfare is an example of a government service that has expanded over the past 50 years. Jointly run programs like Aid to Families with Dependent Children are mostly federally financed but locally administered. Such programs have enlarged the scope of state and local governments, but the expansion of state activity has been counterbalanced by a decline in state and local government autonomy.

State and local policy makers face constant challenges: crime, crack, AIDS, overcrowded prisons, inadequate public education, homelessness, hazardous waste problems, smog, unemployment, farm-belt depression, low prices for oil and gas, bridge and highway deterioration, water shortages, and many others. In summer, hurricanes like Andrew kill scores of people in the South and Southwest; in winter snowstorms paralyze cities in the upper Midwest and New England. Factory closings throw thousands off assembly lines and on to welfare lines. A relentless stream of public wants pour in on statehouses and city halls.

If you listen to debates in state legislatures, attend city council meetings, or observe state and local candidates, you come face to face with people who campaign for better schools, who insist on better crime-prevention programs, who demand that the truly needy receive better care, who become irate about the

FIGURE 10-1
State Government Spending, Fiscal Year Ending 1989

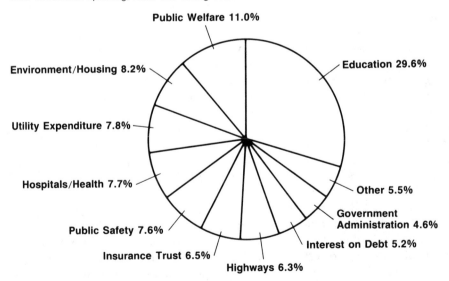

Public Welfare 11.0%

Environment/Housing 8.2%

Education 29.6%

Utility Expenditure 7.8%

Hospitals/Health 7.7%

Other 5.5%

Government Administration 4.6%

Public Safety 7.6%

Interest on Debt 5.2%

Insurance Trust 6.5%

Highways 6.3%

Source: Bureau of the Census, *Government Finances: 1989–1990*, Series GF/90-5 (Department of Commerce, 1991), Table 29.

potholes and decay of our highways and streets, and who are outraged by the hazardous waste dumps near their neighborhoods. Should the district close another school? Where? Will the voters approve a bond issue to construct a new hospital? Should the state superintendent of schools be given authority to establish minimum standards or merit pay for teachers? Should the city or state adopt a comparable worth policy? How can our western states best manage public lands? What can be done about the traffic jams on Main Street? Should commercial growth be encouraged because of the jobs it will bring, or discouraged because of the traffic and pollution it will generate? Hundreds of people— mayors, legislators, judges, civic commissioners, union officials, commercial and residential developers, leaders of chambers of commerce—participate in the process of determining what state and local governments will do.

Since it is obviously impossible to explore each activity of every state, city, county, school district, and township, we will review a few representative activities in this chapter as we examine the basic policy functions of the various levels of government. Figure 10-1 shows government priorities for expenditures in a typical state.

Education

In ancient Greece, Plato and Aristotle insisted that education was a vital task of government. They believed that government itself was an educational institution. Thomas Jefferson, too, was convinced that an educated citizenry was essential to democratic government. But only during the past century has the idea that government should provide tax-supported schools become generally accepted.

For a long time many groups opposed "free" education. They said it would lead to social unrest, undermine the family, give government control over the minds of the young, require a huge bureaucracy, and result in a fatal mixture of education and politics. And was it fair, they asked, to tax people who could afford to educate their own children in private schools in order to educate other people's children?

Today compulsory public education is an established practice (although parents have a constitutional right to pay to send their children to approved private schools). A strong movement has developed to extend public education downward to kindergarten, nursery school, and day care, upward to college and adult education, outward to cover more subjects, and deeper to cover them more extensively. About 37 percent of all state and local government expenditures are for education—a higher percentage than for any other function.[3] Today our public schools spend on average more than $4,867 per pupil per year for elementary and secondary schooling.[4] On average, about 50 percent of these costs are borne by the states and almost 45 percent by local governments, yet there is great variation in how the states finance education. This variation exists in both rich and poor states. It is also important to note that there has been a declining federal contribution to education in terms of the proportion of overall expenditures, but this has not deterred the federal government from legislating federal goals for education. States also vary in the proportion of people over age 25 who are high school graduates, with more than 20 percent difference between states with the highest graduation rates and states with the lowest.

ADMINISTRATION OF EDUCATION

The city, the county, and the township may have some say in local schools, but it is the school district that is chiefly responsible for providing public elementary and secondary education. The school district, of which there are almost 15,000 in the United States, is the basic administrative unit. In each district the voters elect a board of education. This board sets the school tax rate, in most cases independently of the city or county; appoints a superintendent of schools and other personnel; hires teachers; and runs the schools from kindergarten or grade 1 through grade 12.

Each state has a superintendent of public instruction or a commissioner of education. In about a third of the states this official is popularly elected; in almost all states he or she shares some authority with a state board of education. Although actual operation of the public schools is the responsibility of the local community, state officers have important supervisory powers and distribute financial assistance to the communities. State money is passed out according to many formulas, but the trend is toward giving more money to poorer communities. Critics charge that methods of financing public schools in most states are chaotic and unjust, and reformers are pressing for better formulas. Three areas of reform are especially noteworthy: teacher testing, permitting parents to use vouchers to choose which school to send their children to, and national student testing.

Teacher Testing Controversy has arisen in recent years in states like Arkansas and Texas over the question of testing or assessing teachers who are currently in the system. More than 30 states test prospective teachers before granting certification, but only a few test certified teachers. Arkansas began such tests (sometimes called "no pass, no teach" rules) in 1985, and nearly 10 percent of its teachers failed to qualify. Georgia tests teachers in their particular subject areas. And in 1986 Texas required more than 200,000 teachers and school administrators to take a basic-skills quiz. About 3 percent of the Texas teachers failed the exam on their first attempt. The three-hour multiple-choice test consisted of 85 questions about grammar, job-related vocabulary, and other matters. An assessment was also mandated by the governor and the state legislature to restore confidence in public education. The then-governor of Texas, Mark White, who had been bitterly opposed on this issue by many teachers and teacher groups, claimed the exam was necessary to ensure quality education. He said he was pleased with the results.

Some educators and educational reformers say teacher testing will be a fact of life by the mid-1990s. State legislators in states requiring these tests decided to impose them after finding too many teachers inadequately prepared to teach. Many teachers and educational observers find mid-career competence tests offensive. Good teaching, they point out, is an art based more on a teacher's personality, character, and caring than on knowledge. "The best way to judge the effectiveness of a teacher is to see how he or she performs in the classroom," notes the president of the Educational Testing Service.[5]

The debate about teacher competency testing also involves the charge by some critics that such tests are biased against minorities. Defenders deny the charge, arguing that the reason minorities tend to do less well on the tests is not because the tests are biased but because the average minority teacher has had fewer opportunities to become prepared.

Vouchers Some reformers of education argue that we will not see real progress in public education until we inject some competition into the system by permitting parents to shop for schools the way they shop for goods and services in the economy. This reform has been labeled *choice in education* because it would give parents the freedom to choose where to send their kids to school. They would presumably spend their vouchers on the best school, so schools competing for vouchers would have every incentive to improve their product.

Some have proposed that the vouchers should not be limited to parents who place their children in public schools but should be extended to those who choose private schools, including religious schools, for their children. Some states have voted on such voucher systems in the past, and other states and communities have tried different versions of voucher programs. Opponents of vouchers for private schooling argue that this would violate the constitutional separation of church and state and that in some parts of the country vouchers would be used for schools that practice racial segregation. Others oppose the voucher system even for public schools on the grounds that

---

SCHOOLS FOR PROFIT?

Two ambitious entrepreneurs, Christopher Whittle and former Yale University president Benno Schmidt, advocate operating schools for profit. In 1996 they plan on opening 200 schools costing roughly the same amount per pupil as public education, but providing a 15 percent return to their investors. The Whittle schools may stay open year round and 12 hours a day, with a staggered schedule to assist working parents. Mr. Whittle maintains that his program, dubbed the "Edison Project," is the "private research and development arm of the public schools." He envisions a school system in the year 2020 having "several major national providers. Each will have a different design. The parents will have wide choice."

Source: Tim W. Ferguson, "Whittle's Lesson Plan for the Public Schools," *The Wall Street Journal*, June 2, 1992, p. A15.

such a system would have a negative impact on existing efforts to reform the public schools.[6]

Choice programs include the following types:

1. Interdistrict choice plans.
2. Intradistrict choice plans
3. Second-chance plans for students who have been unsuccessful
4. Postsecondary enrollment options for secondary students
5. Magnet school programs aimed at reducing racial and class segregation[7]

Student Testing Another education reform advocated in recent years is standardized national testing of students to measure learning. These tests would be administered to students periodically to permit parents, administrators, and legislators to assess how individual students, classrooms of students, schools, school districts, and states are doing compared to one another. Moreover, once the testing became established, it could be expanded to include a year-to-year measurement of individual students as they progress through the public schools.

Some critics of standardized national tests contend it is unfair and misleading to use such tests to measure learning. Minority students, districts in impoverished areas, and others will not be able to do as well on these tests, which, they argue, will necessarily reflect cultural bias. Other critics worry that the use of such tests will force teachers to "teach to the test." Sensitive to the fact that their students will be compared against the students of other teachers, teachers will attempt to "beat the test" by introducing topics before they normally would. This might work for some students, but would make learning more difficult for others. The main contention of the opponents of national testing, however, is that such measurement will not "induce positive change in education."[8]

Other Administrative Issues State officials are sometimes consulted by local authorities to ensure that new school buildings meet the minimum specifications set by the state. Some state officials have the authority to set the course of study in schools—that is, to determine what must be taught and what may not be taught. In several states, especially in the South and Southwest, state authorities often determine which textbooks will be used as well.

Until the 1950s most local school districts provided only elementary and secondary education, although some of the larger cities also supported junior colleges and universities. Since the end of World War II, there has been a major expansion of community colleges. Now students may attend the first two years of college or receive a technical education within their own communities. The trend is to create separate college districts with their own boards to operate and raise funds for the local community colleges; in a few areas, however, the colleges are part of the regular public school systems.

States support many kinds of universities and colleges, including land-grant universities created by the Morrill Act of 1862. State colleges and universities are governed by boards appointed by the governor in some states and elected by the voters in others. These boards are designed to give public higher-education institutions some independence, even though they depend on the state legislature and governor for their funding. A few states have gone so far as to write provisions securing the independence of their universities into the state constitution.

With over 80 percent of our 15 million college students now attending publicly supported institutions, the control and support of higher education have become significant political questions. State after state has created either a superboard to take over the operation of all public universities or a coordinating board with varying degrees of control over operations and budgets. In addition, governors are trying to impose controls on universities and colleges that university administrators insist are inappropriate. No longer do public universities have the independence they once had to decide teaching loads, implement internal procedures, determine areas of teaching emphasis, and allocate funds.

What of the national government? For a long time the United States left the funding and control of education to states and local units of government, but this has changed in the past generation. The national government's share in financing local education rose from about 2 percent in 1940 to about 8 percent in the 1980s. Then, toward the end of the 1980s, the trend reversed. The federal share of spending on local education declined to 6 percent by the late 1980s.[9]

The federal government, through the national Department of Education and other agencies, makes grants for facilities, equipment, scholarships, loans, research, model programs, and general aid at the elementary, secondary, and higher-education levels. Federal controls over how the money may be spent have come with these federal dollars. Today federal regulations cover school-lunch programs, employment practices, admissions, record keeping, care of experimental animals, and many other matters. Indeed, school authorities note there are often more regulations than dollars. Although the federal government contributes only 6 percent of local school funding, it imposes or accounts for more than 20 percent of the regulations local schools have to contend with.

EDUCATIONAL ISSUES

Educational politics has long been part of our policy-making process. What shall be taught and who shall teach it are often hotly contested questions. Schools are favorite targets for groups eager to have children taught the "right" things. Patriotic groups are concerned about "un-American doctrines" sneaking into the textbooks, classrooms, and school libraries. Others want the schools to teach only facts without regard for values, especially in areas like sex education. Labor leaders want students to get the right impressions about labor

PUBLIC SCHOOLS IN JAPAN

Students in both the United States and Japan attend 12 years of school at the elementary, junior high, and high school level, but that is where the similarities end. Japanese high school students spend 50 percent more time in the classroom than their American counterparts do. One out of eight Japanese seniors have taken calculus, compared to only one in one hundred in the United States. Eighty-six percent of Japanese students report attending "juku"— evening prep schools or Saturday tutorial schools. This added study helps them prepare for the extremely difficult qualifying exams necessary to matriculate into the best junior highs and high schools.

Japanese entrance exams are so competitive that over half of all college-bound seniors fail the first time around and spend additional years of preparation to take the test again. Students have been known to take three and even four years between high school and college to pass the exams to get into top universities like Tokyo University. This additional effort does pay off. The average international high school achievement test scores for Japan are 67/100, with the United States far behind at only 48/100.

Source: Edward R. Beauchamp, Windows on Japanese Education (Greenwood Press, 1991); and Merry White, The Japanese Educational System: A Commitment to Children (Free Press, 1987).

and its role in society. Business leaders are eager for children to see the free enterprise system in a favorable light. Minorities and women's groups want textbooks to present issues about which they are concerned from the perspective they consider correct. Professional educators and civil libertarians, however, try to isolate schools from the pressures of all these outside groups—or at least the ones they don't agree with. They say decisions regarding what textbooks should be assigned, what books should be placed in school libraries, and how curricula should be designed are best left to professionals.[10]

In recent years battles have been fought in many cities over how to integrate public schools to secure racial balance. Busing students from one neighborhood to another to achieve racial balance has been an especially contentious issue. The Constitution does not require public schools to be racially balanced. But the Supreme Court has ruled that where racial segregation is the result of deliberate activity by the authorities, officials have the duty to take appropriate actions, including busing, to overcome the consequences of these unconstitutional violations. Proponents of busing argue that bringing minority students from depressed areas to schools attended by children from more advantaged families raises the achievement of those minority students without impairing the education of the other children. Opponents of busing stress the desirability of neighborhood schools and emphasize the negative consequences of busing, such as encouraging white flight to the suburbs.[11]

A whole series of important issues arises from the growing public concern about the quality of our schools, especially our high schools. The 1983 report of the National Commission on Excellence in Education, *A Nation at Risk*, be-

TABLE 10-1
Salary Comparisons: The Public versus the Private Sector

Public-Employee Average Salaries for 1989	
Administrators	$38,100
Professionals	$30,700
Protective service	$26,700
Private-Sector Average Salaries for 1989	
Managers and professionals	$31,200
Sales	$20,700
Services	$13,600
Manufacturing/labor	$17,500

Source: U.S. Bureau of the Census, *Statistical Abstract of the United States, 1991* (Government Printing Office, 1991), pp. 306, 415.

came the centerpiece of a national debate.[12] The report received widespread public attention and reinforced the public's conviction that much is wrong with our educational system. In stark language the commission called for, among other things, a substantial raising of standards for both students and teachers, a core curriculum, more emphasis on science and mathematics, more homework, a longer school day, and merit systems of teacher pay. The commission's findings were confirmed by other prestigious committees.

The National Educational Association (NEA), the largest teachers' union, disagreed with the commission's merit pay recommendation on the grounds that merit teaching is difficult, if not impossible, to measure, and favoritism taints most merit pay evaluation programs. In addition, Democratic party leaders took issue with President Reagan's recommendations for tuition tax credits and George Bush's view that the national government's role in education is limited. They advocated an increase in salaries for teachers and substantial national programs to strengthen science, mathematics, and foreign-language instruction. They have been less clear about their stand on merit pay. Table 10-1 compares salaries in publice- and private-sector jobs.

In 1986 another national commission called for the first nationwide system for certifying elementary and secondary teachers. This proposed National Board of Professional Teaching Standards won both praise and criticism. States don't want to yield their autonomy over education policies, yet the current absence of transferable standards is a major problem in our highly mobile society.

Nearly all the states have responded to these various reports with stepped-up efforts to strengthen their high school graduation requirements and to encourage longer school days, smaller classes, more student testing, and better financial rewards for good teaching. Plainly, the blue-ribbon reports on education have made a difference. It is noteworthy that proposed educational reforms in the last decade or so are significantly different from the reforms proposed in the 1960s and 1970s in that their focus is more on excellence than on equity for the disadvantaged.[13]

EDUCATION AND GOVERNMENTS

Elaborate attempts have been made to isolate educational agencies from the rest of government. This isolation is strongly supported by well-organized groups: parent-teacher associations, the National Education Association, the American Federation of Teachers, the American Association of University Professors, the American Council on Education, and other university and educational groups. It is also supported by most citizens' general conviction that education should be kept out of the hands of politicians. However, education is of such concern to so many people, and there are so many different ideas about how schools should be run, that it cannot be divorced from the political system. Educational policies, like agricultural, law enforcement, and other policies, are determined by the political processes available and accessible to the people.[14]

Another contentious issue is how to fund higher education. In the United States we have a system in which 15 million men and women can select among 3,000 post-secondary institutions. They can go to small schools, to large ones, to secular ones, to religious ones, to famous ones, to not so famous ones. These schools are all governed by independent boards and funded by a variety of private and public sources. In state after state public and independent schools are finding that they lack resources to provide quality education for all the students who wish to enroll.

Facing us in the 1990s are questions of access and funding for our colleges and universities. Who should go? Only those who can afford it? What about providing outreach programs for minorities who are underrepresented in our colleges and universities? As states confront budgetary problems brought about by increasing health care costs, public-employee wages, elementary and secondary education reform, and crime, one area that may be left behind is higher education. Access to colleges and universities for all students who wish to go has long been the declared goal in many states. But is this goal realistic in today's political and economic environment? Should students be required to pay much more in tuition to cover the costs of their education? And is our higher education system training people for jobs that will exist ten years after they graduate or for soon-to-become-obsolete jobs?

Because of budget constraints, tuition at state universities and colleges has already gone up in most states. At the same time, global competition has prompted a call for expanded federal funding such as we had in the 1950s after the Soviet Union launched Sputnik and threatened to establish superiority in space exploration. While many agree that we need an infusion of new money to update college laboratories, improve libraries, and recruit and keep first-rate

We The People

College Enrollment Rates

Of the 2.4 million high school graduates in 1990, 60 percent were enrolled in college. The college enrollment rate for whites (62 percent) was well above that for blacks (46 percent) and Hispanics (47 percent). Overall, the percentage of high school graduates going to college has risen 11 percent over the past decade.

college professors, there is no consensus about who should pay for this. The federal government has not stepped forward, partly because of its own budget deficit. And the states have been struggling just to keep the existing systems afloat.

One problem with American education is that no one entity governs it. The Congress, the state legislature, and local governments all fund it; an elected or appointed state board shares oversight responsibilities with a locally elected board; and state administrators work with district administrators over whom they have little or no line authority. Governors attend conferences on how to improve what they do not control, while teachers' unions and PTAs pursue agendas that are usually protective of the status quo.

Social Services

What role should government play in making sure all citizens have their basic human needs for housing, health, and nutrition met? How important is the government's social services role compared to its obligation to provide police and fire protection, education, parks and recreation, and other services? For much of U.S. history the human service needs of the nation were left to private charities, which ran orphanages, old-age homes, and hospitals, and in other ways tried to meet the needs of society. Philosophically, this reliance on private charity fit well with the American notion of a limited government. That view changed dramatically during the Great Depression, when the problems of poverty, unemployment, and homelessness affected such a large number of people that the government could no longer act as if these were private matters. Then in the 1960s, with Lyndon Johnson's Great Society agenda, the nation embarked on a second major wave of social service programs, which Johnson labeled a "war on poverty." Today the nation is debating whether the Great Society programs changed much about poverty and is considering alternatives to these efforts.

WELFARE

The number of Americans on welfare has soared from about 2 million in 1950 to about 11 million today.[15] Why such growth? Some say it is because governments at the national and state levels finally recognized their obligation to care for the truly poor. Others point out that welfare systems enslave their participants: government "handouts" rob some recipients of the self-confidence they need to go to work and succeed. In this sense, they say, dependence on welfare has become a curse.

Welfare programs in the United States are among the most emotional and controversial public policy issues. Access to welfare benefits is based on the needs of the recipients as well as on whether they meet certain specified "qualifications." One such qualification is to prove they have no income or that their income is insufficient to meet their needs. Welfare policy, a complex web of federal, state, and local programs, often involves shared or matching financial responsibilities. Most of the administrative burden, however, falls on state and local governments.

The national government picks up the costs for aid to the aged, blind, and disabled. It also pays for Medicare and food stamp programs. Joint federal and state efforts pay for Aid to Families with Dependent Children (the well-publicized AFDC program), public housing, and Medicaid (a federally sponsored program under which states can obtain about 80 percent of the cost of providing medical care for the poor).

States themselves provide for and administer unemployment compensation; assistance supplementing federal aid to the aged, disabled, and the poor; specialized hospitals and institutions for the ill, handicapped, and destitute; and some general-assistance programs for those needy who somehow do not qualify for other welfare programs.

States commonly pick up about 25 percent or more of welfare and related social service costs, making welfare the second largest expenditure for most states. Every state has a department of human services or welfare that either directly administers welfare programs or supervises local officials who administer these programs. County welfare departments determine who is entitled to assistance and deal directly with recipients.

Federal guidelines for welfare assistance are very detailed, but each state has some latitude in determining the size and details of its own welfare programs. Variations in programs among the states are significant, with the wealthier states paying higher benefits (see Table 10-2). Federal policies in re-

TABLE 10-2   Unequal Welfare Benefits in the States

Monthly welfare payment, as of 1989, for a family of three headed by one adult recipient:

Alabama $118	Illinois $321	Nebraska $327	South Dakota $269
Alaska $698	Indiana $274	Nevada $296	Tennessee $176
Arizona $271	Iowa $373	New Hampshire $437	Texas $173
Arkansas $198	Kansas $362	New Jersey $404	Utah $335
California $630	Kentucky $226	New Mexico $242	Vermont $533
Colorado $339	Louisiana $172	New York $486	Virginia $277
Connecticut $537	Maine $418	North Carolina $243	Washington $461
Delaware $310	Maryland $371	North Dakota $378	West Virginia $239
Washington,	Massachusetts $573	Ohio $309	Wisconsin $460
D.C. $375	Michigan $441	Oklahoma $298	Wyoming $336
Florida $269	Minnesota $496	Oregon $396	Guam $207
Georgia $256	Mississippi $117	Pennsylvania $364	Puerto Rico $99
Hawaii $531	Missouri $270	Rhode Island $488	Virgin Islands $169
Idaho $265	Montana $340	South Carolina $193	**U.S. Average $378**

Source: Office of Family Assistance, *Characteristics and Financial Circumstances of AFDC Recipients, 1989* (Department of Health and Human Services, 1992), p. 59.

cent years have sought to diminish the variations among the states, yet notable disparities remain.[16] People on welfare acknowledge that higher benefits in certain states such as Wisconsin encouraged them to move there. This led Wisconsin to institute a lower benefit schedule for newcomers in an effort to discourage "welfare migrants."

About half of the states, including Massachusetts, New York, and California, have experimented with so-called *workfare* programs designed to help welfare recipients develop the self-confidence, skills, and habits necessary for regular employment. Despite criticism, especially by public-employee unions, many states are adopting mandatory or voluntary workfare programs. (The mandatory programs are subject to the most criticism.) Workfare gives able-bodied adults who do not have preschool-aged children the opportunity to learn jobs skills that can lead to employment. A concept like this was advocated in the 1992 Democratic platform. Another proposal, advocated by some conservatives, such as Bush's Secretary of Housing and Urban Development Jack Kemp, and some liberals, such as New York Governor Mario Cuomo, is to create "opportunity or enterprise zones" in our large cities by giving tax incentives to companies to invest in plants and provide job training for the unemployed.

Over the past several years there has been very little federal activity in welfare reform and no new funding. The states have therefore had to deal with increased demands for spending while also trying to innovate to improve the system. The unpopularity of welfare programs with the public, coupled with budget constraints, has limited the states' response. Some states have begun to

WELFARE PROGRAMS: ASSISTING THE POOR

Welfare policy is made up of a combination of federal, state, and local programs. Most of the following programs are paid for by federal funds, but most of the administrative burden falls on state and local governments.

FOOD STAMPS

Coupons that can be exchanged for food at most grocery stores. Food stamps are the nation's largest single welfare program, originating in the New Deal as a way of helping feed the poor. The program is administered by the U.S. Department of Agriculture with the assistance of state and local welfare offices.

HEAD START

Provides educational, nutritional, health, and other social services to children aged three to five in institutions that in many ways resemble preschools. Head Start was originally part of the Economic Opportunity Act of 1964. Roughly half a million children participate in Head Start annually.

JOB TRAINING

All levels of government administer job training programs that range from student aid programs in public schools, to vocational rehabilitation programs for people who are physically or mentally handicapped, to programs under the Job Training Partnership Act, which encourages private firms to hire and train poor people.

MEDICAID

Pays for medical care for eligible poor people, including the aged, the blind, the disabled, and AFDC families. The program is partially funded by the federal government but is administered by state agencies. Medicaid was created in 1965 as an amendment to the Social Security Act.

AID TO FAMILIES WITH DEPENDENT CHILDREN (AFDC)

Provides federal funds administered by states to families with children who meet specified standards of need. Originally part of the Social Security Act of 1935, it was expanded in 1962. Some contend that the program encourages both illegitimate births and the abandonment of families by fathers. In 1989 about 3,799 families received AFDC on average each month.

PUBLIC HOUSING

The national government assists local governments to build housing through a local housing authority that, with state permission, can sell bonds and spend the federal funds provided for the program. Rents collected help to pay for the bonds, but since rents are too low to provide enough money for this purpose, the government must make up the difference. The federal government also has a rent subsidy program to assist poor people in paying rent where public housing units are not available. The program originated in 1937 as part of the New Deal but has since been expanded.

---

cut back on welfare payments. Wisconsin's Governor Tommy G. Thompson has even proposed capping welfare payments for unwed teenage mothers, regardless of the number of children they have. Larger grants would be paid to those who are married.[17] Governor Wilson of California has also proposed a 25 percent cut in his state's welfare payments.[18] Other governors, however, especially after the Los Angeles riots of 1992, proposed new federal-state-local programs to respond to the joblessness and despair of people living in the urban ghettos.

PUBLIC HEALTH

During one hot summer in the 1780s a yellow-fever epidemic struck Philadelphia. The streets were deserted. All who could afford to do so had fled with their families to the country. Every night the sounds of the death cart echoed through the empty city. Few families that remained behind did not lose a child, father, or mother. Only when cool weather returned did the city resume normal activity.

Yellow fever, dysentery, malaria, and other diseases periodically swept American cities in the eighteenth and nineteenth centuries. As late as 1879, yellow fever struck the South hard, and Memphis was nearly depopulated. State after state, following the lead of Louisiana and Massachusetts, established a board of health to deal with such epidemics. Spurred by the medical discoveries of Pasteur and other scientists, authorities began programs for the protection of public health. Open sewers were covered and other hygienic measures were instituted.

Today thousands of local governments—counties, cities, townships, and special health districts—have some kind of public-health program. Every state has an agency, usually called a Department of Health, that administers the state program and supervises local health officials. The U.S. Public Health Service conducts research, assists state and local authorities, and administers federal grants to encourage these agencies to expand their programs. Every state also administers various federal medical-benefit programs for the needy, such as Medicaid. As usual, however, wealthier states tend to take advantage of or match these programs more liberally than poorer states, despite fixed federal incentives to the contrary.

The health care crisis in America has become acute. It involves access—who gets care—and the dramatic rise in costs. Access and cost are related, of course, but wealthy people can afford the costs and gain the access, and poor people who qualify for welfare also have access to health care, although the quality of their care is lower. It is the people in the middle who are more and more worried about whether their insurance will be adequate to cover their health care needs. Governors and state legislators are increasingly worried about the fiscal implications of meeting federal mandates in health care. If costs continue to skyrocket, the federal mandates could bankrupt many states. And if the middle class feels excluded from health care because they are neither wealthy enough to buy it nor poor enough to get it at state expense, there will be an additional policy problem for state and local governments.

Prevention and disease control are still major public-health activities. Doctors are required to report cases of communicable disease. Health department officials then investigate to discover the source of the infection, isolate the afflicted, and take whatever action is called for. Most state health departments give doctors free vaccine and serum; many local departments give free vaccinations to those who cannot afford private physicians. Because the public is more enthusiastic about specific programs than about general disease control, some afflictions, like tuberculosis, venereal disease, and AIDS, have received special attention. Mobile X-ray units take free X-rays of schoolchildren, teachers, and the general public; county health departments provide free or low-cost inoculations, eye tests, and hearing tests. Public health officials try to protect water supplies and ensure the safe disposal of waste and sewage. They protect the community's food supply by inspecting hotels, restaurants, and food markets.

During the past decade, AIDS has received more media attention than even perennial killers such as cancer and heart disease. Certainly the high rate of growth of HIV-positive infections (the virus that leads to AIDS) justifies labeling the disease as "epidemic." The government has responded to the crisis with increased funding to various research programs, both public and private. In 1992 the government alone spent $2 billion on AIDS research, and that amount is expected to grow rapidly in the 1990s. Still many people, including celebrities such as basketball star Magic Johnson, call on the government to dramatically increase funding.

The AIDS epidemic reminds us of the role public health agencies play in informing the public of health hazards, urging precautions, and seeking cures. Health officials predict that over 40,000 or more preventable cases of AIDS are occurring. This only reinforces the point that to teenagers and others the message of "safe sex" is not getting through. States, especially through public schools, have adopted different approaches to educating students about AIDS —including the distribution of condoms in some public schools. Other public health issues surrounding AIDS have to do with the regulation of health care professionals and what records are kept of persons infected with the disease.

State and local governments have gradually moved onto the environmental health front in recent decades, with several states leading the way. California, New York, and Pennsylvania began clean air programs before the federal government acted. Congress has followed the states' lead by gradually adopting more stringent federal regulations, yet the primary responsibility for building facilities and enforcing regulations still belongs to the states. Pollution-control, air, and water agencies have also been created in the states. Although pollution control accounts for only a small portion of total state spending, these allocations have risen in recent years.[19]

Safe Streets and Law Enforcement

In 1835 the famous Texas Rangers were organized as a small border patrol. In 1865 Massachusetts appointed a few state constables to suppress gambling, a job the local police had proved unwilling or unable to do. But not until 1905, with the organization of the Pennsylvania State Constabulary, did a real state police system come into being. It was so successful that other states followed Pennsylvania's example. Many of the powers of state and local government stem from the **police power.** This is the power of states to use physical force if necessary to protect the safety of its citizens. It is on the basis of this power that mayors or governors impose curfews, as in the 1992 Los Angeles riots. But the police power extends to other activities of government, such as regulating public health, safety, and morals.

THE STATE POLICE

State police became a part of our law enforcement system for a variety of reasons. The breakdown of rural law enforcement, the coming of the automobile (and the resulting demand for greater protection on the highways and the creation of a mobile force for catching fleeing criminals), and the need for a trained force to maintain order during strikes, fires, floods, and other emergencies all led to the creation of state police.

The establishment of the Pennsylvania State Constabulary marked a sharp break with traditional police methods. The force was a mounted and uniformed body organized on a military basis. Centralized control was given to a superintendent who was directly responsible to the governor. The Pennsylvania pattern was followed by other states, and these forces are now among the most respected police organizations in the world. They are well equipped and maintain high standards of conduct and discipline.

The organization of state police forces shields them from temptation, builds morale, and helps officers develop a pride that contrasts sharply with the cynical attitude of some urban police. Because of their mobility and professional character and their rigorous systems of recruitment and training, state police are less prone to develop the problems that beset urban and rural police forces.

Some state police systems developed out of the rather modest highway patrols of some decades ago. During the 1930s traffic control in rural regions became an acute problem, and state after state organized highway patrols, usually as subordinate units of the highway or motor vehicle department. Gradually their authority was extended from enforcing the rules of the road to exercising the usual powers of the police. Generally speaking, the state police forces that grew out of highway patrols are not as well trained nor are their standards as high as those established on the Pennsylvania model.

OTHER POLICE FORCES

State police are not the only law enforcement agencies maintained by state governments. There are liquor law enforcement officials, fish and game wardens, fire wardens, independent detective bureaus, and special motor vehicle police. This dispersion of functions has been widely criticized, but each department insists it needs its own law enforcement agency to handle its special problems.

At the local level almost every municipality maintains its own police force;

the county has a sheriff and deputies; and some townships have their own police officers. In fact, there are over 40,000 separate law enforcement agencies in the United States employing more than 500,000 men and women.

FEDERAL-STATE ACTION

The national government has gradually moved into law enforcement, a field traditionally reserved for state and local governments, although the main cost of local law enforcement is still borne by local governments. Today, for example, it is a federal offense to transport kidnapped individuals or stolen goods across state lines. Taking firearms, explosives, or even information across state lines for illegal purposes is also a federal offense.

Despite increased national and state expenditures, crime rates have not diminished. After heated feuds over how best to spend federal funds, and considerable debate about whether past spending made any difference, Congress cut almost all the block-grant assistance monies for state and local law enforcement agencies out of the 1981 budget. These federal cutbacks, which amounted to almost 5 percent of the funds spent at the state and local levels, had the immediate effect of placing virtually all fiscal and administrative responsibility for law enforcement on state and local governments. Federal efforts to make our streets safe fell victim both to anti-inflationary budget cutting and to the realization that the causes and cures for crime elude experts at all levels of government.[20]

Students of crime in America say federal and state spending on crime control have not significantly reduced criminal activity. It may also be fair to conclude, writes one expert, "that crime cannot be effectively addressed by the customary local policies. If I am correct in concluding that change in the crime rate is a national phenomenon that is the product of macrosocial forces beyond the control of local government policy, local planning will be doomed to failure."[21]

In short, what most of us regard as a local problem may never be resolved solely by local initiatives—no matter how bold, innovative, or well funded. President Bush proposed a limited anticrime program for the early 1990s, most of it aimed at hiring more federal marshals, building more federal prisons, and funding various antidrug programs. Local law enforcement officials applauded the initiative, even though it will not have much effect on their own crime-fighting efforts.

Outrage about crime and demands for tougher penalties for drunk driving, child abuse, and drug peddling have been common to the politics of most states and communities. States have passed tougher laws, and many have limited the discretion of judges in sentencing some categories of criminals. All of this has necessitated more prison construction and a dramatic increase in the costs of running prisons, jails, and the court system. Paying these expenses has reduced the funds available in most states for education, health, and welfare.

Planning the Urban Community

Are our cities good places in which to live and work? Crime, pollution, garbage, crowded shopping areas, dented fenders, shattered nerves, slums and blighted areas, inadequate parks, impossible traffic patterns—are all these the inevitable costs of urban life?

For many decades American cities were allowed to grow unchecked. Industrialists were permitted to erect factories wherever they wished; developers were allowed to construct towering buildings that shut off sunlight from the streets below. Commuters, bicyclists, and pedestrians all ended up with transportation systems that did not meet their needs.

The most common method of assuring orderly growth is *zoning*—creating specific areas and limiting the uses to which property may be put in each area. A community may be divided into areas for single-family, two-family, or multifamily dwellings, for commercial purposes, and for light and heavy industry. Other regulations restrict the height of buildings or require that buildings be located a certain distance apart or a certain distance from the boundaries of the lot.

Zoning regulations attempt to prevent garbage dumps from being located next to residential areas, stabilize property values, and enable the city or county government to coordinate services with land use. A zoning ordinance, however, is no better than its enforcement. This is usually the responsibility of a building inspector, who ensures that a projected building is consistent with building, zoning, fire, and sanitary regulations before granting a building permit. In most cases a zoning or planning commission or the city council can amend ordinances and make exceptions to regulations. These officials are often under tremendous pressure to grant exceptions, but if they go too far in permitting special cases, the whole purpose of zoning is defeated. Zoning can also be used as a means of keeping "undesirables" out of a community. This is done merely by manipulating zoning requirements; for example, by mandating that all new homes be built on lots of an acre or more and by prohibiting the building of multifamily homes and apartments.[22]

Government can and does take the lead in community development and community renewal through redevelopment agencies (RDAs), which attempt to use grants and subsidies to encourage builders or industries to locate in a particular area of town or to revitalize a part of town that is aging or in need of renewal. Originally used in the 1960s as a method to combat urban blight, the RDA has become a potent tool of cities in their economic development efforts. Often through the use of governmental power, including "eminent domain," cities force owners to give up land for the city to redevelop. The redevelopment of the land is often financed with the net gain in taxes the city receives after losing the original property tax revenue from the land and subsequently gaining sales tax revenue from businesses that are located on the land. RDAs are often staffed by city council members, and there has been a growing sense in some cities that they are being used more to benefit RDA members than the community at large. Most states now have statutes limiting the amount of tax dollars that can be used to finance RDA projects.

Zoning is only one kind of community planning. Until recently, city planners were primarily concerned with streets and buildings. Today many are concerned with the quality of life, and planning covers a broad range of activities, including methods to avoid air pollution and to improve the quality of water. Planners collect all the information they can about a city and then prepare long-range plans. Can smaller-scale communities be devised within urban centers? Can downtown areas be revitalized, and if so, how? Where should main highways or mass transit be constructed to meet future needs? Will the water supply be adequate for the population 10, 20, or 50 years from now? Is a larger or new regional airport needed? Are hospitals and parks accessible to all? Does the design of public buildings encourage crime or energy waste?

Many communities attempt to create some kind of order out of the chaos of random growth, and most have some kind of planning agency. Federal laws support state regulations for careful long-range planning and require environmental impact statements before any major changes can be made in the roadways or land usage. The standards for these statements or reviews can sometimes be even more demanding than those of the federal government. These regulations provide opportunities for all persons affected by proposed developments to be heard and for the mitigation of any unavoidable adverse effects on the environment.

States have a vested interest in controlling the negative effects of population growth. Florida is a good case in point. Its economy rests largely on its beauty, tourism, and its ability to attract companies to relocate there. Thousands of people per day move into Sunbelt areas such as Florida. "People are loving Florida to death, literally."[23]

Floridians believe growth has caused several problems that cry out for state planning. Two-thirds or more of respondents to a survey done in the 1980s said that the state's population growth had contributed to increased crime, air pollution, declining water quality, and a loss of natural areas. This same survey found that about 50 percent (this figure rose in highly urban areas and decreased in rural counties) of Florida residents thought that government should do something about population growth. When asked what should be done, however, these citizens voiced varying levels of support for planning programs, depending on how the programs would affect their self-interest. California is another state where debates about how to manage growth are part of the political scene.

Critics of urban and state planning are skeptical whether governors, mayors, or state and local legislators can prevent what they sometimes call the "Los Angelezation" of America, by which they mean urban growth without much planning for transportation, environmental protection, or management of water and other resources. Unregulated market forces can cause severe harm to residents, and politics as usual—with governmental entities continually adjusting to the prevailing political pressures—does not ensure sensible growth patterns and the protection of the air, water, and beauty of most states and communities. Even the most idealistic plan may be little more than a reflection of one or more private interests.

Seattle and San Francisco residents have voted in recent years to limit the height and bulk of downtown buildings. These steps to regulate both the size and the pace of urban development are an effort to protect cities from excessively fast growth. The Seattle campaign pitted a host of community and neighborhood groups against downtown business interests and most of the city's elected officials. Opponents of the "slow the growth" referendum, who outspent the proponents ten to one, predicted doomsday side effects such as rising office rents, increased property taxes, and declining investments and local revenues, but 62 percent of local voters were apparently so alarmed by the decline in the quality of life in their city that they ignored these predictions and voted for the restrictions. Said one local resident: "There are things money can't buy that this area's got. You can't buy the slower pace. . . . A lot of people think this is the last outpost. They've escaped other cities that have been ruined and if they let Seattle be ruined, there'll be no place left to go."[24] The Seattle measure leaves somewhat unresolved how new buildings are to be approved, other than on a first-come, first-serve basis. In San Francisco a design review committee of architectural experts selects the projects. Other cities are likely to consider the Seattle and San Francisco precedents, although not those with sagging economies. The area around Washington, D.C., has also experienced growing pains. Local efforts to limit growth were challenged in court, but the Virginia Supreme Court unanimously upheld the slow-growth policies passed by Fairfax County, Virginia.[25]

Obviously, planning and sensible growth depend upon public support. They also depend on market forces. No plan will be effective, however, unless it reflects the interests and values of the major groups within the community. Planning is clearly a political activity. Different groups view the ends and means of planning differently, and agreements on tough policy options are often hard to reach. Moreover, one of the barriers to successful planning is the general fear of government power. Thus effective planning will always be hard to achieve. It requires imaginative collaboration between planners and the popularly elected officials who must bear the responsibility for implementing the plans.[26]

Transportation

State and local governments build highways, public buildings, airports, parks, and recreational facilities. Because highways and bridges around the nation are aging, a federal tax on gasoline was levied to help rebuild these public facilities. State and local governments, in fact, spend more money on transportation than

"INFRASTRUCTURE"

There is much talk these days, especially in state and national legislatures, about rebuilding or investing in our infrastructure. What does this term mean? In the old days people just talked about "public works," and generally the two terms mean the same thing. The Latin word *infra* means below or beneath. In general, *infrastructure* refers to our roads, highways, bridges, water tun-

nels, pipelines, airports, utilities, telephone lines, and similar public works that we often take for granted. It is true that in many places these public facilities are wearing out or deteriorating and massive new investments are needed. The term will become more common as this debate intensifies and the costs become a topic of heated political discussion.

on anything else except education and welfare. Their major transportation program is building and repairing roads.

Until the coming of the automobile, canals and railroads were the major methods of long-distance travel. Local roads were built and repaired under the direction of city, township, and county officials. Able-bodied male citizens were required either to put in a certain number of days working on the public roads or to pay taxes for that purpose.

By the 1890s bicycle clubs began to urge the building of hard-surfaced roads, but it was not until the 1900s and the invention of the automobile that road building became a major industry. The function was gradually transferred from the township to larger units of government. But counties and townships still have important building and maintenance functions.

The national government has supported state highway construction since 1916, and through various federal highway laws passed over the last 40 years, federal aid has increased. States do the planning, estimate the costs, and arrange for the construction work even when they receive federal assistance. In order to receive support, however, states must submit their plans to, and have their work inspected by, the U.S. Department of Transportation. All federally backed highways must meet certain standards governing the engineering of the roadbed, employment conditions for construction workers, and weight and load conditions for trucks.

Under the Federal Highway Act of 1956, states have planned and built the National System of Interstate and Defense Highways. The Interstate consists of 43,000 miles of superhighways linking almost all cities with a population of 50,000 or more. The federal government paid 90 percent of the cost of this system, with most of the money coming from user charges or fees (taxes on gasoline, tires, and trucks) that are placed in a trust fund designated for that purpose.

Few aspects of government are more enmeshed in politics than highway building. Groups such as the American Automobile Association support highway development. Automobile and tire manufacturers, oil companies, motel and restaurant associations, automobile and tourist clubs, trucking associations, and others join hands to advance their common cause. In most states they have been strong enough to persuade legislatures to allocate gasoline taxes, automobile drivers' license fees, trucking fees, and other user taxes for road purposes. But there is always conflict over how the money should be spent. Farmers want secondary roads developed; truckers and tourists favor the improvement of main highways; and merchants prefer that roads come their way.

Today not everyone is pleased by the heavy commitment of public funds to highways. These roads, some say, are in effect a massive subsidy for automobile users and makers; without highways, autos would not be so popular or so widely used. Some people, critics point out, use the highways far more than others, and yet everyone must contribute to the general taxes that help pay for highway construction. Why not tax people in proportion to their actual use of the highways? This is already done to an extent through the gasoline tax. But some people advocate installing a meter in every vehicle at a cost of less than $20 to measure usage of the roadways in order to extract adequate federal user fees. Others favor incentives or restrictions on employers to foster mass transit and car pools. An example is limiting parking space as part of a building permit for a new business.

There is competition among the major transportation sectors—trucks, railroads, air freight—and this competition fuels efforts to enhance the position of one mode over another through tax subsidies or regulations. For instance, the railroads have sponsored an ad campaign warning of the unsafe nature of piggyback trucks. If piggybacking were limited or banned, the railroads would benefit and truckers would be hurt.

Recently some people have urged the federal government to spend a sizable percentage of the highway trust funds on public mass transit systems. Congress at various times and through a variety of programs has permitted the use of some highway trust funds to purchase buses and finance mass transit systems. But even though more attention is being paid to bus systems and other transportation modes besides the auto, any notion that the age of the automobile is over should be cast aside. Generally, urban mass transit programs have had a difficult time in recent years,[27] especially after the Reagan administration sharply slashed urban mass transit funds.

Economic Development

State and local governments have recently been emphasizing economic development. A primary concern of governors and mayors, as well as other state and local officials, is jobs for their citizens. It is not uncommon for governors to

UNITED AIR, DIVIDED STATES

When United Airlines named Indianapolis as the site of its planned $1 billion airplane maintenance facility, a 21-month competition between more than 90 U.S. cities—including "finalists" Denver, Louisville, and Oklahoma City—came to a halt. The United facility will employ 7,000 people when fully operational in 1998, each earning an average of $45,000 a year. Indiana state officials estimate that another 11,680 jobs will be created indirectly by the project.

Indiana persuaded United with a package worth $291 million in financial incentives. Officials from losing states were dismayed not only at the results, but at the method. Kentucky governor Wallace Wilkinson felt that United prolonged the selection process "to the point that they were sure they had squeezed every drop of blood out of every turnip there."* The bidding war between states became so heated and protracted that Wilkinson finally withdrew Louisville from the competition.

* Brett Pulley, "United Air Taps Indianapolis for Facility Site," *The Wall Street Journal*, October 24, 1991, p. A6. See also Stanley Ziemba, "Kentucky All But Quits Race for United Facility," *Chicago Tribune*, October 19, 1991, Sec. 2, p. 1.

spend a significant amount of their time encouraging companies to relocate within their borders, courting corporate officials, going on trade missions to other countries to promote their state's products, and negotiating favorable tax and other incentives with new businesses as well as their own state legislatures. This interest is not new. What is new is the international proportions of these activities. Former Utah Governor Norman Bangerter was fond of saying, "The one thing you will always see on an economic development trip to Tokyo is another governor."

States compete with one another in this way because economic development is the key to increasing the tax base that funds government services. This competition impacts tax rates, regulatory methods, environmental regulation and quality, education and training programs, infrastructure, and virtually every other aspect of government. The economic hard times of the early 1980s and early 1990s, combined with Reagan's New Federalism, led to a "fend-for-yourself" situation among the states in which economic development was seen as the only alternative to raising taxes or cutting services. This is true because of the fundamentally different nature of government at the state and local levels, where, unlike the federal government, budgets must be balanced.

In the mid-1980s nearly every state felt compelled to offer an incentive package aimed at snaring the new General Motors Saturn plant. Tennessee won the competition after granting millions of dollars' worth of subsidies and concessions. Such "competitive federalism" between states has intensified in the 1990s to the point that localities are worried about keeping the jobs they have, not just persuading new companies to move to their area. New York City has offered over \$2 billion in incentives to influence several companies not to leave. Critics of these bidding wars argue that states should spend tax money on rebuilding infrastructure and strengthening education, rather than offering public funds to selected large private companies. They contend that offering incentives to certain companies is a short-sighted policy that slights the small business community and the taxpayers.

Regulation

State and local regulations are adopted on the assumption (sometimes mistaken) that benefits to the general public will outweigh the costs to the individuals and groups being regulated. An overriding public goal is typically viewed as a justification for imposing a regulation on an individual or industry. Thus laws requiring drivers' licenses, compelling motorists to stop at red lights, mandating seat-belt use, or imposing severe penalties on those caught driving under the influence of alcohol or drugs are intended to protect the safety and freedom of innocent pedestrians or occupants of other motor vehicles. Most such laws are accepted as both necessary and legitimate. States have raised the drinking age and stiffened the punishments for drunk driving, in most cases because the federal government tied federal funds to the passage of such legislation. An interest group, Mothers Against Drunk Driving (MADD), also helped to force the issue.

Corporations receive their charters from the states. Banks, insurance companies, securities dealers, doctors, lawyers, teachers, barbers, and various other businesses and professions are licensed and their activities are supervised by state officials. Fears about nuclear waste, "acid rain," and hazardous wastes of all kinds have sparked extensive efforts at regulation within states, as well as court battles with nearby states over the export of unwanted by-products of contemporary energy development. Both farmers and industrial and service workers are regulated. But of all businesses, public utilities are the most closely monitored.

PUBLIC UTILITIES

It is easier to list than to define public utilities. They include (among others) water plants, electric power companies, telephone companies, railroads, and buses. Public utilities are distinguished from other businesses because government gives them special privileges, such as the power of eminent domain, the right to use public streets, and protection from competition. In return, utilities are required to give the public adequate services at reasonable rates. Public utilities are used to supply essential services in fields in which competition is not suitable.

In the United States private enterprise subject to public regulation, rather than public ownership, has been the usual method of providing essential services. Nevertheless, more than two-thirds of our cities own their own waterworks, about a hundred operate their own gas utilities, and more and more are taking over the operation of their transit systems. But other services—intercity transportation, airplanes, telephone—are almost everywhere provided by private enterprise subject to government regulation.

Every state has a utilities commission (usually called the Public Utilities Commission or PUC) to ensure that utilities operate in the interest of the public. In about 35 states utility commissioners are appointed by the governor with the consent of the state senate. In two states they are chosen by the legislatures, and in about a dozen more they are elected by the voters. Formerly PUC posts were considered political plums, and commissioners used them as stepping-stones to higher elective office. The commissions must strike a balance between fair rates for consumers and adequate profits for the utility companies.

Utility commissioners raise or lower utility rates—perhaps the most visible part of their job—but they are also involved in such issues as toxic waste, nuclear power, and truck regulation, as well as telephone, cable television, and other energy-related disputes. The average tenure for commissioners is only about three and a half years, a statistic that suggests the burnout and fatigue involved in the job.

Utility commissioners operate under the assumption that their decisions are not "political," yet nearly every decision they make comes under political attack or stirs political reaction. Several states have enacted laws prohibiting conflict of interest, limiting commissioners' affiliations with the utilities they regulate, and prohibiting them from accepting employment with any company that was under their regulation for at least a year after they resign from the PUC. Other states have established a separate office of state consumer advocates to encourage even greater responsiveness to consumer needs.

The politics of regulation, especially regulation of public utilities, is of growing interest to more and more citizens and consumers. In many areas citizens' groups have formed to make their own presentations and to monitor the operations of the PUC. "The tremendous work load on these commissions," writes one observer, "finds commissioners constantly walking a tightrope between helping a regulated industry get a decent return on investment, and making sure consumers get good service at a fair price."[28]

There has been an increasing interest of PUC activity all across the country, especially in the areas of nuclear power and the rising costs of energy. For example, a Cook County, Illinois, judge overturned a $495 million rate increase granted by the commissions to Commonwealth Edison Company to pay for building a nuclear power plant.[29] And after 17 years of debate over the environmental impact of the San Onofre Nuclear Generating Station, the California Coastal Commission adopted a plan that will mitigate, but not prevent, the ongoing destruction of fish and kelp.[30]

EMPLOYERS AND EMPLOYEES

Despite the expanded role of the national government, state and local governments still have much to say about working conditions.

Health and Safety Legislation States require proper heating, lighting, ventilation, fire escapes, and sanitary facilities in work areas. Machinery must be equipped with safety guards. Some standards have also been established to reduce occupational diseases. Health, building, and labor inspectors tour industrial plants to ensure compliance with the laws.

Workers' Compensation Today all states have workers' compensation programs based on the belief that employees should not have to bear the costs of accidents or diseases incurred because of their jobs. Like the depreciation of machinery and other items, the costs of accidents and occupational diseases are borne by employers and passed on to consumers in the form of higher prices. In the past employees had to prove their employers were at fault if they suffered an accident on the job. Today if people are injured or contract a disease in the ordinary course of employment, they are entitled to compensation set by a

---

WORKPLACE SAFETY

Americans take it for granted that the safety of their workplaces is guaranteed by the government, but a 1991 fire in a North Carolina chicken-processing plant served as a reminder that basic safety features are not always checked by government authorities. In this case, the plant operators had chained the fire doors closed. When the fire started, employees were unable to use them to get out of the building. Most of those killed in the blaze were found near locked or blocked doorways where they had unsuccessfully attempted to escape. In addition to the locked doors, the deaths were precipitated by the plant's lack of an automatic heat detection sprinkler system, the presence of only a single fire extinguisher, and no contingency plan for such a crisis.

The state officials responsible for inspecting such plants admitted that they had not been able to inspect the plant regularly because of a shortage of money and staff. They also pointed to the federal government's failure to hold them to stricter standards as a contributing factor to the plant's unsafe conditions.

Many of the surviving workers expressed great bitterness toward their employers for their seeming lack of care for worker welfare. There is a heightened sense of awareness in the South, where poultry plants are numerous, about plant safety. There is growing support for more regulation and intervention in order to prevent repeats of the North Carolina tragedy. State and local authorities will have to deal with these demands, along with the likely unwillingness of taxpayers to pay higher taxes to finance their implementation.

Sources: Ronald Smothers, "North Carolina Examines Inspection Lapses in Fire," *The New York Times*, September 5, 1991, p. D25; B. Drummond Ayres, Jr., "Factory Fire Leaves Pall Over 'All-American City,'" *The New York Times*, September 5, 1991, p. D25; and Associated Press, "Fire Victims Died Trying to Open Shut Exits," *The New York Times*, September 7, 1991, p. A9.

prearranged schedule. Workers' compensation is once again a controversial issue. Employers are arguing that employee claims of workplace stress are excessive and will make American firms uncompetitive.

Child Labor   All states forbid child labor, yet state laws vary widely in their coverage and in their definition of child labor. Many states set the minimum age for employment at 14. Higher age requirements are normal for employment in hazardous occupations and during school hours. Many of these regulations are now superseded by federal laws for most businesses.

Comparable Worth   The idea of comparable worth is advocated by those who believe jobs traditionally dominated by women (nurses, secretaries, and elementary school teachers, for example) have lower wage rates compared to jobs traditionally dominated by men (plumbers, electricians, and janitors, for example), because of discrimination and role stereotyping. The comparable worth concept is not to be confused with equal pay for equal work.

Environmental Protection   Citizens in many states are becoming more critical of the environmental havoc caused by industrial water and air pollution, chemical dumping, strip mining, and abandoned hazardous waste sites. Normally their complaints turn into requests that the states set up some kind of regulatory and monitoring agencies empowered to impose stiff penalties for violations of environmental laws. In the 1990s some of the effort shifted to individual action—recycling, conservation, saving and planting trees, using public transport. Garbage recycling programs requiring residents to separate glass, plastics, and lawn clippings from the rest of their trash are spreading throughout the United States.

Consumer Protection   Consumer groups are often relentless supporters of regulatory efforts. Consider auto repairs, the biggest single headache for those who handle consumer complaints. Many consumer advocates believe auto mechanics should be licensed by the state to control incompetence and dishonest practices. But would this ensure that repairs are made competently or honestly?

Consumerism, a movement that became prominent in the 1960s, maintains that consumers should be provided with adequate safety information and choices, and should be able to be heard. These principles guide state efforts at regulating services and products. Most states have offices that hear consumer complaints, including lawyers working in the offices of the state attorney general. State governments often establish professional standards and handle complaints about legal and medical services or insurance practices. Recent state activity in protecting consumers has focused on fraud, especially "guaranteed prize schemes," which have been mailed to over 54 million Americans and to which roughly one third respond. When the prize isn't exactly what was promised, the public often turns to the state government for help. Other areas where state governments have been active in attempting to protect consumers include charitable solicitations, "900" telephone numbers, credit-card promotions, and guaranteed loan scams.

Can We Explain Policy Differences?

Political scientists have been attempting to learn why states do or do not enact various policies. Investigators visualize each state as producing certain policy "outputs"—for example, expenditures for welfare, a public housing program, or a civil rights law. They are trying to understand the dynamics of the political process and figure out why one state acts one way while another does something else. Researchers have looked at such variables as levels of urbanization and industrialization, education, economic resources, and home ownership. They have studied structural variables such as types of party systems and innovation in state administration, and political variables such as citizen participation and voter interest in state politics.[31]

The results of earlier studies often suggested that factors such as urbanization, wealth of the state, and geographical region accounted for public policy differences much more than party system or governmental structure. Thus the more urbanized and wealthy the state, the more likely it would be to invest in human resources; whether it was a one-party state or had competitive parties seemed irrelevant. More recent studies, however, suggest that political and structural factors do count. One study concluded that a state's policy outputs are partially determined by the attitudes and behavior of those who participate actively in state politics.[32]

Other scholars find creative leadership can make a difference. A governor who wants to encourage economic development can go abroad on trade missions, open overseas offices, and spend time on promotion and development. Through determined leadership and skillful use of available resources, a governor or a group of state leaders can overcome the constraints that traditionally stifle change.

Policy outputs are expenditures and laws. *Policy outcomes* are the actual changes these expenditures and laws make in the lives of citizens—"the bottom line" of politics. Today political scientists are asking how policy outcomes could be changed by altering some of the conditions over which we have some control. Most of us reject, or want to reject, the proposition that social and economic forces alone determine everything individuals do. Yet we know that social and economic forces are important. In a constitutional democracy, we like to believe the quality of our constitutions, leaders, and political participation can and do make a difference.

Summary

1. We ask our state and local governments to do many things for us, and what we request in the areas of education, public welfare, health and hospitals, public safety, and transportation are the most costly, accounting for more than three-fourths of state expenditures and almost two-thirds of local government spending.

2. In addition, we ask states and communities to keep our streets safe, protect our

natural resources, provide parks and recreation, encourage job opportunities, and protect consumers. There are, of course, great differences in how states and communities set their priorities in these areas. Some communities are so concerned about environmental quality that they are settling for selective growth at the expense of job opportunities. Other communities favor attracting jobs and industry despite the environmental costs.

3. Education has been a major area of state and local government activity and concern. It moved to center stage during the 1980s because of a growing concern that our system was not keeping pace with our needs or our global competitors. As we have moved into the 1990s, several reform efforts originating at the state and local levels have sought to improve our system. Some of the reforms that are now being debated, and in some instances implemented, are teacher testing, voucher or choice systems, and standardized student testing.

4. Concern about America's system of higher education has also grown in the 1990s as states attempt to balance budgets and meet pressing demands in health, welfare, and other areas. Few people question the need for a major investment in laboratories, computer instruction, and libraries at colleges and universities, but the federal government has not offered to pay for these things and most states do not have the resources to do more than stay afloat in this policy area.

5. Welfare, never a popular issue for politicians, became a much debated topic in the 1992 presidential election in part because of the riots that year in Los Angeles. Some argued that our welfare system had failed because it was based on incorrect assumptions. Others argued that we had never invested enough to truly solve the problem. Finding solutions to malnutrition, homelessness, poverty, and unemployment, especially among African Americans, will remain an important concern of state and local governments throughout the 1990s.

6. States openly compete with one another in the area of economic development by offering tax incentives, waiving environmental regulations, and offering other enticements to businesses to locate or stay within their boundaries. Companies, for their part, stress the importance of infrastructure—roads, schools, communications, trained workers—in their relocation decisions. In an era of fiscal constraint building up the tax base is vital. But states are in a dilemma because building or rebuilding an infrastructure is expensive and the tax incentives reduce the tax return the new companies will generate.

7. Political scientists conduct research on the differences among the states and cities in their policy outputs and outcomes. They are interested in why some states invest more in one policy function than in another, and why benefits are distributed in certain ways. Interest is also growing in how citizens evaluate the way their governments provide and administer public services.

For Further Reading

TIMOTHY CONLAN, New Federalism: Intergovernmental Reform from Nixon to Reagan (Brookings Institution, 1988).

DENNIS DRESANG and JAMES GOSLING, Politics, Policy and Management in the American States (Longman, 1990).

THOMAS DYE, Understanding Public Policy, 7th ed. (Prentice Hall, 1991).

VIRGINIA GRAY, HERBERT JACOB, and ROBERT ALBRITTON, eds., Politics in the American States, 5th ed. (Scott Foresman, 1990).

NORMAN R. LUTTBEG, ed., Comparing States and Communities (HarperCollins, 1992).

DAVID OSBORNE, *Laboratories of Democracy* (Harvard Business School Press, 1988).
PAUL PETERSON, ed., *The New Urban Reality* (Brookings Institution, 1985).
THOMAS SWARTZ and JOHN PECK, eds., *The Changing Face of Fiscal Federalism* (M. E. Sharp, 1990).
JACK TREADWAY, *Public Policymaking in the American States* (Praeger, 1985).
CARL E. VANHORN, ed., *The State of the States* (CQ Press, 1989).

Notes

1. Tom Mathews et al., "The Siege of L.A.," *Newsweek*, May 11, 1992, p. 30.
2. Robin Toner, "Los Angeles Riots Are a Warning, Americans Fear," *The New York Times*, May 11, 1992, pp. A1, A11.
3. *Book of the States*, 1991, pp. 304–5.
4. *Statistical Abstracts*, 1991, pp. 132, 134.
5. Gregory Anrig, "Tests Can't Solve Every Problem," *U.S. News and World Report*, May 19, 1986, p. 84.
6. See William Bainbridge and Steven Sundre, "School Choice: The Education Issue of the 1990s," *Children—Today* 20 (January 1991), pp. 28–29.
7. Educational Commission of the States, "Survey of State Initiatives: Public School Choice," in *Public School Choice* (Educational Testing Service, 1990), p. 8.
8. Lynn Davey and Monty Neill, "The Case Against a National Test," in *ERIC Clearinghouse on Tests, Measurement, and Evaluation* (ERIC, 1991), p. 1.
9. U.S. Department of Commerce, Bureau of the Census, *Statistical Abstract of the United States, 1991* (Government Printing Office, 1991), p. 134.
10. Harmon Zeigler and M. Kent Jennings, *Governing American Schools: Political Interaction in Local School Districts* (Duxbury Press, 1974). See also George Kaplan, *Who Runs Our Schools? The Changing Face of Educational Leadership* (Institute for Educational Leadership, 1989).
11. For a look at some of the consequences of busing in Boston and the impact on different families, see Anthony Lukas, *Common Ground* (Knopf, 1985).
12. The National Commission on Excellence in Education, *A Nation at Risk: The Imperative for Educational Reform, An Open Letter to the American People* (Government Printing Office, 1983).
13. Ernest L. Boyer, *High School: A Report on Secondary Education in America* (Harper Row, 1983), based on observations of high schools, contains a detailed series of recommendations. See also the National Science Board Commission on Precollege Education in Mathematics,

Science, and Technology, *Educating Americans for the 21st Century* (Government Printing Office, 1983); and *A Nation Prepared: Teachers for the 21st Century*, a report from the Carnegie Forum on Education and the Economy (1986).
14. "School Reform Movement Requires Added State Support," *State Legislatures*, January 1985, p. 6; and Peggy M. Siegel, "School Reform Momentum Continues," *State Legislatures*, March 1985, pp. 11–15.
15. U.S. Department of Commerce, Bureau of the Census, *Statistical Abstract of the United States, 1991* (Government Printing Office, 1991) p. 373.
16. See Frederick Wirt and Michael Kirst, *The Political Web of American Education* (Little, Brown, 1972); and Zeigler and Jennings, *Governing American Schools*.
17. Isabel Wilkerson, "Wisconsin Welfare Plan: To Reward the Married," *The New York Times*, February 12, 1991, p. A16.
18. Susan Faludi and Marilyn Chase, "Surging Welfare Costs, Struggle to Control Them Join Health-Care Expense as Hot Political Issue," *The Wall Street Journal*, December 11, 1991, p. A18.
19. For discussions of the problem nationwide, see Rochelle J. Stanfield, "Drowning in Waste," *National Journal*, May 10, 1986, pp. 1106–10.
20. For commentary on the embattled and frustrating national effort to make our streets safer in the 1970s, see James Q. Wilson, *Thinking about Crime* (Basic Books, 1975); and Thomas E. Cronin, Tania Cronin, and Michael E. Milakovich, *U.S. v. Crime in the Streets* (Indiana University Press, 1981).
21. Herbert Jacob, "Policy Response to Crime," in *The New Urban Reality*, ed. Paul E. Peterson (Brookings Institution, 1985), p. 251.
22. See Michael N. Danielson, "The Politics of Exclusionary Zoning in Suburbia," *Political Science Quarterly*, Spring 1976, pp. 1–18.
23. See Jane Carroll, "Florida Reins in Runaway Growth," *State Legislatures*, November–December 1985, pp. 21–23.
24. Quoted in Jane Gross, "Seattle Decides to Limit Construction," *The New York Times*, May 18, 1989, p. A10.

25. John F. Harris and John Ward Anderson, "Fairfax Downsizing Upheld, Posing Challenge for Davis," *Washington Post*, November 9, 1991, p. B1.

26. See Albritton, "Subsidies: Welfare and Transportation."

27. See Glen Yago, *The Decline in Transit* (Cambridge University Press, 1983); Comptroller General of the U.S., *Why Urban System Funds Are Seldom Used for Mass Transit* (Government Printing Office, 1977); and Victoria Irwin, "Urban Mass Transit Faces Declining Federal Funds," *Christian Science Monitor*, April 2, 1986, p. 6.

28. Nancy M. Davis, "Politics and the Public Utilities Commissioner," *State Legislatures*, May 1985, p. 20. See also William T. Gormley, Jr., "Policy, Politics, and Public Utility Regulation," *American Journal of Political Science*, February 1983, pp. 86–105.

29. Rob Karwath, "Edison Using Courts to Bog Down Refunds," *Chicago Tribune*, June 23, 1991, p. 2C1.

30. Amy Wallace, "San Onofre Mitigation Plan Wins Approval," *Los Angeles Times*, July 17, 1991, p. A3.

31. M. Kent Jennings and Harmon Zeigler, "The Salience of American State Politics," *American Political Science Review* (June 1980), p. 535.

32. See, for examples, David Klingman and William W. Lammers, "The 'General Policy Liberalism' Factor in American State Politics," *American Journal of Political Science*, August 1984, pp. 598–610; Thomas R. Dye and Virginia Gray, *The Determinants of Public Policy* (D. C. Heath, 1980); and John C. Kincaid, *Political Culture, Public Policy and the American States* (Institute for the Study of Human Issues, 1982).

Glossary
of Key Terms

Advisory opinion   An opinion unrelated to a particular case that gives a court's view about a constitutional or legal issue.

Amendatory veto   State veto power that allows governors to return a bill to the legislature with suggested changes or amendments. The legislators must decide whether to accept the governor's recommendations or attempt to pass the bill in its original form over the veto. Also called *conditional veto.*

Assessment   The value a government places on property for purposes of taxation. The assessed value may or may not reflect the real market value.

Assigned counsel system   Arrangement whereby attorneys are provided for persons accused of crime who are unable to hire their own lawyers. The judge assigns a member of the bar to provide counsel to a particular defendant.

Bicameral legislature   Two-house legislature; form for 49 of the states as well as for the U.S. Congress.

Bicameralism   The principle of the two-house legislature.

Binding arbitration   See *Compulsory (and binding) arbitration.*

Block grant   Broad grant of funds made by one level of government to another for prescribed activities—for example, health programs or crime prevention—with few strings attached.

Categorical-formula grant   Grant of funds made by one level of government to another, to be used for specified purposes and in specified ways.

Caucus (legislative) or conference   Meeting of the members of a party in a chamber of legislature to select the party leadership in that chamber and to take party positions on pending legislative issues.

Caucus (local party)   Meeting of party members in a ward or town to choose party officials and/or candidates for public office and to decide questions of policy (e.g., platforms).

Centralists   Those who favor national rather than state or local action.

Checks and balances   Constitutional grant of powers that enables each of the three branches of government—legislative, executive, and judicial—to stop some of the acts of the other branches and ensures each branch a sufficient role in the actions of the others so that no one branch may dominate. The branches must work together if governmental business is to be performed.

City-manager plan   See *Council-manager plan.*

Closed primary   A primary in which only persons registered in the party holding the primary may vote.

Commerce clause   The clause of the Constitution giving Congress the power to regulate all business activities that cross state lines or affect more than one state, and also prohibiting states from unduly burdening or discriminating against business activities of other nations or states.

Commission charter   Form of city government in which a group of commissioners (usually five) serves as the city council, each commissioner heading a department in the municipal administration.

Comparable worth   The idea that jobs should be paid at the same rate if they require comparable skills and contributions, even if market considerations make it possible to secure employees for one job at a lower rate than for another. The notion of comparable worth is advocated by those who believe jobs traditionally dominated by women—as nurses, secretaries, and elementary school teachers, for example—are held down in wage rates compared to equivalent type jobs traditionally dominated by men—as plumbers and janitors, for example—because of discrimination and role stereotyping.

Compulsory (and binding) arbitration   Process whereby a dispute between management and a union is settled by an impartial third party. When the law dictates that a stalemated labor dispute must be turned over to an outside arbitrator, the process is called *compulsory arbitration.* When union and management are required by law to accept the decision of the arbitrator, it is called *binding arbitration.*

Conditional veto   See *Amendatory veto.*

Confederation   Government created when nation-states, by compact, create a new central government and limit its powers, especially the power to regulate the conduct of individuals directly.

Constitutional democracy   A government that regularly enforces recognized limits on those who govern and allows the voice of the people to be regularly heard through free and fair elections.

Constitutional home rule   State constitutional authorization for local governmental units to conduct their own affairs.

Council-manager plan   Form of city government in which the city council hires a professional administrator to manage city affairs. Also known as the *city-manager plan.*

Crossover voting   A member of one party voting for a candidate of another party. Open primaries encourage crossover voting and may result in a situation in which nonparty members determine the party's nominee for a particular office.

Decentralists   Those who favor state or local action rather than national.

Deficit   The difference between the revenues raised from sources of income other than borrowing and the expenditure of government, including paying the interest on past borrowing.

Deficit spending   Spending by increasing the debt.

Delegate A view of the role of a member of a legislature which holds that, as delegates, legislators should represent the views of constituents even when personally holding different views.

Due process Established rules and regulations that restrain those who exercise governmental power.

Excise tax Consumer tax on a specific kind of merchandise, such as tobacco.

Express powers Powers specifically granted to one of the branches of the national government by the Constitution.

Extradition Legal process whereby an alleged criminal offender is surrendered by the officials of one state to officials of the state in which the crime is alleged to have been committed.

Federal mandate A requirement imposed by the federal government as a condition of receipt of federal funds.

Federalism Constitutional arrangement whereby power is divided by a constitution between a national government and constituent governments, called states in the United States. The national and the constituent governments both exercise direct authority over individuals.

Full faith and credit clause Clause in the Constitution requiring each state to recognize the civil judgments rendered by the courts of the other states and to accept their public records and acts as valid documents.

General property tax Tax levied by local (and some state) governments on real or personal, tangible property, the major portion of which is on the estimated value of one's home and land.

Gerrymander Drawing an election district in such a way that one party or group has a distinct advantage. The strategy is to provide a close but safe margin in numerous districts while concentrating (and hence wasting) the opposition's vote in a few districts.

Habeas corpus See *Writ of habeas corpus.*

Implied powers Powers given to Congress, by the Constitution, that allow Congress to do whatever is necessary and proper in order to carry out one of the express powers or any combination of them.

Indiana ballot See *Party column ballot.*

Information affidavit Certification by a public prosecutor that there is evidence to justify bringing named individuals to trial.

Inherent powers Those powers of the national government in the field of foreign affairs that the Supreme Court has declared do not depend upon constitutional grants but rather grow out of the very existence of the national government.

Initiative Procedure whereby a certain number of voters may, by petition, propose a law and get it submitted to the people for a vote. Initiative may be direct (if the proposed law is voted on directly by the people) or indirect (if the proposal is submitted first to the legislature and then to the people, if the legislature rejects it).

Interstate compacts Agreements among the states. The Constitution requires that most such agreements be approved by Congress.

Iron triangle A mutually supporting relationship among interest groups, congressional committees of subcommittees, and government agencies that share a common policy concern.

Item veto Authority of the executive (usually the governor of a state) to veto parts of a legislative bill without having to veto the entire bill. Presidents do not have the power of the item veto.

Joint committee Committee composed of members of both houses of a legislature. Such committees are intended to speed up legislative action. Some oversee institutions such as the Library of Congress or conduct congressional investigations.

Judicial interpretation A method whereby judges can remove a constitutional provision's restrictive force by a narrow interpretation of its meaning.

Legislative caucus See *Caucus (legislative)*.

Legislative home rule Authority granted by the state legislature to local governments that eliminates the need for local governments to go back to the legislature for additional grants of power. However, state law still takes precedence over local ordinances, and powers given to the local governments by the legislature may be rescinded.

Legislative veto Until it was declared unconstitutional by the Supreme Court in 1983, a provision in a law reserving to Congress, or to a chamber or committee of Congress, the power to reject by majority vote an act or regulation of a department or agency of the national government.

Lobby/lobbying To conduct activities aimed at influencing public officials, especially legislators, and the policies they enact. This is, of course, part of the citizen's right to petition the government.

Lobbyist Person who is employed by and acts for an organized interest group or association or corporation to try to influence policy decisions and positions in the executive and—especially—legislative branches.

Lottery A form of voluntary taxation used by more than 30 states and the District of Columbia; it involves distributing prizes by lot or random chance to the buyers of winning tickets. State income from lotteries typically amounts to less than 3 percent of state revenue; lotteries do, however, generate income without raising taxes. They are also sometimes defended as means of reducing the amount of illegal gambling and of minimizing the influence of organized crime.

Massachusetts ballot See *Office block ballot*.

Mayor-council charter The oldest and most common form of city government, consisting of either a weak mayor and city council or a strong mayor and council.

Merit system A system of public employment in which selection and promotion depend on demonstrated performance (or merit) rather than on political patronage.

Missouri Plan System for selecting judges that combines features of the appointive and elective methods. The governor makes an initial appointment from a list of persons —usually three—presented by a panel of lawyers and laypersons (the panel is usually appointed by the chief judge of the state court of last resort). After the judge has served for a year, the electorate is asked at the next general election whether or not the judge should be retained in office. If a majority vote yes, the judge serves the rest of the term. At the end of the term, if a judge wishes to serve again, his or her name is once again presented to the electorate.

National supremacy Constitutional doctrine that whenever conflict occurs between the constitutionally authorized actions of the national government and those of a state or local government, the actions of the national government take priority.

Necessary and proper clause Clause of the Constitution setting forth the implied powers of Congress. It states that Congress, in addition to its express powers, has the power to make all laws necessary and proper for carrying out all powers vested by the Constitution in the national government.

New judicial federalism The practice of some state courts of using the bill of rights in their state constitutions to provide more protection for some rights than is provided by Supreme Court interpretation of the Bill of Rights in the Constitution.

Office block ballot Method of voting in which all candidates are listed under the office for which they are running. Sometimes called the *Massachusetts ballot* or the *office group ballot.*

Ombudsman Office that handles citizen complaints against the government.

Open primary A primary in which any voter, regardless of party, can vote.

Party column ballot Method of voting in which all candidates are listed under their party designations, making it easy for the voters to cast votes for all the candidates of one party. Sometimes called the *Indiana ballot.*

Plea bargaining Negotiations between prosecutor and defendant aimed at getting the defendant to plead guilty in return for prosecutor's agreeing to reduce the seriousness of the crime for which the defendant will be convicted.

Pluralistic power structure The notion that even though some people do have more influence than others, that influence is shared among many people and tends to be limited to particular issues and policy areas.

Police powers Powers of a government to regulate persons and property in order to promote the public health, welfare, safety, and morals. In the United States, the states, but not the national government, have such general police power.

Populists Adherents of a movement and political party of the 1880s and 1890s. Their geographical base was rural—in the Midwest, South, and Southwest especially. Waging "reformist" efforts against the banks, railroads, and other establishments, populists raised issues that influenced the progressive movement and the Democratic party after 1892.

Preemption The right of a federal law or regulation to preclude enforcement of a state or local law or regulation.

Privatization The contracting out to the "for profit" private sector "public services" that are typically provided by public organizations. Trash collection, ambulance, and fire protection services have been the most common privatizations of public services. The objectives are to obtain the public services at lower costs, and sometimes to shrink the public bureaucracy to encourage additional efficiencies.

Pro bono Term used to refer to the work lawyers (or other professionals) do to serve the public good and for which they either receive no fees or decline fees.

Progressive tax A tax whereby upper-income citizens pay a larger fraction of their income in taxes than do lower-income citizens.

Progressives Adherents of a "good government" movement in the first two decades of this century, who advocated measures that would open up the system and weaken party bosses. They favored nonpartisan elections, participatory primaries, and direct elections of senators. The Progressive party, especially active from 1912 through the mid-1920s, emerged as a visible part of the progressive movement.

Project grant Federal funds given for specified purposes and based on applications.

Property tax rate Usually a tax per $1,000 of assessed valuation or some other such measure of the value of property. Local and state governments can do very little to change an assessment value, but they can raise or lower the rates.

Public defender Public officer whose job is to provide legal assistance to those persons accused of crimes who are unable to hire their own attorneys.

Public goods Services or commodities that individuals benefit from but that cannot be separately sold or given to individuals. Examples are clean air, national defense, and public safety. Many public goods are difficult to provide through privatization; others require government regulation of private economic activity.

Recall   Election held to determine whether or not an official should be removed from office before the end of his or her term. A certain number of voters, typically 25 percent, must petition to hold a recall election.

Recidivist   One who habitually relapses into crime.

Reduction veto   The power of a governor in a few states to reduce a particular money-providing measure approved by the state legislature.

Referendum   Practice of submitting to popular vote measures passed by the legislature or proposed by initiative. Use of the referendum may be required or optional.

Regressive tax   A tax whereby lower-income citizens pay a higher fraction of their income in taxes than do higher-income citizens. In other words, a regressive tax is one that weighs most heavily on those least able to pay.

Revenue sharing   Program whereby federal funds are provided to state and local governments to be spent largely at the discretion of the receiving governments, subject to few and very general conditions.

Revision commission   State commission that recommends changes in the state constitution. The recommendations have no force until acted upon by the state legislature.

Sales tax   General tax on sales transactions, sometimes exempting food and drugs.

Severance tax   Tax on the privilege of "severing" natural resources such as coal, oil, and timber, charged to the companies doing the extracting or severing.

Social stratification   The division of a community among socioeconomic groups.

Split ticket   Voting for some of one party's candidates and some of the other party's candidates.

Standard Metropolitan Statistical Area (SMSA)   A central city—or twin cities—of at least 50,000 people, along with those surrounding counties that are economically and socially dependent on the city.

Straight ticket   Voting for all of one party's candidates.

Strong mayor-council   Form of local government in which the public directly elects the mayor as well as the city council. However, the mayor appoints the department heads with the approval of the council, and in effect serves as the chief executive officer for the city and its administration.

Sunset process   Legislative review process that calls for the termination of a program after a certain number of years, often six or seven, unless it is carefully examined, certified to be doing what it was intended to do, and repassed by the legislature. Many states have adopted this practice. The word comes from the expression that "the sun should set" on programs that have outlived their usefulness.

Tort law   Law, primarily judge made, dealing with damages to compensate people through a civil trial, for legal wrongs done to them, including injuries to person, reputation, or property.

Trustee   A view of the function of a member of a legislature which holds that, as trustees, legislators may believe that they were sent to Washington or the state capitals to think and vote independently for the general welfare, and not as their constituents determine.

Turnout   The proportion of the voting-age public that votes.

Two-party system   Electoral system in which two major political parties dominate.

Unicameral legislature   One-house legislature. Nebraska and almost all cities use this form.

Unitary system   Government with power concentrated by the constitution in a central government; also an election system in which voters elect legislators who, in turn, elect the prime minister or head of state.

Unitary tax   A state tax on the proportion or a corporation's domestic receipts earned in that state. It is a controversial tax, viewed by some as a legitimate means of securing added state revenue and by others as discouraging companies from locating in the state.

User charges   Fees charged directly to individuals who use certain public services on the basis of service consumed. Sometimes called a *user fee* or *user tax*.

Value-added tax (VAT)   A tax on the increased value of a product at each state of production and distribution rather than just at the point of sale, as with a sales tax.

Weak mayor-council   Form of local government in which the mayor must share most of the executive powers of a city with other elected or appointed boards and commissions. The mayor in weak-mayor cities is often mainly a ceremonial leader.

Writ of *habeas corpus*   Court order requiring explanation to a judge why a prisoner is held in custody.

Index